EMBATTLED REASON

EMBATTLED REASON

ESSAYS ON SOCIAL KNOWLEDGE

❦ ❧

REINHARD BENDIX

NEW YORK
OXFORD UNIVERSITY PRESS
1970

The preparation of this volume has been assisted financially by a research grant from the Institute of International Studies, University of California, Berkeley. I am indebted to Hans-Eberhard Mueller, and to my children Erik and Karen Bendix for research and editorial assistance.

R.B.
Göttingen
August 1969

For my sister Dorothy

PREFACE

A collection of essays published over a twenty-year period is a piece of intellectual autobiography. Each theme explored exacts a price of topics and ideas left aside, deliberately or otherwise. Inevitably the result violates Bacon's rule that we should hold in suspicion "whatever the mind seizes and dwells upon with peculiar satisfaction." If that rule were obeyed strictly, intellectual choices would not be worth making. The essays collected here mark a series of such choices and in this sense provide an intellectual profile.

Awareness of subjective predispositions are among the tools of the social scientist. He observes the society of which he is a member, and as a social scientist he must account for the vantage point of his analysis. In doing this he inevitably participates in debates among his peers. The terms of these debates are a response not only to exigencies of the moment, but to debates of the past which gain or loose in relevance with changing patterns of experience. Accordingly, Parts I and II contain a number of essays which formulate the theoretical positions at which I have arrived. I am quite aware that my formulations only outline an approach and do not constitute a theoretical framework or system. So be it. I think it more to the point to face up to uncertainty than grasp at certainties that do not endure.

This intellectual position is not synonymous with immobility. Rather, it attempts to steer a course between the exaggerated trust in human reason and power associated with the belief in science, and the exaggerated cultural despair which has accompanied Western industrial civilizations since its inception. I admit to a profound distrust of the dogmatic righteousness of both extremes. Many scientists show genuine humility before the "facts" and a disarming modesty concerning their own work. But their unswerving dedication to science is inspired by the missionary belief that its cause itself is virtuous. On the other hand, there are those who believe that intellectual dedication to humane values is by itself an indication and guarantee of morality. They do not see their own preconceptions and are oblivious to the inhumanities of moral and intellectual absolutism. These extremist tendencies will not soon diminish. The momentum of the scientific establishment is too great and so is, paradoxically, the impact of a cultural critique that excoriates an industrial society intricately linked with the further advance of science.

As I try to show, these tendencies pose a special dilemma for sociology. Committed to empirical inquiry, this discipline has developed in the wake of the natural sciences whose success it wishes to imitate. Committed to a critical view of society, sociology is under attack nonetheless by those who want to alter the world rather than understand it. In the 1960s the idea that scholarly understanding may help to alter the world in a desired direction has become curiously old fashioned. In the face of these cross currents social theory and the social sciences become worthwhile as objects of study in their own right. Reflection on their position may illuminate the paradox that collectively we seem to believe in science but not in reason, and we advance social knowledge while despairing of human nature.

The essays collected in Part III deal with our changing historical experience. Conceptual problems in the study of social change are on the agenda of the social sciences today. But in an era of declining colonial empires, the proliferation of sovereignties, and the continual regrouping of world powers, our framework for the study of change still derives from the Western experience. An explicit analysis of this Western experience is in my view a safeguard against tacit preconceptions. We cannot in fact erase the traces the past has left on our minds, but we can examine them critically and move forward on that basis. The essays collected in Part III and the larger studies of which they form a part suggest that it is work to be done, not a set of assumptions to be elaborated.

Chapters 1, 3, 4, 6, and 12 have been written for this volume. Others have been published previously, but are reprinted here in revised form. I list below details of the original publications and wish to thank the responsible editors and publishers for their permission to reprint them here.

"The Age of Ideology: Persistent and Changing," in David Apter, ed., *Ideology and Discontent* (Glencoe: The Free Press, 1964), pp. 294–327.

"Images of Society and Problems of Concept-formation in Sociology," in Llewellyn Gross, ed., *Symposium on Sociological Theory* (New York: Harper & Row, 1959). This article was written in collaboration with Bennett Berger.

"Concepts and Generalizations in Comparative Sociological Studies," *American Sociological Review*, XXVIII (August 1963), pp. 532–39.

"Industrialization, Ideologies and Social Structure," *American Sociological Review*, XXIV (1959), pp. 613–23.

"A Study of Managerial Ideologies," *Economic Development and Cultural Change*, V (1957), pp. 118–28.

"Social Stratification and the Political Community," *European Journal of Sociology*, I (1960), pp. 181–210

"Tradition and Modernity Reconsidered," *Comparative Studies in Society and History*, IX (April 1967), pp. 292–346. Published by Cambridge University Press.

Some passages of Chapters 3 and 4 were originally contained in an essay "Sociology and Ideology" in Edward Tiryakian, ed., *The Phenomenon of Sociology* (New York: Appleton-Century, 1970), but they have been recast and expanded considerably. Finally, Chapter 12 was written for a volume edited by Alan Bullock, *The Twentieth Century*, to be published by Thames and Hudson, London, and McGraw-Hill, New York. It is here published with the permission of the editor and the publishers.

CONTENTS

PART ONE

CONDITIONS
OF KNOWLEDGE

◄§ ৡ►

SOCIAL SCIENCE
AND THE IMAGE
OF MAN

◆§ ONE §◆

◆§ LEGACIES OF THE ENLIGHTENMENT

Some two hundred years ago, in his *Philosophical Dictionary*, Voltaire declared that God had to create man with self-esteem, but that self-esteem misleads him most of the time. Passions are necessary, for mankind cannot propagate itself without desire. But passions also lead to quarrels and wars. Still, Voltaire thought his time the "most enlightened century that ever was." God or nature has established a "few invariable principles" of morals and justice underneath all the customs and evils which have "diffused variety over the face of the universe." The office of man's reason is to discover these principles, make them his code of conduct, and teach them to his children. In this view truth and virtue are synonyms. God has so ordered the world that proper inquiry will lead to their discovery.

Social philosophers and social scientists have presupposed a secular version of these beliefs ever since the eighteenth century. By using their reason men can discover regularities of human behavior

This introductory essay draws on three earlier publications, namely, "Social Theory and Social Action in Historical Perspective," *Ethics*, LVI (1946), pp. 208–18; *Social Science and the Distrust of Reason* (Berkeley: University of California Press, 1951); and "The Image of Man in the Social Sciences," *Commentary*, II (February 1951), pp. 187–92.

much as natural scientists have discovered laws of nature. Society, like nature, is uniform underneath the diversity of appearance; man can discover these uniformities; and the resulting knowledge will be "for the benefit and use of life" (Bacon).

From the Age of Voltaire to that of the social scientists of the present, writers have assumed some order in nature and society which is not man made. At one time this abstract assumption involved the idea of a divinely created order. Marx posited the theory of a predictable interrelation between an economic substructure and an ideological superstructure. Freud held that the human personality is formed in accordance with the individual's history of pleasures and pains. Economists employ laws of supply and demand in an idealized market as a useful approximation of the aggregate behavior of real men in real markets. At other levels of abstraction sociologists assume more generally that the order of society is a system of correlated factors to be analyzed by scientific methods. Theories of society as a system or as a pattern of interaction are typical variants of this assumption.[1]

Every social scientist endeavors to clear away the bias and error that would obstruct his inquiry. But he also stands in some personal, affective relation to the society he investigates. This inquiry depends on a prior analysis of bias and error and of what can be done to minimize their distorting effects. The paradox is that the very effort to advance the study of society has deepened our understanding of human fallibility. As a result, man's efforts to understand society have been marked by increased social knowledge and by an increased distrust of reason.

Consider this sequence. In the seventeenth century, Francis Bacon believed that man could free his understanding from distortion (idols), once he understood the nature of these distortions. Man's capacity to reason was divinely ordained and the unhampered pursuit of knowledge would be rewarded by discovering the truth. In the eighteenth century philosophers of the French Enlightenment shared this belief but saw the pursuit of knowledge endangered by the church. They advocated educational reforms and developed a scientific pedagogy as means towards the emancipation of man. For Marx, in the nineteenth century, knowledge itself was a part of society and history. In his view there is no escape from the distortions of ideology because these serve man's most vital interests. The shackles of bias and self-interest can be thrown off only when society as a whole has been reorganized. Revolution rather than elimination of bias or educational reform appears as the safeguard of human reason. With Freud, in the twentieth century, we move still further away from the tradition of the Enlightenment. Now man's quest for knowledge appears as a sublimation or rationalization of his basic organic drives. In this view all knowledge, but especially the knowledge of self and society, appears as an epiphenomenon of the human condition. Therapy rather than educational reform or revolution must safeguard what little room is left for the constructive possibilities of human reason. Freud takes a last precarious stand on the side of human improvement.

No social scientist today can match the sweep and penetration of Marx's or Freud's theoretical constructions. At the same time sophisticated methodologies are available for the elimination of bias. The elaboration of research tools may be considered an extension of Marx's or Freud's insights into the sources of error. But one cannot overlook that in the process terms like "man" or "reason" have gone out of fashion. They involve philosophical concerns which social scientists eschew as "pre-scientific." Yet these larger concerns are implicit in the very drive to be scientific.

Our awareness of human fallibility has increased as the methods to eliminate bias have become more sophisticated. By implication these advances cast doubt upon the rational abilities of the many who cannot rid themselves of their prejudices and achieve an understanding of society. Since interests, emotions, and cultural patterns tend to obstruct the pursuit of knowledge, it requires uncommon ability to keep inquiry free of these obstructions. Inadvertently social scientists have made an invidious distinction between themselves and people at large. They have contributed their share to the decline of the Enlightenment—sometimes through the very effort to continue its traditions.

ᴥᶳ VULGARIZATION OF THE DISTRUST IN REASON

Marx and Freud have had commanding influence upon modern social thought. Both helped to destroy a naïve belief in reason by insight into bias and by analyses which revealed the social and emotional foundations of culture. But neither Marx nor Freud believed that reasoning is futile or improvement by reasoning impossible.

There is a striking parallel between Freud's and Marx's belief in reason. Marx analyzed the impersonal and inadvertent operation of historic forces. Freud analyzed the organic, unconscious operation of human drives. Marx desired a society in which production could be rationally planned for the benefit of mankind. Freudian therapy aims at an individual who is able to subject his organic drives to the control of his cognitive and moral faculties.[2] Marx believed that some bourgeois intellectuals could overcome their class interest and, by comprehending the "historical movement," become leaders of the proletariat. Similarly, Freud believed that by undergoing psychoanalysis therapists could master their emotional involvements and thus become able to help patients achieve a similar emancipation.[3] Thus, the Marxian and Freudian elites depend on individual choices arising from a cathartic experience.

Neither Marx nor Freud dwelt upon *this* aspect of their belief in reason. Marx did not explain why some "bourgeois ideologists have raised themselves to the level of comprehending the historical movement." As Professor Perlman has pointed out, the workers do not ask to be guided by middle-class intellectuals; it is the latter who feel that it is their historic duty to do so.[4] Similarly, Freud did not explain why certain persons attain an exceptional level of self-knowledge and why they should see the cure of souls as their vocation. These unexplained residues suggest that the tradition of the Enlightenment requires a will to believe in reason, and that Marx and Freud were its genuine heirs. When this will to believe is absent, skepticism becomes vulgar and the distrust of reason turns into a distrust of man.

Vulgarization may be the eventual fate of all great ideas.[5] In vain did Marx state "Je ne suis pas un Marxiste." His theory of ideology held that ideas are embedded in self-interest. He explored the relation between ideas and actions because their convergence could become an important lever of social change. In the tradition of the Enlightenment Marx was concerned with man and his perfectibility, but many of those who followed him neglect this purpose. Marx's insight becomes pedestrian when his philosophy of history is abandoned and individuals are seen primarily as products of their group affiliations. This vulgarization omits Marx's passionate concern with the paradox that the organization of production increasingly prevents the full utilization of productive capacities. It omits his attempts to relate political action to this discrepancy and thus fails to see the present as a step towards a future reorganization of society. Where this larger context of change is abandoned, our interests become restricted to what ideas reveal about man's social experience. Such inquiry may have value in certain contexts, but its humane aspirations fall short of those which motivated Marx's work.

Freud once paraphrased Marx: "Moi, je ne suis pas un Freudiste," probably because his ideas have not escaped a similar vulgarization.[6] Much of what prompts man to think and act as he does lies hidden in his unconscious. Psychoanalytic theory provides a framework for interpreting the unconscious impulses inadvertently revealed in a person's conscious life. Freud's therapeutic prescription is detachment towards the self, particularly where this is most painful. There is no guarantee of therapeutic success, but therapy aims at the individual's emancipation from his uncontrolled drives. To this end men must come to terms with their hidden feelings and ideas. Here again great insights become pedestrian once their context is abandoned. The concept of the unconscious is vulgarized when a man's ideas are judged by the motives which prompted him to express them. Ideas are degraded to symptoms when a man's conscious experience is interpreted as a compensatory verbalization of unresolved emotional conflicts. When all knowledge is an epiphenomenon in this sense, we have no reason to expect positive results from a man's painful achievement of self-knowledge.[7]

The vulgarization of Marx and Freud is further support for the distrust of reason which has developed since the eighteenth century.

The perfectibility of man is an illusion, if human fallibility is a basic obstruction to the pursuit of knowledge, rather than an impediment that can be removed. If social relations are only a breeding ground of error and prejudice, men cannot hope to profit from the use of knowledge in society. Nor can an individual benefit from education if his every action is a repercussion of emotional conflicts sustained in early childhood. These statements only extrapolate the underlying pessimism of the social sciences today.

The ramifications of this problem are explored in this volume. But at this point I shall state the resulting paradox in simplified terms. In the social sciences two contradictory views of the nature of man are asserted simultaneously. On the one hand we are told that it is possible to increase our understanding of man and society. Such knowledge promotes intellectual clarity. It can enlarge man's control of human affairs; it can reduce unhappiness and misery; it can increase the joy and fullness of life. Social scientists subscribe to Bacon's stirring denunciation of that "factitious despair, which not only disturbs the auguries of hope, but also cuts the sinews and spur of industry . . . for the miserable vain-glory of making it believed that whatever has not yet been discovered . . . can never be discovered hereafter." But on the other hand we are told that man is a creature of his drives, habits, and social roles in whose behavior reason and choice play no decisive part. As evidence for this view accumulates, it becomes difficult to see why social scientists continue a work that "disturbs the auguries of hope." If all men are mere creatures of circumstance, then social scientists are not exempt from this condition. If all men are subject only to passions, then knowledge of this fact will not prompt us to search for man's reason. Hence we will find less reason than there may be, our hopes will be diminished, and the question will be raised what passions social scientists obey in making their inquiries. A quest for social knowledge which merely expresses the impact of social and psychological determinants can give no promise of enlightenment. Why continue the work of social science, when our view of human nature becomes incompatible with the belief in the constructive possibilities of knowledge?

৩ THE SOCIOLOGICAL PERSPECTIVE

The paradox has special relevance for sociological theory. Sociologists look to Emile Durkheim as a pioneer of their discipline. Durkheim approached the age-old problems of moral philosophy from an empirical standpoint and proposed thereby to lay the foundations of the new discipline. The sociological study of moral facts rests on two assumptions. All actions of the individual must be reduced to their elementary components. Once this is done, questions of morality and politics can be brought nearer a solution.

According to Durkheim, man is born unformed and amoral. The individual acquires the moral standards of his group and culture through interaction with peers and adults as well as through formal education. But in modern society moral standards no longer provide the individual with the guide lines he needs. Under these conditions Durkheim considers the sociological study of moral facts the only resource left to us. That study reveals the sacred character of all morality and the moral authority of the collective over the individual mind, even where secularism and individualism prevail. Durkheim expected the emergence of a new morality, once we have a well-grounded understanding of its collective character.[8]

This approach contrasts with that of Sigmund Freud at every point. Where Durkheim assumes that other ages possessed a sound collective morality in contrast to our own, Freud asserts that the morality of all ages is impaired. Where Durkheim assumes that the individual is born with an unformed nature, Freud asserts that human nature is endowed with definite instincts demanding satisfaction (libido and the death wish). As a result a basic discontent is the mark of civilization. Aggression and license prevail if man's amoral instincts break through the cake of custom and culture. But frustration and neurosis increase if moral rules inhibit or repress man's instinctive drives. Like Durkheim, Freud asserts that the religious beliefs of the past cannot be restored to their former place in human culture. Both scholars consider science the only remedy left to us.[9] But Durkheim sees religion and science as collective representations controlling the individual mind, whereas Freud contrasts the wish fulfillment of religious beliefs with the detached and skeptical approach of science. For Freud religious beliefs and rituals are one of many resolutions to man's internal conflicts, making it possible for men to achieve some balance among their drives (Id), the demands of reality (Ego), and the demands of conscience (Superego). But such balances are precarious, internal conflicts unavoidable, and man's happiness at best a tenuous achievement.

Freud believed that with the aid of therapy the individual may achieve heightened awareness and reduce his anxiety and sense of guilt. He would have had no use for the Durkheimian view that unhappiness rises as the individual's group integration declines, or for the idea that greater integration with the aid of science is the road to happiness. Indeed, in the Freudian canon Durkheim evades the problems of morality by elevating the group at the expense of the individual. To which a Durkheimian might reply that Freud's approach downgrades society's positive contribution to the life orientation of the individual. The two approaches are in conflict because Durkheim considers the mores of society a main buttress of individual morality and mental health while Freud sees them as one source of our mental ills.

Yet both theories appeal to us, because they are scientific in intention and reductionist in procedure. Durkheim (1858–1917) and Freud (1856–1939) belong to a generation of scholars that wanted to put the study of man on a scientific basis, but in opposition to the crude materialism of the nineteenth century.[10] Through a lifetime of research Durkheim analyzed the moral framework which the group provides for the individual. Yet eventually he turned his attention to those aspects of experience which this initial assumption had left out of account. He came to insist that state intervention had rescued the individual from the despotism of the group to which he belonged, though he never relinquished his belief in the superiority of the collective conscience.[11] Durkheim considered the two views compatible because individualistic beliefs as well as state intervention are collective representations.

One can discern an analogous change of emphasis in Freud's work. In each individual there are instinctual drives which undergo a history of release or inhibition. We can understand the personality of an adult only if we trace that cumulative history back to its beginnings in early childhood. However, within this framework Freud emphasized eventually that the resulting personality structure has to be understood in its own right, a view which Anna Freud elaborated in her analysis of ego defenses.[12] Thus both writers began with a completely reductionist analysis of the individual but subsequently qualified this reductionism in the interest of balance and comprehensiveness.

Durkheim and Freud are heirs of the Enlightenment. They came to see, though perhaps not explicitly, that a completely reductionist view of human nature is incompatible with sociology and psychoanalysis as intellectual disciplines. For, such disciplines cannot remain free of contradiction, if steps forward in the analysis of man are steps backward from the belief in knowledge "for the benefit and use of life."

໖ DISTRUST AND INQUIRY

As a social scientist I am concerned with the intellectual fashions implicit in this paradox. We are committed to scholarly and scientific pursuits because we want to achieve clarity and hope to discover regularities of behavior and social development. We want to go forward with efforts to ensure that the consequences of discovery will be benign, in the spirit of hope if not always of confidence. But in the last third of the twentieth century we are not sure that the constructive use of knowledge will prevail over its destructive potential. This uncertainty is long overdue. The opinion is gaining ground that human benefit may not be the only or automatic end product of advancing knowledge.

Such doubts apply to the social sciences in a special way. The uses of social knowledge will not be comparable very soon to those of knowledge in the natural sciences. Yet the social sciences have had massive consequences of their own, over and above their contributions to the management of public affairs. A conception of human impotence is the paradoxical by-product of advancing social knowledge. If physiological drives, emotional involvement, cultural legacies, and the expectations of others compel men to act as they do, they are not likely to make reasoned choices. This image of man is a popular version of theoretical ideas rather than the direct result of scholarly work, but it is still the unwitting by-product of the social sciences. As such it contributes to the antirationalist tendenices of our time, much as the vulgarization of Marx and Freud contributed to the destruction of the Enlightenment tradition.

Social scientists must try to safeguard their work against such ideological contamination. They must be able to explore the analytic utility of a theoretical perspective on the assumption that "all other things are equal." They will be aware that any theoretical perspective leaves residues which are neglected for the time being. The pluralism of theoretical perspective provides a corrective for this neglect. And general assertions about man and society can be treated as provisional abstractions. But such conditions of the tentative and the provisional do not exist in the context of action. Here the abstractions of scholarly inquiry are general assertions about man and society, which affect our lives.

The scholar and the ideologist are distinguished by a difference of commitment. In a scholarly context every theoretical scheme involves a twofold obligation. The implications of the scheme should be pursued with all the devotion of the true believer. But the scheme should be abandoned when its intellectual utility is exhausted. Evidence of this point will be proximate at best, and the productivity of theories continues to be a matter of debate. Therefore, scholars only approximate the terms of their mandate, while the academic community helps to preserve the conditions under which they can continue to do so. By contrast, in an ideological context ideas are linked to action, and commitment to a theoretical scheme is complete. Considerations which challenge the scheme may modify the details, but the theory will remain intact. For a commitment to action demands that we take a stand and make our view of the world a matter of principle, however adaptable we are in practice.

The scholarly intent of social theories is safeguarded only when the distinctions indispensable to scholarship are recognized as arbitrary and abstract, a view typically rejected by ideologists. As an analytic tool the sociological perspective emphasizes the importance of group life, and this restricts our observation of the individual. The social sciences as a whole take account of this dilemma by emphasizing the individual's integration with the group in one discipline, and choice or decision making in another. Individual scholars are in a more difficult position, however, and some of their conceptual devices have become ideological manifestos. To avoid this dilemma we should learn from Marx, Durkheim, or Freud that a reductionist analysis of the individual, carried to its extreme, comes to contradict even the rational capacities of men in science.[18]

As scholars we must guard the insights of the reductionist perspective by close attention to the role of reason and the individual in human association.[14] A lively interest in the history of ideas is a useful methodological safeguard in this respect. It provides a guide to diverse theoretical standpoints and hence a ready corrective for the distortions endemic in each. Disciplines which possess an impressive cumulation of knowledge, may consider the history of the discipline a secondary interest. Disciplines which lack such cumulation, do so at their peril.

❧ IMAGES OF MAN

In the second half of the twentieth century the term "reason" does not have as widely accepted a meaning as it did for the philosophers of the eighteenth century. Indeed, empirical scholars do not concern themselves with the philosophical questions suggested by the term. Yet I do not see how we can be social scientists and not commit ourselves, tacitly at least, to some image of man and hence to a concept of reason. Knowledge may be the result of inquiry. But inquiry itself is initiated by our hopes and fears concerning the promise of knowledge for the good or ill of man. Hence we are bound to make some assumption about a discoverable order that is not man made and some estimate of what men are and what they are capable of becoming. The term reason refers to our estimate of the role of knowledge in human affairs. Images of man are different intellectual constructions which arise from the basic assumptions of social inquiry.[15]

For present purposes three images of man may be distinguished. The Marxist image arises from a belief in reason as a by-product of history. The social scientist's image attributes reason to a quest for knowledge which obeys certain evolutionary regularities. Admittedly, this image is an artifact attributed to social scientists who rarely reflect on these matters. The third image also attributes reason to the quest for knowledge but emphasizes the dependence of that quest upon historical and institutional preconditions. This position is derived from the sociology of knowledge.

1. *In Marx's view the question of reason is historical.* In the long run and in its main outlines culture is determined by the organization of production and the class struggle arising from it. Marx argues that theologies, philosophies, the sciences, and the arts reflect the all-pervasive influence of man's material life, albeit often indirectly. Not only man's conception of the world or of his place in it, but the pursuit of knowledge in all its specific development are affected in this sense. No logic, epistemology, or scientific methodology can free our thinking from mental preoccupations which arise quite unwittingly from the way we make our living. Thus, accurate knowledge is not a simple product of correct thinking.

Marx's insights into the causes of ideology might make it appear that he was preoccupied with *un*reason as a product of history. This is misleading. His lifework was devoted to an analysis of capitalist society and this makes no sense without a belief that knowledge is attainable and can contribute to the emancipation of mankind. Marx had a conception of reason in two phases. He believed that under capitalism people cannot attain a true conception of man and society. As the contradictions of capitalism mount, so does the unreason of the many. Only a few can attain a scientific understanding of society, though it takes a Promethean conception of knowledge to attribute this attainment to the same contradictions. On the other hand, reason will prevail in the socialist society of the future. Classes and the division of labor will be abolished and with them the cause of deceit and illusion in human society. When the exploitation of man by man has ceased, then people at large will enjoy untrammeled human relations, characterized by candor and lucidity. Thus, history is the cause of reason and unreason, since the changing structure of society is the root of all theoretical and practical activity. Marx denies the distinction between theory and practice. As a result, reason in the sense of scientific knowledge and reason in the sense of honest and creative human interactions are presented as closely related aspects of one historical process.[16]

2. *The belief in reason as an attribute of the quest for knowledge is widely diffused, but not clearly identified with the work of any one scholar.* For purposes of orientation a composite view is presented here.[17]

Man's pursuit of knowledge is beset by impediments which can be removed by constant, self-critical awareness. The spirit of this Baconian position is alive today, though a great deal has been added to the early formulations, and important parts of it have been modified. Scholars constitute a community engaged in the steadfast pursuit of knowledge. On the alert against all sources of error they are dedicated to utmost candor, the accurate public disclosure of their methods and results, and the critical assessment of each other's work. The great strength of this position lies in its self-corrective mechanisms. No single evidence of error, misdirected effort, dogmatism, etc. can argue against it. Time and again scholars have shown the capacity to eradicate error, redirect their efforts, and prevent the perpetuation of dogma. There are many scholarly communities; they vary in the degree to which they apply these built-in correctives and approximate the ideal.[18]

Here is the point where the Baconian ideal is linked with an evolutionist conception of knowledge. The history of the natural sciences is marked by the cumulation of knowledge since the seventeenth century. Disciplines which lack a comparable record of cumulation, take this history as their precedent. Sociology is obviously among them. If today a discipline is beset by unresolved methodological problems, dogmatic controversies, or personal polemics we are reminded that like conditions characterized disciplines like physics or chemistry at an earlier time. Redoubled efforts will overcome these defects, much as they were overcome in the more advanced disciplines. This inference assumes that the history of science provides not only an arsenal of models worthy of imitation, but also that sooner or later the pursuit of knowledge will traverse roughly similar phases of cumulative growth. The criteria of successful advance are unequivocal and the progress achieved in this way is endless.[19]

3. *The sociology of knowledge suggests a third position which differs from the evolutionist and Marxian perspectives.* A full recognition of the achievements of the natural sciences is compatible with the observation that there are different kinds of knowing and that the term "reason" can apply to many of them. It may serve our purpose to analyze different types of knowledge and consider the growth of knowledge in that light.[20] We do not know what cannot be known and to this extent subscribe to the idea of progress. But we do not know either that knowledge steadfastly pursued will traverse all the phases of growth exemplified, say, by the history of physics. The pursuit of knowledge is indeed open ended, but its success is not assured.

One can recognize the historical conditioning of knowledge and yet deny that history is the cause of reason. The pursuit of knowledge is affected by factors extraneous to that pursuit, strictly speaking. It depends on a prior belief in the value of knowledge. The direction of inquiry is affected by many social conditions, though these need not determine or bias its results. Intramurally, the pursuit of knowledge is affected by the social relations of a scholarly community at work with their fashions, personality clashes, and approximations to the scholarly ideal. To deny the impact of these factors is incompatible with the evidence. To assert that they must lead to the prevalence of unreason is contradicted by the constructive continuation of scholarly inquiry. Thus, reason is the result of pragmatic approximations which may be favored or obstructed by the historical conditions of knowledge.

These considerations pose special problems for the pursuit of social knowledge, which are explored in the following essays. In "The Age of Ideology" I consider the assumptions with which social theorists have approached the quest for social knowledge. In "Changing Foundations of Scholarly Detachment" I take up the value implications of scholarly inquiry in relation to the changing setting of the academic community.

THE AGE OF IDEOLOGY:
PERSISTENT AND CHANGING

↔§ TWO §↔

↔§ IDEOLOGY AS AN HISTORICAL PHENOMENON

About three centuries ago, Francis Bacon observed that words become idols and obstruct our understanding. Words in common usage designate what is "most obvious to the vulgar." Men of learning, therefore, alter the common meaning of words in order to achieve accuracy through definition. Nevertheless, they often end up in dispute about words among themselves, since definitions also consist of words and these "words beget others." Bacon concluded that "it is necessary to recur to individual instances." [1] In the social sciences, his observations and advice are still valuable and nowhere more so than with regard to the phenomenon of ideology.

Modern scientists—like the earlier men of learning—tend to be impatient with words in their common usage which, as Bacon put it, "stand in the way and resist change." Like Humpty Dumpty in *Through the Looking Glass*, they want the words to mean what they say the words mean. If clarity is obtained thereby, it is well worth the artificiality that results. An artificial terminology, however, has its own risks, even aside from the problem of getting other scientists to agree to it. In order to clarify definitional problems, it is often advisable to refer to "individual instances," and

An earlier version of this essay was published in David Apter, ed., *Ideology and Discontent* (Glencoe: The Free Press, 1964), pp. 294–327.

18

such references are obscured when the terms used have been formulated deductively. In addition, it must be kept in mind that the ambiguous or multiple meanings of words, as they are ordinarily used, are an important part of the evidence. Social scientists should consider this evidence with clear heads, but should not clarify it out of existence. The scientist's legitimate quest for clarity can subtly distort such evidence by supposing that, once the confusions of a term are cleared up, the problems to which it refers have disappeared also.

"Ideology" is a case in point. The word is in such bad repute that writers on the subject are either apologetic about using it or prefer to substitute another term like "belief-system." At the same time, there are writers who continue to use it as if its meaning were well understood. Among them are those who speak of an "end of ideology," by which they mean the decline of political ideas in Western countries. This decline is attributed to the rise of totalitarianism, which diminishes controversy in the antitotalitarian camp; the rise of the welfare state, which institutionalizes the drive toward equality; and the resulting consensus on a "pluralistic" society in which power is sufficiently decentralized to leave room for individual freedom.[2] These factors probably account for the sharp reduction of ideological disputes over some aspects of domestic policy, but there is also evidence of a sharp increase of ideological disputes in other respects. We may be witnessing a change in the arena of ideological conflict, rather than an "end of ideology," even in the Western context. For if intense ideological conflict has declined domestically in some respects, it has probably increased in others, in race relations, for example. While the secret diplomacy of the nineteenth century sought to obviate ideological differences, the "diplomacy" of the Cold War has accentuated them. Again, the waning imperialist doctrines of the nineteenth century are now being replaced by the anticolonial and anti-Western doctrines of the mid-twentieth century. These considerations suggest that the phenomenon of "ideology" has an historical and structural dimension.

A Nonideological World View. If one can speak—even in a restricted sense—of an "end of ideology," then the phenomenon of ideology must also have had a beginning. Is there a common element in all the diverse uses of ideology, by reference to which one can distinguish one cultural epoch from another? Can one speak meaningfully of a "pre-ideological" epoch? [3] The answer is, I believe, that the term is not properly applicable in Western civilization prior to the seventeenth or eighteenth centuries, somewhat in the way that terms like "economy" or "society" or "intellectuals" do not fit the "premodern" period either. All these terms are applicable to the ways in which men think about their society. The shift is one of cultural pattern and intellectual perspective rather than of social or political structure. In practice, it is sometimes difficult to distingush the earlier world view from that more characteristic of the subsequent, "ideological" epoch— especially during the long transitional period that began in the Renaissance when the earlier conviction became attenuated. But this difficulty does not invalidate the distinction. A culture based on belief in the Supreme Deity differs from one in which man and society, along with nature, are viewed as embodying an "ultimate reality" of discoverable laws. As Carl Becker has put it:

> In the thirteenth century the key words would no doubt be God, sin, grace, salvation, heaven and the like; in the nineteenth century, matter, fact, matter-of-fact, evolution, progress. . . . In the eighteenth century the words without which no enlightened person could reach a restful conclusion were nature, natural law, first cause, reason, sentiment, humanity, perfectability (these last three being necessary only for the more tender-minded, perhaps).[4]

This substitution of nature for God is especially important for an understanding of ideology as a distinctive intellectual perspective.

The ramifications of the earlier world view are observable in many different realms. In literature, for example, "reality" had been represented in a heroic and a satiric-comic mode since antiquity, a contrast that disappeared only in the realistic or naturalistic representations of nineteenth-century literature. The object of the older literature was poetic representation of reality as it should be, in terms of ideal contrasts between virtues and vices, between heroes and fools or knaves. Similarly, the facts of economic life were treated in the context of estate-management, in which instructions concerning agriculture, for example, occurred side by side with advice on the rearing of children, marital relations, the proper management of servants, and so forth. The moral approach to human relations was not at all distinguished from the economic and technical considerations of the household. Again, premodern historiography—if the word is not indeed a misnomer —consisted in what we consider a moralistic chronicling of events, an entirely unselfconscious assessment of history in terms of a moral standard accepted as given and unchanging. The basis for this moral standard was belief in a divinely ordered universe, and the common element in these premodern perspectives was therefore the effort to discover "the moral law," which had existed from the beginning of time as the central fact of a world created by God.[5] One may speak broadly of a premodern or pre-ideological epoch as long as this perspective remained intact, as long as even the most passionate controversialists did not question the existence of the moral law and the divine ordering of the universe.

In this view, history consists in the unfolding of the divine law and of man's capacity to understand it and follow its precepts. To be sure, men cannot fully understand the providential design. But through their thoughts and actions, men reveal a pattern or order of which they feel themselves to be vehicles or vessels, even though they understand it only dimly. Man's capacity to reason is not questioned, even though his development of that capacity remains forever partial, precisely as the ends of human actions are not in doubt although in an ultimate sense they remain unknown. It is when human reason and the ends of action are questioned that "ideology" comes into its own.

Sources of Error and the Ends of Action. In ordinary usage, "ideology" refers to:

> 1. The body of doctrine, myth, and symbols of a social movement, institution, class, or large group. 2. Such a body of doctrine, etc.

with reference to some political and cultural plan, as that of fascism, along with the devices for putting it into operation. 3. *Philos.* a. the science of ideas. b. a system which derives ideas exclusively from sensation. 4. Theorizing of a visionary or unpractical nature.[6]

To relate these definitions to the present discussion, it is only necessary to distinguish their several elements. In the sociopolitical and philosophical realms, the definitions refer ideas back to a nonideational basis, whether it be a social movement, an institution, a class, or a physiological and psychological substratum called "sensation." In this view, ideas are derived from some extra-ideational source, however the source or the process of derivation may be conceived. I shall use the term *reductionism* to characterize this approach. Second, the definitions specify that doctrine, myth, symbol, or theory is oriented to the future, in the sense that it embodies a political or cultural plan of action. In this sense, ideology is a type of goal-orientation, a special aspect of the teleology that is characteristic of all human action. I shall speak of *goal-orientation* or *the ends of action* when I refer to this attribute. The last definition refers to theorizing as visionary or impractical, thus raising a question about *the uses of theories*. The accent is polemical, setting up an invidious contrast between a visionary and a realistic approach, the latter term referring presumably to theories and truths (or statements of fact) that are practical or concrete. Here "ideology" is used in its pejorative sense, about which we shall say more presently.

The distinction between the "ends of action" and the "uses of theories and truths" requires comment. The action primarily considered here is the pursuit of knowledge, so that in the present context the "ends of knowledge" are distinguished from the "uses of knowledge." The distinction is necessary even though the relationship between the ends and uses of knowledge is sometimes close. But for the men of knowledge, the pursuit of truth is often a large and ill defined good, which is never fully realized by the uses of truths even in the ideal case, since all knowledge is proximate. Furthermore the "uses of theories and truths" are often in the hands of men of affairs, and even where theories and truths are abused from the point of view of the scientist as a citizen, such abuse does not invalidate the value of knowledge in his eyes, since, under favorable conditions and in the hands of wise men, the same knowledge can be put to constructive use as well. It is advisable, therefore, to refer to the *ends* and *uses* of knowledge as separate, though related, aspects of the action-involvement of ideas.

These three aspects together—the reductionist tendency in the analysis of ideas; plans of action for man and society, including the pursuit of knowledge for the sake of human progress; and the invidious contrast between realism and illusion—are the constituent elements of ideology as I shall use the term.

Historically, the Age of Ideology came into its own when critical questions were raised concerning man's ability to reason and to define and realize the ends of his actions. Reductionism in the analysis of ideas and concern with the ends of knowledge are important elements in Francis Bacon's programmatic statements. Critical questions about the use of theories, especially in society, arose much later toward the end of the eighteenth and the beginning of the nineteenth century.

Bacon's declaration of independence from the scholastic learning of an earlier age has the stirring power of all acts of emancipation. His manifesto seeks to guard scientific inquiry against the errors that typically obstruct human understanding. In his "theory of idols," analysis of the sources of error becomes an important part of the quest for knowledge. We must guard against the influence of interests and wishful thinking that is found in all men (idols of the tribe); against the individual's character and experience, which prompt him to dwell on some ideas with peculiar satisfaction (idols of the cave); against the "ill and unfit choice of words" (idols of the market-place); and against the received systems of philosophy (idols of the theater). In thus classifying recurrent sources of error, Bacon intends only to safeguard the pursuit of truth, and he approaches these critical questions in a spirit of optimism.

> Human knowledge and human power meet in one; for where the
> cause is not known the effect cannot be produced. Nature to be
> commanded must be obeyed; and that which in contemplation is
> as the cause is in operation as the rule.

Accordingly, Bacon refers to the *kingdom of man*.[7] Still basing
his thought on the traditional world view, Bacon believes in man's
capacity to discover the divine order. He wishes only to emancipate the men of this age from a world view which considers all
wisdom already contained in the divine word. He intends "the
investigation of truth in nature" as a new and better means of
discovering the divine wisdom.

But when he considers the ends of human action and admon-
ishes men to seek knowledge "for the benefit and use of life,"
Bacon is totally at variance with the traditional view. He reminds
men to seek knowledge for charity rather than for such inferior
ends as profit, fame or power,[8] but this does not alter the secular
trend of his thought. Bacon is aware that the pursuit of knowledge must be safeguarded against the apprehension that it will
undermine the authority of religion and the state. He claims that
investigations of nature are "the surest medicine against super-
stition, and the most approved nourishment of faith," rather than
a danger to religion as some people fear. And he argues against
those who fear for the power of the state, declaring that investigations of nature can only enhance that power, while "matters
of state" are not a proper subject for science—"these things resting on authority, consent, fame, and opinion, not on demonstration." [9] The very act of emancipation thus raises questions
about human reason and the ends of human knowledge. Rather
than relying on faith in man's God-given capacity to discover the
truth, it becomes necessary to protect this human capacity by
rationally devised safeguards against error. And instead of faith in
a providential design, which is revealed through human action
whether men know it or not, it becomes necessary to make the
ends of the pursuit of knowledge (and more generally, of all
actions) a conscious object that must be protected against base
motives, misinterpretations and unintended consequences.

No scientific inquiry can dispense with the two concerns Bacon formulated in his "Novum Organum." The possible sources of error must be understood and guarded against; this concern is a part of the scientific enterprise. In addition, by the act of engaging in research or inquiry, scientists commit themselves to a line of action that cannot be clearly separated from its social context. The "ends of knowledge" that they pursue are a matter of belief, not of proof. We saw that Bacon raises the hopes of men for the new science but also tries to anticipate and offset the apprehensions of those who fear it. For scientific work depends upon men of affairs and the general public, and Bacon discerns some consequences of this dependence.

> It does not rest with the same persons to cultivate sciences and to reward them. The growth of them comes from great wits; the prizes and rewards of them are in the hands of the people, or of great persons, who are but in very few cases even moderately learned. Moreover, this kind of progress is not only unrewarded with prizes and substantial benefits; it has not even the advantage of popular applause. For it is a greater matter than the generality of men can take in, and is apt to be overwhelmed and extinguished by the gales of popular opinions.[10]

To be successful, the scientific enterprise requires special assistance from its sponsors and the public. Yet, neither the errors to which inquiry is subject nor its dependence upon public support has proved an ultimate bar to a properly conducted inquiry. On the contrary, critical awareness of the scientist's fallibility has helped to promote scientific knowledge, and the public's conditional support has not impeded its gradual advance.

At the threshold of the modern world, the task was to emancipate men from unthinking acceptance of received opinion, stimulate the critical scrutiny of ideas, and encourage the investigation of nature in the hope of benefiting mankind. Bacon initiated an era in which reason replaced faith among the mental and psychological conditions of inquiry, while the ends of that inquiry were defined in terms of "human utility and power," rather than the greater glory of God. In the natural sciences, the Baconian program proved extraordinarily successful. As methods of research were developed and its findings proved reliable, the utility of these findings became an article of secular faith that was questioned less with each advance in scientific knowledge. The appeal of this faith quickly dispelled the remaining commitments of scientists to the earlier world view, as well as Bacon's rather defensive declaration that "matters of state" are outside the province of scientific inquiry.[11]

The new intellectual perspective came to be applied to man and society. There also reason replaced faith as the mental and psychological conditions of inquiry were subjected to critical scrutiny. Yet the result was a paradox. The search for the sources of error proceeded apace as an indispensable means for the advancement of social knowledge. But the ends of inquiry remained uncertain, resting as they do on the borrowed belief, rather than the proven fact, that social knowledge serves "human utility and power." Accordingly, "ideology" came to be used in a pejorative sense, when the scientific approach was applied to man and society. Here also knowledge can be advanced only if the sources of error are known and guarded against. But such knowledge of error has been used as a means of discrediting an opponent, rather than as a methodological safeguard. Here also the advance of knowledge depends on public support. But in the absence of manifest utility that support becomes precarious and provides ready arguments for those who would discredit an opponent's views as "visionary and unpractical."

These questions came to the fore as confidence in progress was extended to those "matters of state" that Bacon had cautiously excluded from his program. I need not here review these extensions in psychology, education, political theory, and philosophy except to note that in philosophy the optimistic search for truth eventually found expression in a science of ideas entitled "ideology." [12] In his *Eléments d'idéologie* (1801, 1803, 1805) Destutt de Tracy gave a systematic exposition of this science intended for use in the schools. He stated in his preface that "ideology is a part of zoology," since human intelligence is a phenomenon of animal life and must be analyzed accordingly.[13] Tracy felt, as did his ideologue colleagues, that such a reductionist analysis of ideas—"studies on the formation of our ideas" as he called it—had arrived at the truth and no longer left room for doubt or perplexity.[14] Yet this perspective was directly associated with the republicanism and atheism of the ideologues. During Napoleon's ascendance to supreme power, a conflict developed between the Emperor and these philosophers, whose association he had cultivated a short time before. The pejorative meaning of "ideology" originated in Napoleon's repeated denunciations of the men who had coined this term to identify a philosophical school.[15] With Napoleon's phrases like "obscure metaphysic" and "idealistic trash" to characterize the work of *les idéologues*, we have the third constituent element of "ideology," one that questions the truth, the utility, and the political repercussions of ideas about man and society.[16]

The implications of this pejorative meaning are illuminated in the work of Edmund Burke, although he wrote before Tracy had coined the term and Napoleon had used it in polemic fashion. Burke opposes the reductionist analysis of ideas with his affirmation of sentiment and prejudice as indispensable bases of the community.

> . . . In this enlightened age I am bold enough to confess that we are generally men of untaught feeling; that instead of casting away all our old prejudices, we cherish them to a very considerable extent, and, to take more shame to ourselves, we cherish them because they are prejudices. . . . We are afraid to put men to live and trade each on his own private stock of reason; because we suspect that this stock in each man is small, and that the individuals would do better to avail themselves of the general bank and capital of nations and of ages. Many of our men of speculation, instead of exploding general prejudices, employ their sagacity to discover the latent wisdom which prevails in them. . . . Because prejudice, with its reason, has a motive to give action to that reason, and an affection which will give it permanence. Prejudice is of ready application in the emergency; it previously engages the mind in a steady course of wisdom and virtue, and does not leave the man hesitating in the moment of decision, sceptical, puzzled and unresolved. Prejudice renders a man's virtue his habit; and

not a series of unconnected acts. Through just prejudice, his duty
becomes a part of his nature.[17]

This famous passage states the case for conservatism but, it is
cited here because it illuminates the pejorative meaning of "ideology."

Burke sets out to shock his readers by using "prejudice" as a
word of praise. In the eighteenth century, the philosophers of the
French Enlightenment sought to discredit and unmask prevailing
opinions of church and state, by theoretical reduction of all ideas
to the basic "sensations" out of which they have been formed.[18]
Accordingly, when Burke praises "prejudice," he seeks to put a
stop to that inquiry into the "sources of error" that the Enlightenment was extending from the natural sciences to philosophy, political theory, and education. At the same time, he provides an
impressive analysis of the hiatus between theory and action. Theory
means detachment, while practical things are accomplished by
commitment; theory deals with principles, while action involves
compromises and modifications in detail; theory enlarges the hori-
zon and endangers action by revealing its contingencies, while
action is limited in its aims; theory makes provisional statements,
while actions are irreversible; theory involves no presumption in
favor of precedent, while action is limited by past behavior; and
where theory rejects errors, prejudices, or superstitions, the states-
man puts them to use.[19]

Burke thus denounces all inquiries into the conditioning of
knowledge as presumptuous and unnatural, a fatal disruption of
the "untaught feelings" and inherited sentiments that alone provide a basis of morality. Similarly, he denounces all theories in
politics because they will jeopardize the "art of the possible."
Such theories project visionary plans, state impractical principles,
and undermine the resolution to act in the face of contingencies.
As a conservative who seeks to preserve the older world view,
Burke thus gives a pejorative meaning to critical inquiries into
the "formation of our ideas" as well as to abstract political theories
that define the ends of social action for the nation as a whole.
The lot of men can be improved only gradually and then only

if sentiments and the ends of action remain undisturbed by rational inquiry—though in making this argument he advances a theory of his own based on a concept of reason as an outgrowth of experience and tradition. In Burke's view, the position of the philosophers of the Enlightenment has wholly pernicious repercussions, and a position that gives rise to such consequences must be false. In this type of argument the truth of an idea is confused with its social and political effects so that the test of truth and evaluation of the effects become interchangeable. Burke's position is, therefore, an early example of the ideologizing tendencies against which he fought vigorously but helped to initiate nevertheless. By the time he wrote, the old world view had lost its hold over the minds of men; it had become difficult to look upon man's reason and the ends of his action as an ultimately unknowable part of the providential design. Even Burke, who sought to uphold this view, was forced to do so with arguments that were at variance with its basic assumptions.[20]

ᴥᔑ IDEOLOGICAL DIMENSIONS OF SOCIAL THEORY

In the social sciences, men have not accepted the value of knowledge to nearly the same extent as in the natural sciences. It can be said that men should explore such knowledge and its possible benefits to the limit, since they never know enough to determine that limit. There was resistance to the advance of knowledge in the natural sciences as well, and in the absence of constructive alternatives the problems before us must be solved by all available avenues of detached inquiry. But these considerations, valid as they may be, do not enable us to ignore the ideological dimensions of social theory.

It is difficult to keep studies of man and society distinct from considerations of purpose and utility. Scholars who inquire into the sources of error in order to enhance social knowledge must do so in the face of considerable uncertainty. They are not in the position of natural scientists who could point to increasing utility as traditional faith declined. Accordingly, in the social sciences, every new insight into human fallibility raises questions about the role of reason in human affairs. Here also inquiry into the sources of error is indispensable. But this inquiry tends to be linked with efforts to allay uncertainty, to state the case for the value of knowledge, and to ensure that it will serve human progress.

In the twentieth century, terms like "prudence" and "reason" no longer possess a widely accepted meaning. The first term refers to the "reason of Everyman," which Hobbes defines as "learning begot by experience which equal time bestows equally on all men." Related to this concept is "cumulative experience" in the sense in which Burke saw institutions embody the judgments exercised by successive generations of men of affairs. Hobbes and Burke refer to "prudence" as the word is used here. Such prudence is distinguished from reason acquired by specialized experience, which Coke defined with reference to the common law as "an artificial reason acquired by much study." The paradox faced by the social sciences can be summed up in the statement that our general estimate of prudence has declined, while our estimate of reason acquired by "much study" has increased greatly.

Distrust of Prudence and Belief in Science. The history of social thought since the Enlightenment is characterized by exaggerated confidence, inspired by progress in the natural sciences. If it is possible to increase our knowledge of nature, then it must be possible to increase our knowledge of man and society. Such knowledge has value as a means of enhancing intellectual clarity and of enlarging man's control of human affairs.[21] Properly employed, knowledge of society can improve the human condition. In this way, many social scientists might subscribe to Bacon's stirring declarations about the "kingdom of man," were it not for their reticence in propounding a borrowed belief for which supporting evidence in their own fields is equivocal.[22] More common perhaps is the approach that emphasizes scientific method, contrasts that method with mere opinion, and urges that the ends and uses of knowledge be considered once our knowledge is sufficiently advanced and secure.[23]

On the other hand, social thought since the Enlightenment has developed an image of man as a creature in whose behavior prudence and choice play no decisive part. In this view the investigation of social life would itself be a product of social and psychological conditioning. But knowledge conceived solely as a product of social life can hold no promise for the improvement of the human condition. The paradox is an ancient one.[24] If we assume that all men are products of their passions, then we shall not search for prudence and shall consider what looks like prudence a mere by-product of passion. Our hopes will be diminished. The question becomes: What passions do we obey in making these inquiries? Unlike their fellows in other disciplines, social scientists are subject to the restriction that their general assertions about man and society affect society directly and apply significantly to themselves as well.

All social inquiry leads to a heightened awareness that easily turns into skepticism, or into an anti-intellectualism of intuition or of technical empiricism. But awareness is also an intellectual tool. Properly handled, it may protect social research against unexamined influences to which social scientists are subject as members of their societies. To this end, it is useful to explore in some depth the ideological implications arising from our inquiries into the sources of error, from our conception of the ends of knowledge, and from our uses of theories.

Since the time of Bacon, inquiry into the sources of error has greatly advanced our knowledge of men and in the process has greatly lowered our estimate of the effect of prudence on human affairs. To appreciate this development, it is necessary to recall the eighteenth-century belief in progress through science. In the view of philosophers like Condillac, Cabanis, Tracy, Helvétius, and Holbach, the good society is the product of man's quest for knowledge. The powers of the altar and the throne stand in the way of this achievement. Representatives of these powers believe they must blind the people and exploit their prejudices in order to keep them subject. To this end, religious fanatics and political rulers interfere with freedom of thought. In the interests of humanity they must be opposed by a deliberate unmasking of prevailing prejudices and by scientific inquiry into the principles of morality which are innate in man. To the philosophers of the Enlightenment, the discoverable order of society consists of these principles, which will be revealed by knowledge of ideas and natural law. In the battle for enlightenment this knowledge is a great power feared by those who stand for the prejudices that obscure the moral order. In this view, prejudices are no longer obstructions of the mind, as they were for Bacon, but weapons with which the leaders of established institutions defend the status quo. Vices and crimes, says Helvétius, are errors of judgment closely akin to prejudices. There must be freedom of thought to combat them; such freedom encourages discussions and disputes, which bear fruit in the advance of truth. And it is God's will that truth results from inquiry.[25]

The truths to be discovered are laws of the human mind like those that Tracy and Cabanis sought through their inquiries into the "formation of our ideas." The ideologues left the use of these discoveries rather vague, content in the belief that their philosophical ideas would be used in the schools once the needed educational reforms had been instituted. Their work contributed to the transition from philosophy to the modern sciences of man and society and became widely influential through the writings of Henri de Saint-Simon (1760–1825). Following the ideologues, Saint-Simon also makes physiology the basic scientific discipline because it involves theories based on observations that can be verified in contrast to the conjectural sciences.[26] This idea of Saint-Simon actually adds little substance to earlier speculations. But—like Bacon before him—he raises men's hopes in the promise of the new science.

> Politics will become a positive science. When those who cultivate this important branch of human knowledge will have learned physiology during the course of their education, they will no longer consider the problems which they have to solve as anything but questions of hygiene.[27]

The implications of this idea are far-reaching, although its generic interest is negligible. Bacon had proposed a reductionist analysis (his theory of "idols") as a safeguard against error; now physiology rather than logic is the discipline appropriate for analysis of the human mind. Since men are animals, their physical attributes provide the clues for a scientific understanding of human qualities. Saint-Simon believes that, in the future, human affairs will be as easily manageable as personal cleanliness. Rarely perhaps has so low an estimate of man been linked with so high an estimate of science and of what scientists can accomplish.

A century and a half after Saint-Simon's death our knowledge of man has increased greatly, but our hopes for the use of knowledge have diminished. While Saint-Simon remains noteworthy as an initiator, Freud's work is relevant here as the most far-reaching development of the reductionist tradition. Where the Enlightenment philosophers sought the laws of the human mind in "sensations," Marx in the organization of production, and Nietzsche in the struggle for power, Freud sought them in man's biological make-up. All human behavior leads to pleasure or pain. Man's subjective efforts to increase the first and diminish the second are primarily reflections of a character that is formed through prior experience of drive-satisfactions (or frustrations) in the growing child's relations with his parents. Character is the product of what has happened to each individual's organic drives of sex and aggression. For the satisfaction or frustration of these drives is the medium through which the individual forms his patterned responses, sees himself, and relates himself to his significant others. All cultural activities and values are secondary compared with these primary sources of gratification and frustration.

Freud is an heir to the eighteenth-century tradition. Based on a theory of personality-formation, his therapy aims at the improvement of the individual. Patients may find a way out of their emotional difficulties when they have opportunities to reassess especially the repressed experiences of early childhood. But common prudence is of minor importance in avoiding such difficulties and of no importance in finding solutions for them, since prudence is at a discount when a person is emotionally involved. Although Freud believes men capable of reassessing their personal histories and—to a degree—reorganizing their lives on that basis, this therapeutic use of cognitive and moral faculties depends on a cathartic experience. And catharsis depends upon a therapeutic transaction in which the patient becomes dependent upon his analyst, while the latter—with a detachment achieved through training and control analysis—seeks to help the patient master himself.

Freud does not offer a psychoanalytic interpretation of the quest for psychoanalytic knowledge; he rests his case upon belief in progress through science. In his arguments against the defenders of traditional religion, Freud puts the case of scientific inquiry in the following terms:

1. It is difficult indeed to avoid illusions, and perhaps the hopes men have for science are illusions also. But men suffer no penalties for not sharing belief in science—in contrast to religion—and all scientific statements, though uncertain, are capable of correction.

2. Defenders of religion and science may agree that the human intellect is weak in comparison with human instincts. But the voice of the intellect, though soft, does not rest until it has gained a hearing. One may be optimistic about the future of mankind, for by its gradual development and despite endless rebuffs the intellect prevails. If, as a defender of religion,

> you confine yourself to the belief in a higher spiritual being, whose qualities are indefinable and whose intentions cannot be discerned, then you are proof against the interference of science, but then you will also relinquish the interest of men.

In the name of this Baconian ideal, Freud states his belief that "in the long run nothing can withstand reason and experience." [28]

3. The illusions of religions are basically infantile; once they are discredited, believers must despair of culture and of the future of mankind. The champions of science are free of this bondage. True, secular education probably cannot alter man's psychological nature. But if we acknowledge this fact with resignation, we do not thereby lose interest in life.

> We believe that it is possible for scientific work to discover some-
> thing about the reality of the world through which we can increase
> our power and according to which we can regulate our life. . . .
> Science has shown us by numerous and significant successes that
> it is no illusion.[29]

Those who are skeptical should remember that science is still
young; in judging its results we tend to use a foreshortened time
perspective. The frequency with which previously established scientific statements are replaced by closer approximations to the truth
is a strong argument for the scientific procedure. "It would be
an illusion to suppose that we could get anywhere else what
[science] cannot give us." [30] Compared with the confidence of
Saint-Simon, Freud's advocacy of science is skeptical and subdued.
For him, the solution of human problems is highly complex, and
no advance of science will reduce the management of affairs to a
question of hygiene.[31]

Saint-Simon's and Freud's inquiries into the "foundation of our
ideas" are linked with their concepts of the ends of knowledge. But
neither writer is directly concerned with the steps taken to guard
knowledge against error, or with the purpose and use of knowledge
which these steps imply. These ideological implications of social
theory are a central theme in the writings of Karl Marx, Alexis de
Tocqueville, Emile Durkheim, and Max Weber. Each of these theorists analyzes the social conditioning of knowledge, but each also
believes in progress through knowledge and thus faces the task of
protecting that belief against the corrosive effects of his own insights.

✎§ THE QUEST FOR OBJECTIVITY AND THE USES OF IDEAS

Karl Marx (1818–1883). The philosophers of the Enlightenment
believed that a just social order can be established through human
reason, as long as discussion is free and once education is reorganized on the basis of the "science of ideas." To these men, prejudice
has its source in vested interests, while the correct understanding
of society results simply from unprejudiced inquiry. This easy optimism was abandoned by Marx.

He conceives of man's intellectual history as a reflection of class struggles. Ideas about society are weapons wielded by contending social classes to attack their enemies and defend their friends. Classes are formed on the basis of the organization of production, which engenders common interests and ideas among individuals who make their living in similar life-situations as capitalists, shop-keepers, craftsmen, wage-earners or others. Each individual lives under circumstances not of his own choosing and shares with others life-experiences arising from the organization of production. It is from this source, that awareness of social relations and ideas about society lead to the formation of classes which affect all other aspects of consciousness as well. Accordingly, for Marx, all aspects of cultural life reflect the class struggle. Men of ideas differ among themselves only in the degree to which they are subject to the compulsions of the class struggle and the manner in which they transform these compulsions intellectually. In Marx's view, knowledge of man and society depends upon and changes with the class structure. This dependence must be analyzed anew in each case. Inquiry into the "foundations of our ideas" (reductionism) is no longer a means to knowledge; it has become a type of knowledge in its own right.

For Marx distinguishes social structures like feudalism, capitalism, and socialism, not only in terms of their respective class structures, but also in terms of the religious beliefs and the knowledge of social reality that "correspond" to these structures. In the feudal period, men are easily swayed by the fantastic images of mythology and religion. Because technology is backward, the masses of the people suffer great deprivations and unwittingly exchange spiritual for material satisfactions. In feudal society, social relations are marked by a pervasive personal dependence, of which the members of that society are fully aware, because it is not "disguised under the shape of social relations between products of labor." [32]

This disguise of social relations arises because capitalist society is

> based upon the production of commodities, in which the producers in general enter into social relations with one another by treating their products as commodities and values, whereby they reduce their individual private labor to the standard of homo-

geneous human labor—for such a society, Christianity with its *cultus* of abstract man, more especially in its bourgeois developments, Protestantism, Deism, etc., is the most fitting form of religion.[33]

Religion prevents men from actively changing the world in which they live. But under feudalism technology is backward and the promise of change small, while under capitalism the real satisfaction of material needs is possible. On the basis of modern technology, capitalism has created an unprecedented productive potential, but its exploitative system of production has also created unprecedented misery because—for the first time in history—misery has become unnecessary. Religion prevents men from seeing that their misery can be abolished; it is an opiate of the people in that sense. In addition, everything is reduced to the status of a commodity that is judged in terms of its price rather than its intrinsic value. The relations between one man and another are obscured, if their transaction appears to them in terms of its price. Thus the "personal" dependence of the worker on his employer appears to both in terms of the wage agreed upon. All human values become quantified and homogeneous, when social relations are mediated by the mechanism of the market. Christianity, however, obscures and perpetuates this alienation.

Under socialism, these conditions are radically altered. Marx's critique of capitalism becomes clearer by means of this contrast. He never speaks in detail about the socialist society of the future, but he claims that religion will disappear along with the reasons for its previous importance—namely, the alienation of men from the product of their labor and from their fellow men.

> Let us now picture to ourselves . . . a community of free individuals, carrying on their work with the means of production in common, in which the labor-power of all the individuals is consciously applied as the combined labor-power of the community. All the characteristics of Robinson [Crusoe's] labor are here repeated, but with this difference, that they are social, instead of individual. Everything produced by him was exclusively the result of his own personal labor, and therefore simply an object of use for himself. The total product of our community is a social product.

One portion serves as fresh means of production and remains social. But another portion is consumed by the members as means of
subsistence. A distribution of this portion among them is consequently necessary.

While the mode of this distribution will vary with the productive
organization and the historical development of the producers,

> The social relations of the individual producers, with regard both
> to their labor and to its products, are in this case perfectly simple
> and intelligible, and that with regard not only to production but
> also to distribution. . . .[34]

Since alienation arises from social relations mediated by trading on
a market, alienation will be abolished once men re-establish direct,
unmediated relationships with their work and their fellows through
control over the processes of production and distribution. Under
modern conditions, such control must be collective. Once such collective control is established, the conditions that favored religious
ideas and appeals will disappear.

> The religious reflex of the real world can, in any case, only then
> finally vanish, when the practical relations of everyday life offer
> to man none but perfectly intelligible and reasonable relations with
> regard to his fellow men and to nature.
> The life-process of society, which is based on the process of ma-
> terial production, does not strip off its mystical veil until it is
> treated as production by freely associated men, and is consciously
> regulated by them in accordance with a settled plan.[35]

Once it is so treated, the need for illusions has disappeared, because
relations among men and between men and nature have become
"perfectly simple and intelligible."

Freedom from illusion about the relations of men in society is
seen as a by-product of the classless society of the future. For Marx,
knowledge of man and society remains ideological, an example of
what he calls "false consciousness," as long as it is conditioned by
the class struggle. No man is exempt from this conditioning while
that struggle continues. In this context, Marx posits a nexus between existing social relations and the ordinary man's ability to
comprehend them. His repeated references to the simplicity and in-

telligibility of social relations suggest that these relations are more intelligible in some social structures than in others. "Intelligibility" refers to the understanding of ordinary men. A kind of prudence uncontaminated by ideology will become possible once class struggles have ceased and men make full use of their rational and creative faculties.

But Marx also contrasts his own scientific analysis with the ideological interpretations of classical economists, utopian socialists, and others.[36] He likes to compare his approach with that characteristic of the physical and biological sciences.[37] In this way, scientific knowledge of society—implicitly distinguished from the ordinary man's understanding of social relations—appears possible under capitalism. Ideological distortion is not therefore an inevitable byproduct of a society rent by class conflict. Despite his distrust of prudence and reason, Marx clings to the eighteenth-century belief that scientific knowledge of society is attainable and will play an important historical role.

> In times when the class struggle nears the decisive hour, the process of dissolution going on within the ruling class—in fact, within the whole range of an old society—assumes such a violent, glaring character that a small section of the ruling class cuts itself adrift and joins the revolutionary class, the class that holds the future in its hands. Just as, therefore, at an earlier period, a section of the nobility went over to the bourgeoisie, so now a portion of the bourgeoisie goes over to the proletariat, and in particular, a portion of the *bourgeois ideologists, who have raised themselves to the level of comprehending theoretically the historical movements as a whole.*[38]

In this view, the workers will provide the political momentum for the great historical change to come. They will cause a revolutionary upheaval against the material and psychological inhumanities to which they have been subjected, but they do not possess the intellectual tools to direct that upheaval. This direction will be provided by bourgeois ideologists who respond to the dissolution of their own class, the miseries of the proletariat, and the historical opportunities arising from the intensified class struggle and the underutilization of man's productive potential.

Accordingly, Marx clings to both horns of the ideological dilemma. He insists on the reductionist analysis of ideas as emanations of the class struggle. Illusion will vanish from our understanding of society only when freely associated men regulate society in accordance with a settled plan.[39] But social knowledge would have no constructive role now, if truth will be attained only in the society of the future. Marx does not accept this implication, which would cut the ground from under his own claim as a scientist and political leader. His work is a life-long insistence upon man's capacity to forge the intellectual instruments for the reorganization of society. Accordingly, he shifts back and forth between reductionism and the belief in the constructive role of ideas. Under capitalism the working class provides the lever for the reorganization of society (reductionist analysis), but the labor movement cannot be successful unless guided by the results of scientific inquiry (belief in reason). In responding to the contradictions of capitalist society (reductionist analysis), bourgeois ideologists "raise themselves" to an understanding of the historical movement (belief in reason).

Marx believes in the historically constructive role of human intelligence but his inquiries undermine that belief. By treating all knowledge as a distorting reflex of the real world, he casts doubt upon the ends and uses of knowledge and of all human activities. Since, under capitalism, men pervert rather than enhance the "benefit of life," all positive use of intelligence is precarious. Subsequent history and the vulgarizations of his followers have obscured the fundamental tragedy of Marx as a man of knowledge. He wants to know—accurately and dispassionately—but he also wants to make sure that the knowledge gained will play a constructive role in human affairs. Yet his theory casts doubt upon the belief in reason to which his life's work is dedicated. Perhaps these contradictions explain the passion of Marx, the wild polemics against his opponents, the promethean hope, and the undercurrent of despair. Consideration of a near contemporary, Alexis de Tocqueville, will reveal the work of a man who grappled with similar problems but did not conceal from himself the tragedy of the man of knowledge who seeks to enhance the role of prudence in human affairs.

Alexis de Tocqueville (1805–1859). Tocqueville is a seeker after truth, he believes in reason, and he wants to enhance the "benefit and use of life"—quite as much as Marx. But while Marx is an heir of the Enlightenment, Tocqueville is an heir of its critics. Where Marx carries forward the eighteenth-century belief in science and develops particularly the "science of ideas," Tocqueville makes no reference to the scientific approach and, if anything, opposes the reductionist analysis of ideas, as Burke had done. Where Marx follows the model of the natural sciences and insists upon the objectivity of his materialistic approach despite the manifest passion of his writings, Tocqueville patterns himself after writers like Montesquieu and avows his passionate concern with moral problems.

Yet Tocqueville knows that the pursuit of knowledge must be guarded against the passions of partisanship aroused in the wake of the French Revolution. It is characteristic of the man that his discussions of method and his claims to objectivity appear not in his published writings but in his correspondence with friends. Tocqueville does not claim to be a scientist and does not publicize his procedures and erudition so that his objectivity may be checked by others, as in the natural sciences. Yet inquiry free of bias is indispensable to sound judgment, and Tocqueville states the reasons why he believes himself to be dispassionate.

> They ascribe to me alternately aristocratic and democratic prejudices. If I had been born in another period, or in another country, I might have had either the one or the other. But my birth, as it happened, made it easy for me to guard against both. I came into the world at the end of a long revolution, which after destroying ancient institutions, had created none that could last. When I entered life, aristocracy was dead and democracy as yet unborn. My instinct, therefore, could not lead me blindly either to the one or to the other. I lived in a country which for forty years had tried everything and settled nothing. I was on my guard, therefore, against political illusions. Myself belonging to the ancient aristocracy of my country, I had no natural hatred or jealousy of the aristocracy; nor could I have any natural affection for it, since that aristocracy had ceased to exist, and one can be strongly attached only to the living. I was near enough to know it thoroughly, and

far enough to judge dispassionately. I may say as much for the
democratic element. It had done me, as an individual, neither
good nor harm. I had no personal motive, apart from my public
convictions, to love or to hate it. Balanced between the past and
the future, with no natural instinctive attraction towards either, I
could without an effort look quietly on each side of the question.[40]

Accidents of birth and historical circumstance are here advanced as
the basis of objectivity. In reductionist analysis, the social conditioning of knowledge is ordinarily perceived as a source of error
and bias, but Tocqueville attributes to that conditioning his own
freedom from bias.[41] He readily acknowledges that other circumstances might have led him to adopt the aristocratic or democratic
prejudices falsely attributed to him. That it did not happen is the
result of attributes entirely unique to his personal situation. True
to his aristocratic heritage Tocqueville guards against bias in a
manner that is incompatible with the equalitarian tenets of science.
For in science safeguards against error and bias are accepted only if
they are open to public inspection and therefore in principle accessible to everyone who adopts the required procedures.

   But if Tocqueville is aristocratic in his claim to objectivity, he
also makes good his contention that he is dispassionate. In his view,
the development of human societies toward greater equality is an
established fact, decreed by providence. Unlike his fellow aristocrats, he does not deny what he considers inevitable, quarrel with
it or resist it to the last. He seeks to understand the conditions of
equality in all their implications, as in his great work *Democracy in
America*. He concludes, it is true, that under these conditions a
government "cannot be maintained without certain conditions of
intelligence, of private morality, and of religious belief." But hc believes that these conditions can be attained, since "after all it may
be God's will to spread a moderate amount of happiness over all
men, instead of heaping a large sum upon a few by allowing only a
small minority to approach perfection." [42] Tocqueville thus accepts the goals of democracy but attempts to "diminish the ardor
of the Republican party" by showing that democracy is not an
easily realized dream and—while conferring benefits on the people

—is not likely to develop the "noblest powers of the human mind." At the same time, he attempts to "abate the claims of the aristocrats" by showing that democracy is not synonymous with destruction and anarchy but compatible with order, liberty, and religion. Democracy of this kind, rather than an unspeakable tyranny, can be achieved if the aristocratic opponents will not resist what they lack the power to prevent. By making the "impulse in one quarter and resistance in the other . . . less violent" Tocqueville seeks to ensure a peaceable development of society.[43]

This balance in the political sphere is matched by Tocqueville's capacity for self-scrutiny, which helps him preserve the objectivity of his pursuit of knowledge. Aristocratic background and a realistic assessment of men lead to a somber view indeed. "I love mankind in general, but I constantly meet with individuals whose baseness revolts me." [44] Or, "If to console you for having been born, you must meet with men whose most secret motives are always actuated by fine and elevated feelings, you need not wait, you may go and drown yourself immediately." [45] But Tocqueville also reminds his friends and himself that in fact such high motives are predominant in a few men and that they occur even in a large majority of men from time to time. Consequently, one "need not make such faces at the human race." [46] Nor is it only a matter of general attitude. One should be aware that our estimate of men has unwitting effects upon human affairs and upon ourselves.

> Some persons try to be of use to men while they despise them, and others because they love them. In the services rendered by the first there is always something incomplete, rough, and contemptuous that inspires neither confidence nor gratitude. I should like to belong to the second class, but often I cannot. . . . I struggle daily against a universal contempt for my fellow-creatures. I sometimes succeed, at my own expense, by a minute uncompromising investigation into the motives of my own conduct.[47]

When Tocqueville tries to judge himself as if he were an indifferent spectator or opponent, he is more inclined to "drop a little in my own esteem" than to place too low an estimate on other men. And elsewhere he declares that "man with his vices, his weaknesses, and his virtues, strange combination though he be of good and evil, of grandeur and of baseness, is still, on the whole, the object most worthy of study, interest, pity, attachment, and admiration in the world, and since we have no angels, we cannot attach ourselves, or devote ourselves to anything greater or nobler than our fellow-creatures." [48]

Aristocrat though he was, Tocqueville put himself on a par with the masses of men, who were the objects of his most passionate concern. Considering the march toward greater equality inevitable, he devoted his life to the furtherance of men's understanding of the democratic societies that were emerging, so that they might be safeguarded against the dangers of despotism. He did not base his claim to be heard either on his background or on his standing as a scholar but solely on the strength of his concern, his personal detachment, and the persuasiveness of his reasoning. Tocqueville found a very direct relationship between his ideas and political action, even though he disclaimed not so much the ambitions, as the qualifications of great statesmanship.

> No! I certainly do not laugh at political convictions; I do not consider them as indifferent in themselves, and as mere instruments in the hands of men. I laugh bitterly at the monstrous abuse that is every day made of them, as I laugh when I see virtue and religion turned to dishonest uses, without losing any of my respect for virtue and religion. I struggle with all my might against the false wisdom, the fatal indifference, which in our day saps the energy of so many great minds. I try not to have two worlds: a moral one, where I still delight in all that is good and noble, and the other political, where I may lie with my face to the ground, enjoying the full benefit of the dirt which covers it.[49]

Here, then, is detachment in the pursuit of knowledge, a passionate concern for the "good of mankind" and a direct effort to use knowledge to this end. For Tocqueville, politics is the natural arena in which that knowledge must be applied in order to affect the course of human affairs.[50]

Tocqueville's assessment of this task is strikingly different from that of Marx. Committed to the proletarian cause as the lever for the reorganization of society, Marx nevertheless distinguishes

sharply between the untutored proletariat and the bourgeois ideologists who analyze the capitalist economy and understand history.
Despite his populist stance and his insistence that ultimately proletarian class consciousness and the scientific understanding of capitalism develop in response to the class struggle, Marx makes clear
that, for the time being, what workers *are* is far more important
than what they *think*.

> It is not relevant what this or that worker or even what the whole
> proletariat *conceive* to be their aim, for the time being. It matters
> only *what* the proletariat *is* and that it will be forced to act his-
> torically in accordance with this *being*. The aim and the historical
> action of the proletariat are clearly and irrevocably outlined by its
> life situation as well as by the entire organization of present-day
> bourgeois society.[51]

Tocqueville, on the other hand, makes no distinction between men
of knowledge and the masses of the people—despite his aristocratic
background. He is convinced, furthermore, that, to influence the
course of events, it will not do to "cure all our ills" by institutional
means, for institutions exert "only a secondary influence over the
destinies of men." For him, the "excellence of political societies"
depends upon the "sentiments, principles, and opinions, the moral
and intellectual qualities given by nature and education to the men
of whom they consist." [52]
Accordingly, Tocqueville believes that men will be able to avert
the dangers of despotism implicit in democracy, if they develop
the moral and intellectual qualities necessary to the task. His own
inquiry into the natural tendencies of a democratic society seeks
to point out these dangers so that by timely discovery and confrontation "we may look our enemies in the face and know against
what we have to fight." [53] Tocqueville sees these "natural tendencies" in precarious balance with the forces opposing them.[54] It
is not possible to predict the outcome. In the face of uncertainty
he wishes society to behave "like a strong man who exposes himself
to the danger before him as a necessary part of his undertaking and
is alarmed only when he cannot see clearly what it is." [55] On another occasion, Tocqueville makes clear the significance of this po-

sition. The eighteenth century had "an exaggerated and somewhat childish trust in the control which men and peoples were supposed to have of their own destinies." That idea may have led to many follies, but it also produced great things. Since the revolution, however, so many generous ideas and great hopes have miscarried that men have been led to the opposite extreme.

> After having felt ourselves capable of transforming ourselves, we now feel incapable of reforming ourselves; after having had excessive pride, we have now fallen into excessive self-pity; we thought we could do everything, and now we think we can do nothing; we like to think that struggle and effort are henceforth useless and that our blood, muscles, and nerves will always be stronger than our will power and courage. This is really the great sickness of our age. . . .[56]

It is this sickness against which Tocqueville takes his stand, an heir of the Enlightenment in the tradition of Montesquieu.

Nevertheless, Tocqueville's life was marked by profound pessimism. At the age of thirty-one, he wrote to a friend of his desire to persuade men that respect for law and religion must be combined with freedom and that to grant freedom is the best way of preserving morality and religion. "You will tell me that this is impossible; I am inclined to the same opinion; but it is the truth, and I will speak it at all risks. . . ."[57] At the age of forty-three, at the time of the 1848 Revolution, he wrote to the same friend that, if he had had children, he would warn them to be prepared for everything, for no one can count on the future.

> In France especially, men should rely on nothing that can be taken away; [they should] try to acquire those things which one can never lose till one ceases to exist: fortitude, energy, knowledge, and prudence. . . .[58]

And toward the end of his life, at the age of fifty-one, he wrote to Madame Swetchine:

> No tranquillity and no material comfort can in my mind make up for the loss [of liberty]. And yet I see that most of the men of my time—of the most honest among them, for I care little about the others—think only of accommodating themselves to the new sys-

tem and, what most of all disturbs and alarms me, turn a taste for slavery into a virtue. I could not think and feel as they do, if I tried: it is even more repugnant to my nature than to my will. . . . You can hardly imagine how painful, and often bitter, it is to me to live in this moral isolation; to feel myself shut out of the intellectual commonwealth of my age and country.[59]

We see that Tocqueville passionately believed in freedom and rejected the reductionist analysis as false wisdom tending toward "the unfair circumscription of human power." Yet throughout his life he was haunted by the impenetrability of the future and by the melancholy realization that the truths he had discovered were *not* being used for the "good of mankind." As a result, despite his relations, neighbors, and friends, his mind had "not a family or a country." [60] The contrast with Marx is startling, if we consider that this life-long exile who had family but few friends and, one suspects, few neighbors, derived courage and confidence in his mission from the very determinism that Tocqueville rejected, from the conviction that he had "comprehended theoretically the historical movement as a whole." It is hard to resist the conclusion that the wish for power through knowledge was father to Marx's determinist and reductionist theories, while Tocqueville's quest for truth without the promise of power was linked with his willingness to face the tragedy of moral isolation.

Emile Durkheim (1858–1917). The experience of moral isolation is as central a problem for Durkheim as for Tocqueville. Writing some of his major works during the years of the Dreyfus Affair (1895–1906), Durkheim witnessed a threat to moral standards fully as great as did Tocqueville when he observed the consequences of the French Revolution and the failure of French society to achieve institutional stability. Like other critics of the Enlightenment, both men are preoccupied with questions of morality. Yet the two differ profoundly. For Tocqueville, moral isolation was an intense, personal experience, as well as an object of study. As a champion of liberty, he was conscious of the degree to which liberty is jeopardized by the moral weaknesses associated with the drive for equality. He believed that his contemporaries had abandoned the ideals of the eighteenth century, and he felt the loneliness of his position. For Durkheim moral isolation appears to have been a less personal experience than for Tocqueville. Belief in science furnishes the moral basis of Durkheim's approach. He is the champion of sociology, and he endeavors to introduce his chosen discipline into the scientific community. Durkheim states this purpose clearly:

> Our principal objective is to extend scientific rationalism to human behavior. It can be shown that behavior of the past, when analyzed, can be reduced to relationships of cause and effect. These relationships can then be transformed, by an equally logical operation, into rules of action for the future. . . . It therefore seems to us that in these times of renascent mysticism an undertaking such as ours should be regarded quite without apprehension and even with sympathy by all those who, while disagreeing with us on certain points, yet share our faith in the future of reason.[61]

We shall see that, in Durkheim's view, it is science and not—as with Tocqueville—liberty, morality, and religion that will reconstruct the moral order.

To establish sociology as a science is Durkheim's central concern. In his very first publication, his Latin thesis on *Montesquieu's Contribution to the Rise of Social Science,* Durkheim emphasizes the distinction between science and art.[62] Life goes on, decisions about what to do must be made quickly, and the reasons for our actions are hastily assembled. "We improvise a science as we go along," but such collected arguments, by which men of action support their opinions, "do not reflect phenomena . . . but merely states of mind."

> Even in abstract questions, no doubt, our ideas spring from the heart, for the heart is the source of our entire life. But if our feelings are not to run away with us, they must be governed by reason. Reason must be set above the accidents and contingencies of life.[63]

Accordingly, science must be advanced in complete independence and "in utter disregard of utility." The more clear-cut the distinction between science and art, which Durkheim defines as decisions on what to do, the more useful science will be for art.

Durkheim proceeds to define "the conditions necessary for the establishment of social science." Each science must have its own specific object. The only objects that admit of scientific study are those that constitute a type, that share "features common to all individuals of the same type," that are finite in number and ascertainable. But description of types must be supplemented by interpretation, which presupposes stable relations between cause and effect, for without them everything is fortuitous and does not admit of interpretation.[64] No social science is possible if societies are not subject to laws. No one questions the possibility of natural science; the principal assumptions underlying these sciences have been tested and never found false; hence they are "also valid, in all likelihood, for human societies, which are part of nature." [65] Like Marx before him, Durkheim takes the established natural sciences for his model, and he is specific in his use of this model.

> So long as everything in human societies seemed so utterly fortuitous, no one could have thought of classifying them. There can be no types of things unless there are causes which, though operating in different places and at different times, always and everywhere produce the same effects. And where is the object of social science if the lawgiver can organize and direct social life as he pleases? The subject matter of science can consist only of things that have a stable nature of their own and are able to resist the human will.[66]

Even then a method of investigation is needed that does not exist ready-made but must be developed as social science grapples with the great complexities that confront it.

In his *Rules of Sociological Method*, Durkheim elaborates this point by stating the basic theoretical assumptions of his work.

1. Social phenomena are a reality *sui generis*, and they cannot be explained by reference to less complex or nonsocial phenomena— exactly as psychological phenomena can be understood only as such rather than by a reduction to physiological processes, for example.

2. Sociology is the study of social groups, albeit groups composed

of individuals. The group, however, is a new, synthetic reality, arising from the *association* of individuals.

3. At its own level, society must be observed with regard to the
consciousness a collectivity forms of itself, much as the individual
is observed through his consciousness. The collective thought embodied in language is an obvious example of such collective consciousness.

4. Language, moral rules, religious beliefs and practices, myth,
folklore, proverbs, popular sayings, and other aspects of culture are
external to the individual and exercise a *moral constraint* upon
him. These collective "representations" exist when the individual
comes into the world, and he acquires them unwittingly. That he
is constrained to acquire them becomes apparent when his violation
of cultural norms is censured.[67]

In later comments on his work, Durkheim seeks to correct the
impression that his collectivist approach totally subordinates the
individual. Society exists only in and through individuals; the collective derivation of their thought and feeling is as natural to them
as the air they breathe.[68] Accordingly, "society" is immanent in the
individual at the same time that it transcends him by virtue of its
greater duration and power of constraint. Even Durkheim's efforts
to qualify his emphasis on the collectivity re-emphasize how far he
has carried the analytical reduction of individual consciousness.

Symptomatic in this respect are two explicit discussions of individualism. Durkheim considers the cult of the individual a great
threat to social solidarity, especially in the context of economic
competition. But he also appears to reconcile himself to this cult
of the modern world by showing that individualism itself is a product of society.[69] Durkheim considers the problem again in his last
writings, in which he discusses the frequent antagonism of social
relations. Our bodily appetites are self-centered and therefore individualistic; our minds are preoccupied with ideas that are socially
derived and therefore universal. Accordingly, *individuality* results
from the biochemical nature of every person; it is a by-product of
those purely physical attributes that make every man unique. *Personality*, on the other hand, has its source in the feelings and ideas

that the members of a collectivity share. This conception is consistent with Durkheim's theory that the idea of the soul's independence from the finite body (immortality) is derived from the
fact that society continues while individuals are born and die.[70] In
this way, Durkheim rejects the earlier reductionism of the ideologues, which attributed all intellectual and moral activity to a
substratum of bodily sensations. His own sociological reductionism
cites man's biological attributes as the only source of individuality.
Paradoxically, the individual is here located in what all men have
in common, while his psychological and intellectual faculties become the locus of a common humanity, despite the fact that cultural differences rather than physical attributes have spread variety
over the face of the earth.

This concluding paradox of Durkheim's work brings us back to
the ideological dimensions of social theory. How does Durkheim's
sociological theory affect his conception of the ends of knowledge
and the uses of his ideas? He analyzes how European society is characterized increasingly by a moral decline attributable to the increasing division of labor. If modern society is to become "healthy"
again, legal regulations are required that will encourage co-opera-
tion; and social solidarity must be fostered by voluntary associations of occupational groups.[71] To achieve these effects men must
rely on knowledge, since traditional beliefs have lost their efficacy.
Durkheim points out that:

> Man seeks to learn and man kills himself because of the loss of
> cohesion in his religious society; he does not kill himself because
> of his learning. It is certainly not the learning he acquires that dis-
> organizes religion; but the desire for knowledge wakens because
> religion becomes disorganized. Knowledge is not sought as a means
> to destroy accepted opinions but because their destruction has
> commenced.[72]

Here and throughout Durkheim's work the basic cause of a declining morality is seen as a *loss of social cohesion* of which the decline
of religion, the tendency to commit suicide, and the quest for
knowledge are different symptoms or consequences. But if this view
is valid, then why does Durkheim hope that knowledge, which is

among these consequences, can construct a new and vigorous morality? His answer is:

> Far from knowledge being the source of the evil, it is its remedy,
> the only remedy we have. Once established beliefs have been car-
> ried away by the current of affairs, they cannot be artificially re-
> established; only reflection can guide us in life, after this. Once
> the social instinct is blunted, intelligence is the only guide left us
> and we have to reconstruct a conscience by its means. Dangerous
> as is the undertaking there can be no hesitation, for we have no
> choice. . . . [Science] has not the dissolvent effect ascribed to it,
> but is the only weapon for our battle against the dissolution which
> gives birth to science itself.[73]

Durkheim adds that one must not make a "self-sufficient end" out
of science or education. They are only means or guides to aid us
in our efforts to reconstruct a "social conscience."

But what can we hope from a science which tells us that moral
standards remain intact only as long as sacred beliefs are shared by
the members of a collectivity? Durkheim shows skepticism to a degree when he refers to intelligence and science as the *only guide or
weapon left to us.* His work demonstrates that moral norms are viable if the social cohesion of groups is intact, but that this cohesion
must decline as a result of the division of labor. At the end, Durkheim's subjective faith in reason remains, but intellectually it is
undermined by the theory and evidence that he developed in order
to sustain it.

Max Weber (1864–1920).   Of the four theorists considered here,
Max Weber concerns himself most directly with the problem of objectivity. He does not view scientific neutrality as a by-product of
the historical process as does Marx, of circumstance and personal
quality as does Tocqueville, or of the effort to establish sociology
after the model of the natural sciences as does Durkheim. For
Weber, objectivity results from the deliberate efforts of the scholar.
While Tocqueville claims objectivity as a concomitant of personal
experience, Weber seeks to achieve it through methodological clarification and self-restraint. But like Tocqueville, Weber emphasizes

the importance of ideas and sentiments for an understanding of social life—in contrast to Marx and Durkheim, who continue the reductionist tradition of the ideologues. It is true that Weber, as
well as Tocqueville, appreciates the insights of this tradition. Nevertheless, both consider ideas an irreducible factor in social life,
and it is above all in his analysis of ideas that Weber's claim to scientific objectivity must be assessed.

The intellectual vantage point of these theorists is clearest perhaps in their treatment of religion. For Marx, the "religious reflex"
provides a spurious gratification of human desires, a spiritual justification of the inhumanities of man's social condition. Now that
technology can fulfill these desires, religion has become unnecessary
and will disappear. Tocqueville considers religious faith among the
highest manifestations of the human spirit and is aghast at the
abuses and perversions to which it is subjected. To preserve liberty
as relations among men become more equal, it is necessary to
strengthen religion and morality. Toward the end of his life,
Tocqueville became more religious though he recognized the
growth of secularism among his contemporaries. For Durkheim, religion is an object of study, as enduring a phenomenon as Tocqueville believed it to be, but not a personal concern. Science cannot
accept the literal truth of religious beliefs, but it recognizes and
analyzes their symbolic truth. For Durkheim, religion arises from
the reality of group life: "It is society which the faithful worship;
the superiority of the gods over men is that of the group over its
members." [74] Weber's approach to religion contains all these elements. Like Marx, he recognizes the material interests involved in
religious beliefs and institutions, especially the economic interests
of religious functionaries. Yet, like Tocqueville, he also considers
religious ideas as an aspect of human creativity. Personally areli-
gious, Weber takes as scientific an interest in religion as does Durkheim. But Durkheim focuses on primitive religion in order to understand its "essence," while Weber concentrates on the age of religious creativity (Confucius, Buddha, Old Testament prophets)
in order to understand the characteristics of Western civilization.
This attempt to analyze the highest manifestations of human spir-

ituality gives special point to Weber's concern with the problem of scientific objectivity.

All inquiry is initiated by the subjective orientation of the investigator. In the natural sciences, this orientation depends on the results previously obtained, the unresolved problems suggested by these results, and the ingenuity of the researcher. In the social sciences, cumulation is evident primarily in the collection of data. In the interpretation of these data, it is less evident and more difficult to sustain. The questions raised for investigation depend more upon considerations of cultural relevance (*Wertbezogenheit*) than upon previous findings. The different approaches to religion mentioned above exemplify the mutability of such considerations. But if the same questions are raised about the same data, then equally competent men will arrive at the same conclusions—provided that value-judgments (*Werturteile*) do not intrude. It is at this point that Weber sees the major obstacle to objectivity.

His most explicit statements in this respect are a criticism of professional malpractice. Nationalist professors in Imperial Germany were unable or unwilling to distinguish between their civic and academic responsibilities, and Weber attacked their propagation of political opinions under the guise of science. In many settings, it is relatively easy to meet this criticism. The speaker or writer himself declares what his values are and warns his listeners or readers that they must not mistake certain statements for judgments authenticated by scientific findings. Value-judgments must be assessed by each person in the light of his own evaluations. Weber insists passionately on the separation of value-judgments from scientific inquiry, for he is as deeply concerned with the one as with the other. Failure to observe this separation appears to him an abuse of science *and* a monstrous desecration of what men hold most dear—in contrast to Tocqueville who sees in that same separation a "false wisdom" and a "fatal indifference." At this point, the hiatus between the two men's ideas could not be greater—despite affinity in other respects.

Weber is directly concerned with the formulation of concepts for research; Tocqueville is not. For Weber, the exclusion of value-judgments is the pre-condition of scientific inquiry about man and society. Concepts must enable us to identify types of social phenomena unequivocally and without intrusion from "the will and the affections" (Bacon). Such classification and identification are elementary scientific procedure. The zoologist hardly requires a reminder that his own liking for fox terriers has no bearing on the classification of dogs. A social theorist like Weber, however, may wish to identify the magnetic appeal that commanding personalities have had for masses of people throughout history. Where the fact of this appeal is unquestioned, the concept "charisma" applies, whether the reference is to a holy man like St. Francis of Assisi or a "great bird of prey" like Alexander the Great.[75] Weber insists that the enormous ethical gulf between two such figures must be considered in its own moral terms, clearly separated from the finding that they have at least one trait in common.

The value-neutral formulation of concepts is as crucial for Weber as is the theoretical foundation of sociology for Durkheim. Both men are committed to the advancement of knowledge, but the difference between them is marked. For Durkheim, social science becomes possible to the degree that "realities can be reduced to a type" consisting of "the features common to all individuals of the same type." A social science that characterizes a typical social phenomenon, "cannot fail to describe the normal form of social life . . . ; whatever pertains to the type is normal, and whatever is normal is healthy.[76] Durkheim subscribes to a philosophical realism that identifies the type with the prevailing characteristics of the phenomenon. Consequently, he considers it indispensable for social science

> to discover *in the data themselves* some definite indication enabling us to distinguish between sickness and health. If such a sign is lacking, we are driven to take refuge in deduction and move away from the concrete facts.[77]

This position Weber rejects *in toto*. Terms like "health" or "sickness" when applied to society are for him, criteria of moral worth by which men arrive at ethical judgments.[78] These criteria should not be confused with the normal or typical forms of social life. For Weber social phenomena exist in a continuity that allows no natural demarcation.[79] Instead of positing natural types with a more or less stable arrangement of their elements, as Durkheim would have it, Weber posits ideal types—benchmark concepts constructed out of a one-sided simplification and exaggeration of the evidence as it is found in society.

This basic difference in orientation has several consequences. For Durkheim, the purpose of ascertaining natural types is to understand the features common to all individuals of a given type. By recognizing the similar social constraints to which all these individuals are subject, we can explain their actions in terms of cause and effect. This knowledge enables us to understand what is normal and healthy in social life and to act accordingly. For Weber the purpose of constructing ideal types is to interpret the meaning of actions, to understand what sense it makes for men to act as they do.[80] The simplifications involved in this procedure give order to the multiplicity of phenomena. By referring to these artificial benchmarks, the analyst can assess the actions which are documented or observed.[81] An example is the ideal type of the charismatic leader and the routinization of his appeal. In Weber's view, the analyst can assess the degree to which a given action approaches the ideal type of a personal or institutionalized charisma without himself evaluating these approximations. The purpose of this procedure is not to achieve causal explanation, however. Weber makes quite clear that for him sociology is an auxiliary discipline, one that uses the comparative and classificatory procedure to distinguish between what is general and what is unique. In this way, sociology establishes what is recurrent in different societies, while history explains the unique event.[82]

It follows that Weber's conception of purpose is more cautious than that of Durkheim. The idea that men pursue knowledge for its own sake or for intellectual clarity cannot be found in Durkheim, who puts major emphasis upon enlarging man's control of human affairs. Weber subscribes to all three objectives. But he is circumspect with regard to the practical uses of social science in keeping with his emphasis on the hiatus between the detachment of the scientist and the commitment essential to the man of action. Having once taken the position that truth is not a by-product of history, and that types and criteria of "social health" do not reside in the data themselves, Weber is consistent. The scientist can ascertain the facts, point out the assets and liabilities of alternative actions, clarify value-positions in terms of their internal consistency and possible consequences. He can do no more; his role is that of adviser, assistant, or expert if he is consulted. For Weber, there is no direct link between knowledge and power in human affairs.[83]

Compared with the hopes of the Enlightenment this position is one of great resignation. In contrast to Marx and Durkheim, Weber does not have a strong faith in the power of knowledge in society. He shares Tocqueville's pessimism in this regard, though not his melancholy. In Weber's case, the hiatus between fact and value, between the scholar and the man of action is not a token of indifference, as Tocqueville sees it. It is evidence rather of Weber's simultaneous commitment to scholarship and action. In his life-long effort to achieve a creative relationship between these spheres, Weber put a premium on preserving the integrity of both and thus exposed himself, as only Tocqueville had done before him, to tension and utter frustration. To assert and search for the meaningfulness of the individual's life in a world without God, to recognize the compulsions of human existence yet assert man's capacity to act, to advance social science yet probe into the irrational foundations and consequences of knowledge—this acceptance of tension left its mark on Weber's personal life. Like Tocqueville before him, he paid a price for tolerating the ambiguities of reason in human affairs that Marx and Durkheim were less willing to accept.

◆§ LEGACIES AND EMERGING PROBLEMS
Scientific inquiry presupposes a belief in science. Most people adhere to this belief in the expectation that "knowledge is power." In the social sciences, confidence in this maxim has been undermined.

Efforts to advance social knowledge have led unwittingly to changes in conceptions of human nature. Inquiry presupposes the control of bias. To control bias, we must understand its sources. In this respect, our understanding has advanced from Bacon's theory of idols to Nietzsche's and Freud's views of the organic conditioning of knowledge. The sciences of men have grown together with a skeptical view of human nature, and the latter raises questions about the utility of social knowledge.

These questions have been evaded where belief in progress through science and distrust of common prudence have gone hand in hand. The view that the mass of humanity is subject to social laws has been linked—implicitly perhaps—with the assumption that an elite of social scientists can understand these laws and enhance knowledge, human utility, and power. But through the work they do, social scientists belie the assertion that *all* men are subject to social laws. This exception reveals an "infusion of the will and the affections" against which Francis Bacon warned three centuries ago. But when everything is expected of science and nothing of man, we must take stock of our assumptions. Trust in science and distrust of prudence is a "stage play" that "wonderfully obstructs the understanding," like Bacon's "idols of the theatre." Emancipation from received opinion in this regard and repeated examination of the mental set with which we approach the study of society are indispensable methodological tools.

Such re-examination has been attempted in this discussion by reflection on the historical and theoretical dimensions of ideology. As we contrast the nonideological world view with the questioning of human knowledge and power that marks the "Age of Ideology," we cannot conclude that the "end of ideology" is in sight.[84] Rather, the efforts to control bias and questions about the ends and uses of knowledge expose the action-involvement of all ideas. This involvement exists in all the sciences, but poses special problems in those fields in which every general statement applies to the man of knowledge as well as to the subject he investigates.

The paradox of the liar, as the ancient philosopher Zeno formulated it, is an integral part of theories about society. All social theorists are bound to begin with postulates on how they propose to investigate society dispassionately. For, in the "Age of Ideology" they seek truth through the quest for objectivity rather than praise God through discovery of His wisdom. This effort leads to two typical variants, at least. The reductionist approach seeks to control or exclude error by reference to an impersonal source or safeguard. Truth as a by-product of the class-struggle and of methods used in the natural sciences are the examples we mentioned. The approach through self-knowledge seeks to ensure objectivity by cautions that the investigator applies to himself. Truth as a by-product of personal experience and opportunity and of methodological inquiry and self-discipline were our examples. Such approaches do not resolve the ambiguities of knowledge in human affairs; rather they accentuate these ambiguities through dogmatism or mitigate them even at the price of personal resignation. The belief in reason has been on trial ever since social philosophers began to employ the natural sciences as their model. Their hope was to discover universal principles of morality or regularities in the behavior of men and societies. This hope presupposed remnants of an earlier belief in man's God-given capacity to discover uniformities underneath the diversity of appearances. The resulting knowledge would enhance man's moral stature. Eventually this view was superseded by the secular belief that knowledge would enhance man's "technical mastery of life" (Weber) and that such mastery is worthwhile. These latter assumptions are on trial today. We are learning that social theories are not alone in having failed to resolve the ambiguities inherent in the secularization of knowledge. The ambiguities of the nonideological world view had to be resolved by faith, but in the absence of faith we must live with the ambiguities of the human condition.

In his essay, "Science as a Vocation," Max Weber wrote some fifty years ago that scientists are professionally dedicated to the advancement of knowledge. They do not ask what ends this knowledge will serve, because increased "technical mastery" is to them a self-evident good. When we observe the pain of those struck down by an incurable disease, we yearn for the day when these remaining scourges will have been eradicated. All of us are tender toward the sick, because the means to help them are or may be within reach; if we lacked that confidence, we could not permit ourselves to be so tender. There is a world-wide unanimity in favor of death control, and this unanimity is the spirit that has initiated and sustained the growth of medical knowledge. Yet, in the two centuries that have elapsed since the beginning of modern medicine, the *effect* of advancing knowledge has been equivocal. From ancient times until the end of the seventeenth century, the world population did not exceed 500 million people; by the 1920s, it had increased to more than two billion. A report from the United Nations predicts that, by the year 2000, it will exceed six billion. This twelvefold increase in world population over a period of 350 years occurred with the aid of medical knowledge. On humanitarian and political grounds, it is impossible to withhold such knowledge from countries whose productive capacity does not keep step with their reproductive capacity. Such countries face the Sisyphean task of narrowing a gap while it increases. A century after the *Communist Manifesto*, a specter *is* haunting the world: the age-old prospects of famine, epidemic, and political tyranny or chaos.

Most of us recoil at the suggestion that this prospect is also a product of knowledge. Most of us hope that advances of knowledge will enable men to banish this specter from the face of the earth. We know we must make the attempt, we want to advance our technical mastery for "the benefit and use of life." Bacon made that declaration when the population of Europe was only beginning to increase after centuries of stagnation or cyclical variation. We too support this declaration. The "inherent value" of knowledge is equivocal in a world in which medicine by its effects on population can foster starvation, albeit indirectly, and in which increasing "technical mastery" may lead to the annihilation of life. Yet who will abandon the benefits of science because men are unable to control the powers science has unleashed? No advocate of ending the nuclear arms race, no man who warns against the effects of nuclear testing has been heard to suggest that, along with these destructive uses of knowledge, we discard its constructive uses also. It is unusual to call the benefits of science into question, but today we are all aware that the "technical mastery of life" can lead to consequences beyond human control. So far, few men have grappled with the corollary that the advancement of knowledge may one day destroy man's "technical mastery of life." [85] The ends and uses of knowledge (and that means the ideological dimensions of intellectual effort) call for critical examination—more urgently than ever.

CHANGING FOUNDATIONS
OF SCHOLARLY DETACHMENT

&§ THREE ȝ&

In the 1960s a strange affliction spread around the world. At many culture centers of Western civilization an epidemic of verbal violence occurred, accompanied by political demonstrations and novel forms of civil disobedience.

Similar events have occurred elsewhere. In Indian universities student riots are endemic, as are disturbances in Latin American universities. Within the Soviet orbit, post-Stalinist protest movements in countries like Poland, Czechoslovakia, and Yugoslavia have been based on student participation to a considerable extent. But the Indian riots have involved bread and butter issues. In Latin America university politics have long provided a proving ground for the politicians of tomorrow. And Polish, Czech, Yugoslav, and Spanish students aim at such bourgeois, nineteenth-century values as freedom of speech and of association.

By contrast, American, German, and French universities have witnessed an upsurge of student agitation in the midst of affluence and in a manner that transcends conventional politics—even those of the far left. Since the fall of 1964 the "movement" has responded to several conditions—among them the American national elections, agitation for civil rights, and the war in Vietnam, to refer only to the American experience. But while these conditions and the specific causes of disturbance at the University of California in Berkeley provided an immediate background for the spreading crisis of the universities, the roots of that crisis are more deep-

62

seated. They can be traced to cultural transformations at least two generations old, and they may also be related to the crisis of conscience that has been precipitated by the decline of colonial empires since World War II.

These roots are analyzed here in specific reference to the conditions and implications of scholarly detachment. I shall examine the consensual basis of academic communities, relate this discussion to the values of scholarship, and then turn to the changes in belief which have affected the intellectual legitimacy of scholarship. Finally I shall look into the question of what place academic self-government has in a democracy. In that context I shall return to the larger moral and political issues which student agitation has brought to the fore.

⤙§ CONSENSUAL CONDITIONS OF SCHOLARSHIP

All scholarship depends on communication concerning the findings and methods of study. Every statement made in this context invites consent and helps to define the circle of those who agree, while to some extent marking off those who do not. But such reasoned statements usually do not make explicit the logical, psychological, and social preconditions of reasoning. My purpose is to analyze the preconditions which favor a reasoning based upon scholarly detachment.

In the analysis of these preconditions Karl Mannheim's concept of a "socially unattached intelligentsia" (*freischwebende Intelligenz*) may be contrasted with Karl Popper's analysis of objectivity as the achievement of a scientific community. Both ideas refer to the relation between the social conditions of intellectual discourse and the partisanship or objectivity resulting from it. Mannheim tries to answer the question of how far "scientific politics" are possible; Popper is concerned with the achievements of the natural sciences.[1]

The idea of a "socially unattached intelligentsia" is not a strong concept. Men of letters became "socially unattached" when they were emancipated from their subservience to the church and to private patrons—an emancipation related to the emergence of modern journalism and a literate public. This development was quite compatible with new types of attachment and partisanship. Some writers may be affected by changing fashions in an anonymous mass market; others become spokesmen for particular groups; various professionals become attached to specific institutions like universities and foundations. Some even form groups of their own and remain "socially unattached" deliberately, such as bohemians on the margins of academic or artistic institutions. They share a cultural elitism and moral isolation which separates them from the surrounding materialism. Bohemianism is an important type of group formation in modern society, but its lack of attachment has little or nothing to do with objectivity in any type of knowledge. To be sure, a "socially unattached intelligentsia" goes together with a high degree of intellectual freedom and with an opportunity of seeing the relative validity of many viewpoints. But a "pluralistic culture" itself does nothing to ensure that this opportunity is utilized. It may only be conducive to intensified partisanship.

On the other hand, Popper has pointed out that scientific objectivity is *not* the result of an individual's lack of social attachments. Proximate objectivity results rather from an individual's participation in a scholarly community. Such a community is based on the inculcation of standards of discourse and investigation including the public disclosure of methods and results.

The social and psychological mechanisms of this scholarly community work very imperfectly, but they appear to obey certain rules that have proved effective. In an analytical study of the history of science Thomas Kuhn has shown that the scientific community is characterized by repeated but irregularly timed alternations between "normal science" and "scientific revolutions." With reference to the first concept Kuhn writes:

> Some accepted examples of actual scientific practices—examples which include law, theory, application and instrumentation together—provide models from which spring particular coherent traditions of scientific research. . . . The study of paradigms . . . is what mainly prepares the student for membership in the particular

scientific community with which he will later practice. . . . Men whose research is based on shared paradigms are committed to the same rules and standards for scientific pursuits. That commitment and the apparent consensus it produces are prerequisites for normal science, i.e. for the genesis and continuation of a particular research tradition.[2]

Terms like coherent tradition, community, commitment to the same rules and standards, and consensus suggest that group formation is a basic condition of scientific work. Such work rests on shared assumptions and considerations of relevance that have proved useful in the elaboration and application of theories. At the same time, theories usually leave certain residues unaccounted for. Occasionally their elaboration leads to observations that cannot be assimilated readily to "normal science." Scientific revolutions occur when questions arising at the margins are made the focus of attention by someone who offers a new theory that resolves old puzzles, or is more comprehensive. On that basis scientific work is given a new direction and a new group forms in the community of scholars. Kuhn's distinction between "normal science" and scientific revolutions reveals the major dynamic element in the consensual basis of that community, while Popper's emphasis on "intersubjective testability" shows how that consensus can be made effective.

The consensual basis of scholarly investigations and discourse is always proximate. It is most highly developed in the natural sciences. The social sciences and the humanities are less successful, varying greatly in the degree to which they aim at, and achieve, consensus on theories and methods. Where the capacity to achieve such consensus is very limited, academic disciplines tend to consist of more or less incompatible interpretations competing for attention. Scholarly discussion then perpetuates the controversies dividing these interpretations. For a working scholarly community this situation is an embarrassment and moral burden, since it fosters contention and discontent rather than a spirit of joint endeavor.

These dangers are enhanced by the typical uncertainties of

scholarly work, which greatly contribute to the "ambivalence of scientists."[3] Robert Merton has shown that scholars must choose between:

1. attention to detail and the excessive accuracy of the pedant;
2. the ready communication of ideas and the tendency to rush into print;
3. a receptivity to new ideas and the tendency to be swayed by intellectual fads;
4. a thorough knowledge of one's field and the tendency towards excessive reading and erudition;
5. a self-effacing interest in the pursuit of new knowledge and excessive interest in establishing claims of priority. Each of these issues poses the problem of the "Golden Mean" at the same time that the very qualities encouraged by a commitment to scholarship imply an invitation to excess.

Merton suggests that the ambivalence over priority claims is symptomatic of the difficulty in maintaining scholarly standards. The scientist's commitment implies an unselfish pursuit of knowledge and hence a readiness to welcome scientific advances from whatever source. If the advance of knowledge is his paramount interest, the scientist himself must endorse the speedy obsolescence of his own contribution. Consequently, a high degree of competitiveness is built into the structure of the scientific enterprise. Where every scientist's contribution is readily superseded, he will be anxious that his contribution, however large or small, receive its "proper" recognition. His anxiety is often as great as the intensity of his endeavor, and the "proper degree" of recognition is always debatable. Yet conflicts over priority claims are incompatible with the shared dedication to truth and the colleagueship which represent the ideals of the scholarly community. As Merton has demonstrated, these persistent conflicts over priorities arouse quite intense feelings of guilt, especially in the most eminent scientists. Since scientists are in fact competitive, their feelings of guilt suggest that they do indeed believe in the ideal of a selfless pursuit of knowledge.

All this presupposes scientific disciplines in which new knowledge clearly adds to, or supersedes, previous knowledge. In such disciplines the normative conflicts of the scientist's role can be resolved. But in many of the social sciences this is not the case. The social scientist's approximation of his ideal role is more difficult to judge and the moral burden of the conflicts he faces is correspondingly greater. Where standards are ambiguous, excesses like pedantry, premature publication, faddism, and "conspicuous erudition" (in Veblen's sense) are difficult to recognize. To be sure, even natural scientists must distinguish between the appropriate and the excessive; these are matters of judgment and experience. But in the social sciences there is the additional complexity that frequently such problems must be faced against a background of self-doubt and disputed standards.

Where uncertainty is endemic, each scholar faces decisions of academic propriety unaided and rather anxiously. When should incomplete and uncertain results be published? What degree of accuracy is appropriate to the problem at hand? How does one distinguish between the desired openness to new ideas and a faddist multiplication of intellectual idiosyncrasies? Or how does one distinguish between needed knowledge and needless erudition in a field beset by ambiguous advances and the rediscovery of old ideas? Finally, in a discipline like sociology, one may not even approximate the dangers of pride implicit in disputes over priority. Instead, one should probably ask whether or not a self-effacing pursuit of knowledge is jeopardized by the images and the prestige borrowed from the more successful natural sciences. In raising such questions no social scientist can be entirely easy in his mind.

As yet, there has not been an explicit discussion of the *moral* decisions involved in scholarship itself, so that scholars and their students can develop the moral sensibilities needed within the house of reason and science. As it is, the individual scholar simply uses his judgment—however conventional or wayward—in work of his own, and then submits that work to the critical judgment of others. Where the capacity to achieve definitive advances is small, such judgments depend upon the persuasiveness of the criteria on which they are based. Scholars and their scholarly critics are com-

mitted to the social sciences to the extent that they feel obliged
to improve their ideas through critical and self-critical communication among scholars. As Max Weber once put it, "truth is only
that which *claims* to be valid for all those who *want* truth." [4]
From that commitment a sense of obligation can arise, which leads
to improvement in scholarship and teaching—even in the absence
of clear criteria of advance.

Kuhn's analysis of "scientific revolutions" has suggested that
ideas develop along with the formation of scholarly groups.
Through graduate training, examinations, publications, and scientific meetings individuals come to adhere to certain standards of
scholarly work. Here a *reductionist* perspective is employed. Other
kinds of reductionism have often been used: reference may be
made to the community support on which a scientific project depends, or to the psychology of inventions—to cite two divergent
examples. The common feature of the reductionist approach is the
endeavor to relate ideas to a nonideational basis like the social and
historical conditions favoring their development and reception. In
addition, all scholarship involves a general *goal orientation*. Scientists and scholars are engaged in the pursuit of knowledge. With
them the idea of unlimited progress is an article of secular faith
based on the manifest cumulation of knowledge. They prefer the
knowledge resulting from scholarship and scientific inquiry to
ignorance or false certainty. Their commitment to the pursuit of
knowledge is based on that preference; it is not a matter of scientific demonstration. Yet such a preference can be questioned.
Even for those who accept it, it remains problematic, because
scholarship lacks clear priorities and the uses of knowledge are
uncertain.

✺§ THE VALUES OF SCHOLARSHIP

The goals of scholarship are general, like the preservation of life
or the understanding of beauty. Such goals are endorsed by everyone, but can militate against the moral consideration of a specific
situation. Even if such goals are applicable, it is often difficult to

know how to apply them. Within this ill-defined framework the scholar is free to choose his purposes of inquiry without outside interference. This freedom may lead to the choice of an approach on which all reasonable men would agree. But the choice may also be one over which reasonable men would dispute violently or to which they would react with indifference. Convenience, playfulness, and personal idiosyncrasy, even given the most selfless devotion to knowledge, can enter into such choices, as well as into the reactions of reasonable men. Freedom to choose the purpose of inquiry stands high on the list of academic values despite this diversity, because knowledge derived from scholarly inquiry is often advanced in surprising ways. The lack of freedom to pursue knowledge wherever it may lead is stultifying.

But despite the importance of free inquiry there are limits beyond which such freedom becomes self-defeating. A scholar's work cannot long survive an articulate and unsympathetic inspection of the motives which produced it, although introspection and articulate reflection on the choice of scholarly purposes are important tools of his work. Nor can men be scholars without believing in the value of the knowledge they pursue. And this belief limits freedom because scholars must exclude ends extraneous to inquiry itself, and in this sense must remain "ethically neutral." Freedom of inquiry is, thus, limited to "the freedom to pursue the value of science within relevant limits, without their being overridden by values either contradicting, or irrelevant to, those of scientific investigation." [5]

Freedom to choose the purpose of inquiry also raises questions of priorities among possible areas of study and the amounts of time to be spent on each. Career requirements, teaching duties, and foundations or other agencies establish routine deadlines and thus restrict the scholar's liberty. Within these limits it is necessary, however, that the individual scholar is left free to decide his own priorities of time and purpose. To think otherwise is to open the pursuit of knowledge to political decisions on the content and importance of different lines of inquiry. This issue is a matter of great concern today.

Finally, knowledge is equally capable of humane and inhumane applications. Efforts to pursue knowledge that is only capable of humane applications always founder on the impossibility of knowing in advance what knowledge is possible, and how it can be used. The pursuit of knowledge wherever it may lead, and hence the suspension of specific guide lines, can be justified by this unpredictability of scholarly work.

In the face of these uncertainties, most scholars pursue their work in the belief that it will enhance the vague goals shared by thinking men. Such commitments to scholarly work only make sense if there is the hope or expectation that in the long run the constructive uses of knowledge will prevail. Scholarship presupposes a belief in progress through knowledge and in the perfectability of man. It does not flourish alongside a preoccupation with its own potential evil, nor where doubts concerning the value of knowledge prevail.

Detachment is necessary to free the scholar of purposes extraneous to inquiry, and to maintain scholarly standards. This basic assumption of the academic pursuit of knowledge lies at the heart of the modern university. We will accept this assumption as legitimate as long as we cherish the pursuit of knowledge which it facilitates. Since the nineteenth century, there have been critics of dispassionate inquiry who questioned the value of knowledge produced in an academic setting, and hence challenged the university's right to existence, among them Kierkegaard, Marx, Nietzsche, and Freud. In one particular their views are similar: they assert that truth however conceived is inseparable from a process (for example, class situation, psychological maturation) that conditions knowledge. They deny the possibility of scholarly detachment because, as they see it, scholars, like all men, cannot free themselves from these conditions.

Marx and his followers challenge the scholarly community, both from within the university and from without. To them every intellectual posture (including their own) is determined by a single historical process and thus functions as a weapon in the class struggle.[6] Since all men are committed actors on the stage of history, whether they know it or not, the quest for knowledge in all its forms is a by-product of history. To the scholar the bias of analytical concepts may appear provisional, but to the Marxist it appears at best as an inadvertent expression of very mundane interests and at worst as an effort to divert attention from the vested interests served by scholarly work. In this view universities are institutions of learning only superficially. At a deeper level they are involved in the contentions of society and their vaunted posture above the battle is false. Partisanship should be made explicit, since all claims to nonpartisanship are hypocritical.

Implicit in the Freudian approach is a similar critique of the university, despite the obvious differences between Marxism and psychoanalysis. For Freud every intellectual posture including his own is only part of an entire psychological process, and hence functions as an element in the psychic "economy" of the individual. The quest for knowledge cannot escape each individual's cumulative balance of pleasures and pains. According to Freud, the path to knowledge in psychology lies in an explicit admission of the emotional or psychological meaning which that quest has for the individual. In the field of academic psychology, however, a university does not really encourage such admission. Specifically, academic careers preclude the self-awareness induced by the analysis and control analysis of psychoanalytic training, which the followers of Freud have come to regard as indispensable to the pursuit of knowledge in their field. Thus they argue for the extramural recruitment and training of psychoanalysts. For that reason psychoanalysis is as opposed to the academic establishment as is Marxism.

These critiques of the university claim that the theories employed by academic scholars involve false pretensions and hence a flawed intellectual perspective. An "adequate" examination would reveal, according to the Marxist or Freudian canon, that scholars are biased by implicit class interests or emotional involvements, despite their pretensions to objectivity. Indeed, those pretensions are said to be deliberate or unwitting disguises of such bias. But as long as scholars and these critics start from irreconcilable premises there is no chance of a genuine clarification. Every intellectual position has its prior assumptions. The critics of the scholarly community may question the conditions and assumptions on which that community is based. Yet they can do so only on the basis of other conditions and assumptions, which are also subject to critical scrutiny. A proper critical approach would have to compare the assumptions of the critics with those of academic scholars. Perhaps it would be useful to compare the foibles and achievements of Marxist or Freudian critics with those of academic scholars. That study cannot be undertaken here. But universities would stand up well in such comparison, because scholarship allows for a self-critical correction as Marxism and Freudianism do not.

True, the immobilities of academics arouse much impatience; the proper performance of university functions is frequently distorted by vested academic interests. But it is a fact that over the last half-century many academic disciplines have been fundamentally transformed, especially in the United States. Part of the reason for such changes is that the modern university has become an institution of specialized learning, and thus of rapidly cumulating knowledge as well.

Ideally, a university protects the pursuit of knowledge against abuse from within by the maintenance of academic standards, and against interference from without by upholding academic freedom. The first implies a self-denying ordinance: academicians are enjoined to view their immunities as a responsibility to be discharged, not as a privilege to be exploited. Accordingly, when a teacher pursues entirely personal ends under the guise of his prestige as a specialist, he jeopardizes that sanctuary from within.[7] Not only does he misuse his students as a captive audience in order to air his personal views; he also undermines the university's ability to protect his own freedom to engage in scholarly work. Such tendencies are a grievous breach of professional responsibility. Secondly, the protection of scholarship from outside interference implies the recognition that academic freedom is accepted, if perhaps grudgingly, by the powers that be, because it has proved indispensable for the productive pursuit of knowledge. Like other institutions, universities only approximate their ideals. Their claims may be impaired by the foibles of academicians, by the intrinsic uncertainties that beset academic standards, and by doubts surrounding an elitist institution in an equalitarian society. But these difficulties remain secondary as long as the ultimate justification of a university is accepted, that science and scholarship promote the pursuit of knowledge, and that knowledge is desirable.

Today, this justification is being questioned. Universities are increasingly criticized less for their failings than for their accomplishments. Their central function of teaching and scholarship becomes an issue when the value of knowledge becomes controversial. Whereas criticism from outside the academy is of long standing, questioning of its foundations from within is a relatively new development. This has resulted in part from changes since about the turn of the century in man's cognitive relation to the world around him, a theme I shall turn to in the next section. Recently, however, such questioning has also resulted from a social critique level at certain assumptions of scientific method, and this critique requires a brief elaboration.

All scientific and scholarly work presupposes a commitment to the quest for knowledge. Natural scientists have been able to make this commitment easily. They take the desirability of knowledge for granted; past success gives them confidence in the methods of science, and the community at large generously supports research which creates such obvious benefits. To the extent that the immediate consequences of increased knowledge are benign or neutral, few questions are raised concerning long-run consequences. Yet philosophers and social critics have debated these long-run consequences since the eighteenth century. Since the invention of the atomic bomb this questioning has been revived and carried over into the scientific community. Scientists have become aware that man's capacity to control the powers unleashed by dispassionate inquiry is highly problematic.[8] As Professor Harry Rubin of my own university wrote in a letter to the Chicago Alumni Magazine:

> We scientists often assume that our group represents a selection of some higher order of humanity. Yet, we have no control over the fruits of our labor and have bestowed upon the world a dowry of atomic warfare, inflammable polymers (napalm), biological and chemical warfare. We have done little or nothing to improve the lot of most of the world. We assume our smugly righteous attitude of pure objectivity and say here is the fruit of our work— take it and do with it what you will, we accept no responsibility.[9]

Here is an expression of moral outrage at a situation as old as the fashioning of tools, which have always been capable of good use or ill, depending upon the user. Professor Rubin singles out the use of science in warfare and even denies the great benefits that have also resulted from science. He accuses scientists of misusing the mandatory neutrality of their scholarly work as a cover for civic irresponsibility. No doubt there are instances of this kind. But the larger question is obviously how scientists who do not control "the fruits of their labor" can be responsible for the uses to which their results are put. Scientists are indispensable for the advancement of knowledge and this gives them an intellectual significance which indeed contrasts starkly with their political insignificance as citizens.

The questions arising in this context threaten the legitimacy of the scientists' activity. For doubts arise concerning the value of knowledge and of the methods needed to search for it, when even apparently constructive uses of the sciences lead to consequences that are destructive in their repercussions. Roger Revelle has called attention to such negative effects of scientific advance. Synthetic rubber has impaired already underdeveloped economies that were heavily dependent on rubber exports. Antibiotics and public health measures keep children alive and prolong life expectancy but greatly aggravate the population problem. Western technological superiority causes a "brain drain" the poor countries can ill afford.[10] The list of negative side-effects could be continued.

Concern among scientists over these long-run implications is rising; but at this point most scientists are likely "to put on blinders" (Weber), because too radical a questioning of the benefits of knowledge is not a viable basis for its pursuit. If the very scientists who raise such questions continue their work, it is because they are sustained by the momentum of the "scientific establishment" in modern universities.

So far, the social sciences have not been affected directly by the critical questioning to which I have referred. Frequently they model themselves after certain conventional conceptions of the natural sciences. When Bacon sought to promote science against its many political and religious opponents, he emphasized the benefits of knowledge and explicitly denied that knowledge would endanger faith or political stability.[11] This fundamental belief in the progressive role of knowledge strongly influences the social sciences. Even incisive critics of modern society have shared that belief. In Marx's view knowledge was misused only because the vested interests of capitalist society were opposed to the fully constructive use of science and technology. The destruction of those interests would guarantee that the pursuit of knowledge will benefit mankind. On the other hand, Max Weber differentiated the technical mastery achieved by science from the ultimate question of whether it makes sense to achieve such mastery. In his skeptical view of progress, technical mastery through specialized knowledge might have unmanageable consequences. Still, even Weber remained committed to the advance of science. Marx and Weber were rationalists *and* skeptics whereas, generally speaking, social scientists adhere to the Baconian vision of progress through knowledge without qualifications. Their optimistic view may face mounting difficulties in the future.

The social sciences are vulnerable where they take the "hard sciences" as their model but fail to meet its requirements. By aspiring to an imitation of natural sciences many social scientists put themselves in a false position. Their disciplines possess only a modest utility and attain but a modicum of rigor.[12] The differences between natural and social sciences remain considerable, even

though on theoretical grounds a strong argument for the unity of
knowledge can be advanced. It is the latter argument which
provides a major motivation for social scientists. But while the
world view of the nineteenth century is still espoused by social
scientists, it has been challenged by theoretical physics for two
generations. As prominent natural scientists express their doubts
concerning the benefits of an uncontrolled pursuit of knowledge,
the rationale of the social sciences may also be in jeopardy. Social
scientists may confront an "inflationary threat" if the demand
for their research increases along with a questioning of the belief
in progress through knowledge.

Changing attitudes towards science and scholarship are affecting
the fundamental assumptions of modern universities, that is, the
consensual basis of the scholarly community. This scholarly consensus is beset by an ambivalence characteristic of all normative
behavior. Scholars resolve their ambivalences, or live with them,
in ways that differ between the natural and social sciences. Over
and above such differences, scholars are committed to the pursuit
of knowledge on the tacit assumption that the benefits will exceed
the hazards resulting from increased knowledge. This goal orientation is inculcated and sustained by the academic community, but
has been subject to attack by a succession of cultural critics since
roughly the middle of the nineteenth century. Such critiques can
be countered by a defense of the positive functions of scholarly
detachment. Yet this defense is weakened to the extent that
scientists question the belief in the progressive or constructive role
of knowledge.

Clearly, the traditional ideal of scholarly detachment is doubted
when it is no longer obvious that knowledge is desirable, when
it has been demonstrated that objectivity concerning physical
occurrences is a problematic idea, and when the institutional conditions which alone make scholarship possible are threatened. Two
questions are at the core of the difficulties now confronting scholarship. On the intellectual side, man's cognitive relation to the
world has changed, and thus the scholar's quest for objectivity is
open to question. On the institutional side, the crisis in academic

self-government threatens rational discourse as a basis of scholarship, and beyond that jeopardizes the viability of democratic government.

◄§ THE QUEST FOR OBJECTIVITY

It is a common assumption of the Western intellectual tradition that both nature and society possess an understandable order. Over the years, this assumption has changed; we have seen emphasis on such ideas as a divine order of nature, the development of Reason in history, the long-run determination of a cultural superstructure by a society's economic substructure, and others. Despite this diversity we can speak of *one* underlying assumption in the sense that a discoverable order was assumed to exist independently of the perceiving mind. It is this assumption which Einstein's theory of relativity altered fundamentally. In the words of J. Bronowski:

> Physicists since Newton have been describing the world as a network of events. But physics does not consist of events; it consists of observations, and between the event and us who observe it there must pass a signal—a ray of light perhaps, a wave or an observation. This is the insight which Einstein showed in 1905. It came to him when, looking at the discrepancies within physics then, he asked himself how in fact one would set about doing what Newton took for granted, namely comparing the time in two places far apart. Once the question is put, everyone can answer it: you cannot make any comparison at two different places without sending a signal and observing its arrival. . . . Event, signal, and observer: that is the relationship which Einstein saw as the fundamental unit in physics. Relativity is the understanding of the world not as events but as relations.[13]

Einstein's discoveries revolutionized the nineteenth-century conception of science, one that had been based on the old assumption of an order that is discoverable by an observer detached from the objects of his investigation.

This assumption is now considered an instance of "naïve realism" by the pace-setters of scientific advance. When Einstein formulated the result of his work, he stated that with it "the last remainder of *physical objectivity* [my italics] had been taken from the concepts of space and time." Ernst Cassirer, who quotes this passage, makes clear that for epistemology this phrase poses a problem:

> Planck's neat formulation of the physical criterion of objectivity that everything *that can be measured* exists, may appear completely sufficient from the standpoint of physics; from the standpoint of epistemology, it involves the problem of discovering the fundamental conditions of this measurability and of developing them in systematic completeness. For any, even the simplest, measurement must rest on certain theoretical presuppositions . . . which it does not take from the world of sense, but which it brings to this world as postulates of thought. In this sense, the reality of the physicist stands over against the reality of immediate perception. . . . [Thus] the physicist does not have only to hold in mind the measured object itself, but also always the particular conditions of measurement.[14]

In emphasizing that physical thought must determine its own standards of measurement before observations are made, the theory of relativity did *not* renounce the objectivity of knowledge.

> For the truly objective element in modern knowledge of nature is not so much things as laws. Change in the elements of experience and the fact that no one of them is given in itself, but is always given with reference to something else, constitute no objection to the possibility of objectively real knowledge in so far as the laws establish precisely these relations themselves. The constancy and absoluteness of the elements is sacrificed to gain the permanency and necessity of laws.[15]

An outsider cannot judge whether this view has since been impaired by the controversies among physicists concerning the use of probability measures at the sub-atomic level.[16] But scientists are certainly united in their insistence upon experimental verification. The effect which the act of observation has upon the results of observation is only recognized on that basis. And while the disputes concerning the interpretation of results involve presuppositions, they are always referred back to the experimental evidence. Thus scientists are bound by the requirements of their method to define and calculate the relationships between event, signal, and observer.

The physicist's theory of relativity encourages a subjective view of knowledge *only* in the sense that it has overturned the earlier, naively realistic view of a nature comprehended by a mind detached from nature.[17] But artists have little interest in the scientist's claims, and outside the scientific sphere its self-imposed restraints are not observed. Instead, painters and imaginative writers have developed their own expressions of "relativity" and its world of multiple relationships. They have been fascinated by the notion that there are many possible ways of viewing the world, that no one perspective is the whole truth, or perhaps even that it is no more true than any other (perspectivism). Considering the diffusion of these ideas since the early 1900s, it is surprising that their intellectual impact on some sections of the academic world has been delayed for so long.

The destruction of the object as conventionally conceived is one consequence of these developments. Cubism expresses this approach in one way:

> Technically, cubism is a breakdown of three dimensional space constructed from a fixed point of view. things exist in multiple relations to each other and change their appearance according to the point of view from which we see them—and we now realize that we can see them from innumerable points of view, which are also complicated by time and light, influencing all spatial systems.[18]

From here the road has lead to the exploration of numerous permutations of perspective in painting, sculpture, and literature. Such experiments include photographic montage effects, the reshuffling of time sequences, the interplay among dream states, memories and freely associated sense impressions, and many others. At times this active and endless quest for new perspectives results in a noncommital experimentalism—an approach that also produces elaborate "put-ons" more designed to outrage or poke fun at the viewer than to represent an artistic work. Any more limited approach would seem to deny man's capacity for creating new perspectives and thus falsify the artist's new sense of freedom from the ideal of representation.

The quest for objectivity takes on new meaning in this context. Against the background of naïve realism the effort to be detached meant compliance with Bacon's demand that the scientist must guard against the "idols of the mind." But against the background of the new world view, loosely interpreted, the effort to keep the understanding steady and clear becomes an act of experimentation with ever new perspectives. Only this endless quest can represent the absence of definitive solutions adequately. From the standpoint of a radical perspectivism, a quest for scholarly objectivity or detachment appears bound to the arbitrary limits of a given perspective explored in depth—evidence of willful bias or arid rationalism.

Another aspect of these developments is the promethean glorification of the artist together with the destruction of the individual in the world the artist creates. The first goes back to the romantic exaltation of the artistic personality with its emphasis on passion at the expense of reason and utility.[19] In the nineteenth century this emphasis on the individual also found expression in the work itself: not only the writer but also his heroes, not only the painter but also the subjects of his portraits were seen as personalities and thus as initiators of creative activity. And as long as the self was idealized, the scientist's ascetic code of conduct, his effort to be a detached observer, represented an act of self-denial.[20] This self-confident subjectivism has certainly declined during the twentieth century. But while the artist's promethean self-conception is not as strong today as it was in the romantic period, the main change has occurred in the conception of the individual. Man is seen immersed in a world of objects, his mind continuous with his surroundings, not detached from them.[21] In this context the quest for objectivity also acquired new meanings. For where the individual searches for his identity in vain, the effort to be detached from the self becomes an act of fusion with the world, whether in the sense of a mystical union or of lonely despair. And from that vantage point the quest for scholarly objectivity or detachment appears as a denial of true feeling and as intellectual egotism.

These intellectual and artistic ramifications have considerable psychological appeal, especially to students. The most advanced ideas of modern science and art seem to make a mockery of the scholarly quest for objectivity. If the scholar's quest is an illusion, then its continuation appears as an hypocritical defense of the status quo and hence a proper occasion for attacking the academic "establishment." In this respect, the destruction of the object and the declining sense of individual identity can be made to appear as a more or less coherent attack upon the standards of academic scholarship.

Those who see the act of observing in terms of its effects on the phenomenal world, and who therefore engage in an "experimental perspectivism," consider theirs a more candid quest for objectivity than the prolonged specialization of the scholar. And those who see man as part of the world of objects, and who therefore submerge themselves in an "oceanic feeling" (Freud) of some kind (for this the hippies provide a good example), think their denial of self more authentic than the denial implicit in scholarly self-discipline. Thus an approach to inquiry which considers every intellectual perspective a try-out to be replaced by others blends with the quest for authentic experience. Both approaches interpret the impossibility of definitive solutions as their warrant for a radical subjectivism.

But neither the authenticity of experience nor the adoption of replaceable perspectives possess a principle of cumulation or standards of consensual validation. Rather, it is individualistic isolation and self-concern which give rise to the view that any experience or perspective may be considered authentic and hence worthwhile, as in the current phrase of "doing your thing." There is a type of tolerance when everyone pursues his own experience without considering the experience or opinion of others as relevant to himself. But one also gets various forms of self-intoxication, from drugs or verbal violence to the consummate ease with which spokesmen of the New Left identify the agonies of faraway peoples as a moral symbol of their own activities.[22] At the same time, many of these personal, artistic, or political utopiates are quite compatible with a strident intolerance of more pragmatic and rational perspectives.

❧ A CRISIS OF LEGITIMACY IN ACADEMIC SELFGOVERNMENT

Recent events at universities in many Western countries have made clear that it will not do for academicians to dismiss these currents of opinion, or embrace them as views that have a right to be heard like all others. Neither studied neglect, nor argument, nor the principle of toleration can disguise that political expressionism undermines the foundations of rational discourse, and of the rule-making procedures based on such discourse. This crisis of the university is *not* a simple outcome of the intellectual trends I have traced. Rather, these trends have created a climate of opinion in which the authority embodied in the ideals of scholarship and academic self-government has lost some of its earlier legitimacy.

Changes in the institutional structure of universities have greatly contributed to this crisis of legitimacy. Since World War II the sciences have flourished because foundations and the government have poured increasing funds into research. Greater funds from outside sources are not an unqualified gain. Comparing the scholar with the worker in his lecture "Science as a Vocation," Weber pointed out that under modern conditions the handicraft stage of scholarship as well as of production has passed. As research and scholarship come to depend upon resources beyond the direct control of the scholar himself, the structure of the academic community is altered. Increasingly, decision making on what research is worthwhile devolves upon people who are not engaged in research themselves but "specialize" in research administration. These people may be foundation officials, government officials, or university professors who are co-opted to sit on committees. They organize research units, and process applications for these units, thus having a considerable effect on those who do research. Scientists and scholars are naturally attracted by the opportunities and facilities provided by grants. Consciously or unwittingly a consensus of judgments concerning research develops between them and the research administrators. Now, such group formation is inevitable—if it were not this consensus, it would be another— and this tells us nothing about the quality of judgments arrived at. Nevertheless, there is often a subtle transformation of the academic community, to the extent that an important segment of intellectual decision making is removed from that community's exclusive jurisdiction and becomes lodged in these other organizational contexts.[23] This organizational change leads to a declining autonomy of academic scholars, a development which in the United States has coincided with an increase in their general prestige and the increasing availability of extramural funds.

In this setting two questions are asked by critics of the modern university: (1) of what use and how real is the university's autonomy, when research and teaching are affected increasingly by the extramural politics of the scientific establishment? and (2) of what use is objectivity, if the knowledge it produces can lead to destruction? Universities have never been and cannot be completely autonomous. But with such autonomy as they have, they have demonstrated the long-run utility of scholarly detachment and inquiry. Even in the absence of direct utility, scholarly detachment in the social sciences and humanities can contribute to the art of living together. Nevertheless, the dispassionate search for knowledge is shunted aside all too often, especially with regard to controversial issues, although no one can foresee the potential benefits of such knowledge. As to the second question: he who questions the value of objectivity because the resulting knowledge can destroy, also questions the foundations of constructive knowledge. Since anything that can be used can be abused, we would need to abandon everything if we were to prevent the possibility of misuse completely.

These considerations are certainly among the values of science and scholarship in universities. Yet these values are persuasive only as long as a certain tolerance for their ambiguity exists. When the pressure of unresolved political and social issues increases, that tolerance will wane, as will the public acceptance of academic freedom. As Chancellor Heyns of the University of California, Berkeley, said on one occasion:

> In its simplest terms, the satisfactory solution to a complex problem . . . requires freedom to choose among a large number of alternatives. It is a fact of our life that the range of alternatives available to us is progressively narrowing as a result of two factors. The intransigent determination of radicals to make extreme demands and to provoke confrontation. This means that the number of alternatives they will consider is very narrow. The other set of forces is more complex; it consists of public opinion, informally stated, and manifested in the position of their representatives. The range of solutions they can accept is more and more limited, as public anxiety grows and as the obvious need for the protection of the community grows.[24]

Made amid public calls for more vigorous action by the authorities and calls for freedom from interference by some faculty members and students, the statement well illustrates the increasing obstruction to compromise between polarizing factions. This conflict over the universities is part of a larger setting.

The war in Vietnam, the explosive race issue at home, and now campus unrest have brought to the fore the impatience and moral indignation of a largely conservative public that finds it difficult to accept the intractability of America's position at home and abroad. At the same time, faculty members and students with strong moral commitments and little opportunity for political participation have come to use the university as a stand-in for the politics to which they have insufficient access, or which they reject altogether. A university cannot resolve the problems of society at large. But the outraged conservatives and the equally outraged radicals can link relatively minor problems of university life with these larger political issues, and thus give vent to their opposing frustrations.

The conservatives identify unrest in the universities as the decline of law and order at home and as manifest treason in relation to the nation's concerns abroad. The radicals make it appear that protest against the university symbolizes protest against the draft, the war in Vietnam, and the "establishment" of American society. The nation as a whole may have the capacity to moderate that conflict. But in the university, the opposing factions undermine the precarious foundation of detachment without which it would soon be impossible to distinguish between a scholarly community at work and commitment to an intolerant ideology.[25]

In this setting two problems of private government rend the university and threaten democracy. One problem concerns the right of private bodies to make rules that are binding on their participants (or members). This right implies the authority of such bodies to discipline or exclude individuals under certain conditions. The other problem derives from the first. If private bodies have the right to make binding rules, then there are institutional limits to the principle of toleration. For, the exercise of that right necessarily leads to the exclusion of types of behavior considered basically incompatible with the developing purposes of the organization and its constituents. Universities are institutions detached from the more insistent claims of social and political controversy precisely because they want to achieve maximum safeguards for the expression of all opinions. In periods of mounting stress they are particularly vulnerable, however, because they can remain intact only as long as all members of the university accept that principle of toleration and adhere to the standards of a scholarly community at work. When some members reject those standards as incompatible with the political and moral demands of the hour, the very rules and purposes of academic institutions tend to become politicized.

Like other private bodies, universities have the right to govern their own operation and (within limits) to regulate the conduct of their participants. As in other institutions the enactment and enforcement of rules require constant attention and improvement. But leaders of current student agitation do not aim at the reform of universities; they seek rather to turn issues of academic self-government into public affairs of the body politic.

Two arguments are typical in this respect. One seeks to prevent universities from making rules binding upon students which in any way violate the students' constitutional rights as citizens. Students are citizens, so the argument runs; universities are the natural forum of their activity; hence students are entitled to make the university into an instrument of their political activity.[26] The other argument demands that students be granted popular sovereignty in matters of educational policy. In this instance, the legitimate claim to be heard is made the basis for an academic class struggle, which projects the image of an "alienated academic proletariat" pitted against the entrenched privileges of the "academic ruling class." In this way constitutional provisions like the Bill of Rights and the franchise are applied directly to the "governance" of private bodies, and the distinction between such bodies and the public affairs of the country as a whole is disregarded.

The universities' limited purposes of teaching and scholarship are jeopardized, when confrontations on issues of academic self-government are made to stand for political issues in the national arena. Such issues easily crowd out the legitimacy of more limited concerns. Yet the rights and privileges of citizenship are no more appropriate to the governance of universities than the limited purposes of the latter are appropriate to the arena of national politics. To think otherwise is tantamount to a destruction of privacy, that is, to an enforced coordination (*Gleichschaltung*) from below which rejects special purposes at the several levels of society in the interest of addressing the issues before the nation. In this way private bodies are denied the right to make binding rules for their participants—a denial that is also characteristic of Fascist or Communist regimes.

Social theorists have advanced two contradictory evaluations of private organizations. In Tocqueville's classic analysis, the achievement of collective purposes through voluntary organizations is viewed as a major safeguard of democracy. For such organizations provide the individual with means to achieve his ends far greater than those available to him personally. Therefore, the individual need not appeal to the still greater and more dangerous powers of the national government. Robert Michels's "iron law of oligarchy" expresses a much more negative evaluation. All private organizations are ruled by small oligarchies which pervert formally democratic methods in order to continue in office and achieve ends fundamentally incompatible with the purposes of their members. Both interpretations seem to me inadequate. The first is too benign. Voluntary organizations often serve special interests, and nothing prevents them from calling on the national government for assistance. They may do neither, but they can do both. The second interpretation is too cynical. Oligarchy stands for leadership as well as for abuse of power. Nor are oligarchies as powerful as the Machiavellian tradition suggests. The effort of ruling minorities to stay in power entails attempts to win adherents, and oligarchic rule can be guided in part by the "anticipated reactions" (Friedrich) of the relevant publics.

In relation to these views of private organizations universities have a rather good record. As special interest organizations they can make a greater claim to altruistic objectives than most other organizations. And their acceptance of government assistance is surrounded by safeguards against political interference. Also, in keeping with the teaching function, academic oligarchies are relatively responsive to student demands.[27] Their failures are more often due to a lack of concerted leadership than to an oligarchic abuse of power.

These general considerations are not, however, the most relevant as far as the institutional protection of scholarly detachment is concerned. For the university disturbances of recent years have revealed a failure of nerve and conviction on the part of some faculty, which undermines the university's purpose and function. E. K. Scheuch has pointed out that student agitation expresses a growing cultural ambivalence among segments of the educated middle class. Most activists come from affluent families, and their radical rhetoric suggests a solidarity with disadvantaged groups which is illusory. But these protests find some resonance among middle-class adults and considerable sympathy among intellectuals. There are many reasons: the declining significance of general education in the context of decision making by experts, the dehumanizing consequences of technology, the fear of large organizations, the waning sense of purpose when consumers find new purchases less and less enticing and when scholars and scientists feel troubled by the dangers attending new knowledge. The list is long and has been full of familiar themes of intellectual protest since the end of the eighteenth century.[28]

To this I would add that the problems facing educated, middle-class adults in Western industrial societies are compounded by the collective sensitivities arising from the decline of colonialism. There is a growing awareness of the cumulative liabilities left over from centuries of Western expansion. To understand this one need only contrast the confident intellectual justifications of social inequality at the beginning of this century with the agonized revulsion at the war in Vietnam in the 1960s.[29] That war has for many a symbolic significance both as a holding action in the retreat of Western civilization and as a last manifestation of aggressive expansionism which goes far beyond the particular facts of the case. As the Swiss writer, Karl Schmid, has stated:

> We should be willing to agree quickly that European culture which today we are ready to raise as our flag and which is supposed to immobilize our antagonist at the moment of attack,—that this culture appeared outside Europe during the last centuries in the form of unscrupulous power and technical violence. Is there a sentence of that Greek-Roman-Mosaic-Christian-Humanist catechism . . . , which Europe did not turn into its opposite a hundred times over in [its ventures] abroad? No Parthenon and no Uffizi Palace, no Bach and no Goethe, no Champs Elysée and no Salzburg festivals can alter this fact.[30]

Where this reliance on the cultural accomplishments of Western civilization is of little avail in the balance of moral accounts one can hardly expect that the values of scholarship and its institutional protection will remain unaffected.

This is the general setting in which it is proposed that universities reform themselves through "participatory democracy." The principle of equality inherent in citizenship is to be introduced as a guide line for the participation of students at all levels of educational decision making. Indeed, some go so far as to suggest that today the failure of universities as educational institutions can now be compensated for only by turning the "governance" of these institutions itself into an educational process.[31] The fact that such a proposal is made by some highly respected members of a university faculty (in collaboration with student spokesmen) is more important in the present context than that the proposal is not likely to be implemented. For the proposal reveals acute uncertainty concerning the positive purposes of teaching and scholarship.

Those purposes imply the inequality of teacher and student which it is a university's function to recognize and gradually to diminish, even though as citizens, teacher and student are equals. As citizens teachers and students ideally adhere to the principles of toleration. But as members of an academic community, teachers must be committed to standards of excellence which ideally enable and oblige them to discriminate and pass judgments. Ideally, students must be imbued with a desire for learning strong enough to overcome or tolerate the frustrations that are incident in being judged. For the university, a crisis of legitimacy arises when significant minorities on both sides question these commitments.

I have suggested that this crisis is part of a larger failure of nerve in Western civilization. In the years ahead, the values of scholarship and the quest for objectivity may have to be defended by those who have learned to live the life of reason with more humility and kindness than those who pioneered the age of science. For these pioneers also incurred the hubris of Western expansion and of an overweening confidence born of materialist beliefs and successes. But then again, it may be that for a time (how long?) only those disciplines will continue to thrive which are sufficiently technical to be immune to the intrusions of politics. For where partisanship becomes an effective deterrent to scholarship, we may get universities of technical indispensability, in which humanistic concerns are restricted to areas too esoteric to interest the politicians.

Half a century has passed since Weber gave his lecture on "Science as a Vocation," but little of his insight seems diminished in retrospect. Science remains the affair of an intellectual aristocracy. It demands concentration, hard work, inspiration, and passionate devotion to a task that can only be accomplished if all extraneous considerations are excluded. For Weber, science expresses the attempt of Western man to eliminate magic and fathom what seems mysterious. In this sense our civilization depends on the accumulation of knowledge to satisfy our curiosity. But the preeminence of science does not mean that each of us understands much about our complex environment. In fact, we have less knowledge of our surroundings in a practical way than primitive man had of his, because our world and the knowledge available have become much more extensive. This individual ignorance amidst a plethora of knowledge is a result of specialization.

Specialization has also separated the modern scholar from his means of production: he no longer owns the libraries and laboratories he uses. Scholarship has become part of increasingly large-scale academic and research enterprises. Weber was aware that both the ordinary person and the scholar have become more dependent. The ordinary man, including the specialist outside his own field, is ever more affected by science and social conditions he does not understand. The scholar is ever more affected by institutions he does not control.

Weber's insight into the spiritual uncertainty at the core of the scientific endeavor is of profound importance. The very success of the sciences has "chained [us] to the idea of progress." Every scientific achievement poses new questions and calls for investigations that will supersede it. "It is not self-evident that something subordinate to such a law [of progress] is sensible and meaningful in itself. Why does one engage in doing something that in reality never comes, and never can come, to an end?" Tolstoy had said that for men on this endless frontier death has no meaning; the goal of progress demands man's immortality. In Weber's view science cannot answer Tolstoy's question: in a scientific world view the goal of life remains undefined. Instead, "the individual life of civilized man [is] placed into an infinite 'progress,' . . . for there is always a further step ahead. . . ." As a result, men intensify their efforts in the pursuit of knowledge, ever approaching what they cannot reach. By refining methods of inquiry, science and scholarship advance a knowledge that helps to control life and achieve intellectual clarity.[32] Yet today even these goals are in question. Some unintended consequences of science seriously hamper the effective control of nature and society. An intellectual clarity, in the absence of moral guide lines and political judgment, proves unable to cope with this and other predicaments of modern civilization.

In this context scientists have been called upon to assume responsibility for the consequences of their work. Some scientists have made public their decision not to undertake certain lines of research. But most feel that the utilization of knowledge cannot be their responsibility as scientists.

> Science has achieved its great power by insisting on defining for itself the problems it proposes to solve, and by refusing to take on problems merely because some outside authority considers them important. But that power, and the precision of thought on which it depends, is purchased by a refusal to deal with many aspects of such problems.[33]

The pursuit of knowledge, wherever it may lead, must exclude concerns extraneous to inquiry if the pursuit is to be successful.

In a number of ways this exclusion has become more difficult in recent decades. The question of priorities among different lines of inquiry involves the allocation of funds. This is a political concern extraneous to inquiry itself, but scientists cannot ignore it. Engineering, medicine, and other technical professions base themselves on scientific results, but are directly concerned with purposes extraneous to science. Politicians often resort to the testimony of scientists and professionals in the hope that political decisions can be based entirely on knowledge and thus be greatly facilitated. For the same reason scientists and professionals are encouraged to move into positions with administrative and political responsibility.

There is more respect for specific knowledge than for the judgments and general responsibility of politicians. The results are that scientists and professionals may be induced to make decisions in the name of science which go beyond their expertise.[34] These and other factors have impaired the capacity of scholars and universities to protect inquiry from concerns that are extraneous to it. Yet the need remains. The methods of scholarship have proved indispensable to the pursuit of knowledge, even though the results of inquiry and the uses of knowledge are unpredictable.

The question is whether under these circumstances the impulse behind inquiry, the belief in progress through knowledge, can remain vigorous enough. This is the agonizing problem of scholarship in the modern world. The knowledge it alone can produce, is as indispensable as ever. But the optimism of the Enlightenment which so far sustained the quest for knowledge, has been undermined by the great powers of destruction which science has made available, by the change in man's cognitive relation to the world, and by our collective incapacity to solve problems of decision making which science proper cannot solve. For scholarship the task ahead will be to moderate the unconditional quest for knowledge by an intensive concern with priorities, but without impairing the quest itself. Its task will also be to develop an ethics of conduct which can relate the scientist's indispensability and the powers created by knowledge to the weakness of the scientist as a man.

PART TWO

A THEORETICAL
PERSPECTIVE

SOCIOLOGY AND IDEOLOGY

✧§ FOUR §✧

Academic disciplines depend upon the existence of scholarly communities. A modern university comprises a congeries of such
communities. For the university to function, the several scholarly
communities must share a common ground in the disinterested
pursuit of knowledge. Teachers and students in the different disciplines may communicate little or not at all. But while they live
with their different interests and obligations, all of them can share
an interest in increasing knowledge through scholarly detachment.
Such an interest overrides the ambiguities and frustrations of
academic life; it makes the obstacles to communication among
different specialties appear secondary.

A modern university has its common basis in the liberal idea
of independent inquiry, free discussion, and academic self-government. Like other tenets of liberalism, this idea is subject to attack
from the right and left. We are all familiar with outside attacks
of religious and political fundamentalists upon the inherent radicalism of free inquiry and the institutional safeguards of that
freedom. More recently we have become families with equally
doctrinaire attacks upon free inquiry from the left and from
within the university. Here the right to dissent is turned into an
obligation. The competence and proper function of teachers is
rejected if they fail to display the required degree of political
relevance and commitment. As in the attacks upon German universities and parliamentary institutions in the early 1930s, the
legitimacy of free inquiry and discussion is rejected because the

problems before us demand decisive action, not more words and knowledge. In this setting—to quote an editorial in The Times Literary Supplement—

> it has become increasingly necessary to bring alive the notion of academic freedom as an intellectual necessity; and this in a situation where it is crowded not only from without but from within, and not only from those who find its activities too radical but too conservative.[1]

To accept this mandate as a sociologist poses special problems because of the ease with which theoretical positions in that field are turned into ideological commitments. An awareness of historical legacies and institutional conditions can guard against this hazard to a degree, as the preceding essays suggest. But we must also come to terms with the theoretical distinction between sociology and ideology. The liberal principle of academic freedom is a vantage point of considerable promise for sociological theory however precarious it may be politically. To show this I shall examine the distinction between sociology and ideology, the implications of "perspectivism" in modern thought, and the scholarly responsibilities which are consonant with a liberal position.

✑§ IDEOLOGIES AND THE IDEOLOGY OF ANALYSIS

Sociology seeks to develop a systematic knowledge about men in society. It includes the study of ideologies, since doctrines, ideals, and myths are elements of collective action. Ideally, competent scholars will arrive at the same conclusions, if they agree on the materials to be considered and the questions to be addressed to these materials. Sociological studies which are undertaken with this expectation in mind, presuppose an academic setting. Only there can such studies be free of an immediate concern with social utility. Controversial as this freedom is, sociological studies can thrive only where such relative detachment is considered possible and, in a broad sense, worthwhile.

The term "ideology" has many meanings. Some of them are

not easily distinguished from the sociological analysis of ideas. Ideology proper refers—in the words of Raymond Aron—to

> the longing for a purpose, for communion with the people, for something controlled by an idea and a will. The feeling of belonging to the elect, the security provided by a closed system in which the whole of history as well as one's own person find their place and their meaning, the pride in joining the past to the future in present action:[2]

these are aspects of ideological commitment. Every idea bears on action and hence links the past to the future. Ideas may be seen in this context exclusively. Their content or validity will then be of little interest in themselves. Instead, ideas will be assessed primarily for what they reveal about the conditions and effects of intellectual effort. This is the conventional, pejorative meaning of ideology which originated in the seventeenth century with the destruction of a "monopolistic culture" claiming universal validity. The "age of ideology" dates from that period and may be considered a synonym of "pluralistic culture." [3]

The social sciences as we know them arose in the later phase of this pluralism. They have not flourished wherever one world view held exclusive sway. The sociology of knowledge is an example of the social sciences at work. It includes a sociological study of ideologies which also views ideas from the standpoint of their relation to action. But in this case the causes and consequences of an idea are of interest in themselves. They are not made the basis for judging the content or validity of the ideas concerned. The distinction between an ideological and a sociological approach becomes clearer when we note that the latter steers a course midway between an idealist and a reductionist interpretation of ideas.

The *idealist* approach considers ideas as a world apart which must be analyzed and understood entirely in their own terms. Typically, "high culture" in all its aspects has been viewed in this manner, as for example in the history of philosophy or of art styles. Some anthropologists have approached customs or material artifacts or folklore in the same way. Again, in social interaction men form ideas of themselves and others: an analysis of these ideas lies at the center of sociological interest. The dictum of W. I. Thomas that situations which men define as real are real in their consequences, applies to ideas as well. As long as men live by what they believe to be true, their beliefs are real in their consequences. Where the object is to analyze these beliefs, the sociologist takes the content of such beliefs as seriously as do the actors who adhere to them.

The *reductionist* approach, by contrast, considers ideas epiphenomena. Ideas are analyzed primarily in terms of their existential conditions in an effort to account for, and correct, distortions which impede the pursuit of knowledge. In this respect the social sciences have inherited an intellectual tradition of self-scrutiny which extends from Francis Bacon to Sigmund Freud.[4] In their extreme form, psychological and sociological analyses of ideas leave no room for a consideration of content. Elton Mayo's statement that he was no longer interested in what a man said, but only in why he said it, is an example of such reductionism.[5]

The sociological analysis of ideas achieves its proper level, I believe, when it combines these two approaches. It is committed to the task of interpreting the phenomenology of social life, because men are prompted to act as they do by the beliefs they hold. And where equal attention is given to ideas and ordinary beliefs, to high and to popular culture, the peculiar bias of the idealist tradition can be minimized or even avoided. At the same time, sociological analysis always makes use of questions and concepts which are not themselves derived from the beliefs of the actors. In this way implications and relationships come into view which the participants either fail to notice altogether or interpret in a manner that itself forms part of the evidence to be analyzed. This side of sociological analysis is indebted to the reductionist tradition, since it examines the social foundation and function of beliefs. Here the other-oriented behavior of social actors is the proper object of analysis, though attention to the personal meaning even of very conventional behavior can reduce the peculiar bias of the reductionist tradition.

Analysis at the level of ideas *and* analysis of functional interrela-
tions provide the sociologist with a built-in corrective for the
exaggerations implicit in the idealist and reductionist positions.
This midway position of sociological analysis interprets culture
as possessing a relative autonomy. The arts and sciences as well as
the symbolic framework of everyday life are products of a tradition,
mediated by language and transmitted from generation to generation. Sociology examines the group-specific differentiation of the
cultural process within this relatively autonomous complex.

Such analysis depends upon the detachment made possible by
a working scholarly community. Like other scholars, sociologists
commit themselves to the methods of science and scholarship, because they consider the knowledge they seek worth obtaining.
Specifically, in the analytic study of ideologies, sociologists constitute a scholarly community to the extent that they negotiate an
uneasy and no doubt erratic path between idealism and reductionism, between critical reasoning cut off too soon and reasoning cut
off not soon enough. But this intermediate position or vantage
point is tied to a liberal conception of academic freedom. In a
world torn by strife the universities can render a service to the community only if they are institutions of detachment.[6] If the sociologist's analysis of ideologies is such a service, and I assume that
it is, then we must note that he is not involved in action himself.
His understanding becomes possible because he is in a position to
apply alternative perspectives to the experience of those who are
involved. Activists and ideologists will deny the legitimacy of this
position, in part because it challenges their own absolute claims.
They argue, as we have seen, that scholarly detachment is spurious.
In response, sociologists must examine what in their capacity as
scholars they often take for granted, namely the value of sociological knowledge and the institutional preconditions of obtaining
such knowledge.

Every intellectual enterprise makes prior assumptions. The concepts employed by sociologists in the analysis of ideologies are the
working tools of their scholarly community. The *provisional* use
of these concepts expresses their detachment and primarily analytic

interest. But each concept is based on prior assumptions, however tentatively it is put forward. As Kenneth Burke observed a generation ago, concepts are partly illuminating and partly disguising, "a way of seeing is also a way of not seeing," and in this sense any abstraction comes at a price.[7] The question is how definite an advance in knowledge is obtained thereby. In disciplines that are relatively noncumulative, such advances may be equivocal or difficult to discern. We are committed to analysis despite these uncertainties in the hope of advancing sociological knowledge. In this sense it may be appropriate to speak of an "ideology of analysis."

A reminder may be added concerning the strategies with which this problem has been faced or evaded. There are those who will have no truck with onesidedness. Some sociologists (and philosophers) would reject clear concepts and explicit definitions as incompatible with the "evidence." For them the facts of society constitute an unstructured aggregate so that every concept is artificial and imposes "merely academic" distinctions. These are typically contrasted with the fluid and fuzzy, but lifelike and hence real "definition of the situation" by the proverbial man in the street. In this view the ideal stance of the sociologist is a kind of academic walkie-talkie after the manner of Studs Terkel.

Others will accept the necessity of employing abstractions but use various strategies to minimize the resulting distortions. Enumerative syntheses are frequently employed in this respect, resulting in comprehensive lists of all available standpoints. This is a common bane of textbooks and not in very good repute. A more imaginative synthesis (with hazards of its own) consists in a system of sociological theory which seeks to incorporate the concepts developed in the past from a perspective chosen for this purpose, as Parsons did in *The Structure of Social Action*. At a different level of abstraction Merton's formalization of basic sociological insights is another important approach. Again, Weber's ideal types posit simplified distinctions derived from historical evidence, which serve as benchmarks for surveying the range of actual variation and for formulating hypotheses. The impulse *behind* these well-known strategies (but not the strategies themselves) may be called an "ideology of analysis." For divergent as these approaches are, *they have in common an effort to advance knowledge by imposing a grid of abstractions on the evidence—despite an equivocal record of achievements.* Current confrontations over the principles of academic freedom are in fact contentions (once again) over the right to free inquiry—which in our context means the right of sociologists to the provisional exploration of alternative analytical perspectives.

❧ PERSPECTIVISM IN MODERN THOUGHT

An intellectual rationale of perspectivism was clearly articulated in the decades before World War I. Beginning in the 1880s Wilhelm Dilthey developed a philosophy which took the history of philosophy as its point of departure. In his view all possible philosophical perspectives have been developed already. Instead of formulating a world view of his own, the contemporary philosopher had the task of developing a *typology of possible philosophies,* based on the range of past philosophical perspectives. One might characterize Dilthey's position by paraphrasing Marx's thesis on Feuerbach: in the past philosophers have interpreted the world, what matters now is to understand the range of possible philosophies. Dilthey's approach arose from a decline of philosophical impulse and a positivist belief that the nature of the human mind was best revealed through a systematic study of its past manifestations.[8]

Dilthey's work became influential only in his later life and did not become widely known outside Germany. Nevertheless, it was part of a widespread cultural tendency that is best characterized by reference to artistic trends of the same period.

> The ideas behind cubist painting are reflected in all the modern arts. . . . By its revolution in thought and method of representing the world cubism created a cinematic style. . . . The cubists . . . broke open the volumes of things by spreading objects upon shifting interrelated planes that did not violate the surface of the canvas. . . . By *representing the several faces of things simultaneously,* the cubist dealt with the old problem of time and motion in new ways; objects "moved" but they were also immobilized in

a complex design, . . . their plural aspects conceived together. If
the cubists assassinated "objects" so "much the worse for the objects"—as Picasso said to Zervos. This destruction was actually
the reorganizing of the world by the mind. . . . *The cubist object
no longer has a single or simple identity.*[9]

Cubist painting thus provides a pictorial analogue to a philosophy
which sees man and the world broken up into a number of typically
possible philosophical positions. As the cubists destroy the traditional wholeness of the object, so Dilthey notes the destruction of
comprehensive philosophical systems.

What became true of philosophy and the arts in the years preceding World War I was bound to affect the social sciences as
well. In the methodological essay with which he introduced his
editorship of the prestigious *Archiv für Sozialwissenschaft und So-
zialpolitik* in 1904, Max Weber formulated what may be called a
"spotlight" theory of truth for the social sciences. The historical
world presents an unstructured aggregate of actions from which the
historian selects the particular configuration he wishes to study.
That selection is subjective, guided by the concerns that underlie
an historian's research into the past. Inevitably, these concerns
change in response to the changing cultural and historical scene.
Yet once the questions are asked, the usual criteria of scholarly
excellence apply. In principle, competent scholars asking the same
questions can arrive at the same answers, provided the object
chosen for study is analyzed in terms of explicit theoretical constructs. In Weber's view two subjective conditions must be presupposed. The knowledge to be obtained must be considered
worthwhile. And the choice of abstraction and of scholarly strategy
contains an irreducible imaginative component.

Having thus stated the value assumptions of inquiry in the social
sciences Weber formulates a "perspectivist" interpretation of
knowledge:

"Within the infinite abundance of happenings we aim at a meaningful understanding of that which is significant for us. In the
empirical social and cultural sciences the possibility of such understanding is bound up with *the unremitting employment of stand-*

points which in the last analysis are oriented towards [cultural] values (Wertideen). Empirically, these values are experienced as components of all meaningful human actions and as such subject to observation, but their validity cannot be derived empirically. The "objectivity" of knowledge in the social sciences is compatible with the practice of always relating the empirically given to those values.[10]

Thus, Weber emphasizes the analytic utility of clearly delineated "standpoints," but he rejects explicitly the "constant chase after new viewpoints and conceptual constructions." [11] The two views are compatible if one remembers that by value relevance (*Wertbeziehung*) Weber designated the conscious attention of the scholar to the problems that appear to him of moment in an historical period. In an age of scientific specialization social scientists would not always remain conscious of the intellectual and moral commitments which determine their focus of inquiry. They must struggle against this neglect, if they are to be worthy of their calling. But in the long run the questions which initiate inquiry, will change. What is significant to one generation, may not be salient to the next.

> At some time the color changes: [men] become uncertain of the significance of the viewpoints that have been used without reflection. The path looses itself in the dusk. The light of the great problems of culture has passed on. Then science also prepares itself to change its standpoint and its conceptual apparatus in order to look down from the heights of thought upon the current of events.[12]

Weber refers to the ideal scientist who desires the early obsolescence of his own achievements, because his quest for knowledge is prompted by the belief in progress. In the natural sciences that quest is cumulative, earlier results being superseded by later ones. In the social and cultural sciences only some results are superseded by newer and better knowledge. More often it is a shift of interest to new cultural problems which makes a scholar's results obsolete, as is the case in history which is rewritten when current concerns make the events of the past appear in a new light. Weber systematized this notion into a perspectivist approach to the social

sciences. Man and society lack a "single or simple identity." Instead, they are broken up into a number of aspects, one as valid
as the next, as long as each is of central concern. And these "great
problems of culture" change from one historical configuration to
another. Thus, Weber recognized a historically conditioned multiplicity of concerns which precludes an integrated view of man and
his world. A more systematic view of society and history appeared
to him a falsification of the human condition. His nominalist conception of social reality was at one with those tendencies of
modern thought which make the methods used to comprehend the
world part of the world as we understand it.

This Weberian position may be contrasted with the work of
Karl Mannheim, who developed a specifically political interpretation of the sociology of knowledge. Different political ideologies
reflect divergent class positions, as is the case with bureaucratic
conservatism, conservative historicism, liberal-democratic thought,
the socialist-communist conception and fascism. This approach to
the ideologies of social classes was shaped by the political controversies of Weimar Germany, but did not account for the social
position of intellectuals. As Marx noted already, intellectuals
identify with different social classes, often in disregard of their
own social origins. In attempting to account for this phenomenon
Mannheim referred to a "socially unattached intelligentsia"
(*freischwebende Intelligenz*) consisting of educated men who
were free to choose their class identity.

Yet a sociology of knowledge which analyzes the conditions of
diverse perspectives, presupposes a vantage point of its own. Accordingly, in a later essay, Mannheim tried to show that the same
freedom which makes some intellectuals into partisans of different
camps, prompts others to adopt a more objective approach. The
latter consists of a *relational* view of a society's universe of discourse. By seeing the diversity of simultaneous perspectives, and
by analyzing the group interests at work in each, a scholar can
develop a many-sided model of social reality and overcome the
relativism of a reductionist approach to ideas. Mannheim's "relationism" searches for a vantage point from which this reductionist

approach is still compatible with a concept of society as a "single identity." We cannot be entirely free of divergent perspectives, but the relational approach is to carry us as far as possible towards a holistic view of society. In contrast to Dilthey and Weber, Mannheim attempts to escape from the tendency of modern thought that "destroys the object" (that is, society as a whole) and accepts a multiplicity of perspectives as the only reality accessible to us. Mannheim was unwilling to abandon the fiction of a comprehending mind clearly separated from society and nature as objects of study.[13]

The perspectivist approaches of Dilthey, Weber, and Mannheim have a family likeness with the striking reversal between means and ends characteristic of modern science and art. At one time the word "technique" was used to designate the means or tools needed to accomplish a given purpose. Admittedly, "technique" in this purposive sense is still with us. But now the tendency is increasingly to vary or try out methods of inquiry, in order to see what unexpected results may be obtained.[14] This procedure has proved very productive, but where it is adopted in the absence of pragmatic tests, it becomes difficult to know when to stop. Experimentation with the techniques of inquiry can become an end in itself, a tendency dangerous to the maintenance of standards that can command a general assent.

Certain extreme implications of "technological subjectivism" have become apparent in modern art. A basic theme of this development is that "for the modern painter, novelist, and scientist the world exists to be violated by the mind, which excerpts from it what it needs." This summary characterization by Wylie Sypher is well illustrated in André Gide's *Le Journal des Faux-Monnayeurs*, in which the author through the notes of Edouard expresses the world view of experimentalism in art. "Only this remains—that reality interests me inasmuch as it is plastic, and that I care more —infinitely more—for what may be than for what has been. . . ." The fictitious *Journal* contains notes towards a novel Edouard plans to write, which will display a "formidable erosion of contours," a sum of destructions, and "a rivalry between the real world and the representation of it which we make to ourselves. The manner in which the world of appearances imposes itself upon us, and the manner in which we try to impose on the outside world our own interpretation—this is the drama of our lives." [15]

Similarly modern poetry finds ever new ways of expressing this dramatic conflict. In 1859 Baudelaire introduced the term "modernity," in order to characterize the novel problem facing the artist. How can he discern elements of beauty in the wasteland of the metropolis with its commercial and technical civilization? Baudelaire's answer and that of many others was to achieve the greatest possible distance from the banality of the real, while using references from that reality to achieve expressions of poetic sensibility.[16] Baudelaire implemented this program in the thematic sequence of his *Fleurs du Mal*. The poems move from the contrast between idealization and dejection through futile escapes into the external world of the city, the internal world of an artificial paradise, and a fascination with destruction to the last two sections which express a revolt against God and the quest for peace in death and the unknown.[17] From the refined and intelligible language of Baudelaire's despairing vision a long road has led to the artistic experimentalism of today. But the many variations of modern art have their common theme in the destruction of man, artist, audience, language, representation, and appreciation by a creative fantasy whose right it is to produce the nonexistent and make it prevail over a banal reality.[18]

Experimentation with techniques of inquiry and imposition of interpretations upon the outside world are alike in their reversal of means and ends. Purpose is abandoned in the interest of exploring what may be obtained by a free experimentation with the means. Yet, at the core, arts and sciences diverge completely. For in back of this seemingly endless experimentation with means of expression one finds—"the exploitation of an uncertainty" (Gide). As Sypher comments, the artist

> will improvise, improvise upon an ordinary motif until he has examined its possibilities. Like the cubist, Gide is impartial.

What he called his irresolution, an incapacity or unwillingness to endorse any one perspective, was typical of the cubist temperament, the indecision of the early twentieth century intellectual who, having accepted the notion of relativism, was aware of all the attitudes that could be held, but perhaps not acted upon: neutrality in art and life, and a clever investigation of alternative angles on every problem.[19]

In the sciences experimentation with techniques of inquiry may have an element of playfulness as well. But the scientist's techniques are based on earlier experiments as part of accepted knowledge and his technological subjectivism is limited by the principle of cumulative knowledge. In the arts previous experiments may be imitated for a while, but eventually previous patterns become a deterrent against imitation in the interest of further experimentation. It is the difference between an interest in valid knowledge as against new forms of artistic experience and expression.

In the social sciences perspectivism has several different aspects. One may think of experimentation with the techniques of inquiry, as in psychological tests or the construction of models for studies of economic development. One may think of instances in which theoretical models reflect specific social interests. But one may also consider that social theories, however experimental or existentially determined, project an interest in seeing the world in a certain way. In this respect academic immunities may allow the scholar to approach social theories as trial presentations of the world, to be assessed in terms of analytic utility. But academic immunities cannot also prevent an extramural political manipulation of such tentative theoretical models. Therefore perspectivism in the social sciences is not as remote from group interests as is the "technological subjectivism" of the natural sciences. Nor is the social scientist's experimentation with perspectives as private a means of expression as it is in the arts. Every statement of fact about society is considered controversial by someone, and this holds doubly for the abstractions of social theorists, which affect the interests of large numbers.[20]

◄§ SCHOLARLY RESPONSIBILITIES

The mutability of perspectives in social theory and their political or social exploitability suggest that theories about society have attributes which must be considered in their own right. Social scientists must take such meta-theoretical factors into account. At the same time, they are well-advised to distinguish in their scholarly work between propositions about objects (object-language) and propositions about statements (meta-language). Both kinds of propositions may use highly formalized or ordinary forms of speech, though if they employ the latter it is not always easy to distinguish the two. The logical attributes of the two kinds of statements are different. A proposition about objects, that is, a statement asserting that something is thus and so, should not also contain a statement about that proposition. Or conversely, statements concerned with the logical and existential attributes of propositions should be separated formally from statements about objects.[21]

How do these considerations apply to sociology? The content of a proposition in sociology is logically distinct from the conditions under which that proposition is asserted, and also from the criteria by which its validity is ascertained. In their proper place all three are relevant. The content of propositions must meet criteria of validity which will lead to agreement. A scholarly community is engaged in continual debate concerning these criteria. In addition, sociologists will reflect upon the conditions and consequences of sociological knowledge. This is the question which concerns us. What do we learn when we understand the conditions under which a given perspective in social theory is propounded and examine the uses to which that perspective is put?[22] These questions lead back to the Marxian and Weberian position examined earlier.

Sociologists are indebted to Marx's reductionist approach to ideas. Their approximation of detachment will become credible to the extent that they show acute awareness of the social contexts of knowledge. But this reductionist orientation need not and should not be associated with the Marxian theory of history. Marx's interpretation of ideas as the direct or indirect reflection of class interest has outlived its usefulness in a society to which nineteenth-century models of the division of labor, the class structure, and social evolution do not apply.[23] Nonetheless, we need a candid account of the conditions and consequences embedded in the theoretical frameworks of sociological analysis.

Weber attempted to give such an account in opposition to both positivism and historicism. He emphasized the subjective element in the social sciences, which in this respect are no longer as distinct from the natural sciences as they were in Weber's time. The focus of scholarly inquiry is defined by the problems and values that concern us. Also, concepts and generalizations are indispensable, whatever the particular constellation of facts. The quest for objectivity occurs only in this subjective context. But once the problem is set, an analytic approach can prove itself by scholarly productivity. Beyond this, Weber noted only that new issues come to the fore as we respond to changed historical constellations, prompted by curiosity, anxieties, beliefs or convictions. These promptings are matters of motivation, not validation. Weber's position calls for reflection upon the values implicit in scholarship and thus contains a partial answer to Marx's reductionism. Scholars may not hide behind anonymous historical forces, whose "agents" they are supposed to be. They perform a creative function. But appropriate as this emphasis is, it also evades Marx's insights which pointed up, even as they exaggerated, the social and political manipulation of ideas.[24]

Is it possible to go beyond these earlier reflections? The social conditioning of knowledge, while important, is neither direct nor precise. True, for a time the emerging industrial societies of the nineteenth century witnessed contentions among ideologically defined classes, which made social theories appear as by-products of group interest. But even then it was misleading to underestimate the range of choice made possible by the perspectivism of a pluralistic culture. Ideas may, of course, reflect the impact of social interests. This is obvious in managerial ideologies or communist party jargon, for example. The transparent manipulation of such language sets off the guarded or cynical response of the readers as well as the Aesopian language of those who attempt to be critics within the gates. However, the impact of social interests on the development of ideas is frequently obscure. Inferences must then do the work of bridging the gap between the social conditioning of ideas and the ideas themselves. Verbs like reflect, correspond, indicate, suggest, and many others are used to assert a relationship which is difficult or impossible to verify. In the Marxian tradition this difficulty is frequently evaded by an analysis of social structure which is seen as integrated and dominated by a ruling class. Ideas are attributed directly to the interests of particular groups. But this approach exaggerates the integration and determinism of social structures and thereby underrates the degree of freedom introduced by the intellectualization of any pattern, including those favored by massive social interests.[25] A general reductionism illuminates little, because it can never be wrong.

Rather than follow this line of thought I wish to emphasize the consequences of social knowledge and especially the moral dilemmas arising from these consequences. This shift to a *projective* approach considers knowledge as a cause or means, not as a result or by-product. Both perspectives have their legitimacy. But today science and scholarship should be preoccupied with the consequences of the pursuit of knowledge, not only with what might obstruct it.

Reasons for this concern have been suggested earlier. To these should now be added a consideration of the scholar's responsibilities. W. H. Auden has commented on the special relevance of Sören Kierkegaard's work for men endowed with special talent in the arts and sciences.

> The fact that such a gift is granted to one and not to all means that it is ethically neutral, for only those demands are ethical which apply to all human beings. It is meaningless to say that it is the duty of an artist or a scientist to exercise his talent, for there is nothing he wants to exercise more. The question of duty can arise only in circumstances in which it might be his duty not to exercise it. . . .
>
> The spiritual dangers for the man of great talent are two. He is tempted to take personal credit for a gift which he has done

nothing to deserve, and so to conclude that since he is superior to most others at art or science he is a superior human being to whom ethical or religious norms do not apply. And he is tempted to imagine that the particular activity for which he has a talent is of supreme importance, that the world and all its inhabitants are of value only insofar as they provide material for art or science or philosophical speculation.

At exposing such pretensions, Kierkegaard is better than anybody else; here, indeed, he is a prophet, calling the talented to repentance. No person of talent who has read him can fail to realize that the talented man, even more than the millionaire, is the rich man for whom it is so difficult to enter the Kingdom of Heaven.[26]

The ramifications of this insight have special significance for the civic responsibility of scholars.

Natural scientists face a dilemma as they advance knowledge in their several fields. The results of their work are used and misused by others; scientists have "no control over the fruits of their labor." Their reactions vary. They may feel uneasy, withdraw from certain branches of research, or enter the political arena in hopes of gaining more influence over the funding and utilization of research. In any case, their *civic* responsibility concerning the *uses* of knowledge remains tolerably distinct from their *scholarly* responsibility concerning its *advance*. This is not to minimize the dilemma. The more successful research becomes, the more it enhances the powers of man to effect changes in nature. And as those powers increase, so does man's technical progress together with man's potential inhumanity to man. But, the scientist's civic responsibility is relatively limited. As a citizen his voice is one of many, and as a scientist-citizen he is honor-bound not to transgress the limits of his expertise. The increasing discrepancy between his civic and his scholarly powers is another side of scientific progress. The opposite possibility would mean that the scientist's civic role should be commensurate with his scholarly one. In such a technocratic society public policies would be decided by those responsible for technical and scientific advance. Here Auden's admonition is appropriate. The use of scientific results is too important a matter to be left to the discretion of those largely preoccupied with the advance of science.[27]

Can these considerations be applied to social theory? Here a comparison between theory in sociology and physics may be instructive. The two fields differ in the power their results put at our disposal. Yet a social theorist's civic responsibility may be as great or greater than that of the physicist. The physicist's research activity is neutral in the sense that the utilization of his results remains to be determined. It is moreover quite uncertain whether and when research results can be used at all. The sociologist faces a different situation. In sociology the utilization of research is modest; results may not be used even when they could be useful. But the political exploitability of theory is great. It is, therefore, difficult to keep civic and scholarly responsibilities distinct. A theoretical perspective of man and society is never only a trial presentation of the world for scholarly purposes. It is also a belief system which men can use to advance their interests. An example can clarify such potential consequences of a social theory.

Organic analogies have recurred throughout the history of social thought, but they were given a new impetus during the nineteenth century. Romanticism drew an invidious contrast between a medieval, organic and a modern, fragmented society. In the middle ages, each individual belonged to a group with defined functions and all groups were considered integrated in a transcendental order. By contrast, modern society was characterized by division of labor, competition, and individualism. Each individual is self-centered and weak, lacking in ties to neighborhood and community. Social groups are tenuous, involving a limited commitment of their members, and lacking any enduring relation with one another. This contrast is a major theme of Western intellectual history from the eighteenth century to the present.

Since the last third of the nineteenth century organic analogies have also been used as models of *modern* society. Starting from the competitiveness and individualism of a capitalist economy, social theorists employed evolutionary analogies in order to account, as they thought, for the evidence of material progress and

Western power. Division of labor and competition were seen as the basis for each individual's role in society. "Survival of the fittest" accounted for the success of the few and the subordination or failure of the many. The mounting discrepancies of power and progress among nations could be "explained" in the same way, and this seemed to make sense of Western expansion and non-Western economic backwardness. Both the romantic and the Darwinian approaches sought to account for each individual's and each nation's relative position. That is, both views "explained" the inequalities dividing men and the interdependence of functions among them. But in doing so they made use of models as different as a hierarchy of the community based on a shared view of the world and a natural hierarchy arising from an unceasing competitive struggle.

Today, it is necessary to add a third, holistic interpretation of society. Modern science and technology have developed self-regulating mechanisms which differ in kind from those dependent upon human control of their on-going operation. Unlike an automobile which cannot function without a driver, these modern mechanisms operate on the basis of built-in responses to stimuli generated by the mechanism itself. Examples are the thermostat, automatic control systems built into airplanes, and others. Once the proper dials have been set manually, the heat of the house and the altitude of the plane are maintained at a given level. The mechanisms turn on or off in response to deviations from that level. This development of modern technology has encouraged views of society as a self-regulating system. Earlier analogies had likened society to a hierarchy of functions in an organic whole or a hierarchy arising from the struggle for existence. Now we get analogies with an equilibrium-maintaining mechanism or with the equilibrium-maintaining functions of the body.[28] The analytic utility of this latest model—depending on the field—can be considerable. But at this point I want to explore the ideological exploitability of ideas which are not as easily separated from their historical context as are the theories of physics.[29]

What are the implications of the larger historical context for the civic responsibility of social scientists? Whether conceived in nostalgic, Darwinian, or technical terms, the organic model of society was an intellectual by-product of societies rapidly increasing in wealth. The countries at the receiving end of Western expansion would have been hard put to develop a view of society as integrated around central values, with individuals and groups distributed by rank and function in accord with their contribution to the survival of their society.[30] In Asia and Africa the economic and political dominance of the West has challenged and undermined the values of native tradition, jeopardized the indigenous economy, and divided the society as a whole into "traditional" and "modern" sectors. An organic model of society is not easily applied to countries, whether or not they became colonies, which are heavily dependent upon Western industrial societies and the world market.

Nor is it easy to apply the model to industrially advanced countries with their conflicts of interest and cultural discontinuities.[31] During the nineteenth century, these societies resolved their internal problems with great difficulty, always inconclusively, and sometimes also through a community of interest in overseas expansion. How can one speak of each individual and group having a function to perform on the basis of a shared outlook on life, when these societies were characterized by major conflicts over the distribution of rights? How can one distinguish the internal and external attributes of societies that greatly advanced the technology of communication? The idea of societies as equilibrium-maintaining systems was not developed in the nineteenth century, but after World War II. This conception of man and society has been put in question by the role of government in the economy and by international relations unbalanced through superpowers, a proliferation of other power centers, and the threat of nuclear war. As ideas and techniques are diffused rapidly among the segments of a population or across political boundaries, existing conflicts are frequently intensified.[32] Organic analogies tend to overstate the consensual basis of modern societies, mistake interdependence for harmony, and underrate the permeability of national boundaries.

These substantive considerations will be elaborated below. Here I wanted to illustrate that in social theory the provisional quality of the scholarly context is not as easy to maintain as in the sciences. Our responsibility is great in disciplines in which the ideological repercussions of theories are frequently more far-reaching than the utilization of research. To meet that responsibility requires awareness of repercussions and a spirit of moderation in keeping with the fact that theories are trial presentations of the world. All social theories arise in an historical context and lend themselves to manipulation. That is no argument against any of them. But scholars are obliged to preserve the context and value of inquiry if they are to meet their civic responsibilities.

IMAGES OF SOCIETY
AND PROBLEMS OF CONCEPT
FORMATION IN SOCIOLOGY

৵ই FIVE ৡৢ৾

Sociologists frequently modify old concepts, or offer new ones, because the standard concepts neglect or omit some range of facts now considered important. To remedy this deficiency, a new formulation is offered though in due time it may be challenged in turn. This conceptual instability is attributable to the youth of the discipline, its want of rigor, the emergence of new problems. It is also due to certain metatheoretical views which influence social theory, but often without the explicit consideration they deserve. These views are expressed in divergent images or interpretations of what is significant or "real" in society.

৵ই DEFINITIONS OF THE "SOCIAL FACT"

These divergent views lead to conflicting definitions of the "social fact." Georg Simmel, for example, was explicitly concerned with

Written together with Bennett Berger and originally published in Llewellyn Gross, ed., *Symposium on Sociological Theory* Copyright © 1959 by Harper & Row, Publishers, Inc., pp. 92–118. My colleague Bennett Berger has given his permission to this republication of our joint essay in the present revised form. Aside from stylistic changes and some necessary amplifications two changes have been made. I have adapted the essay to the context of this volume, and the last two sections have been rewritten with a clearer emphasis on comparative studies. Some pages on Max Weber's work have been deleted also, because their content overlapped with other essays in this volume. The responsibility for this revision is mine alone.

delimiting the subject matter of sociology as an independent discipline. He identified it as the process of interaction among individuals. Accordingly he criticized conventional concepts like the
state, administration, the church, and others as lacking "real"
social content. For these official "social formations" take on meaning only when they are studied in terms of interactions among
individuals.[1] On these grounds Simmel argues for interaction as
the proper focus of sociological inquiry. At the same time he
argues against the familiar assumption that society is an abstraction, but the individual is "real." In his view every abstraction
simplifies and exaggerates "the facts" in order to formulate concepts of analytic utility. In this respect the "individual" is as
much of an abstraction as society. Yet "interaction" is an abstraction as well. And Simmel considers it the object of sociological
inquiry because it represents a realistic approach to the study of
society.

Simmel's problem is not fortuitous. All concepts are based on
some evidence, arranged to facilitate understanding. In that sense
all concepts are realistic and abstract. To argue nonetheless that
the interaction approach is more realistic than more traditional
concepts, suggests other than logical considerations. Definitions
of man and society are also social acts. Just as research is initiated
by some sense of what is significant, so sociological theorizing is
guided by a strong sense of what is "real" in society. Each theorist's definition of the "social fact" is a clue to his image of
society.[2]

Emile Durkheim was concerned with the individual's group
affiliation as the foundation of morality. For Durkheim the central fact is that a society's beliefs and practices are imposed on
the individual. Certainly he recognizes that beliefs are internalized
and conformity is limited by individuation. But the reconstruction
of social morality is Durkheim's overriding concern and with it
the question how we can find or reestablish social norms which
provide firm guidelines of conduct. This concern differs sharply
from the impulse behind the work of Max Weber, and accordingly the two scholars offer divergent definitions of the "social

fact." For Weber the central fact is the meaning which individuals in society attach to their own actions and those of others. In the course of Western civilization that meaning has changed as magic has disappeared and rationalism has risen in many spheres of life. A major aspect of rationalism is the coexistence in modern Western society of several antagonistic values or world views. Weber's fundamental respect for the individual and his relative autonomy requires that the scholar withhold his value judgment in the interest of fully understanding the meaning of actions, of conflicting norms and "many Gods" as individuals experience them. What for Durkheim was a decline of social morality demanding constructive action, was for Weber a fact of modern society to be analyzed in its own right—apart from the problem of what policies and what findings of social science might help to alter that fact.

Men like Simmel, Durkheim, and Weber define the "social fact" in accord with their orientation to substantive problems. Such definitions generate pseudo-controversies, when differences among theorists are discussed without regard for their different *purposes* of cognition. There is no single sociological theory. There are only schools of sociological theory because the most eminent scholars in the field choose their theoretical orientation in accord with substantive concerns and with their sense of what is real or significant in society.[3]

In his *Structure of Social Action* (1937) Talcott Parsons undertook to terminate this "war of schools." He sought to show that Pareto, Durkheim, Marshall, and Weber agree on certain ideas in their analyses of social action. More recently, Parsons endeavored to establish a common theory of action among outstanding representatives of anthropology, sociology, and psychology. The resulting "action-frame-of-reference" has been linked in turn with a theory of society as a system. But this work of integration is based on yet another interpretation of society. In this case the definition of the "social fact" is derived from the belief that the concept "system" is indispensable for a scientific theory of society.[4]

The approaches reviewed here exemplify a common tendency of social theorists. Starting from divergent and specific purposes of cognition, they develop theoretical categories basic to the whole discipline. This practice is of doubtful value. One alternative is to approach theories of man and society from the universalist standpoint discussed below. This approach is not new. The perspective we make explicit is familiar to every major sociological theorist.

◄§ THE PERSPECTIVE OF DUAL TENDENCIES

The task of sociological theory is to attend to the social and individual aspects of human behavior. To say that behavior is socially conditioned means that the individual takes his cues on how to act from the expectations of others. But these cues are not determinants. He may comply with, evade, or resist the expectations of others and this room for maneuver is an aspect of his independence. Attention to both the restrictive and the permissive aspects of culture and society also involves a definition of the "social fact." Man and society are not finite systems. Rather they are capable of indefinite (though not infinite) elaboration through tendencies or forces which are linked and opposite at the same time.

This insight has a venerable intellectual history. It has been expressed in Empedokles's view of a world divided by love and hate and in Freud's theory of death and eros, in the medieval idea of a universal determinism coupled with individual freedom and in Marx's view of men as partly free and partly involuntary actors under given historical conditions, in the Confucian concepts of Yin and Yang and in Kant's idea of "unsocial sociability." The variations increase but the theme remains.[5] At the end of his analysis of freedom and equality in American society Alexis de Tocqueville formulated this theme as his own basic creed:

> I am aware that many of my contemporaries maintain that nations are never their own masters here below, and that they necessarily obey some insurmountable and unintelligent power. . . .

> Such principles are false and cowardly. . . . Providence has
> not created mankind entirely dependent or entirely free. It is
> true that around every man a fatal circle is traced beyond which
> he cannot pass; but within the wide verge of that circle he is
> powerful and free; as it is with man, so with communities.[6]

The same theme has been reflected in sociological theory.
Simmel emphasizes the double effect of multiple group-affiliations.
In modern society such affiliations strengthen an individual personality and give it the capacity to sustain great internal tensions.
But these affiliations can also threaten the personality far more
than in a society with less group-differentiation.[7] Robert Park
combined this idea of his teacher Simmel with the related concepts of Ferdinand Tönnies. In studies of the city, of newspapers,
and of race relations Park distinguishes between individuating and
socializing aspects of interactions.

> Competition and communication, although they perform different
> and uncoordinated social functions, nevertheless in the actual
> life of society supplement and complete each other. . . . Com-
> petition seems to be the principle of individuation in the life of
> the person and of society. . . . Communication, on the other
> hand, operates primarily as an integrating and socializing prin-
> ciple.[8]

In social psychology George H. Mead makes a similar distinction
between the organic actions of the individual (the "I") and the
orientation towards a "generalized other," which the individual
has internalized through interactions (the "Me").

The same perspective is found in Max Weber's work. In emphasizing the subjective meaning of action Weber distinguishes
two aspects. The individual makes sense of his actions, and he
responds to the expectations of others. In practice these two aspects of meaning may be inseparable, but analytically they are
distinct.[9] The distinction is reflected in Weber's substantive work.
His study of the Protestant Ethic emphasized the autonomy of
ideas. The Great Reformers as well as "the [common] people of
that period had very specific ideas of what awaited them in the
life after death, of the means by which they could improve their

chances in this respect, and they adjusted their conduct in accordance with these ideas." [10] In other respects Weber emphasized the
influence of social structures on the development of ideas. He
showed, for example, that the political and military autonomy of
Occidental cities was an important precondition of bourgeois
class consciousness and prepared the way for the ideas of Puritanism.[11]

The perspective of dual tendencies can be exemplified from
the work of sociologists but on the whole it runs counter to major
trends in the field. Contemporary sociology accounts for the conduct of individuals in terms of their group membership and cultural participation. Concepts like culture pattern, subculture, social
role, reciprocal expectations, social class, status group, communication, human relations, and many others make it appear that individuals act as group-influences dictate. This interpretation likens
the individual to the actor on the medieval stage who read his
text from the rolled script in his hands.[12]

A case in point is Ralph Linton's influential attempt to formulate the relation between the individual and his culture. Culture
is described as "the way of life of any society." It consists of "the
normal anticipated response of *any* of the society's members to a
particular situation." Culture provides these members with "an
indispensible guide in *all* the affairs of life." Linton continues:

> I realize that in the foregoing discussion of society and culture
> emphasis has been laid mainly upon the passive role of the
> individual and upon the way in which he is shaped by culture
> and social factors. It is time now to present the other side of the
> picture. No matter how carefully the individual has been trained
> or how successful his conditioning has been, he remains a distinct
> organism with his own needs and with capacities for independent
> thought, feeling and action. Moreover, he retains a considerable
> degree of individuality. His integration into society and culture
> goes no deeper than his learned responses, and although in the
> adult these include the greater part of what we call the personal-
> ity, *there is still a good deal of the individual left over.*[13]

In this way culture and society determine and, therefore, explain
the normal responses of all individuals. What they fail to explain

is left over as a residue. This is indeed a "good deal," since Linton himself emphasizes that no two individuals in a culture are exactly alike. Such residues are unavoidable where we deal with the formulation of hypotheses in particular inquiries. But they are not admissible at the most abstract level where sociology focuses attention on the universals of man's social condition. The *basic* concepts of sociological theory should be applicable to all societies.

◄§ PAIRED CONCEPTS

Concepts of such comprehensiveness will be empty. They cannot encompass the full range of social experience by singling out some dominant feature while leaving others aside. Indeed, any single concept necessarily excludes as well as includes. Yet the paired concepts of sociological theory achieve what single concepts cannot. Paired concepts so conceptualize what we know about the variability of social phenomena that they encompass social and individual aspects of interactions and institutions. Examples are: socialization and individualization, primary and secondary relations, status and contract, symbiosis and cooperation, etc. Concepts of this kind have been developed without analysis in depth. At least three difficulties have stood in the way.

Paired concepts invite dichotomous classifications. Interactions are either intimate or impersonal, organizations either formal or informal, social strata either ascriptive or oriented towards achievement, societies either folk or urban. Social actions or relationships approximate one or another of these reference points and various factors may be related to the degree of approximation observed. At the end of such investigations the concepts appear less serviceable than at the beginning. "Urban" elements are found in folk societies, informal relations are present in formally rational bureaucracies, and so forth. Since this use of dichotomous classifications is misleading, a number of sociologists wish to discard paired concepts altogether.

A second difficulty arises from the failure to distinguish between paired concepts and the formulation of hypotheses. Communities may be distinguished by their degree of isolation, heterogeneity, literacy, and so forth. But in using the terms "folk" and "urban" society Robert Redfield indicated that these traits tended to vary together. As isolation increases, so does homogeneity for example. The extent to which this occurs, is an empirical question which paired concepts cannot answer. To explain this correlation, or its absence, we would need hypotheses concerning the social and psychological links between isolation, heterogeneity, and the other attributes of community life.[14] In this respect paired concepts provide only a preliminary mapping of areas of social life in which analysis may be productive.

Thirdly, many paired concepts have not been fully analyzed. New paired concepts frequently overlap with, but also differ from, past formulations. Sir Henry Maine's distinction between status and contract has much in common with Durkheim's contrast between organic and mechanical solidarity, Tönnies's contrast between *Gemeinschaft* and *Gesellschaft*, MacIver's contrast between culture and civilization, and Redfield's contrast between folk and urban societies.[15] Admittedly these broad contrasts have many drawbacks. But their universal applicability makes them potentially useful. Where such universalism is intended, it is a good rule of thumb to search for missing opposites, when single concepts are proposed.[16]

Related to this is the logical distinction between dichotomous (contradictory) and contrary incompatibilities. Dichotomous contrasts refer to two mutually exclusive attributes, such that the existence of one is incompatible with the existence of the other. Contraries refer to proximate contrasts such that the existence of one attribute militates against, but does not preclude, the existence of one or several others. Although paired concepts are formulated in dichotomous terms they are likely to involve such proximate contrasts rather than logical incompatibilities.

Dichotomous contrasts abound only in normative contexts; they are rarely, if ever, found in social action. The reason is that all rule making must distinguish between conformity and deviance and classify actions accordingly. However, the ease of formulating norms of right and wrong stands in sharp contrast to the difficulty of fitting any particular action into this preconceived scheme. For empirically, social actions show continuous gradations and human relationships are marked by much ambiguity and ambivalence. Mankind is neither entirely dependent nor entirely free; social interaction is partly communicative and partly asocial; both the "I" and the "Me" are involved in social action. The paired concepts of sociology do not, therefore, formulate dichotomous choices; they express the perspective of dual tendencies with its emphasis upon links between proximate contrasts. How do we deal with this insight conceptually and in the formulation of hypotheses?

✎§ PAIRED CONCEPTS OF INTERACTION

Primary relations may be defined as personal and intimate. They involve "responses to whole persons rather than to segments," "communication [that] is deep and extensive," as well as a primacy of personal satisfactions.[17] These formulations refer to a universal: it is difficult to think of societies in which relations of this kind are entirely absent. Scholarly analysis will focus on the degree and kind of primary relations in different social contexts. It will also safeguard its detachment by avoiding the tacit implication that intimate relations are necessarily benign.

The definition of a universal can only be an element in a proposition. Take the assertion that the family is the major locus of primary relations, and assume a definition of the family that is clearly separated from this proposition. Such facts as formal property settlements in a family, or a materialistic attitude towards the choice of marriage-partners would be neglected by the statement. Such secondary relations are impersonal and instrumental by definition, whatever personal and emotional qualities may be imparted to them. These two concepts may be formulated as a universal proposition: all relations between men in society are both intimate and impersonal.[18] Such a proposition has a double utility.[19]

A. *It is based on generalized, inductive knowledge and points to a problem with which men in all societies deal.* In this sense it is a guide to relevant questions.[20] For example, romantics would say that two people genuinely in love have a relationship entirely free of impersonal elements. This idea would be contradicted by the asserted universality of impersonal relations. And primary relationships from which such impersonal elements are indeed absent, can then be expected to create special social and psychological problems. One might generalize and say that love relationships tend to be fragile unless buttressed by suitable formal arrangements, or that the survivor of a love relation faces special burdens if he must cope with his loss without meaningful rites of burial and mourning. Yet primary relations militate against such impersonal considerations. Happily married couples often neglect the legal settlement of their mutual obligations which suggest a lack of trust or an intolerable, i.e. impersonal, consideration of death.

Related questions arise when elements of intimacy intrude in secondary relationships. Such intrusion is often faked for personal advantage, as in the "folksy" approach of radio advertisers. But intimacy can imply conventional obligations and serve as a bar against exploitation. In the United States such uses of intimacy pose special problems in hierarchical organizations. Equalitarianism and the human relations approach have led to personalized work relations, but without personal and social distance it is often difficult to apply criteria of efficiency. Yet if intimacy in secondary relations is minimized, as in German managerial practice, other social problems and psychological burdens arise. The two conditions produce very different dilemmas of action.[21]

B. *Universal propositions reveal the limitations of the concepts we use.* If all social relations are both intimate and impersonal, we may examine a primary relationship for its frequently hidden, secondary attributes and vice versa. The paired concepts may be

conceived also as two ends of a scale on which social relations
may be ranked in terms of relative intimacy and impersonality.
For example, the relative isolation of a community can be ranked
in terms of the number of communications with the world outside. Yet two communities with the same number of communications may possess different kinds of contact.[22] No measure of a
community's isolation is meaningful without analysis of the contacts involved, just as a primary relation is understood best in
relation to its more impersonal attributes.[23]

The paired concepts of sociological theory thus serve as the basis
for formulating hypotheses. A classic example of such preparatory
or preliminary analysis is contained in Max Weber's discussion of
class and status. In his last formulation of these concepts Weber
defines the two terms as follows:

> "Class" means all the persons in the same class situation. "Class
> situation" means the typical probability of 1) procuring goods,
> 2) gaining a position in life and 3) finding inner satisfactions,—
> a probability which derives from the relative control over goods
> and skills and from their income-producing uses within a given
> economic order. . . .
>
> "Status" (ständische Lage) shall mean an effective claim to
> social esteem in terms of positive or negative privileges; it is
> typically founded on 1) style of life, hence 2) formal education,
> which may be (a) empirical training, or (b) rational instruction,
> and the corresponding forms of behavior, 3) hereditary or oc-
> cupational prestige.[24]

In these definitions Weber uses two conditions of collective action
as ideal-typical antitheses. The market knows of no personal distinctions. Transactions on the stock exchange are reduced to a few
standardized phrases or gestures. Distinctions among brokers are
factual and impersonal, depending on their respective credit
rating. "The factor that creates 'Class' is unabiguously economic
interest, and indeed, only those interests involved in the existence
of the market." [25] At the same level of abstraction exactly the
reverse is true of the status order, in which men are grouped in
terms of their prestige and style of life. To safeguard their status

such men will reject all claims to "status honor" based on economic acquisition and power alone. Stratification based on the status order would be undermined quickly, if a wealthy man could claim more "honor" than those whose status rests on family lineage and style of life.

Thus, economic interests militate against the dominance of status-distinctions, especially in periods of rapid economic change. Considerations of status "hinder the strict carrying through of the sheer market principle," especially in periods of relative economic stability.[26] But these antithetical tendencies are also linked. Actions based on economic interests frequently aim at the preservation or acquisition of "honor." Weber points to the example of English stock brokers who safeguard fair dealing on the market by excluding "unreliable" elements from membership in their voluntary and exclusive associations. In turn status-groups use their social prestige to monopolize economic opportunities. Thus, the East German landowners (*Junkers*) exploited their aristocratic status to maximize their economic interests as landowners. To understand the linkages and antitheses between class and status it is necessary to define each unambiguously, i.e. *as if* they were mutually exclusive and *as if* each of them were governed by a principle of internal consistency.[27]

◆§ PAIRED CONCEPTS OF INSTITUTIONS

Many sociological concepts refer, not to social action or relations, but to more or less enduring institutions like bureaucracy, types of urban society, specific status-groups like aristocracies, etc. The sociologist can only observe actions, but is bound to use concepts of institutions or social aggregates when he analyzes the conditions of action, of their enduring results.[28] Paired concepts can be applied at this institutional level of analysis as well.

A case in point is Weber's analysis of bureaucracy. The elements of his definition are generally familiar and are repeated here in abbreviated form. A bureaucracy tends to be characterized by:

a. Defined rights and duties, which are prescribed in written regulations;

b. Authority relations between positions which are ordered systematically, and hierarchically;

c. Appointment and promotion which are regulated and are based on contractual agreement;

d. Technical training or equivalent experience as a formal condition of employment;

e. Fixed monetary salaries;

f. A strict separation of office and incumbent in the sense that the employee does not own the "means of administration" and cannot appropriate the position;

g. Administrative work as a full-time occupation.[29]

These conditions of public (and private) employment have been instituted only gradually in the course of Western civilization. To understand "bureaucracy" fully it is necessary to contrast these conditions with those prevailing under traditional authority.

a. "In place of a well-defined functional jurisdiction, there is a conflicting series of tasks and powers which at first are assigned at the master's discretion. However, they tend to become permanent and are often traditionally stereotyped."

b. "The question of who shall decide a matter or deal with appeals—whether an agent shall be in charge of this, and which one, or whether the master reserves decision for himself—is treated either traditionally, at times by considering the provenience of certain legal norms and precedents taken over from the outside; or entirely on the basis of the master's discretion . . ."

c. "The household officials and favorites are often recruited in a purely patrimonial fashion: they are slaves or dependents (*ministeriales*) of the master. If recruitment has been extra-patrimonial, they have tended to be benefice-holders whom he can freely remove."

d. "Rational technical training as a basic qualification for office is scarcely to be found among household officials and favorites."

e. "Household officials and favorites are usually supported and equipped in the master's household. Generally their dissociation from the lord's own table means the creation of benefices . . . It is easy for these to become traditionally stereotyped in amount and kind." [30]

These contrasting conditions of employment under legal-bureaucratic and traditional authority also involve linked and opposite tendencies of action. But this level of abstraction refers to a contrast derived from historical experience, not to the universals of man's social condition.[31]

Paired concepts of institutions serve only as benchmarks that can facilitate detailed analysis. The correlations to which they refer are proximate and unstable. The attributes of bureaucratic or of traditional authority need not occur together. Even when the rights and duties of officials are defined clearly, appointments and promotions may be handled arbitrarily. Even when a ruler assigns different tasks arbitrarily, he may be legalistic in delegating authority. Also, such institutional complexes are relatively unstable. Written regulations may be altered through personal influence, though the intent is to preclude such influence. Tasks can be assigned arbitrarily to curtail the independent power of subordinates, but officials may still succeed in limiting the discretionary authority of their ruler. To a degree these dissociations and instabilities may be overcome by secular tendencies which favor several of the attributes of the bureaucratic or of the traditional type.

Statements of such tendencies are descriptive, not definitional. They make no assumption of logical consistency like the statement that the market knows no personal distinctions if purely economic considerations predominate. Yet statements of secular tendencies also go beyond description. They combine observed attributes into a model or pattern which may be contrasted with one or more alternate patterns.

Keeping contrasting patterns in mind may be considered the analyst's equivalent of always remembering the mutability of historical patterns. For example, the salary scales of officials are readily fixed and administered under modern conditions. Yet, fringe benefits, promotions, and job classifications are subject to bargaining or personal influence; their cumulative effect could nullify the basic salary scale. Much will depend upon the efforts of those who administer the scale. If they were completely successful fringe benefits, promotions and job classifications would be codified minutely and bargaining would have little influence. Much will depend also on those who bargain over the rules and their implementation. If they were completely successful, a condition of traditional authority might be reestablished with renumerations dependent upon arbitrary judgments. In this sense institutions represent the more or less enduring balance of social relations which are the result of past contentions. Institutions are never complete or permanent and analysis must take account of the forces which circumscribe them.[32]

✍ THE STRUCTURE OF CULTURE AND SOCIETY

What are the implications of paired concepts for an understanding of culture and social structure? From the perspective of "dual tendencies" the integration of culture and society is a matter for investigation.[33] A holistic approach discourages such investigation. Durkheim's work provides a striking example. In his *Rules of Sociological Method* Durkheim makes crime a "normal" aspect of culture. Without crime there would be insufficient awareness and enforcement of social norms. How much crime is "needed" to help maintain the norms of society? To answer this question Durkheim distinguishes between normal and pathological degrees of crime, between social health and disease. Yet he fails to establish criteria which would allow us to make that distinction.[34]

The perspective of "dual tendencies" suggest a different approach. Crime is always both: an opportunity for the maintenance of social norms and a hazard to their integrity. Nothing more can be said of *all* societies. Every society faces the problem of achieving a balance between reaffirmation and hazard. This achievement is the work of men who make history but under conditions not of their own choosing—to cite the still telling phrase of Marx's *18th Brumaire of Louis Bonaparte*. The maintenance of morals is not due to a "normal degree" of crime. Rather, the violations of norms result in interaction in which the balance between denial and affirmation is once more at issue. Not only criminals and deviants, but judges and policemen vary in the degree to which they contribute to the integrity of social norms, or detract from it. As the recent history of school-desegregation has made all too clear, failure of the authorities to enforce the law undermines confidence in its efficacy, but vigorous enforcement of a law that remains controversial all too easily casts doubt upon the legitimacy of the law itself. As we thread our way between that Scylla and Charybdis, the integrity of norms and with it the unity of culture hang in the balance—hardly a view that is compatible with Durkheim's approach.

This reference to "balance" may suggest the idea of a social system in equilibrium mentioned earlier. This idea differs from Durkheim's moral concerns. He reacted to the social disorganization of France with a passionate desire to reconstitute the normative order. His theories of religion, of suicide, and of education are only intelligible in that context. Nothing like this moral preoccupation is evident in systems theories which derive their models from biology and from self-regulating mechanisms.[35] Against this background Max Weber's work takes on added significance, because it is informed by a conception of "balance" which is incompatible with Durkheim's approach as well as with the image of society as a "system." [36]

Instead of the word "culture" Max Weber uses such terms as mores (ethics), convention, or style of life.[37] These terms are general designations of different ways of life. Each man's participa-

tion in his society involves a personal commitment to the be-
havior-patterns, ideas, and interests of a particular status group.
By virtue of their styles of life, such groups "are the specific
bearers of all conventions. In whatever way it may be manifest,
all stylization of life either originates in status groups or is at
least conserved by them." [38] Such styles of life may become representative for a whole society. The domineering and paternalistic
manner of the *Junkers* influenced many aspects of German society.
Certain ideas of ascetic Protestantism gained widespread influence
in modern capitalism; they "prowl about in our lives like the
ghost of dead religious beliefs." [39] Weber summarized one aspect
of his sociology of religion by designating the status groups which
were the principal exponents of world religion.[40] Thus, the influence of ideas and behavior patterns can reach far beyond the status
group with which they originated. But Weber construes culture
as an outgrowth of group power and group conflict in their historical development, and hence relates a given style of life to the
group from which it has spread. The culture of a society is interpreted as a more or less enduring result of past conflicts among
status groups.[41]

This formulation also implies a conception of the individual's
relation to his culture. Individuals always engage in attempts to
redefine their roles. Social roles limit the alternatives available
to the individual, but they also provide opportunities for maneu-
vering and initiative. Through their social roles individuals participate in the interactions among dominant, symbiotic, and subordinate status groups, each with vested interests in its style of
life. As individuals and groups seek to enhance their interests,
they also reformulate and institutionalize their position in society.
Sometimes this is deliberate. Negro protest movements in the
United States seek to alter the Negro's collective position vis-à-vis
the white majority. When Negro spokesmen use the nationalist
movements of colored peoples around the world, they want to
enhance their own dignity as well as change their status as a
lower caste. Sometimes the relation between action and status

is quite indirect. Officially, government administrators in the United States implement legislative policy. Yet their status and role is characterized better by the continual pulling and hauling among prominent administrators, Congressional committees, and organized interests. This interplay of many groups continually redefines the role of administrators in the making of public policy and thereby gives them a place in the American social structure. Thus, culture can be related to society and power by an analysis of the strategies of argument and action which individuals and groups use to define their respective roles as advantageously as possible.

The inequality of status groups is found in all societies. Frequently a particular status group and its style of life is dominant for prolonged periods and the pattern it imprints on the culture may endure long after that dominance has passed. This is one reason for the coherence of societies, though the dominance of such groups is often partial and even subordinate groups exert cultural influences of their own. To characterize the structure of a society it is necessary to consider the changing interactions among dominant and subordinate groups, and this depends, as Weber's work did, on a wide-ranging use of the comparative method. As suggested below, the perspective of "dual tendencies" is the theoretical foundation of this method.

✍§ IMPLICATIONS FOR COMPARATIVE ANALYSIS

The perspective of "dual tendencies" contrasts with theories of evolution, although the familiar dichotomies of social theory have often been an aspect of evolutionism. Concepts like status and contract or pattern variables like ascription and achievement always refer to differences between social structures, and hence to changes over time. By contrast, the perspective of "dual tendencies" uncovers the element of uncertainty in all societies. Kenneth Burke calls attention to this approach with his phrase "perspective by incongruity."

Any performance is discussible either from the standpoint of what it *attains* or what it *misses*. Comprehensiveness can be discussed as superficiality, intensiveness as stricture, tolerance as uncertainty—and the poor pedestrian abilities of the fish are clearly explainable in terms of his excellence as a swimmer. A way of seeing is also a way of not seeing. . . .[42]

This is a conceptual strategy, but it is also a social scientist's critique of utopian thought. It asks us to consider *every* social phenomenon as transient. Social action evokes or provokes reactions; it has intended and unintended, valued and devalued consequences. It follows that sociological inquiry should search each fact for what it may become as much as for what it is, for what it hides as much as for what it reveals. In this sense paired concepts and the perspective of "dual tendencies" are a theoretical adaptation to the Janus-faced quality of social life, as the concept of "systemic equilibrium" is not.

This consideration casts doubts upon analyses which assess facts in terms of their contribution to the adaptation (function) or impairment (dysfunction) of a society. Take the statement that frequent industrial strikes prevent maximum production. To turn this descriptive statement into a generalization, we would have to demonstrate that at certain levels strikes are quite compatible with the successful adaptation of the society, but at other, higher levels they are not. However, we do not have a criterion of "successful adaptation" that is free of wishful thinking. Strikes may interfere with maximum production in the short run, whereas in the long run they may help accelerate capital investment and increase overall productivity. Also, strikes may increase cooperation by providing an outlet for accumulated grievances and establishing a new plateau for labor-management relations. The long-run balance between negative and positive effects on production, capital investment, and cooperation is uncertain. And in the face of that uncertainty the temptation is great to advance judgments with an air of assurance: e.g. strikes jeopardize the consensus required for social integration.[43] From a scholarly standpoint such judgments are ideological shortcuts of doubtful value.

In the absence of unequivocal criteria of social health or societal survival it is best to accept uncertainty. The strains and conflicts of society account for the uncertainty of social change, because the same facts may help to maintain or impair the social structure. Party activity, agitation for civil rights, the representation of organized interests are ways by which pressure for change is exerted. Such pressure is an opportunity for the accommodation of grievances or conflicts and a hazard for the institutional machinery by which accommodations have been achieved in the past. Both successful accommodation and the impairment of that machinery are always possible. In this sense social facts are seen as points of transition to the adaptation or impairment of a social structure.

Probably there are limits to what is possible in any one society, but it is difficult to specify them in advance or even with the wisdom of hindsight. While comparative analysis suggests that the actions of individuals fall within a range of tolerance, the limits of this range are in a continual process of redefinition. Men in society repeatedly define what individuals are prohibited to do; yet people often fail to comply with what is expected of them. Sociological theory should comprehend both tendencies by focusing on the boundary-extending as well as the boundary-maintaining activities of individuals. Culture and society enable individuals to experiment with what is possible, but social controls also limit the range of tolerated behavior without defining that range clearly.[44]

This image of society is the theoretical counterpart of comparative analysis. The link between the two is exemplified by the work of Alexis de Tocqueville and it is worthwhile to make this explicit. In the first volume of his *Democracy in America* Tocqueville had dealt with the institutions of a democratic society, principally in a descriptive manner. But in the second volume he had used

> the ideas derived from American and French democracy only as data, . . . [in order] to paint the general features of dem-

ocratic societies; no complete specimen of which can yet be said
to exist. This is what an ordinary reader fails to appreciate. Only
those who are much accustomed to searching for abstract and
speculative truths, care to follow me in such an inquiry.[45]

To know how men will act tomorrow and how they will deal with
coming events, one must be in a position to see continually what
they are doing and thinking. At the same time one must take a
bird's-eye view of affairs in order to understand the "sentiments,
principles, and opinions, the moral and intellectual qualities"
which are given by nature and by an education that has lasted for
centuries.[46]

In his second volume on America Tocqueville was concerned
with this truth for the long run. The progressive development of
democracy appeared to him inevitable, and he favored it. But he
was concerned to show that it was not a brilliant and easily realized
ideal, that such a government was not viable "without certain
conditions of intelligence, of private morality, and of religious
belief." [47] As a nation France had not yet attained these conditions. Indeed, in France the democratic revolution had gone astray,
uncertainly alternating between despotism and anarchy, with no
signs at all as to when and how a stable social order might again
be established. But while he was extremely pessimistic about the
prospects of his own country, Tocqueville derived a more hopeful
outlook from his studies of America.

Indeed, his insights into American democracy arose in part from
contrasting her institutions with those of France.

In my work on America . . . though I seldom mentioned France,
I did not write a page without thinking of her and placing her
as it were before me. And what I specifically tried to draw out, and
to explain in the United States, was not the whole condition of
that foreign society, but the points in which it differs from our
own, or resembles us. . . . I believe that this perpetual silent
reference to France was a principal cause of the book's success.[48]

American conditions provided Tocqueville with a picture of the
"sentiments, principles, and opinions, the moral and intellectual

qualities," which could sustain democratic institutions. By contrast French society exemplified the qualities which *might lead* to a "species of oppression unlike anything that ever before existed in the world." [49] And by superimposing French portents on American actualities Tocqueville projected his picture of the despotic possibilities inherent in democratic institutions generally.

His analysis of American society contains comparisons with analogous conditions in another country and "speculative truths" concerning possible developments in the future. In his view such speculation cannot be more than a judgment of limits and possibilities.

> I own, that this old world, beyond which we neither of us can see, appears to me to be almost worn out; the vast and venerable machine seems more out of gear every day; and although I cannot look forward, my faith in the continuance of the present is shaken. I learn from history, that not one of the men who witnessed the downfall of the religious and social organizations that have passed away, was able to guess or even to imagine what would ensue. Yet this did not prevent Christianity from succeeding to idolatry, servitude to slavery, the barbarians from taking the place of Roman civilization, and feudalism in turn ejecting the barbarians. Each of these changes occurred without having been anticipated by any of the writers in the time immediately preceding these total revolutions. Who, then, can affirm that any one social system is essential and that another is impossible?[50]

This reasoned conviction holds a precious balance between hope and despair. Tocqueville did not think it possible to predict in the future of society. It depends upon men and nations whether their drift towards equality leads to servitude or freedom.[51] Yet he also believed the possible directions of social change to be limited in number. By means of "speculative truths" one can extrapolate observed tendencies. It is fictitious to assume that nothing would interfere with their ultimate realization. But extrapolation is useful as a means of mapping out possibilities of thought and action, however proximately. Tocqueville's approach fits in well with a view of culture and social structure as more or less enduring results of past conflicts, and with a definition of the "social fact" as a point of transition to their adaptation or impairment.

The approach to social theory presented in this chapter is also an approach to the role of knowledge in society. We adopt an attitude of hope *and* uncertainty concerning the constructive potentialities of social knowledge. We do not know enough to be sure of what cannot be known. We stand between the pessimists who think sociology as a science impossible and the optimists who think it is a science already. But we do not believe that man must only know enough in order to solve pressing social problems.

The approach presented here is obviously tentative, requires considerable elaboration, and does not stand or fall on superseding all other approaches. We candidly regard it as experimental and would like to have it read in the same spirit. As stated at the beginning, it is related to an intellectual tradition which views men and society in terms of tendencies or forces which are linked and opposite at the same time. This tradition has special relevance for contemporary sociological theories which have generally sided with the conservative tradition of the nineteenth century. The task is to emancipate sociological theory from the limitations of this intellectual heritage. But the import of these concluding remarks is not to label given theories or thinkers as conservative, liberal or anything else. It is to make plain that the definition of the "social fact" embodies each theorist's image of society which has its distinct utility and unique blindness.

CULTURE, SOCIAL STRUCTURE, AND CHANGE

The history of sociology is marked by a basic controversy between those "who stress conflict and change . . . and those who stress integration and stability." The first group ranges from Marx to Dahrendorf and "tends to rely more on the 'person' or 'group' perspective." The second ranges from Durkheim to Parsons and "tends to rely more on the 'social-structural' or 'cultural' framework." The task is to develop "a more profitable synthesis of these two perspectives than we have been able to effect in the past." [1]

Each set of theories leaves as a residue what the other considers its main focus of attention. Weber belongs to the first set rather than the second. But in his day the bifurcation of schools was not as clearly marked as it is in ours. And while his studies do not contain a theoretical synthesis, they do move in that direction. Neither the "person" or "group" nor the "social structural framework" are left as unexplained residues. The following discussion attempts a systematization of Weber's approach which reflects much of my own image of society.

This essay was written especially for this volume. It is a continuation of my studies of Weber's work, beginning with *Max Weber, an Intellectual Portrait* (Garden City: Doubleday & Co., 1962). Several related essays on Weber and on topics of central interest to him will appear in Reinhard Bendix and Guenther Roth, Scholarship and Partisanship (Berkeley: University of California Press, forthcoming).

⚜§ CULTURE: IDEAS, BELIEFS, AND ACTIONS

To a foreign visitor a culture appears unified at first; then, gradually, this impression weakens or disappears. The longer he stays, the more he learns to distinguish the diversities previously obscured by a uniform strangeness. Eventually he recognizes diversity in the great and the little tradition, as Redfield has phrased it. In the great tradition of the arts and sciences, styles and conflicting schools of thought abound. There is a disjunction between the cultural elite and the large number of those who are more or less passive participants in the great tradition. In the little tradition of popular culture, language, and convention there is much diversity in everyday behavior, grouped by class or region or ethnic origin. These and other diversities become apparent even to the casual observer. Others are more difficult to discern. Our beliefs are often hard to reconcile with one another and may be at odds with our actions as well. Such incongruities arise in part because cultural patterns are a patchwork of legacies and contemporary adaptations. They arise also because each of us plays many roles, leading to incompatibilities between our self-perceptions and the expectations of others.[2]

These diversities and incompatibilities are glossed over by the assumption of an underlying consensus. It has been argued that all social behavior depends upon common understandings. Two speakers using the same language communicate because they share an understanding of words and syntax. But where communications are marked by hostility and incomprehension, it is misleading to speak of consensus. The term suggests shared understandings which go beyond the elements of language, a minimal degree of mutual comprehension and shared belief. These phrases should not be used as synonyms of culture. Rather, analysis must show how a degree of unity coexists with the diversities characteristic of complex cultures.

Weber's studies of religion make a contribution in this respect. In this section I deal with *The Protestant Ethic* as a study of cultural change, with the distinction between cultural elites and the people at large, and with the question of how new ideas can influence the latter. Each of these themes bears on the meaning of "shared beliefs" as an object of study.

◄§ A PARADIGM OF CULTURAL CHANGE

The theme of *The Protestant Ethic and the Spirit of Capitalism* is familiar. By their development of theological ideas Luther and Calvin espoused an innerworldly ascetism. Men were enjoined to seek the salvation of their souls by diligently serving God in their worldly callings. Having analyzed this meaning of certain theological doctrines, Weber proceeded to show its inadvertent affinity with the "capitalist spirit." Secondly, he examined the pastoral admonitions of English divines in the seventeenth century. These encouraged conduct in keeping with the Reformed doctrine and favorable to a methodical, self-denying maximization of gain. Eventually, religiosity declined, but the pattern of conduct remained.

Several levels of analysis may be distinguished. Weber examines the theological doctrines of the Reformers in terms of the ideas and actions which they encourage in the ordinary believer. He focuses attention on the innovative contribution of religious leaders and on the formation of religious movements among the people at large. In a religious civilization changes may be induced by external conditions, but

> the most important source of innovation has been the influence of individuals who have experienced certain "abnormal" states . . . and hence have been capable of exerting a special influence on others. These influences. . . . overcome the inertia of the customary. . . . Very often a collective action is induced, which is oriented toward the influencing person and his experience and from which, in turn, certain kinds of consensus with corresponding contents may be developed.[3]

In time such consensus may be institutionalized in religion or law, leading to a feeling of obligation among members of the community and joint action against nonconformists.

The Reformers had been followed by disciples who proselytized the religious truth revealed to them. Proselytizing implies a distinction between religious disciples, who preach the new truth, and the people at large who are set in the old ways. How can abstract, theological ideas influence the beliefs and actions of ordinary people? And if they do, what is the intensity and duration of that influence? In attempting to answer these questions Weber develops an analytic paradigm which may be summarized as follows:

1. Cultural innovation is the result of extraordinary individuals like Luther or Calvin who were religious virtuosi.

2. Their virtuosity consisted in the first place in the expression of their extraordinary personal qualities through the development of theological doctrines.

3. Analysis at the level of meaning can be pursued in many ways. Weber singles out the explicit and implicit incentives of Reformed doctrine for the conduct of the believer.

4. The reformers together with their disciples and followers constitute an elite of articulate spokesmen intent upon spreading the message.

5. Pastoral sermons by ministers of the church are the most direct vehicle of communicating the new religious ideas to the people at large.

6. Weber attributes the influence of doctrine upon conduct to the intense concern with salvation characteristic of the seventeenth century. Once that intense concern waned, implications of Reformed doctrine remained influential in secular guise.

✎§ ELITES AND MASSES

Emphasis on elites has major significance for Weber's approach to the study of culture. In *The Protestant Ethic*, but still more in his comparative studies of China, India, and ancient Israel, Weber analyzes eras of religious creativity. Confucius, Lao Tse, Buddha, the Old Testament prophets, and others express the divergent world views of the great civilizations. At the same time, Weber begins his most systematic discussion of religion with an explicit refusal to define it. Not religion, but religious behavior as a type of social action is his major concern.

> The most elementary forms of behavior motivated by religious or magical factors are oriented to *this* world. "That it may go well with thee . . . and that thou mayest prolong thy days upon the earth" (Deut. 4:40) expresses the reason for the performance of actions enjoined by religion or magic. Furthermore, religiously or magically motivated behavior is relatively rational behavior, especially in its early manifestations. It follows rules of experience, though it is not necessarily action in accordance with a means-end schema. Rubbing will elicit sparks from pieces of wood, and in like fashion the mimetical actions of a magician will evoke rain from the heavens. . . . Thus, religious or magical behavior or thinking must not be set apart from the range of everyday purposive conduct, particularly since even the ends of the religious and magical actions are predominantly economic.[4]

Thus, religious behavior has a mundane meaning for the ordinary person. Nor is religious experience a thing apart, since "the notion of 'supersensual' forces that may intervene in the destiny of people" is seen "in the same way that a man may influence the course of the world about him."[5]

To understand religion and magic from their own standpoint we must enter into the mind of the believer and religious functionary. The person performing a magical act will distinguish "between the greater or lesser ordinariness of the phenomena in question."[6] Not every object can serve as a source of special powers. Nor does every person have the capacity to achieve the ecstatic states which in primitive experience are the condition for achieving certain effects. The believer can hope for comfort and benefits only from the particular object or person which possesses charisma. The sense of religious awe and reverence is due to the hopes and fears with which he regards that object or person. Weber

focuses attention on religious elites because believers single out
the power to assist them in their need, not only because innovation and leadership are the work of individuals.

The idea that such power exists is associated with "the notion
that certain beings are concealed 'behind,' and are responsible
for, the activity of the charismatically endowed natural objects,
artifacts, animals, or persons." [7] But the beings or spirits which are
the source of charisma are also at the command of those endowed
with charisma. Thus, the necromancer turns ecstasy into an enterprise, because in the eyes of the layman ecstasy "represents or
mediates charisma" and thus authenticates his special powers over
the spirits. In their afflictions or their everyday affairs men seek
assistance from the spirits. Consequently they go for help to those
who can communicate with spirits and demons.

Where such beliefs prevail, elites form easily. The charisma of
an object or person may be seen as a natural endowment that cannot be acquired. In that case it is a question of the criteria by
which its presence may be recognized. To know these criteria is
a special art which is readily monopolized. But charisma may also
be produced artificially. Objects or persons are assumed to possess
a dormant propensity which can be awakened by special rites or
ascetic practices. In that case it is a question of performing these
rites or practices in an authentic manner. Again, this puts a
premium on knowing what is authentic, and such knowledge is
a secret power that cannot be widely shared.

The formation of elites lies at the root of religious experience,
because the believers are convinced that the good things of life
can be attained only with the aid of higher powers. Subjective
convictions of this kind must be understood in their own terms.
In Weber's view critics of his *Protestant Ethic* had neglected that

> people in the past had after all very concrete ideas of what awaited
> them after death and of the means by which they could improve
> their chances in this respect. They adapted their behavior ac-
> cordingly. For the development of culture it became important,
> in what forms this adaptation occurred depending upon the
> various views on the preconditions which—if fulfilled—would

guarantee their salvation. For us moderns it is exceedingly difficult to put ourselves in their place and appreciate the agonizing power of these metaphysical conceptions.[8]

Thus, maxims concerning time, work effort, and the sense of duty in one's calling had been at one time a matter of religious devotion among the Puritan faithful. These maxims are still current, but are largely devoid of religious significance today. At the end of his essay Weber refers to them as the "ghost of dead religious beliefs." Between then and now one can suppose that intense religious beliefs have gradually given way to a process of secularization, though Weber's studies did not extend this far.[9]

Part of this transition must be a declining belief that the good things in life are affected by higher powers. With this decline the difference diminishes between the popular regard for religion and for other realms of high culture. All works of high culture involve arcane knowledge. Therefore, a presumption of some mysterious power is associated also with the painter, the concert artist, the writer, and others creatively engaged. But ordinary men are not intensely concerned with these realms of high culture. Since they do not expect benefits to accrue to them from knowledge or skill in the arts, they have no sense of that power which they believe manifest in the magician or prophet or priest.

Perhaps this explains the popular attitude towards the artist. People are at once slightly apprehensive and belittling. By virtue of his skill the artist possesses mysteries which make him somewhat formidable. But this skill does not give him power in the religious sense. This makes him appear quaint or even suspect, because mysteries without power are a form of charlatanism. In the eyes of the public the modern scientist may be closer to that of the magician, because his knowledge is mysterious *and* powerful, but the quasi-religious significance of this attitude still needs to be explored.

Weber's approach to religion highlights the fundamental difference between cultural elites marked by arcane knowledge and the masses who lack such knowledge. In the case of religion people look with much fervor and concern for themselves upon the promises and guidelines held out to them. Weber does not deal with the difference between elites and masses where people have a "take it or leave it" attitude towards the activities of the cultural elite.

The hiatus between high culture and everyday experience is probably much greater in periods of secular culture than in periods of intense religiosity. In the former there is little cultural integration in the sense that arts and sciences are apart from everyday experience despite popularization and an equalitarian credo. In the latter there is considerable integration in the sense that religious symbols provide a universal language for high and low alike. The study of such periods can advance our understanding of cultural integration by analyzing how aspects of high culture, like new theological doctrines, can affect the daily experience of the ordinary believer.

⌘ DOCTRINE AND CONDUCT

It makes sense to ask how cultural creations are transmitted to the masses, if there is a proselytizing impulse on one hand and an audience eager for the message on the other. But the influence of doctrine on conduct is not a simple process even in periods of intense religiosity. In *The Protestant Ethic* Weber approached this problem in a deliberately limited way. The existing literature warranted the assumption that religious dissent and successful entrepreneurship were somehow linked.[10] He assumed further that religious doctrines made a *prima facie* difference to the people of the seventeenth century, concerned as they were with the salvation of their immortal souls.

On the basis of these assumptions Weber pursued three lines of inquiry. First, what incentives to daily conduct were implicit in the Reformed doctrine of Luther, Calvin, and their followers? Here analysis spelled out what these doctrines would mean to a true believer. Second, how did the Puritan divines of the seventeenth century translate these doctrines in their sermons and pastoral counselling? Here analysis moved away from theology in order to examine how religious doctrines were presented to the congregations. Third, how did the communities of the faithful respond? Here analysis moved still closer to the study of behavior by examining how the congregations censored or commended the conduct of their members. Weber believed that only letters and diaries would contain more direct evidence on the nexus between doctrine and conduct, but he did not undertake that task.[11]

Weber's problem is of general interest for the study of culture. An element of unity arises where the gulf between high culture and everyday behavior is bridged by doctrinal influence on behavior. Weber's essay demonstrates such influence, but only generally. His assumption that all people in the seventeenth century cared deeply for the salvation of their souls is too undifferentiated to carry conviction. It is more promising analytically to differentiate degrees of religiosity even in a universally religious population. This was apparent to the Puritan divines of the seventeenth century who were concerned with the quality of religious belief and attacked the spiritual slumber of their flocks. As William Haller has put it on the basis of an extensive study of seventeenth-century sermons: "the endeavor of the preachers was . . . to arouse men out of their indifference by warning them of the wrath to come. After that they were engrossed with two supreme dangers to morale, the failure of confidence and the excess of confidence." [12] What follows is an analytic commentary on this quotation.

1. In Weber's view Catholicism had provided people with a safety valve through the Confessional. The religious views of the Church were accepted as a matter of course. People would engage in their daily rounds of virtues and vices, knowning that at regular intervals moral accounts could be balanced and forgiveness obtained, for the most part without hazard to their eternal souls. "The agonizing power of metaphysical conceptions" had to be brought home to such people, before their fate in the hereafter became a matter of urgent concern. Periods of universal religiosity are not necessarily periods of a uniform religious intensity. It is more plausible to assume that few people were indifferent and a considerable minority was truly faithful, while the majority was

moderately, one might say conventionally, concerned. What the Puritan divines probably did was to move this majority towards a greater religious concern, and specifically those who were anti-Papist on various secular grounds.

2. How could they do that? The success of the preachers becomes puzzling, once we abandon the notion that a period of universal religiosity is also one in which all people are moved by intense religious concerns. Ordinarily, preaching by itself does not move people out of their customary ways. In *Ancient Judaism* Weber himself analyzed a comparable intensification of belief. He showed the conjunction between prophecy and the historical experience of the Jewish people. The prophetic message of impending doom received its frightful poignancy by the savage military destruction which followed. The events of the English Reformation were entirely dissimilar, but the historical experience of the English people also led to an intensification of belief. The Reformation of the sixteenth century was initiated by political considerations without religious ethos. For three decades, politically inspired church policies succeeded one another without a definite stand on the part of the government itself. Competing doctrinal systems created a welter of conflicting opinions in the absence of genuine religious leadership. As a result, a mounting desire for certainty went together with widespread religious anxiety, as Herbert Schoeffler puts it. In this setting various groups of believers came to hold fast to different sets of beliefs and practices, once they had chosen them as their religious sheet anchor in the midst of change. Thus, propitious circumstances helped to arouse people out of their religious slumber.[13]

3. The preachers had to deal with the spiritual consequences of this development. Now that conventional piety was no longer enough, a large number of believers had become anxious. Some became genuinely frightened and lost confidence. Others tried to maintain their customary stance and became confident of their virtue under a veneer of piety. Accordingly, Haller's statement describes a threefold preoccupation of the preachers. They would arouse the people's religious concern repeatedly, or people would

slide back into conventional religiosity. The preachers would give confidence to those who lost heart. And they would attack others who arrogantly believed that their good fortune was evidence of virtue.

In this way we get a differentiated view of the relation between doctrine and conduct. *The Protestant Ethic* demonstrates the direction of doctrinal influence. But it assumes rather than demonstrates an intense religious concern among the faithful. As Schoeffler suggests, the history of the English Reformation provides circumstantial evidence for an intensification of religious concern among large numbers. Where such intensification occurs, people reorient their beliefs and actions in response to new ideas.

The preceding discussion has used Weber's *Protestant Ethic* as a paradigm of cultural change, rather than for its intrinsic interest. A new set of ideas is first articulated by a cultural elite and eventually influences large numbers of people. Through diffusion and the decline of religiosity these ideas lose their original force, though in secular form their influence continues. This pattern probably recurs in other spheres of high culture, though with less widespread influence upon people and with less difference between periods of intense concern and of secularization.

At any one time a culture represents a congeries of beliefs and actions that originated at different times and with different cultural elites. Complex cultures lack integration because the most antagonistic world views and personalities exist side by side in the same society.[14] This condition accounts for the continuing efforts to achieve greater integration, for example, through the articulation of a common tradition. Like consensus, integration is a matter of degree.

In secular societies not much integration is likely in view of the gulf between cultural elites and the masses. But while a great deal of high culture develops with little or no influence upon the people, it is otherwise with the structure of authority and the system of stratification. People subject to authority or of low status tend to accept "the ruling ideas of the ruling class," to use a phrase of Marx. And unlike the cultural elites, holders of authority and persons of high status tend to back their claims to allegiance by an implied threat of force. The following section continues the analysis of shared understandings as an attribute of social structure.

SOCIAL STRUCTURE

At different levels of a society there are likely to be varying degrees of integration. These can be analyzed, once the conceptual problems are resolved. But at the level of society as a whole the meaning of integration or coherence is questionable. Societies can resemble the living people in Hoffmannsthal's trenchant epigram: "The main difference between living people and fictitious characters is that the writer takes great pains to give the characters coherence and inner unity, whereas the living people may go to extremes of incoherence because their physical existence holds them together." [15] Likewise, geographic contiguity, conventions and institutions hold societies together, even as they go to extremes of incoherence.

✐§ MODELS OF SOCIAL STRUCTURE

Social scientists have developed three models which seek to account for the coherence of social structures: the interdependence model, the exchange model, and the coercion model. These three are not mutually exclusive, nor are they as simple as I shall present them here.[16] Following this discussion I turn to an analysis of authority and of stratification.

The first model is based on the reciprocity of expectations among individuals. Individuals learn their roles in society by conforming to what others expect of them. As they mature, they will use the expectations of others partly as cues for further action; this greatly facilitates interaction and mutual comprehension even where it does not lead to conformity. Both role learning and shared understandings are frequently attributed to the values learned by the individual and incorporated in social institutions.[17] In this way society's capacity to function as an interdependent system is greatly facilitated. Critics of the interdependence model have pointed out that reciprocity of expectations is not synonymous with agreement. There is much indifference or absence of contact which makes the simple idea of reciprocity problematic. Nor is the interdependence of society a product of reciprocal expectations alone. The division of labor creates complementary roles in the absence of direct interaction. Still other types of interdependence are the result of environment, demographic patterns, institutional and intellectual legacies. In addition, we are often affected by the interactions of others without being aware that they have occurred and impinge on our lives. Accordingly, the interdependence model, important as it is, has limited applicability.

The exchange or market model is a special case of the interdependence model. As developed by classical economists and liberal social theorists, the exchange model posits interactions among equals as the basis of the social structure. The classic case is Rousseau's theory of the general will which implicitly presupposes the equality of property owners. The man of property who maintains that all men of property should have their rights of property defended, has the best of both worlds. He can be egoistic and altruistic at the same time.[18] But this benign condition changes the moment the man of property interacts with someone who owns nothing. Both are free to acquire property, but only one enjoys rights of ownership. In this way equality in one respect is accompanied by inequalities in many others. The resulting cleavages may be handled by negotiation, as in labor-management relations. But such negotiations depend upon accepted rules of the game, and these are not derived from interactions in the market. Accordingly the market model can account for the coherence of societies only to a limited extent.

The coercion model proceeds in an opposite direction. It emphasizes the inequalities which make for a cumulation of benefits on one side and deprivations on the other. Where interactions are marked by such inequalities, reciprocal expectations foster conservative and radical postures. The few want to buttress their good fortune and the many strive for equality and justice. Between men divided by good and ill fortune even accommodations are colored by tension so that the social structure appears to be dichotomous.[19] But in fact there are many ties between them. Authority wants to be considered legitimate and considers the reactions of those it can command; the subordinate temper their resistance by the degree to which they accept dominant values. While the possibilities of coercion and revolt remain in the background, the coercion model is weakest where societies are marked by accommodation.

The choice among these models often depends on the purpose of inquiry. The economist will find the exchange model suitable for his purpose. The child psychologist or the sociolinguist will probably opt for the interdependence model. Students of war or international relations may choose the coercion model. The three models may serve their purpose as long as they account for shared beliefs which have a specifiable meaning. But they are inadequate as general theories of social structure.

At this level, Weber borrowed from all three models but with a logic of his own. Interdependence, exchange, and coercion are for him aspects of social action. They may lead to constellations of interests and levels of agreement among individuals or groups. The shared understandings existing in a society vary widely in intensity and generality; except for rare occasions they are probably least intense where they are most general. As a rule social actions do not occur at the level of society as a whole, though Weber does not make this point explicit. Rather, he contrasts the shared understandings of society with the shared understandings of authority. Two attributes distinguish the latter: administration and a belief in legitimacy which makes that administration valid for the polity. Weber's theory of social structure focuses attention on social actions at the two levels of society and authority.

The belief in legitimacy plays a role at both levels. Divisions among individuals or groups of unequal social, economic, and political position are a prime characteristic of societies. Authority and stratification involve institutionalized ways of resolving or at least managing tensions arising from that inequality. A general theory of social structure should interpret the ties of feeling or sentiment among people divided by cleavages of legal position, status, and interest.

✎§ AUTHORITY AND LEGITIMATION

References to a belief in legitimacy are always suspect. They are difficult to separate from self-serving apologetics because persons in authority are *prima facie* evidence of power and inequality. Still rulers and ruled demand a rationale, and the cynics are wrong who would have us think that explanations and symbolic acts are automatically discounted. Rulers want to exercise authority with a good conscience; indeed many of them want to be loved. The ruled want to have some sense of equity and compassion in high places, a proximate, if tacit, *quid pro quo* for the act of obedience. Even democratic governments are surrounded by pomp and circumstance. These along with statements to the press, gala receptions, official hearings, and many other manifestations of authority are ways of meeting the desires of both groups. But it is true that modern forms of publicity easily jeopardize the credibility of justifications in high place. And modern forms of government with their massive bureaucracy certainly emasculate the sense of give and take between the authorities and the public. Accordingly, the belief in legitimacy fluctuates, and evidence for its importance is most telling when that belief has vanished and institutions crumble.[20]

The concept of legitimacy refers to shared beliefs of rulers and ruled, and such beliefs tend to be ambiguous. Weber defines the term tautologically. "Social action may be guided by a belief in the existence of a legitimate order." Such an order exists when "conduct is oriented towards determinable maxims." He acknowledges that much of the time a people's regard for their institutional order will be based on expediency or habit. But the viability of a legitimate order will be enhanced if the people consider those maxims "as in some way obligatory or exemplary" for themselves.[21] Since an insititutional order is legitimate only to a degree, there is no clear distinction between legitimacy and illegitimacy in contrast to the law with its dichotomy between valid and invalid rules.[22] Therefore, the legitimacy of an institutional order fluctuates with the sense of civic obligation in contrast to a merely customary or expediential compliance.[23]

Beliefs in legitimacy appear tenuous, since they wax and wane as different groups respond to the public issues before them. Nevertheless, an institutional order remains intact to the extent that a belief in certain maxims for the long run is shared by office holders and the public, notwithstanding the great social and political distance dividing them. When this belief contains an element of shared hope or trust, people will get along with the tensions of authority and to this extent help maintain the social structure. Weber's discussion of charismatic and legal authority exemplifies the tenuous quality and the importance of beliefs in legitimacy.

⋙ CHARISMATIC AUTHORITY

Genuine charisma makes its appearance when a leader and the people at large become convinced that the accommodations of everyday politics will no longer do. Then consummate belief on one side, and the promptings of enthusiasm, hope, or despair on the other, call imperatively for unconditional commands and obedience.

> The term "charisma" will be applied to a certain quality of an individual personality by virtue of which he is considered extraordinary and treated as endowed with supernatural, superhuman or at least specifically exceptional powers or qualities. These are such as are not accessible to the ordinary person, but are regarded as of divine origin or as exemplary, and on the basis of them the individual concerned is treated as a "leader".[24]

But charisma is not a supernatural, superhuman, or exceptional quality of an individual. It is rather a quality which he claims and others attribute to him.

Charismatic authority depends upon a shared understanding between leaders and followers.

> It is recognition on the part of those subject to authority which is decisive for the validity of charisma. This recognition is freely given and guaranteed by what is held to be a proof, originally always a miracle, and consists in devotion to the corresponding revelation, hero worship, or absolute trust in the leader. But where charisma is genuine, it is not this which is the basis of the claim to legitimacy. This basis lies rather in the conception that it is the duty of those subject to charismatic authority to recognize its genuineness and to act accordingly. Psychologically this recognition is a matter of complete personal devotion to the possessor of the quality, arising out of enthusiasm, or of despair and hope.
>
> No prophet has ever regarded his quality as dependent on the attitudes of the masses toward him. No elective king or military leader has ever treated those who have resisted him or tried to ignore him otherwise than as delinquent in duty. Failure to take part in a military expedition under such a leader, even though the recruitment was formally voluntary, has universally met with disdain.
>
> If proof and success elude the leader for long, if he appears deserted by his god or his magical or heroic powers, above all if his leadership fails to benefit his followers, it is likely that his charismatic authority will disappear. This is the genuine meaning of the divine right of kings (*Gottesgnadentum*).[25]

This passage might suggest that followers recognize a leader as charismatic, because they see "powerful results achieved in the absence of power." [26] But recognition by the followers and the leader's own claims and actions are in fact ambivalent.

To recognize the charisma of a leader is the duty of his followers. But the desire for a sign confirming the existence of charisma easily contaminates a personal devotion born of enthusiasm, despair, or hope. In turn, the leader demands unconditional devotion from his followers. He will construe any demand for a sign of his gift of grace as lack of faith and a dereliction of duty. Yet his "charismatic authority will disappear . . . if proof or success eludes him for long."

Charismatic authority is thus not a label to be applied, but a problematic relationship to be studied. A leader may feel the call, or people at large search for someone to satisfy their longing for a miracle. Such a search for charisma may prove of no avail. Moreover, the followers' desire for a sign and the leader's demand of unconditional faith may jeopardize the reciprocal expectations on which authority is based. Genuine charisma appears only when one man feels possessed by a mysterious gift, and his belief in that gift is shared by those who follow him.[27]

Charismatic authority exemplifies the meaning of legitimacy at its most tenuous. Weber emphasized that it becomes more enduring only when the gift of grace and the devotion to duty become institutionalized, as in the apostolic succession of the Papacy and the ritualized piety of Catholic believers. In addition, charismatic authority occurs more or less frequently as a sudden intrusion into stable political structures, as when a charismatically gifted king appears in a traditional monarchy, or an exceptionally gifted political leader appears in a constitutional system.

Weber did not anticipate, however, that under modern conditions belief in charisma could be combined with secular bureaucratic structures leading to a terrifying corruption of both. A charismatic leader will claim unquestioned validity for his every utterance. At the same time he avoids all tests of his authority by making the agencies of government responsible for every implementation. In the eyes of his followers the leader's claim is unimpaired. All failures are attributed to subordinates who violated the leader's trust. But these subordinates also try to evade responsibility by reference to the absolute commands they are obliged to obey. For a time the day of reckoning may be put off. The claim to authority is divorced from all tests of its validity. And the responsibility of subordinates is obscured by the omnipotence attributed to the leader. In this way the dangers inherent in charismatic authority are compounded by those inherent in bureaucratic administration, leading to a reciprocal escalation of abuses for which Hitler's regime is the most striking modern instance.

In all these instances authority is sustained by shared beliefs in the special powers of an individual, though these beliefs weaken where charisma is institutionalized, or become perverted where charisma is corrupted. I turn now to the beliefs in legitimacy which sustain the legal order.

◌§ LEGAL AUTHORITY

The authority of the law is an example of a relatively stable structure. It rests on several, interdependent ideas. Law is embodied in a consistent system of abstract rules. Any legal norm may be established by agreement or imposition. The result is an impersonal order of rules which are binding on the persons in authority as well as on those subject to it. The obligation to obey is limited in each case to the relevant jurisdiction.[28] The persistence of legal authority is due to three factors: its rules are implemented by administrators, officials and citizens are subject to the same rules; and the rulers and ruled share a belief in the legitimacy of the legal order.

Weber states that the law rests "on a belief in the legality of enacted rules and the right of those elevated to authority under such rules to issue commands."[29] These highly abstract maxims become meaningful only through a general belief in the "rules of the game." In practice that involves trust in the fairness with which conflicting legal claims are adjudicated. To a certain extent this fairness is institutionalized, as in the respective functions of judge and defense attorney under the same body of laws. The judge sees to the maintenance of the law and of procedural rules in reaching a verdict. The defense attorney has the special task of protecting the substantive rights of his client to the full extent of the law. Thus, the maintenance of laws and rules as well as the defense of individual rights are principles built into the rules governing the conduct of trials.

These principles involve conflicting imperatives. For example, legal enactments are administered by an administrative staff, defined by such formal characteristics as delimited spheres of competence and personnel selection based on tested qualifications. At the same time there is "the tendency of officials to treat their official function from . . . a utilitarian point of view in the interest of the welfare of those under their authority. . . . This tendency to substantive rationality is supported by all those subject to authority." [30] Thus, administrators are bound by rules and obliged to uphold them in their own decisions and procedures. On the other hand, they adjudicate disputes or implement policies in keeping with substantive goals like justice or equity or maximum benefit. Consequently administrators, like judges and others in legal authority, are pulled in divergent directions as they seek to reconcile the attributes of formal and substantive rationality.

Laws or rules are formal to the extent that in all procedural or substantive issues "only unambiguous general characteristics of the facts of the case are taken into account." This can mean that only tangible characteristics are considered legally relevant, like the utterance of certain words or the execution of a signature. Or it can mean that a logical analysis of meaning discloses those characteristics of the facts which are legally relevant, thus leading to highly abstract legal concepts. These formal aspects of laws or rules stand in sharp contrast to all substantive decision making, based on ethical imperatives or on considerations of expediency.[31]

The viability of a legal order depends upon the success with which these opposing principles are reconciled in practice. According to the decision of the U.S. Supreme Court, Negro children have the formal right to attend integrated schools. In Little Rock, Arkansas, segments of the white population opposed integration, despite the law decreeing it. Not to call out the troops would have violated the government's formal obligation to enforce the law; but to have done so frequently would reveal the persistent discrepancy between the law and important segments of public sentiment. Both strategies undermine respect for the law. In practice the formal rights of Negro children have been promoted by many expedients short of enforcement by troops or police, apparently in the hope that gradually the gulf between law and public sentiment would diminish.

Thus, legal enactments formulate normative aspirations for the community as a whole. Together with the procedures regulating adjudication and enforcement they constitute the law's system of abstract rules. Action in conformity with these norms and procedures preserves the integrity of the rules and represents the law's formal rationality. At the same time, there is a hiatus between these abstract rules and the world in which Negro children have a claim that is denied by others. This hiatus is not a recognized part of the law. But since it exists, enforcement practices are adapted to effect some workable or manageable relationship between legal norms, procedures, and the conflicting claims in the public arena. This balancing of conflicting claims with the rules as a constant point of reference is the practical reconciliation between the law's formal and substantive rationality. The task of the legal order is to preserve the system of legal norms while managing and adjudicating substantive conflicts of rights and interests.[32]

The development of formal rationality in law, administration, economic enterprises, the sciences, and other spheres is one meaning of the term "rationalization." Throughout his work Weber points out that by promoting formal rationality lawyers, officials, entrepreneurs, scientists, and others also protect and advance their own position and function. In this sense rationalization is inseparable from the self-interest of specialists and their struggle for power. On the other hand, there are many who believe their interests diminished by formally rational action. Those subject to an impersonal implementation of rules will demand a personal consideration of the particular case, regardless of the effect this might have on equity or the calculability and consistency or rules. Sometimes men in high places are sensitive to the ideas and interests left out by adherence to formal criteria, and become champions of ethical or political imperatives. Accordingly, under legal authority tensions recur between the requirements of formal rationality and the concern with achieving certain ethical or social goals.

⁍ DUAL TENDENCIES REVISITED

Weber endowed concepts like charismatic or legal authority with a "not only but also" quality for which it is difficult to find an unequivocal designation. Such concepts do not refer to a specific set of attributes. Instead they refer to patterns of action and reaction which have an unstable "feed back" mechanism as their common denominator. The claims of charismatic leaders and the expectations of their followers affect each other, and in a different way so do the body of formal laws and the ways in which people regard the rules of the game in relation to their conflicting interests. Charismatic or legal authority are legitimate as long as the conflicting claims of authority and of those subject to authority are accommodated.

Since these concepts refer to characteristics of a social structure, they are also relatively empty. The legitimacy of legal authority may fluctuate as various accommodations are achieved between formal and substantive rationality. But legal authority as a structure remains intact as long as a tension is maintained between the integrity of the law and the substantive claims of individuals or groups. That structure will be destroyed only when the formal rationality of the law is made so paramount as to deny all substantive claims, or when these claims are made so paramount as to destroy the system of rules. This is the sense in which Weber's concepts of social structure encompass tendencies or forces which are linked and opposite at the same time.

So far social structure has been discussed in terms of the ties of feeling and sentiment between the few in positions of authority and the many who are subordinate to them. Social stratification likewise involves great differences of status and also poses problems of legitimation.

⁍ STRATIFICATION AND LEGITIMATION

Authority and stratification may converge or diverge, but their problems of legitimation are analytically distinct. Whereas public authority must act for the whole community, social and economic privileges are *prima facie* evidence of narrow self-interest. Yet those who enjoy such privileges also want to make it believable that they deserve their good fortune.

For long periods, religious beliefs legitimated inequality. To the happy few good fortune seemed evidence of divine blessing, while the sufferer was hated by the gods. This interpretation satisfied a general craving.

> Strata with high social and economic privilege will . . . assign to religion the primary function of *legitimizing* their own life pattern and situation in the world. This universal phenomenon is rooted in certain basic psychological patterns. When a man who is happy compares his position with that of one who is unhappy, he is not content with the fact of his happiness, but desires something more, namely the right to his happiness, the consciousness that he has earned his good fortune, in contrast to the unfortunate one who must equally have earned his misfortune.[33]

Yet religious beliefs could also give satisfaction to the lowly. While rulers and owners would see suffering as evidence of a secret guilt, the poor could look upon it as a promise of salvation. The poor were the pure in spirit to whom the good fortune of others appeared as the sure road to damnation. Obviously the lot of the common people was often extremely hard to bear, and to the secular mind the consolations of religion appear threadbare. But religion provided a universe of discourse from which people of good and ill fortune could derive diametrically opposed conclusions. In periods when religion provided a universal symbolic language people sharply divided by status and learning were yet part of the same cultural milieu.

Religion was not alone in providing a common language. Secular powers like kingship and a landowning aristocracy were considered legitimate in their own right. The capacity to decide and command was frequently combined with a ceremonious display and a distinguished bearing which overawed and inspired the populace. A medieval lord's "profession"

> not only qualified him admirably for the defense of his own class interest—he was not only able to fight for it physically—but it

also cast a halo around him and made him a ruler of men. The
first was important, but more so were the mystic glamour and
the lordly attitude—the prestige with all classes of society and
in every walk of life. That prestige was so great and that attitude
so useful that the class position outlived the social and technological conditions which had given rise to it and proved adaptable,
by means of a transformation of the class function, to quite
different social and economic conditions. With the utmost ease
and grace the lords and knights metamorphosed themselves into
courtiers, administrators, diplomats, politicians and into military
officers of a type that had nothing whatever to do with that of the
medieval knight. . . .[34]

This aristocratic capacity to rule could flourish where kings and
nobles combined social and economic privileges with a consecrated
right to rule. Here authority and high social class reinforced each
other. Subsequently the two diverged as the artistocratic capacity
to rule came to be considered an attribute of family tradition,
maintained and enhanced by education. The old consecrated order
lost its legitimacy as aristocratic conduct became an aspect of social
privilege, and eventually even the utility of an aristocratic bearing
declined.

In a secular period neither religious imagery nor aristocratic
culture can legitimate inequality. Good fortune has no transcend-
ent sanction in the eyes of the many who carry the burdens of the
world.

There is surely no trace of mystic glamour about [the industrialist and merchant] which is what counts in the ruling of men. The
stock exchange is a poor substitute for the Holy Grail . . . the
industrialist and merchant, as far as they are entrepreneurs, also
fill a function of leadership. But economic leadership of this type
does not readily expand, like the medieval lord's military leadership, into the leadership of nations.

I have called the bourgeois rationalist and unheroic. He can only
use rationalist and unheroic means to defend his position or to
bend a nation to his will. He can impress by what people may
expect from his economic performance, he can argue his case,
he can promise to pay out money or threaten to withhold it, he

> can hire the treacherous services of a *condottiere* or politician or journalist. But that is all and all of it is greatly overrated as to its political value. Nor are his experiences and habits of life of the kind that develop personal fascination. . . .[35]

In the political field this argument is persuasive. With the decline of kingship and aristocracy public authority has become divorced from wealth. The industrialist as a type enjoys great influence due to economic success. He does not enjoy the prestige of authority.

But high social and economic status still has much prestige. As before, the happy few want to be entitled to their good fortune, while the many want to reverse their lot, or at least compensate for their ill fortune. A secular language of legitimation has replaced the earlier religious and political one. In the early period of industrialization entrepreneurial ideologies of deserved success on one side of the class structure were matched by panegyrics to labor's right to the whole product on the other. Conflicting claims were put in a language of material gain, with each group rewarded for its contribution. This was not a stable legitimation of the social order, but its influence continues to the present day.[36]

The apotheosis of the self-made man idealized personal qualities like diligence and frugality, and above all the value of material advance. This materialist appeal was successful, however much the secular version of the Protestant Ethic came to be discounted. Here is the root of the worker's quest for citizenship and of the intellectual's alienation from the industrial society. Here also is the source of recurrent tensions between them.

As Western societies industrialized and the welfare state emerged, workers gradually accepted the legitimacy of stratification. They adopted as their own the consumption ideals of the upper strata. Here again no more is meant by acceptance than that they contrived to get along with the tensions engendered by the class structure. On the other hand, intellectuals have challenged those ideals throughout, even though they enjoyed high levels of consumption. Cultural standards conflict with the prevailing materialism. Thus, the stratification of industrial societies is legitimate at

one level, but lacks a corresponding intellectual and cultural justification. And this discrepancy accounts for the paradox that economically successful societies have fragile social structures.

MODELS OF SOCIAL CHANGE

The culture of complex societies as well as their systems of authority and stratification are marked by cleavages so great that the
degree of unity achieved becomes a prime object of study. Our discussion suggests that the coherence or integration of societies is a
precarious achievement since geographic contiguity, conventions,
and institutions may hold societies together without unifying them.
Thus the sources of change are ever present, though change itself is
neither necessary nor continuous.

A generation ago theories of evolution and the work of Herbert
Spencer were out of fashion in American social theory. By the late
1960s evolutionist theories were a major preoccupation once again.[37]
The scholarly concern with economic and political development,
rather than the earlier idea of progress through competition, probably accounts for this revival.[38] Max Weber's work contains contributions to the analysis of social change which have not received
the attention they deserve. One can be described as "breakthrough
and routinization." The other concerns the direction in Western
history which he called "rationalization." I shall comment on
each theme in turn, and then relate Weber's approach to the perspective of dual tendencies discussed above.

◄◄§ BREAKTHROUGH AND ROUTINIZATION

Societies are characterized by continuity and the prevalence of
conventional behavior. Daily activities are marked by much routine
even in the midst of change. Yet at times there are extraordinary
needs or situations which jeopardize complacency and convention.
It is then that a person endowed with charisma may appear, or may
be found by the people searching for a solution. Weber focuses
attention on those historical instances that seem to exemplify the

contrast between charismatic breakthroughs and the prevalent continuity of social life. He emphasizes the instability of charismatic domination and its tendency to be transformed into more stable structures.

> Charismatic rulership in the typical sense . . . always results from unusual, especially political or economic situations, or from extraordinary psychic, particularly religious states, or from both together. It arises from collective excitement produced by extraordinary events and from surrender to heroism of any kind. This alone is sufficient to warrant the conclusion that the faith of the leader himself and of his disciples in his charisma—be it of a prophetic or any other kind—is undiminished, consistent and effective only *in statu nascendi*, just as is true of the faithful devotion to him and his mission on the part of those to whom he considers himself sent. When the tide that lifted a charismatically led group out of everyday life flows back into the channels of workaday routines, at least the "pure" form of charismatic domination will wane and turn into an "institution". . . .[39]

The prototype for this pattern of change was the charismatic figure of Jesus, the small band of his apostles, the role of charismatic beliefs in the conventicles of early Christianity, and the later institutions of Catholicism.

The concept of "charismatic leadership" appears equally applicable to other founders of the great world religions, like Buddha, Confucius, Moses, and Mohammed, though the religiosity of each is distinctive. At the beginning a great religious innovator achieves a high point of inspiration. Later on, an eager band of disciples seeks to preserve that inspiration beyond the lifetime of the founder. The institutions set up to accomplish such preservation necessarily substitute office for person, ritual for inspired words or actions. Training in doctrine and conduct develop, and rites of initiation become regular means to achieve the desired commitment and solve the problem of succession. In the Catholic church exceptional qualities become embodied in offices and functionaries, in the sacred service and the thoughts and acts of ordinary believers (*Veralltäglichung*). Such routinization weakens the extraordinary power of charisma. Those who seek its spiritual and material benefits may, therefore, challenge conventional teaching and the institutions of the church by appeals to the original source of religious inspiration.

The pattern here described is familiar in a number of nonreligious contexts as well. Lenin was a charismatic leader. He possessed exceptional qualities and the Bolshevik revolution was a high point of ideological commitment. Major changes in the political and economic organization of Russian society were initiated. But in the course of time, routinization set in. The charisma of Lenin faded into the background despite the verbal adulation of decades and the physical preservation of his body. The original communist tenets have been undermined by monotonous recapitulation and by the abuses of bureaucratic and dictatorial rule. However, massive industrialiation and Russian nationalism may have taken the place of Marxist-Leninist legitimation, at least in part.

Still other examples come to mind. In his theory of economic development under capitalism Schumpeter has attributed exceptional qualities to entrepreneurs who break through "business as usual" by developing new methods of production and distribution. Yet each innovation is a starting point of a new "business as usual." Vested interests cumulate once more and resist the further changes needed to initiate new economic developments. Something like this has also been suggested in the case of science. Earlier I referred to Thomas Kuhn's distinction between normal science and scientific revolutions. The first involves a paradigm of theory and method which has been accepted by a scientific community at work. The second involves a breakthrough of new theory and method achieved by some pioneer who takes as his point of departure the difficulties and unexplained residues left out of account by normal science.[40]

Jacob Burckhardt did not use the term "charisma." But he would have considered instances of such pioneering leadership as moments in which history breaks free of the encrustations of the past. And he emphasized as Weber did that the men who accomplish such breaks may be great birds of prey as well as saints and heroes.[41]

Charisma can be the grace of divine inspiration or the terror of self-deification; it may liberate pent-up forces for good or unleash frenzies of destruction. Similarly, the routinization of charisma may embody the original message or ossify into a monopolistic organization of self-serving votaries. But I write "or" without conviction. The human condition is so beset by motivational ambivalence and situational ambiguity that these antitheses exist side by side, even in the same person.

Weber had as acute a sense of this condition, as did Freud, but his concern was the fate of reason in society, not the cure of souls. He certainly accepted the idea that in human affairs reason can advance through revolutionary change and its subsequent transformations. But social change, and specifically the advance of reason, can also occur through cumulative innovation. This is the pattern of change suggested by Weber's concept of rationalization.

✌§ RATIONALIZATION

The term has many meanings whose most common denominator is probably the idea of systematization. Men behave rationally, when they take into account and weigh the end, the means, and the secondary results of their actions. Weber contrasts this instrumental rationality with a rationality of ultimate values. The latter consists of actions governed by commitment to an ultimate end and by plans of action consistent with that end.[42] Therefore, one aspect of rationalization "is the substitution for the unthinking acceptance of ancient custom, of deliberate adaptation to situations in terms of self-interest." Another is the substitution of "a deliberate formulation of ultimate values (*Wertrationalisierung*)" for "every sort of unthinking acquiescence in customary ways." [43]

In his use of "rationalization" Weber went far beyond these rudimentary meanings. His critique of the idea of progress restricts the term to technology and makes it a synonym of increasing differentiation.[44] His introduction to the sociology of religion suggests links between rationalization in Western science, music, architecture, law, administration, and economic enterprises.[45] Elsewhere, he pursues the possible meanings of this process in economic and political institutions, in the law, and in religion. In all these spheres it is possible to substitute deliberation for unthinking acceptance and thus systematize not only very mundane pursuits but also the most otherworldly orientations of mind and spirit. All types of rationalization are specific historical developments rather than aspects of an evolutionary scheme.

The difference appears clearly in Weber's sociology of law. The general development of law from charismatic legal revelation by law prophets to the systematic elaboration of law and the professional administration of justice is a succession of stages superficially similar to the evolutionary models put forward in the nineteenth century. But this line of development appears only as a convenient summary towards the end of the volume. In Weber's view such schemes explain nothing. Rather, the development of law has been affected by power struggles between the *imperium* on one hand, and kinship groups, folk communities, and status groups on the other; by struggles between theocratic and secular powers; and thirdly by differences among the strata of legal notables which have become significant for the legal development of different societies.[46]

Rationalization, then, is not a uniform developmental process. Its various forms contribute to the persistence and change of societies. In Weber's view social structures are marked by the continuity of conventional behavior. Probably legal norms arise when habits of conduct are experienced as binding and when conventions are turned into rules and acquire the guarantee of coercive enforcement. Here rationalization acts as a conservative force. But this hypothetical view of social continuity does not answer "the question of how anything could ever change this inert mass of canonized custom which, just because it is considered binding, seems as though it could never give birth to anything new." [47] New lines of conduct including new legal norms may arise unconsciously. Either actual changes of meaning are not perceived or an old law is applied to a new situation in the belief that this was always done. Also, external changes may lead to new rules. But the decisive cause of legal innovation has always been "a new line of conduct which then results either in a change of the meaning of the existing rules of law or in the creation of new rules of law." [48]

Here is a pattern of innovation through "formally elaborated law constituting a complex of maxims consciously applied in decisions." Such elaboration "has never come into existence without the decisive cooperation of trained specialists." [49] These specialists are of many kinds: officials, legal notables, elected or appointed judges, occasionally priests, private attorneys, and others. All of them contrast sharply with the role of the law prophet in various types of folk justice. In the early development of law the judge sees to the adherence of certain procedures, but only the law prophet is believed to possess the wisdom required for rendering a verdict. At the conclusion of the trial he answers the decisive question of guilt or innocence through charismatic inspiration.[50] Such law finding is an essential part of justice where adjudication is considered a matter of magical revelation which alone can preserve the integrity of custom and belief. Here charisma is not an innovative break with tradition. In the development of law, it is rather the trained specialist who innovates through rationalization, while the charismatic interpreter guards the tradition through inspiration and extraordinary powers. Thus, according to Weber, bureaucratic or legal rationalization as well as charismatic leadership can become revolutionary forces, but bureaucracy, law, and charisma may also be bulwarks of tradition.[51]

✎§ CHANGE AND HISTORY

Weber's two models of change have an "open-ended" quality in common. Charisma may be a source of innovation, but priests or kings may also use their exceptional gifts to maintain the social order. Also, rationalization may involve cumulative innovations as legal specialists substitute formal rules for the unthinking acceptance of social norms. Yet such substitution may be a means of preserving the status quo as well. Both models can be patterns of conservation as well as change. At the same time they remain distinct in their emphasis on inspiration or systematization. It is doubtful that Weber would have attempted to integrate these dual tendencies. He used them as guide lines for research, not as models to be elaborated deductively.

Weber's approach is incompatible with evolutionist theories of change. As Robert Nisbet has shown conclusively, the latter assume change to be natural, directional, immanent, continuous, necessary, and proceeding from uniform causes.[52] None of these attributes fit Weber's approach. The two models briefly described above start with the view that the persistence of custom is the prevailing condition. Where change occurs, Weber studies it as a charismatic break with tradition or as the rationalizing work of notables. In neither case is change immanent, continuous, necessary, or the result of uniform causes. In addition, Weber emphasizes that the direction of change is reversible. Thus, charismatic breaks with tradition lead to an institutionalization which begins a new tradition. Also, his sociology of law is preoccupied with the process of rationalization, but ends with an analysis of "anti-formalistic tendencies" in modern law.[53]

The rationale of Weber's approach is akin to the classic idea of a mutability of fortunes. To the ancients day and night, the seasons of the year, the passage from childhood to senescence and death were instances of an eternal recurrence which characterizes the universe. In the face of such forces human action is basically presumptuous, a challenge to the gods, and hence a danger to man. Yet men must act, withdrawal is cowardly, and anxiety unmanly. In a universe indifferent to human kind, man's virtue consists in fortitude and his wisdom in equanimity. Men and nations should always remember the opposite extremity of fortune, for those of good fortune must still meet their end and the lowly may one day be victorious.[54]

Where the classics sought equanimity in the face of mortal hazards, Weber formulates concepts to find landmarks in the flux of events. But facts are ascertained at the price of a world of facts neglected. And every pattern the scholar can discern in the course of history must take account of chances missed, opportunities foregone, and aspirations unfulfilled. Weber endeavors to formulate his concepts rigorously enough to be useful tools of analysis, but flexibly enough to allow for corrections of their necessary arbitrariness. His principal aim is scholarly. But his effort is animated by the conviction that every fact or pattern ascertained must be seen against a background which gives it meaning. It must be seen also in the light of the questions asked and the concepts employed.[55]

Multiple, but finite, interpretability lies at the core of an empirical world possessed of continuous gradations and hence lacking natural benchmarks or distinctions. In such a world the scholar is obliged to imprint distinctions of his own devising which have nothing to commend them but a scholarly productivity for which we possess only proximate criteria. In the classical view man's actions disturb the "seamless web" of a universe governed by superhuman forces which have to be propitiated. For Weber the world is a "seamless web" governed by an infinite number of determinants. The scholar who would comprehend that world must impose his abstractions, well knowing that they are indispensable and arbitrary.

PART THREE

STUDIES OF
MODERNIZATION

❧ ☙

CONCEPTS AND GENERALIZATIONS
IN COMPARATIVE
SOCIOLOGICAL STUDIES

◄§ SEVEN §►

Like the concepts of other disciplines, sociological concepts should be universally applicable. The concept "division of labor," for instance, refers to the fact that the labor performed in a collectivity is specialized; the concept is universal because we know of no collectivity without such specialization. Where reference is made to a principle of the division of labor over time—irrespective of the particular individuals performing the labor and of the way labor is subdivided (whether by sex, age, skill or whatever)—we arrive at one meaning of the term "social organization." We know of no society that lacks such a principle; furthermore, we can compare and contrast the social organization of two societies by showing how their division of labor differs.

It is possible to remain at this level of universal concepts. A whole series of mutually related concepts can be elaborated deductively in an effort to construct a framework of concepts applicable to all societies. But such efforts in "pure theory" should be subjected to periodic checks of their analytic utility. For example, the concept "ascription" means an assignment to roles based on the attributes rather than the performances of a person. *Logically* other concepts can be related to "ascription": emphasis on personal attributes is incompatible with emphasis on universal

An earlier version of this essay was published in *American Sociological Review*, XXVIII (August 1963), pp. 532–39.

standards, a neutral or impersonal attitude, and equalitarianism. Empirically, however, the meaning of these terms and their inter-relations is in doubt. To be useful analytically, universal concepts require specifications which help us bridge the gap between concept and empirical evidence. Emphasis on the ascriptive criterion of birth may refer equally well to a person of ancient aristocratic lineage and a person whose family acquired its title by purchase. In one cultural setting emphasis on beauty may outweigh emphasis on high birth; in another it may not. Such differences, rather than the predominance of ascriptive criteria as such, provide the clues for a sociological analysis of diverse social structures.

These considerations point to a persistent problem in sociology. Concepts and theories are difficult to relate to empirical findings and much empirical research is devoid of theoretical significance. Many sociologists deplore this hiatus. But the difficulties persist and tend to reinforce the claims of "pure theory" and "pure methodology," respectively. Comparative sociological studies represent an attempt to develop concepts and generalizations at a level between what is true of all societies and what is true of one society at one point in time and space. In fact, many sociological concepts imply such an "intermediate level" of analysis, though frequently they are used as if they applied universally.

◄§ CONCEPTS OF LIMITED APPLICABILITY

Concepts of socio-historical configurations are a case in point. Stratification is present in all societies, but stratification by "class" is present only in some. Classes depend upon the voluntary coalescence of interests among individuals and thus they differ from stratification by "estate," or court-rank, or clan-affiliation. Again, the exercise of authority requires subordinate agents everywhere, but their organization in a "bureaucracy" is a more specific phenomenon. Bureaucracy under the rule of law applies principally to the countries of Northwestern Europe from the nineteenth century onward. However, several *elements* of bureaucratic organization can be found centuries earlier, as T. F. Tout has documented in his *Chapters in the Administrative History of England*. Also, elements from the "bureaucratic" complex have been adopted in many countries throughout history—with varying success to be sure.

Such historical delimitations of the applicability of a concept are clear only in principle; they are very vague in practice. Though it is possible to date the inception of "bureaucracy" in England from the Northcote-Trevelyan Reforms of 1861, even so marked an institutional innovation is no more than a "high-water mark" of changes in English administration whose century-old continuity can be documented easily. The delimitation in time and space of other sociological concepts presents even greater difficulties, since most such concepts are not reflected in legal or administrative documents.[1] Thus it is both difficult to identify the space and time dimensions of certain sociological concepts and difficult to deny that they possess an historically limited applicability. It may be argued that this is all the more reason for treating such concepts as unanalyzed composites of several analytic dimensions which need to be untangled conceptually, and once untangled each of these dimensions would be universal. Perhaps so, but it has yet to be demonstrated that this gain in universality is not obtained at the expense of analytic utility. So far it appears to me that it is necessary to use "composite concepts" if one wishes to apply concepts rather than elaborate them deductively. Hence I see the utility of logical decomposition more in the clarification of concepts than as a ground for abandoning them.

Usually, we meet these difficulties by constructing a contrast-conception. "Bureaucracy" is hardly a usable concept as long as it stands alone. It gains clarity when we contrast it with the "patrimonial" form of government because in this way we learn of a non-bureaucratic type of government administration that has a century-long development of its own. Again, stratification by "class" is a better analytic tool when contrasted with alternative types of stratification. While such paired concepts are never wholly satisfactory, they do enable us to delimit the space-and-time dimension of a given concept to some extent.[2]

Comparative analysis reveals also that many concepts are generalizations in disguise. Urbanism is a case in point, as are other concepts of complex structures, such as industrial society, bureaucracy, democracy, feudalism, caste society, etc., together with related "developmental" terms, such as urbanization, industrialization, and so on. These concepts define social structures with regard to their several distinguishing characteristics. If we are to refer to social structures, we must define a cluster of attributes that distinguishes one structure from another.[3] It is a fiction to suppose that these attributes generally occur together; after all, the conventional definition, say, of urbanism puts into abstract terms what we have learned about some Western cities as distinguished from nonurban types of settlement. Hence, comparative sociological studies are needed to delimit the applicability of those attributes; here we are back to the space-and-time dimension of sociological concepts.

Even more important, such studies would examine the implicit and, in my judgment, unjustified generalization that the several attributes of "urbanism" tend to occur together.[4] Recent observations in India suggest that our use of the term "urbanization" may be excessively culture-bound. In India kinship ties between urban and rural residents remain strong. Examples: In a recent flood disaster in Poona about one-third of the people made homeless (some 30,000) simply rejoined their families in the villages; in Bombay, textile workers on strike go back to their villages for the duration of the strike; in many cities husbands go to work by themselves, leaving their wives and children in the countryside. A recent survey of the "urban social situation in India" concludes that rural-urban differences with regard to such key factors as caste and joint family have not in fact developed as expected.[5] We know about somewhat similar phenomena from the earlier history of Western cities also and hence it is tempting to predict that with sufficient economic development and urbanization this tie to the country will be broken in India as well.

Thus what began as a definition has subtly turned into a generalization about "urbanism." Yet predictions on this basis are hazardous. For in the West the religious consecration of family ties had

COMPARATIVE SOCIOLOGICAL STUDIES

been broken long before modern urbanization occurred. If by individualism we understand *this* destruction of the fetters of kinship, then individualism was a precondition as much as a consequence of urbanization. And as urbanization in India occurs in the absence of comparable preconditions we must expect that it will take unfamiliar forms. Furthermore, it is difficult to anticipate these forms. In the UNESCO Seminar Report on this subject we read the following:

> Although the great cities of Asia have large size, high density and heterogeneous populations these characteristics (which according to Wirth essentially give rise to the urban way of life), have not produced the basic changes in interpersonal relations, the nature of human beings and the social institutions, as in the Western context. Despite these relatively high densities, life has not necessarily become largely secularized, great differentiation of function has not taken place and the way of life has not changed markedly for many of the indigenous population groups.[6]

Although the report goes on to deny "increased sophistication, rationality of behavior, cosmopolitanism in outlook, or innovation and social change," with regard to these cities, these qualities of "urbanism" surely exist. But they may be more suffused with elements from the traditional culture than in Western cities, and at the same time certain sections of the urban elite may live at a greater social and cultural distance from the common people in Indian than in European or American cities. In addition, as an outsider examines the statistics of unemployment, housing conditions, and population with sympathy for the human condition, he naturally wonders whether the resilience of kinship- and caste-ties under urban conditions represents the one remaining social security for the individual in fierce competition for the scarce opportunities available.

If these impressions are near the mark, then every increase in population, every further crowding of the cities will militate against that individualism most needed to curb population and make Indian cities "urbanized" in our sense of that word. To dismiss all this as a transitory phenomenon that will give way to more familiar features of city life presupposes what we need to examine, namely that the cluster of attributes constituting "urbanism" represents a valid generalization of interrelated social changes. Rather, it is probable that the cities of India have structural antecedents of their own that will eventually blend with the familiar physical attributes of cities under the impact of modern industry—and in this way will create a distinctive type of urbanization.

If we admit this possibility, then we face difficult questions of nomenclature and social theory. We would have to conclude that terms sociologists have adopted or adapted from ordinary speech (e.g., city, village, industry, bureaucracy, etc.) are not readily applicable in their usual connotations. Since such terms have more connotations than we are aware of in ordinary usage, it is indispensable for scholarly purposes to make these connotations explicit. As a result, when we use the term "urbanism" with reference to India we should not also apply connotations of the term that are inappropriate. Some social theorists would cite these difficulties as their reason for discarding ordinary terms altogether and substituting for them a new language. But that approach raises even greater difficulties; it is remote from ordinary experience and it interferes with effective communication since it makes references to that experience unnecessarily obscure. These terminological problems do not exist in isolation. They are often a symptom of unresolved theoretical questions. Comparative sociological studies, I believe, can make their own specific contribution to their resolution.

◄§ CONTRIBUTIONS OF THE COMPARATIVE APPROACH

Among these contributions at least three may be distinguished. First, comparative studies illuminate the meaning of sociological universals. They exhibit the range of "solutions" that men have found for a given problem in different societies. Second, many sociological concepts are composite terms. Comparative studies provide an important check on the generalizations implicit in these terms. Third, insofar as our concepts are of limited applicability, such studies characterize these limits and specify the empirical referents of contrasted social structures.

1. Comparisons between "related" phenomena in different societies are made possible by referring them to some sociological universal. These are not generalizations in the ordinary sense, but refer to the problematics of the social condition. A very detailed, deductive elaboration of "universals"—such as that of Talcott Parsons—deals with these problematics as if they were logical attributes of all societies conceived as "systems." [7] Comparative sociological studies are less deductive and ambitious. Typically, they take a single issue that is to be found in many (conceivably in all) societies and seek to illuminate it by showing how different societies have dealt with the same issue. When Max Weber wrote on the secular causes and consequences of religious doctrines, he identified what we may call the inner-worldly incentives implicit in religions. This issue is examined in the Western religions (culminating in Puritanism), which are contrasted with the inner-worldly incentives implicit in other religions, such as Hinduism or Buddhism. When, in his *Ancient City*, Fustel de Coulanges wrote of the steps by which a consecrated deity of the community gradually prevails over the worship of separate deities of family and tribe, he identified what we may call the social—or in this case the religious —preconditions of civic unity. Coulanges examines this issue over time and in a comparison between Greek and Roman society. Or, to take a modern work, when Hannah Arendt discusses anti-Semitism in Europe and race-relations in South Africa, she identifies what we may call the moral crisis of discrimination. Those who discriminate and those who are discriminated against, lose, or are made to lose, their humanity. One group claims and exploits as virtues what are accidents of birth. The other loses the standards of one community without quite acquiring the standards of another.[8]

In these and similar studies a recurrent issue of the human condition is identified in order to examine how men in different societies have encountered that issue. These studies will have to give full weight to both the *conditioning* of actions and the fact that men have *acted* in face of the agonizing dilemmas that confront them. To maintain this balanced approach, comparative studies should highlight the contrasts existing between different human situations and social structures. And in view of the artificiality of conceptual distinctions they should move back and forth between the empirical evidence and the benchmark-concepts which Max Weber called "ideal types." [9]

2. Many sociological concepts are composite terms formulating a limited body of the evidence. If we use such terms without regard to this limitation, we make unwarranted generalizations—however inadvertent. Here comparative studies help us to be on guard. For example, if city life as we know it goes with secularism, are there other types of city life which go with the maintenance of religious beliefs? [10] More generally, if X goes with Y, can we also find evidence that X can go with non-Y? The second type of evidence would not invalidate the first. But by considering both we protect ourselves against spurious generalizations. The gain is not only negative, however.

In *Contributions to Indian Sociology*[11] the question has been raised, for example, whether the term "village" is applicable to Indian society, because in all too many instances the minimum degree of cohesion commonly associated with this term is absent. Such a question should not remain on the conceptual level, however. People's orientations toward kin and caste always compete to some extent with the demands of the village as a community articulated by political authority. Accordingly, two relatively antagonistic principles of "community" are at work. Research into the prevalence of one or another of these principles might enable us to formulate a typology of villages which would reveal the special features of Indian villages.[12]

An example from Max Weber's sociology of religion shows the analytic usefulness of comparative studies for the construction of such typologies. Weber points out that in ancient times religious prophecy involved oracles concerning future political and military events. Three types of prophecy may be distinguished. In the bureaucratic kingdoms of Egypt and Rome emotional prophecy of the Biblical type did not appear because the religious police suppressed prophets as dangerous demagogues. In Israel such prophecy had a long tradition, on the other hand, because it was supported by families of pious notables and the monarchy was not strong enough to suppress it. Ancient Greece represents a type of prophecy "midway" between that of Egypt and Israel. Only the famous oracle at Delphi was permitted to prophesy, but the ecstatic states of the priestess, Pythia, were considered portents which had to be controlled and interpreted by the priesthood. The three cases are distinguishable in terms of the degree of political or religious control exercised over the prophets. These are primarily political distinctions differing from the religious distinction between the *ethical* prophecy of Judaism and the *exemplary* prophecy of India. Both the political and the religious dimensions provided Weber with an analytic tool that enabled him to study prophecy comparatively, as a clue to the distinctive social structures of ancient societies.[13]

3. Social structures have a space-and-time dimension, as discussed earlier. To formulate concepts appropriate to such structures it is necessary to allow for the variations which are compatible with—or even characteristic of—each type of structure.[14] The enumeration of a cluster of interrelated attributes is not sufficient for this purpose.

Max Weber's analysis of legal domination exemplifies a concept of "structure" in which the variations typical of the rule of law are incorporated. A belief in legality means first and foremost that certain formal procedures must be obeyed if the enactment and execution of a law is to be considered legal. While legal rule-making tends to eliminate the idiosyncrasies of personal rule, it also militates against the exercise of judgment in the individual case. But the interest in developing a consistent body of rules that is the same for everyone may engender an interest in rule-making for its own sake—just as too much regard for equity in the individual case can jeopardize the integrity of the rule-making process. Hence, the rule of law endures as long as piecemeal solutions for these conflicting imperatives are found and neither the concern with equity nor with the formal attributes of rule-making is allowed to predominate. In this way a social structure is understood not as a natural system with defined limits and invariant laws governing an equilibrating process, but rather as a system of historical dimensions which we examine in terms of the piecemeal solutions men have found for the characteristic problems of that structure.[15]

Where analysis emphasizes the chronology and individual sequence of such solutions, it is in the domain of the historian; where it emphasizes the pattern of these solutions, it is in the domain of the sociologist. Comparative sociological studies are especially suited to elucidate such patterns because they tend to increase the "visibility" of one structure by contrasting it with another. In this way, they may help us identify the issues confronting men in their efforts to develop their country in the direction of one pattern or another. Comparative sociological studies are likely to impart a salutary degree of nominalism to the terms we use by exposing concepts and generalizations to a wider range of evidence than is sometimes customary.

◦§ COMPARATIVE STUDIES OF THE "POLITICAL COMMUNITY"

The comparative approach here envisaged starts with the identification of a universal, as in the classic studies cited earlier. The friction between private interest and public authority is the universal I have chosen in my own studies. Where each individual or group takes the law into their hands until checked by the momentarily superior force of an opponent, anarchy reigns and a *political community* does not exist. Some subordination of private interest to public authority is the *sine qua non* of such a community. Governments vary greatly with regard to the subordination they demand and the rights they acknowledge. The term "political community" may be applied wherever the relations between rulers and ruled involve shared understandings concerning this "exchange." These understandings concern the *legitimacy* of public authority, its organization and demands upon the individual; they exist side by side with the fact that individuals find their private interests enhanced through cooperation with others. Accordingly, men are engaged in the pursuit of "ideal and material interests" leading to social relationships based on a coalescence of interests, and they are engaged in actions "governed by the conception that a legitimate order exists." [16] This formulation points to the universal problem of reconciling private concerns and the actions that sustain public authority.

In a comparative study of changing social structures since the French revolution the following inquiries[17] may be distinguished:

1. If the subordination of private interest to public authority is a characteristic feature of political community, then it should be possible to distinguish between types of political communities by types of subordination. It is important, for instance, to formulate the type of subordination characteristic of the "medieval political community," to contrast this with the subordination characteristic of the Western nation-state and, if possible to formulate the "crisis of transition," in which the "medieval" subordination gives way and is superseded by one typical of the nation-state.[18]

2. If two social structures differ in the type of subordination characteristic of them, then they will differ also in the type of protest they provoke among the subordinated. Accordingly, the millenarian movements, social banditry, and populist legitimism characteristic of medieval political life may be contrasted with the quest for national citizenship characteristic of protest-movements in some countries of Western Europe during the nineteenth century.[19]

3. Though social structures may be distinguished one from the other, no structure is static. A further task is to analyze the transformation a given structure undergoes without losing its distinguishing characteristics. In the present case this may be attempted by comparing the manner in which kindred Western European societies have extended national citizenship to those segments of the population which previously had been excluded from the rights of citizenship. In the early type of nation-state these rights

were available only to social notables, whereas subsequently these rights became an attribute of all adults as citizens of the nation-state.[20]

These illustrations of comparative sociological studies aim at propositions that are true of more than one but less than all societies. This essay will have served its purpose if it directs attention to a type of inquiry which—at the macro-sociological level— seeks to hold a balance between grand theory and the descriptive accounts of area-studies.

The three kinds of studies here suggested are capable of extension in many directions. For example, the distinction between the medieval political community, the modern nation-state and the crisis of transition is applicable principally to the countries of Western Europe, and one should explore the limits of this applicability. But one may also apply an analogous approach to other areas of the world which differ from the Western European pattern, to be sure, but which nonetheless possess common structural characteristics of their own.[21] With regard to these characteristics is should be possible to formulate models of the pre-modern social structure, of the transition which followed, and of the modern social structure which has developed to date.[22]

Note: The essays reprinted in Part Three are examples of such studies from my work. "Industrialization, Ideologies, and Social Structure" and "A Study of Managerial Ideologies" present in brief compass perspectives and conclusions from *Work and Authority in Industry*. "Social Stratification and the Political Community" does the same with reference to *Nation-Building and Citizenship*. "Tradition and Modernity Reconsidered" goes beyond these earlier studies in an attempt to provide a framework for the study of modernization. Finally, "Social and Political Change in the Twentieth Century" is an attempt to understand the current scene by a broad use of the framework employed in the two volumes mentioned above.

INDUSTRIALIZATION, IDEOLOGIES, AND SOCIAL STRUCTURE

Since World War II American social scientists have become preoccupied with the industrialization of underdeveloped areas. Considering the recent history of our disciplines, this is a relatively novel undertaking. It involves the study of social change in complex social structures on a comparative basis. One approach to such a study consists in the selection of a social problem encountered in several societies but resolved differently in each, such as the authority relationship between employers and workers and the ideologies of management which justify that authority.[1]

The present paper considers the changes of ideology that have occurred in Anglo-American and in Russian civilization over a two-hundred year period. The historical significance of ideologies of management, and their empirical significance as an index of social structure are examined. I then turn to the problem of bureaucratization and to the difference between totalitarian and non-totalitarian forms of subordination in industry.

◄ई CHANGES IN IDEOLOGY

At the inception of industrialization in England an ideology of traditionalism prevailed; John Stuart Mill called it the "theory of dependence." According to this view the laboring poor are chil-

An earlier version of this essay was published in *American Sociological Review*, XXIV (1959), pp. 613–23.

dren, who must be governed, who should not be allowed to think for themselves, who must perform their assigned tasks obediently and with alacrity, who must show deference to their superiors, and who—if they only conduct themselves virtuously—will be protected by their betters against the vicissitudes of life. This interpretation of authority is self-confirming and self-serving.[2] But it sets up the presumption that the dependence of the poor and the responsibility of the rich are the valid moral rules of the social order. In the course of industrial development these ideas were gradually modified. As the responsibility of the rich was increasingly rejected by the advocates of laissez-faire, the dependence of the poor was turned from an inevitable into a self-imposed fate. As it was "demonstrated" that the rich cannot care for the poor without decreasing the national wealth, it was also asserted that by abstinence and exertion the poor can better their lot. The same virtues, which in the 18th century were extolled so that the lowly will not aspire above their station, were praised by the middle of the 19th century because they enable a man to raise himself by his own efforts.

In England, and even more in America, this praise of effort led toward the end of the 19th century to an apotheosis of the struggle for existence. The militant language of an ethics of the jungle was applied to the relations between employers and workers. Riches and poverty merely reflect differences of ability and effort. The employer's success is evidence of his fitness for survival, and as such justifies his absolute authority over the enterprise. This assertion of authority has a clear-cut meaning only as long as most managerial functions are in the hands of one man. The idea becomes ambiguous as the use of expertise in enterprises increases and the managerial function becomes subdivided and specialized. Just when employers claimed absolute authority over their enterprises, the "scientific management" movement sought to give them expert advice on what to do with that authority. Under these circumstances the doctrines of Social Darwinism gradually lost their appeal, in part because changes in industrial organization gave rise to a changing imagery of men in industry. From the Gilded Age to

the 1920s, workers and managers were self-evident failures or successes in a struggle for survival, in which they were the recalcitrant
objects or the exasperated originators of managerial commands.
Today they have become individuals-in-groups whose skills must
be improved and allocated systematically and whose productivity
must be maximized by appropriate attention to their psychological
makeup. Thus, over the past two hundred years, managerial ideologies in Anglo-American civilization have changed from the "theory
of dependence" to laissez-faire, to Social Darwinism, and finally to
the "human relations" approach.

In the Russian development we also find the assertion of
paternal authority and of child-like dependence, and in much the
same terms as in England. But in Russia this ideology of traditionalism was a very different thing from what it was in England because of the Tsar's assertion of supreme authority over all the
people. This authority remained intact regardless of how many
privileges the Tsar granted to the landlords and regardless of how
rarely he interfered in fact with the use and abuse of these privileges. Ideologically the Tsar maintained his preeminence through
repeated assertions concerning his paternal care and responsibility
for all of "his" people. Through repeated petitions and sporadic
revolts the people used this Tsarist claim in order to obtain redress
for their grievances against landlords and employers. Also, because
of the early centralization of authority under the Muscovite rulers,
the whole distribution of wealth and rank among the aristocracy
turned upon the competition for favors at the Court and hence
reenforced the Tsar's supremacy.[3]

During the second half of the 19th century this pattern of
Tsarist autocracy had far-reaching consequences. The dislocations
incident to the emancipation of the serfs (1861) and the development of industry brought in their train assertions of absolute
authority by the employers, efforts of the workers to organize
themselves, and sporadic attempts of the government to regulate
the relations between them. Although ostensibly acting on an
equitable basis, the government in fact supported the employers
against the workers. Much of this is again broadly familiar from

the English experience; but Russia's historical legacies prevented the shift in ideology which has been described for England. As long as Tsarist autocracy remained intact neither the rejection of responsibility by the Tsar and the ruling strata nor the demand for the self-dependence of the workers developed. Instead, the Tsar and his officials continued to espouse the ideology of traditionalism. Quite consistently, Tsarist officials sought to superintend both employers and workers in order to mitigate or suppress the struggles between them. That is, the officials aided *and* curbed the employers' exercise of authority as well as the workers' efforts to formulate grievances and organize protest movements.

Tsarist autocracy was overthrown in the Russian revolutions of 1905 and 1917. Although vast differences were brought about by the revolution, the managerial ideology of Tsarism lived on in a modified form. In theory, Tsarist officials had regarded employers and workers as equally subject to the will of the Tsar; loyal submission to that will was the mark of good citizenship. In theory, Lenin believed that all workers were equal participants in the management of industry and government; their loyal submission to the Communist party represented their best interest and expressed their sovereign will. The logic of Lenin's as of the Tsarist position is that under a sovereign authority the same person or organization can and should perform both subordinate and superordinate functions. For example, Soviet labor unions approach the ideal of workers' control of industry when they are called upon to participate in the management of industry. But they also function in a managerial capacity when they inculcate labor discipline among their members under the authoritative direction of the Communist Party.

Ideologically this position is defended on the ground that the party represents the historical interests of the proletariat against the short-run interests of individuals and factions. In this orientation one can still see survivals of Tsarist autocracy since all wisdom and responsibility reside in a small group or indeed in one man who, like the Tsar, knows better than private persons what is the good of all, and cares for the well-being of the people. But there is also an important difference. The leaders of the Russian revolution were faced with the task of developing self-discipline and initiative among workers if a suitable industrial work-force was to become available.[4] They proceeded to inculcate these qualities by the direct or indirect subordination of everyone to the discipline of the Communist party. This policy continued the Tsarist tradition by making all matters the object of organizational manipulation rather than of personal striving; but it also represented a break with the past in that it was no longer restricted to personal submission.

⋙ HISTORICAL SIGNIFICANCE OF IDEOLOGICAL CHANGE

What are the historical implications of this analysis of managerial ideologies? All industrialization involves the organization of enterprises in which a few command and many obey. The ideas developed by the few and the many may be considered a symptom of changing class relations and hence as a clue to an understanding of industrial societies.[5]

Historically, ideologies of management became significant in the transition from a pre-industrial to an industrial society. The authority exercised by employers was recognized as distinct from the authority of government. This was a novel experience even in Western Europe where there was precedent for such autonomy in other institutions. The industrial entrepreneurs were "new men" rather than a ruling class buttressed by tradition. This was also the period during which the discipline of sociology originated. Under the impact of the French revolution society came to be conceived in terms of forces that are independent from, as well as antagonistic to, the formal institutions of the body politic. Some early elaborations of this key idea enable us to see the historical significance of ideologies of management.

The authority of employers rests on the contractual acquisition of property, which the 18th century philosophers made the conceptual basis of the social order. In Rousseau's view that order ought to be based on a general will which presupposes that the individual acts for the whole community. In such a society, as George Herbert Mead has pointed out, ". . . the citizen can give laws only to the extent that his volitions are an expression of the rights which he recognizes in others, . . . [and] which the others recognize in him. . . ." [6] This approach provides a model for a society based on consent so that the power of rule-making is exercised by all and for all. This foundation of society upon a "general will" was directly related to the institution of property. As Mead has stated,

> If one wills to possess that which is his own so that he has absolute control over it as property, he does so on the assumption that everyone else will possess his own property and exercise absolute control over it. That is, the individual wills his control over his property only in so far as he wills the same sort of control for everyone else over property.[7]

Thus, the idea of a reciprocal recognition of rights specifically presupposed the equality of citizens as property-owners.

This implication gave pause to some 18th and 19th century philosophers. They noted that the reciprocity of rights among property owners based on freedom of contract does not apply to the relations between employers and workers. As early as 1807 the German philosopher Hegel formulated the problematic nature of this relationship in a manner which anticipates the modern psychology of the self, just as Rousseau's "general will" anticipates the sociological analysis of interaction. Hegel maintains that men come to a recognition of themselves through a process whereby each accepts the self-recognition of the other and is in turn accepted by him. That is, each man's sense of identity depends upon his acceptance of the identity of others and upon their acceptance of himself. In Hegel's view this reciprocity is lacking in the relation between master and servant. The master does not act towards himself as he acts towards the servant; and the servant does not do towards others what his servitude makes him do against himself. In this way the mutuality of recognition is destroyed and the relations between master and servant become one-sided and unequal.[8]

In Western Europe this inequality of the employment-relationship coincided with the ideological and institutional decline of traditional subordination. Yet while the old justifications of subordination crumbled and new aspirations were awakened among the masses of the people, their experience of inequality continued. According to Tocqueville this problem had a differential impact upon masters and servants. In the secret persuasion of his mind the master continues to think of himself as superior; but he no longer recognizes any paternal responsibilities toward the servant. Still, he wants his servants to be content with their servile condition. In effect, the master wishes to enjoy the age-old privileges without acknowledging their concomitant obligations. And the servant rebels against his subordination, which is no longer a divine obligation and is not yet perceived as a contractual obligation.

> Then it is that [in] the dwelling of every citizen . . . a secret and internal warfare is going on between powers ever rivals and suspicious of each other: the master is ill-natured and weak, the servant ill-natured and intractable; the one constantly attempts to evade by unfair restrictions his obligation to protect and to remunerate, the other his obligation to obey. The reins of domestic government dangle between them, to be snatched at by one or the other. The lines that divide authority from oppression, liberty from license, and right from might are to their eyes so jumbled together and confused that no one knows exactly what he is or what he may be or what he ought to be. Such a condition is not democracy, but revolution.[9]

In the 19th century men like Hegel, Tocqueville, and Lorenz von Stein pointed out that the spread of equalitarian ideas was causing a transition in the relations between masters and servants. This transition may be called a crisis of aspirations. In Tocqueville's words the servants "consent to serve and they blush to obey. . . . [They] rebel in their hearts against a subordination to which they have subjected themselves. . . . They are inclined to consider him who orders them as an unjust usurper of their own rights." [10] As a consequence most European countries witnessed the rise of a "fourth estate" which struggled against existing legal liabilities and for basic civil rights, above all the right to suffrage. In a parliamentary debate on Chartism, Disraeli remarked that this struggle was invested with a degree of sentiment usually absent from merely economic or political contests. To the extent that such complex movements can be characterized by a common denominator this sentiment referred, I think, to the workers' quest for a public recognition of their equal status as citizens.[11] Where this and other rights became accepted, such recognition compensated for the continued social and economic subordination of the workers and thus assuaged the crisis of aspirations. Moreover, the political utilization of these civil rights could lead to a recognition of basic social rights. Today these are embodied in the institutions of social welfare characteristic of many Western democracies.[12] The initial crisis of aspirations continued, on the other hand, where civil rights were rejected or where their acceptance was postponed for too long, leading either to an eventual revolutionary upheaval as in Tsarist Russia, or to a more or less damaging exacerbation of class-relations as in Italy and France.

The question of 19th century Europe concerned the terms on which a society undergoing industrialization will incorporate its newly recruited industrial work force within the economic and political community of the nation. Ideologies of management are significant because they contribute to each country's answer to this question. In England the workers were invited to become their own masters, if they did not wish to obey; in Russia they were told that their subordination was less onerous than it seemed, because their own superiors were also servants of the almighty Tsar.[13]

◆§ EMPIRICAL SIGNIFICANCE OF IDEOLOGIES [14]

What are the implications of this approach? Ideologies of management may be considered indexes of the flexibility or rigidity with which the dominant groups in the two countries were prepared to meet the challenge from below. This "preparedness" or collective tendency to act is analogous to the concept of character-structure in the individual: it may be defined as an "inner capacity" for recreating similar lines of action under more or less identical conditions.[15] The ideologies of management, which reflect this "inner capacity," naturally provoke new challenges and these in turn lead to new managerial responses, so that at the societal level there is a replication of the action-reaction process so typical of interaction among individuals.

An analysis of this process must deal with those explicitly formulated ideas that are as close as possible to the collective experience of employers and workers. This social philosophizing of and for the ordinary man as a participant occurs at a level somewhere between his attitudes as an individual and the sophisticated formulations of the social theorist. Such philosophizing is exemplified by what Andrew Ure wrote in his *Philosophy of Manufactures* or by what the publicity-men for General Motors say in their pamphlet *Man to Man on the Job*. The serious analysis of such documents is at variance with the prevailing tendency to dismiss them as obviously biased and hence unworthy of consideration on their own terms. In this respect Marx was a forerunner of the intellectuals born in the 1850s and 1860s. Freud, Durkheim, Pareto, and others searched for some underlying principle or force that could explain the manifest beliefs and actions making up the external record of individual and collective behavior.[16] Accordingly, ideologies of management might be dismissed because they *merely* express a class-interest, or because they do not reveal the *real* attitudes of the employers, or because they disguise *actual* exploitative practices, or because all this talk tells us nothing about man's behavior or about his personality structure. These various objections have in common an intellectual preoccupation with covert forces that can explain the manifest content of the social world.

Modern social science owes to this intellectual tradition many important insights, but also many of its aberrations. Where the phenomena of the social world are treated merely as the reflection of "hidden forces," speculation easily becomes uncontrolled while observable evidence is dismissed as "irrelevant" or "uninteresting" on theoretical grounds. The difficulty is familiar in Marx's theory of history which treated the "false consciousness" of the workers as an epiphenomenon that was bound to be superseded in the course of history. Similarly, the Freudian approach devalues a behavioristic study because it deals with the appearance rather than the underlying motivations of social action. Again, the use of organic analogies in the study of society treats all actions as dependent adjustments to other actions (or environmental conditions). Consequently this approach devalues all deliberate and innovative activity, which is yet another dependent adjustment. In inexpert hands these approaches lead to a cavalier construction of the evidence which can always be more easily imputed to the "underlying determinants" than analyzed in detail on its own ground.

Yet human experience occurs at this phenomenological level—and the study of ideologies of management illustrates that it can also provide an approach to our understanding of the social structure.[17] The managerial interpretations of the authority relationship in economic enterprises together with the workers' contrast-conception concerning their collective position in an emerging industrial society constitute a composite image of class relations which has changed over time and which differs from country to country. Each ideological position may be examined in terms of its logical corollaries as these relate to the authority of the employer and in a wider sense to the class position of employers and workers in the society. Where these corollaries create major problems for the complacent self-interest of the group, one may expect the development of tensions, and perhaps of change, ideologically and institutionally.[18]

Such ideologies are in part expediential rationalizations for the problems confronting the entrepreneur, and in part the result of cumulative response-patterns among social groups. In this way ideologies are formulated through the constant interplay between current contingencies and historical legacies. Although "men make their own history under circumstances directly given and transmitted from the past," Marxian dogmatism consistently sacrificed the first to the second part of this generalization.[19] Accordingly, ideologies of management can be explained only in part as rationalizations of self-interest; they also result from the legacy of institutions and ideas which is "adopted" by each generation much as a child "adopts" the grammar of his native language. Historical legacies are thus a part of the social structure: they should not be excluded from a discipline that focusses attention upon the persistence of group-structures. In the following section an attempt is made to show the link between historical legacies and the structure of industrial societies by relating ideologies of management to the bureaucratization of industry.

ᴇᴚ IDEOLOGIES, INDUSTRIAL BUREAUCRACY, AND TOTALITARIANISM

Since the 18th century Anglo-American and Russian civilizations have witnessed a growing managerial concern with the attitudes as well as the productivity of workers. It is possible to relate this change of ideology to a large number of the developments which comprise the transition from an early to a mature industrial society. The changing structure of industrial organizations was only one of these developments. Yet the bureaucratization of economic enterprises is of special importance for any attempt to "interpret the difference of fact and ideology between a totalitarian and nontotalitarian form of subordination in economic enterprises." [20] Bureaucratization is also especially suitable for a comparative study of authority relations in industry, since it involves comparable processes in two such different civilizations as England and Russia. This choice of focus deliberately eschews a comprehensive theory of society in favor of selecting a problem which, if suitable for comparative analysis, will also lead to an analysis of social structure. For, if comparable groups in different societies confront and over time resolve a common problem, then a comparative analysis of their divergent resolutions will reveal the divergence of social structures in a process of change.[21]

Problems of a systematic management of labor come to the fore where the increasing complexity of economic enterprises makes their operation more or less dependent upon an *ethic of work performance*. That is to say, management subjects the conditions of employment to an impersonal systematization, while the employees seek to modify the implementation of the rules as their personal interests and their commitment (or lack of commitment) to the goals of the organization dictate. As everyone knows, there is no more effective means of organizational sabotage than a letter-perfect compliance with all the rules and a consistent refusal of the employees to use their own judgment. "Beyond what commands can effect and supervision can control, beyond what incentives can induce and penalties prevent, there exists an exercise of discretion important even in relatively menial jobs, which managers of economic enterprises seek to enlist for the achievement of managerial ends." [22] In the literature on organizations this exercise of discretion by subordinates is known by a number of terms: Veblen called it the "withdrawal of efficiency;" Max Weber referred to it as the bureaucratic tendency towards secrecy; Herbert Simon might call it the "zone of non-acceptance." I have suggested the phrase "strategies of independence" so as to get away from the negative connotations of the other terms, since the exercise of discretion may serve to achieve, as well as to subvert, the goals of an organization.

Now, the great difference between totalitarian and nontotalitarian forms of subordination consists in the managerial handling of this generic attribute of all authority relations. In some Western countries management presupposed a common universe of discourse between superiors and subordinates. Managerial appeals to the cooperation of subordinates have ranged from evangelism and the tough-minded laissez-faire approach of 18th century England to the latest refinement of the "human relations" approach. Whether good faith existed is less important than that such appeals were made, though it is probable that in England and the United States large masses of workers in one way or another accepted managerial authority as legitimate even if they were indifferent to, or rejected, the managerial appeals themselves.[23] In Russia, on the other hand, historical legacies did *not* encourage a comparable universe of discourse. From the time of Peter the Great to the period of rapid industrial growth in the last decades preceding World War I appeals were addressed to the workers' duty of obedience towards all those in positions of authority.

These appeals assumed the workers' bad faith and lacking sense of duty. Accordingly, officials and managers attempted to eliminate the subordinates' strategies of independence.

This managerial approach is related to the totalitarian type of bureaucratization. In such a regime the will of the highest party authorities is absolute. The party may disregard all formal procedures as well as its own previous rulings. Where norms may be changed at a moment's notice, the rule of law is destroyed. Totalitarianism also does away with a single line of authority. Totalitarian regimes use the hierarchy of the party in order to expedite and control at each step the execution of orders through regular administrative channels. The object is to prevent officials from escaping inspection while compelling their intensified effort to implement orders. A totalitarian government is based, therefore, on two interlocking hierarchies of authority. The work of every factory, of every governmental office, of every unit of the army or the secret police, of every cultural or social organization is programmed, coordinated, and supervised by some agency of government. But it is also propagandized, expedited, criticized, spied upon, and incorporated in special campaigns by an agency of the totalitarian party, which is separately responsible to higher party authorities.

The rationale of this double hierarchy can be stated within the framework of Max Weber's analysis of bureaucracy. An ideally functioning bureaucracy in his sense is the most efficient method of performing large-scale organizational tasks. But this is true only *if* the tasks involve more or less stable norms which maintain the rule of law and an equitable administration of affairs. These conditions are absent where tasks are assigned by an omnipotent *and* revolutionary authority. Under the simulated combat conditions of a totalitarian regime the norms that govern conduct need not stay put for any length of time, although a drive for maximum achievement is directed at each goal in turn. In response, subordinates use their devices of concealment for the sake of systematic, if tacit, strategies of independence. They will do so for reasons of convenience, but also because the directives of the regime are "irrational" from the viewpoint of expert knowledge and systematic procedure.[24] The party, on the other hand, seeks to prevent such strategies of concealment. This is the rationale of a double hierarchy of government, which places a party functionary at the side of every work unit in order to prevent concealment and apply pressure. The two hierarchies would be required, even if all key positions in government and industry were filled by party functionaries. For a functionary turned worker or official would still be responsible for "overfulfilling" the plan, while the new party functionary would still be charged with keeping that official under pressure and surveillance.[25]

In this way totalitarianism replaces the old system of stratification by one based on criteria of activism and party orthodoxy. The ethic of work performance on which this regime relies is one of material incentives and of a political supervision that seeks to prevent evasion from below as well as from above. For example, the collective "bargaining" agreements of Soviet industry are in fact declarations of loyalty in which individuals and groups pledge themselves publicly to an overfulfillment of the plan. The subsequent organization of public confessions, the manipulation of status differences between activists and others, the principle of collective leadership, and further devices seek to maximize performance and prevent the "withdrawal of efficiency." The individual subordinate is surrounded almost literally. Aside from ordinary incentives he is controlled by his superior and by the party agitator who stands at the side of his superior; but he is also controlled "from below" in the sense that the social pressures of his peer group are manipulated by party agitators and their agents. This institutionalization of suspicion and the consequent elimination of privacy are justified on the ground that the party "represents" the masses, spearheads the drive for Russian industrialization, and leads the cause of world communism.

A comparative analysis of social structures pays attention to the historical continuity of societies as well as to the concatenation of group structures and deliberate, self-interested action in the process of social change. Studies of managerial ideologies provide an example of such analysis. During the last two centuries Anglo-American and Russian civilization were characterized by an increased managerial concern with the attitudes of workers. In Western civilization authority relations between employers and workers remained a more or less autonomous realm of group activity even where the "human relations" approach replaced the earlier individualism. In Russia the employment relationship has been subjected throughout to a superordinate authority which regulated employers and workers. Superiors could be transformed into subordinates or (more rarely) subordinates into superiors, when governmental policies seemed to warrant such action.

This comparison has a specific historical rationale. Ideologies of management became significant when the equalitarianism of property owners, brought to the fore by the French revolution and by the legal codifications which followed, was contrasted with the inequality of the employment relationship. A heightened awareness of this inequality coincided with the decline of traditional subordination of the lower classes and hence with aspirations for social and political as well as legal equality. In England these demands for equal rights of citizenship on the part of the lower classes eventuated in a painful reconstitution of class relations; in Russia the same demands were rejected and finally led to the revolutions of 1905 and 1917.

Ideologies may be considered indexes of a readiness to act, which together with the ideological responses of other groups can provide us with a clue to the class relations of a society. Ideologies are an integral part of culture, which should be analyzed on its own terms as an index of the social structure, much as the neurotic symptoms of an individual are analyzed as an index of his personality. Such ideologies are rationalizations of group interests, they are circumscribed by historical legacies, and their logical and empirical implications provide clues to a country's developing social structure.

Studies of managerial ideologies are also suitable for a comparison of totalitarian and non-totalitarian regimes. All industrial enterprises undergo a process of bureaucratization and all bureaucracy involves the use of discretion in the execution of commands. The Anglo-American and the Russian tradition have differed in terms of whether or not managerial appeals have presupposed the good faith of subordinates. Where that supposition has not been made, the drive for industrialization has employed a double hierarchy of government. The purpose is to apply maximum pressure on subordinates and to forestall their evasion of commands by supplementing executive with political controls at every point in the chain of command.

English, American, and Russian industrialization have been marked by bureaucratization, and bureaucratization certainly threatens the development of initiative. The Soviet case also illustrates that this threat may provoke countermeasures. One might speak of an institutionalization of initiative in the totalitarian party and speculate that the dynamic drive of the Soviet regime can be jeopardized if the regime were to relax the simulated combat conditions which justify that drive.

A STUDY OF MANAGERIAL
IDEOLOGIES

☙ NINE ❧

In the course of industrialization employers and their spokesmen develop ideas in order to justify the exercise of authority over the workers and enhance the latter's obedience and efficiency. All ideas which relate to these two issues are called entrepreneurial ideologies in the early phase of industrialization, and managerial ideologies when economic enterprises are fully developed. These ideologies have been examined in four countries: in England during the Industrial Revolution (approximately from the 1780's to the 1850's), in Tsarist Russia from the reign of Peter the Great (1685 1725), to the Revolution of 1905, in the United States from about 1900 to the present, and in East Germany in 1953–54. Thus, the theme of the study may be suggested by a short phrase: managerial ideologies—East and West, then and now.

I want to consider the intellectual context of a broadly comparative study of managerial ideologies and economic development and draw some conclusions with reference to England and Russia during the early and mature phases of their industrialization.

☙ THE INTELLECTUAL CONTEXT

From the controversy between Schmoller and Menger in the

This chapter is based on Reinhard Bendix, *Work and Authority in Industry* (New York: John Wiley and Sons, 1956), Chaps. II–IV. An earlier version of this essay was published in *Economic Development and Cultural Change*, V (1957), pp. 118–28.

1880's to the 1954 Bulletin No. 64 of the SSRC entitled *The Social Sciences and Historical Study*, a voluminous literature has dealt with the feasibility of relating social theories to historical materials. All seem agreed—though clearly for divergent reasons—that the relations of the social sciences to history are not what they should be.

The matter is not merely of methodological interest. Events since World War II pose the problem whether and in what respects the process of industrialization in the developed countries provides lessons for the future industrialization of the economically under-developed areas.[1] This problem can be addressed if analytical tools are developed for an interpretation of the process of industrialization and if further headway is made with regard to the comparison of like processes in different historical contexts.

An outstanding example of such analysis is Max Weber's work on the economic ethic of world religions. Weber's interest was twofold: to explain the unique development of capitalism in Western civilization in one of its aspects and to show how the close fit between social structure and religious orientation had effectively impeded similar developments in other civilizations. The analysis of cultural peculiarities of capitalist civilization in the West was, thus, broadened so that comparisons with other civilizations would elucidate the relation between prevailing religious doctrines and the ethics of economic conduct.

Weber's interest in this approach arose from the observation that farm-laborers in East Germany preferred the freedom of the day-laborer to the subservience of the worker on annual contract, even where this choice diminished their total earnings. This preference seemed to point to the importance of culturally conditioned values in economic life. Weber also noted that among prominent industrial leaders in the Rhineland, Protestants predominated over Catholics. What was the nature of this contrast at the time of its origin, when religious beliefs were intense and affected the everyday life of the people? From these inquiries the thesis emerged that the answers of preachers to questions of conscience posed by members of their congregations reflected the more or less acute anxiety to which certain doctrines of Calvinism gave rise. And this anxiety was relieved under the combined pressure of doctrine and circumstance by frugal living, intense work-effort, and a thorough discipline in all aspects of daily life, the innerworldly asceticism of the early entrepreneurs.

I am not here concerned with this thesis as a substantive issue, for today the same problem is likely to suggest lines of inquiry which differ markedly from those Weber initiated. In the interval between his essay of 1904 and the second half of this century we have witnessed the successful industrialization of Japan and of Russia. In these countries the development of technical and economic rationality has been the product of political organization and collective sanctions. It has not been the consequence of efforts to relieve anxieties engendered by a demanding conscience and an inscrutable God. Moreover, even for the West, Weber's thesis applied principally to the pioneers of capitalism. Religious ideas certainly played a part in creating the self-discipline, the rational style of life, among the early entrepreneurs. But even in England it was, broadly speaking, the secularization of these ideas which helped to create the work discipline of the masses. The term "secularization" may not entirely fit the parallel process in Russia, though it may be suggested that the religious absolutism of Tsarist autocracy was transformed into the secular absolutism of a Communist dictatorship. Obviously, it was the latter which affected the discipline of the masses. And in Japan that discipline may be attributed perhaps to the political manipulation of a religiously sanctioned theory of obligation, which penetrated downwards from the ruling groups, and which imposed on all people a deferential self-discipline with regard to superior ranks in the society.

These processes have involved forms of discipline other than those considered by Weber. He was concerned with the distinctive human type that had come into prominence under Western capitalism. That type could be traced to the day-to-day sanctions by which the Protestant sects inculcated among their members a self-disciplined rationality peculiarly fit for the promotion of capitalist enterprises. The religious systems of other civilizations had given rise to different types of deliberateness, for example the Confucian emphasis upon detachment and orderly expectations in relations among relatives. Each of the great religions encouraged a distinctive ordering of man's daily life. Weber's analysis examined which ends of personal and social life were served by the several religious doctrines. This very special emphasis has not always been understood. It was due to Weber's interest in showing the relatively independent influence of ideas upon conduct. It did not attempt to explain the origin and expansion of the industrial system.

The contemporary interest in economic development is very different from Weber's study of the "human type" peculiar to Western capitalism. The contrast will be apparent when we ask how work-discipline may develop by methods other than the religious inculcation of ethical demands. This question is a useful guide to research in this field, even though at present we are hardly in a position to answer it on a comparative basis.[2] In the study under review I have been concerned with the managerial ideologies which have defined the discipline and coercion of the masses in the process of industrialization. These predominantly secular ideologies should not be regarded as a merely verbal accompaniment of coercion. Rather they have tended to persuade, not only those whose interests they served, but also the masses of the people for whom they are the dominant ideas of their time.

The creation of a non-agricultural work-force is a process which may be studied comparatively if the evidence is examined in terms of certain elementary abstractions. The authority-relationship between employers and workers is the proper focus for an analysis of the mass-discipline and -persuasion which are necessary conditions of industrialization. By "industrialization" I refer to the process by which large numbers of workers since the 18th century have been concentrated in single enterprises and have become subject to the directing and coordinating activities of entrepreneurs and managers. By "large number" I refer to any number of workers in excess of that which still permits face-to-face relationships between employers and workers. Within this general context my object has been to analyze one recurrent aspect of industrial societies. All economic enterprises have in common a relation between the employers who exercise authority and the workers who obey. And all ideologies of management have in common the effort to interpret the exercise of authority in a favorable light. At this most general level it is largely a matter of finding arguments in support of two related contentions. One of these refers to the position of those in authority who are alternately shown not to rule at all, or to do so only in the interests of large numbers. The other refers to the position of the many who obey orders, and who are alternately shown to obey only when they consent to do so, or because such obedience provides them with the greatest opportunities of advancement. Apparently, such ideologies interpret the facts of authority and obedience so as to neutralize or eliminate the conflict between the few and the many in the interest of a more effective exercise of authority. To do this, the exercise of authority is either denied altogether on the ground that the few merely order what the many want; or it is justified with the assertion that the few have qualities of excellence which enable them to realize the interests of the many. This is the common theme which makes ideologies of management comparable despite the different patterns of industrialization and despite the variety of specific interpretations.

I should like to comment on these "truisms" in two respects before turning to a discussion of some of my findings. A few command and many obey wherever economic enterprises are set up. As suggested earlier, the few will not be satisfied to command without a higher justification, while the many will be sufficiently uncooperative to provoke such justifications. There are two sides to these "truisms" and accordingly I have tried to distinguish between an early and a mature phase of industrialization. In the early phase the creation of an industrial work-force implies a more or less drastic separation of the worker from the traditional setting of his previous economic activities. His subjection to the authority of an employer involve work-conditions and disciplines which contrast sharply with the experience of the peasant or craftsman. For the employers the early phase typically involves a situation in which

the profits of industrialization accrue to them, but their risks and
their self-imposed demands are also great. Under these conditions
the burdens of rapid change fall upon the workers, while the employers seek to justify their exercise of authority over the workers.
But at this time the "few" are more concerned with winning
recognition for their activities from the public at large than with
labor-management and its problems. Thus, the separation of the
workers from the traditional setting of their economic activities
and the justification of industrialization to the public at large
typically belong to the initial phase.

In the mature phase of industrialization the many have more
or less accommodated themselves to factory discipline, but they
tend to withdraw effort and efficiency because they are dissatisfied
with their share of material and psychic income in the society.
Planned and impersonal methods of managing the work-force also
belong to this more developed phase of industrial society. The
"few" have won recognition from the society at large, and the
management of large-scale organizations including the efforts to
ensure the efficiency of the work-force have become of major concern. Labor-management under these conditions is no longer divorced from "public relations" and any new challenge to the
position of employers and managers will tend to be met by
appeals which justify the managerial as well as the other practices
of business leaders.

A second point should be noted also. The "truism" that the
few will persist in justifying their authority, while the many
will tend to "withdraw their efficiency" presupposes that frictions
between managers and workers are endemic in large-scale economic
enterprises. Such frictions may assume many different forms, and
the managerial practices and ideologies designed to cope with them
will vary likewise. My study examines these frictions and their
managerial resolution during the early and mature phases of industrialization, in the context of Anglo-American and of Russian
civilization. But it is clear that differences between cultures and
the particularity of historical events permit systematic comparisons

and contrasts only in so far as the assumption is correct that
frictions between managers and workers in large-scale economic
enterprises are universal.[3]

✌§ CIVIC INTEGRATION AND THE WORK-ETHIC

I shall describe two sets of conclusions, the first relating to the
early, the second to the more mature phase of industrialization.

Industrialization in its early phase poses a very general problem.
It is accompanied by the creation of a non-agricultural work force
which is usually forced to bear the consequences of great social
and economic dislocations. These dislocations terminate the traditional subordination of the "lower classes" in the pre-industrial
society. Though this development varies considerably with the
relative speed and the social setting of industrialization, its result
is that the "lower classes" are deprived of their recognized, if
subordinate, place in society. A major problem facing all societies
undergoing industrialization is the civic reintegration of the newly
created, industrial work-force. For industrialization brings with it
the education of the masses which has very frequently resulted in
claims to the social and political recognition of workers as citizens.
Hence, the early phase of industrialization tends to be a period
of transition from a society in which the inequality of classes is
relatively stable, to a society in which the status of different classes
and the relations among them have become highly uncertain. As
we saw, Alexis de Tocqueville described this condition of society
with great insight over a century ago.[4]

In an emerging industrial society this problem confronts the ruling groups with typical alternatives. One frequently recurrent response is an outright opposition to industrialization and the attempt to retain or restore traditional relations between the classes,
if not in practice then at least in theory. Equally recurrent is the
approach of those who seek to advance industrialization, who utilize the traditional subordination of workers for their own ends,
but who reject the traditional obligations of the ruling class. The

comparison between England and Russia during the early phase of industrialization shows that these entrepreneurial ideologies vary with the social structure and the historical legacies in question.

In *England* the traditional subordination of the people was disrupted by rapid industrialization. At the level of ideology the rising entrepreneurial class rejected the obligation of the rich to protect the poor and maintained that the latter were solely responsible for the poverty from which they suffered. Initially, this ideological rejection of the newly recruited industrial work force was counterbalanced by the continued strength of traditional views: aristocratic spokesmen contended for the right of the poor to protection by the rich, while workers used this image of traditional class-relations as a weapon in their attacks upon the employers. Eventually the English entrepreneurs found a new and positive formula which differed from their earlier views in being compatible with the civic position of the working class as well as with their own interests. This formula consisted in a basically equalitarian appeal which invited the workers to emulate the qualities of their employers and thus attain success for themselves.

In *Russia* the traditional subordination of the "lower classes" was retained in theory and practice long after legal and economic changes had terminated the conditions under which that subordination had been successfully defended in the past. The common dependence of all social groups on the supremacy of the Tsar meant that the relations among them remained subordinate to the government at a time when the ideological and institutional emancipation of workers and peasants, as well as of employers, was in progress. Landowners and employers insisted as much as the government officials upon the continued subordination of the "lower classes." In the absence of a civic position appropriate to the changed, even though subordinate, role of workers and peasants in an emerging industrial society, the masses finally revolted, not against their oppressors as they had in the past, but against the person of the Tsar, the symbol of the social order which they had previously upheld.

The English and the Russian development illustrate the generic problem arising from the break with traditional subordination. On what terms will a society undergoing industrialization solve the problem of incorporating its newly recruited, industrial work-force within the economic and political community of the nation? Merely to insist on the continued subordination of the "lower classes" when their traditional way of life has been changed profoundly, is fraught with danger to a society as the Russian case illustrates. But to accentuate this change by holding the workers responsible for the deprivations from which they suffer is also hazardous, unless as in the English case this ostracism of the workers is counteracted vigorously by other forces within the society. Russia and England exemplify extreme alternatives. Elsewhere the traditional subordination of peasants and workers was modified without being abandoned, and the demand for the self-dependence of workers was mitigated by governmental measures designed to cushion the impact of rapid economic change.

Industrialization thus creates a revolutionary potential as a consequence of the problems engendered in the early phase of its development. The resolution of these problems may take a long time. Partial resolutions of the problem only lead to partial dissipations of the revolutionary potential as in Germany and France. In such cases the unresolved problems of the early phase linger on long after economic enterprises have been well-developed. The revolutionary potential of the proletariat will disappear, on the other hand, where this work-force is more or less rapidly reincorporated in the national community. These considerations have far-reaching implications for our understanding of the social and political history of capitalism.

Entrepreneurial ideologies are an element in a society's capacity to reincorporate a newly created, industrial work-force. This capacity to accord civic recognition to an "internal proletariat" (Toynbee) is an outgrowth of each country's historical legacy which manifests itself in the developing relations among the social classes and the government. The revolutionary dangers of industrial civilization materialize when the various dominant groups are unable or unwilling to compromise. This inflexibility and hence the suppression of social unrest are actually greatest at the inception of industrialization. But the resulting conditions are highly unstable and may have cumulative, long-run repercussions. The revolutionary threat to an emerging industrial society involves the workers' quest for civic recognition in that society. It involves a struggle between classes over rights of which the workers claim to have been deprived unjustly (though in fact they never possessed them previously), and which they seek to gain through a political struggle for a more equitable distribution within capitalist society.

This interpretation is at variance with the Marxian analysis. Marx had predicted that the revolutionary threat to capitalist society would increase as capitalism advanced. I have suggested that in Europe this threat grew out of conflicts during the incipient phase of industrialization.[5] Marx believed that the political awakening and the increasing radicalization of the workers were a response to the economic crises and the cumulative deprivations of advancing industrialization, which would eventually lead to an overthrow of the capitalist system. Yet, there is evidence that political radicalism may decrease with a rapidly developing capitalist economy, while it appears to be intensified where the economic development is retarded and workers are denied the rights of equal citizenship. Finally, Marx predicted that as capitalism advanced the capitalist ruling class would become increasingly fearful for its supremacy, reluctant to make concessions to the workers, and unwilling to advance industry technologically. But this study suggests that the willingness of entrepreneurial classes to compromise may increase along with the capitalist development. The rejection of compromise or the most reluctant yielding to pressure result from historical legacies which antedate industrialization, though they have a profound effect upon the relations among social classes in the course of industrialization.

In the early phases of English industrialization the entrepreneurial concern with the workers was not managerial primarily, if by "managerial" we mean the deliberate organization and control of the work-force in an enterprise. The early entrepreneurs could ignore these problems as long as managerial responsibility as well as the risks of managerial failure fell to the lot of subcontractors. The problems of labor-management came to the fore wherever all work operations were concentrated within the enterprise and depended to some extent upon an *internalized* ethic of work performance among the workers. Under the conditions of factory production such an ethic involves a number of variables. Workers must be willing to do the work assigned with a degree of steady intensity. They must have a positive interest in accuracy and exercise reasonable care in the treatment of tools and machinery. And they must be willing to comply with general rules as well as with specific orders in a manner which strikes some reasonable balance between the extremes of blind obedience and capricious unpredictability. This last qualification brings the general attributes of an ethic of work performance within the framework of an industrial organization. For under conditions of factory production the intensity of work, its accuracy, and the careful treatment of tools and machinery cannot remain the attributes of an individual's performance. Rather, these qualities of work must be coordinated with the production schedule, and that coordination depends to some extent on the good judgment of each worker in his every act of complying with rules and orders. It is probable that in England this ethic of work performance developed among the masses of workers out of the combined legacies of craftsmanship, the Puritan ethic, and the rising ideology of individual striving and success. But these legacies had become effective among industrial workers (and to a certain extent the workers had become adapted to the disciplines of factory work) *prior* to the growth of modern, large-scale industry. It is easiest to appreciate the significance of timing in this respect by considering the contrast with the development in Tsarist and Soviet Russia.

The doctrines of autocratic rule assumed the total depravity of workers and serfs. An ethic of work performance was not expected of the laboring masses. It was assumed, rather, that they owed the utmost exertions to their masters and that they needed to be punished severely if they failed in their obligations. Autocratic rule relied upon the omnipresence of fear and coercion to make workers and serfs act as they ought to act. Its ideological appeals exclusively stressed the sacred duty of submission.

> . . . in their instruction to the people [the clergy] should remind them how sacred is the duty of submitting to the authorities, and above all to the Highest authority; how necessary is a trusting and united respect for the government, which of course knows better than private persons what is the good of all, and cannot but wish the well-being of its subjects; and how dangerous is credulous acceptance of injudicious or ill-intentioned advice, from which proceed folly and disorders. . . .[6]

The distinctive feature of this and many similar appeals was the emphasis upon submission to the government as the principal rule of conduct. Subordination to the master was but a token of the worker's submission to the Highest authority. This political interpretation of obedience precluded ideological appeals concerned with the inculcation of work habits, and Russian employers expected that coercion and fear rather than conscience would prompt the worker to exert himself.

It is instructive to consider the comparison with England. There also, the assumption was widespread in the late 18th and early 19th centuries that the laboring poor were depraved. Complete submission to the higher classes and the government was demanded without equivocation. A real concern with the attitudes of workers only arose (as it did in Russia) when the people showed signs of rebelliousness. Yet, these similarities are superficial. In England, the depravity of the poor was rarely mentioned without reference to the good qualities which every self-respecting man can develop, and the demands for submission were couched in terms which made submission synonymous with ideal qualities of work and conduct.[7] Just as there was little distinction between the ruling classes and the government, so there was also little distinction between the work performance expected of the ideal laborer and the submission to the authority of government which was expected of the laborer as a citizen. In Russia, these distinctions were fundamental. The employers failed to appeal to the conscience or self-esteem of the

workers, because the reliance on fear and coercion effectively precluded the demand for an internalized ethic of work performance.
The demand for submission, on the other hand, was only related to
civil obedience and religious orthodoxy, but not to other aspects
of personal conduct. It may be suggested that the employers acted
as they did because their self-esteem depended upon an exercise of
authority patterned after that of the landowners and the Tsar. And
the officials of the Tsarist government were concerned with the conduct of the people only insofar as the maintenance of public order
made that concern necessary. To have gone beyond the suppression of disturbances would have been outside the established routine of officials, for whom an unconditional submission to the Tsar's
supreme power was an unquestioned maxim.

Under these circumstances, an ethic of work performance did
not become a managerial problem in Russia until after the revolution of 1917 and hence until industrialization had become synonymous with the development of large-scale enterprises. It is instructive to read Lenin's reflections on this problem written in 1918.

> The Russian is a bad worker compared with workers of the
> advanced countries Nor could it be otherwise under the Tsarist
> regime and in view of the tenacity of the remnants of serfdom
> The task that the soviet government must set the people in all
> its scope is—learn to work. The Taylor system, the last word of
> capitalism in this respect, like all capitalist progress, is a com-
> bination of subtle brutality of bourgeois exploitation and a num-
> ber of its greatest scientific achievements in the field of analyzing
> mechanical motions during work, the elimination of superfluous
> and awkward motions, the working out of correct methods of
> work, the introduction of the best systems of accounting and
> control, etc. The Soviet Republic must at all costs adopt all that
> is valuable in the achievements of science and technology in this
> field. The possibility of building socialism will be determined
> precisely by our success in combining the Soviet government and
> the Soviet organization of administration with the modern
> achievements of capitalism.[8]

In the years following the revolution this program was acted upon
in several directions.

It will be useful to illustrate the Bolshevik approach to problems of management and of productivity. In June 1923, first in the ranks of the Red Army and then in offices and factories, small groups were formed which resolved to fight for the "proper use and economy of time." Soon, similar groups were constituted in many parts of the country. It is probable that the formation of these groups was entrusted to the "activists" of the trade union and the party, a device which Communist ideology explains as the leadership of the masses by the most advanced segment of the working class. These groups were formally organized in the *Time League*, whose members were obliged to keep a "time-card" on which they would record their daily activities. Each member was further obligated to protest against, and to report, every waste of time he encountered. Here is the text of a leaflet with which the *Time League* sought to eliminate the "organizational illiteracy" of the Russian people:

Time,
System
Energy

What do these words mean?
Time:
Measure your time, control it!
Do everything on time! exactly, on the minute!
Save time! make time count, work fast!
Divide your time correctly, time for work and time for leisure!
System:
Everything according to plan, according to system!
A notebook for the system. Order in your place of work!
Each must work according to plan.
Energy:
Pursue your goal stubbornly!
Try hard. Don't retreat after failures!
Always finish what you have started!
Communist Americanism, realism and vigilance![9]

Again, a comparison with the Western industrial development is instructive. To "make time count," to use leisure "so as to work better afterwards," to be orderly and work according to plan, to show perseverance in the face of reverses: these were the familiar admonitions of the Puritan divines in 17th century England. Two centuries were to elapse before men like Frederick W. Taylor turned their attention to problems of industrial organization and labor management. Another way of making the same observation is to state that in the West two hundred years of moral and religious education preceded the rise of modern large-scale industry with its unprecedented demands upon the discipline of the individual worker. In Russia, on the other hand, both developments coincided, mass education of the workers and the technical and administrative organization of large-scale industry occurring at one and the same time.[10] Thus, in the West mass education of the people was the result of unplanned growth which "scientific management" could take for granted. In Russia the development of labor discipline and of "scientific management" were attempted at the same time under the leadership of the dictatorial party and subject to its supervision.

This coincidence between industrialization and the bureaucratization of economic enterprises, between the inculcation of an ethic of work-performance and the introduction of complex technology and administrative organization has occurred under dictatorial rule. The Party fears the organization of common understandings by political means. This has meant specifically that the decision-making authority of the managers is not only controlled by the planning agencies from above, but must be in line with the "experience of the masses," as this "experience" is represented and manipulated by the Party. The workers are not only subordinated to the managers, but are also called upon—under the guidance of the Party, of course—to criticize and help correct the administrative and technical work of management. As noted earlier, the social differences between managers and workers are disguised symbolically by the subordination of superiors and the super-ordination of subordinates, a disguise made possible by the total subordination of all social ranks to the political controls of the Party. Under this system differences of power, of status, and of rewards are at least as great as in any "class society," but conflicts over the distribution of rewards are suppressed and class-differences are denied by making the work-performance of each individual or group a test of loyalty and a testimonial to the Party.

Under the conditions of Western civilization the distribution of rewards is in dispute and conflicts of interest are intense. The belief is more or less accepted by management and labor that the authority of managers over their subordinates not only reflects the imperatives of industrial organization, but also the existence of class-differences. For when managers make their appeals for cooperation they identify themselves automatically as persons in authority who formulate the interests of the organization they lead. And yet there also remains a vague residue of understanding between managers and workers as members of the same community. Managers appeal to the good faith of their subordinates in order to enlist their cooperation. Workers and their representatives continue to appeal for the acceptance of their position by the public and by management. Presumably, these appeals continue to be made because both sides believe that they have a chance to be heard some of the time, because they appeal to their own group and express its feelings rather than change the ideas and feelings of the other group, and also because both sides more or less accept a certain level of frustration. This acceptance of differences in belief and interest together with the continued appeal by each side for cooperation and understanding suggests that for all the ambiguity of ideas and the ambivalence of feelings there exists a common universe of discourse.

This common universe of discourse can be understood more clearly if one examines entrepreneurial and managerial ideologies in Anglo-Saxon civilization over a two hundred year period. In 18th century England views concerning the position of the poor—the "swinish multitude" as Burke called them—were much the same as those I have described for Tsarist Russia, with the significant exception that the "benevolent protection" of the people was regarded as an obligation of the aristocracy, not of the king. Beginning with the writings of Adam Smith, Edmund Burke, and T. R. Malthus, the idea began to spread that the people should be self-dependent. Too much attention has been paid to the hypocrisy of a call for self-dependence which coincided with the massive distress of the industrial revolution. For the recently uprooted peasants this appeal had considerable force and in the 1830's it was buttressed further by appeals of free-trade spokesmen for the political support of the working class. By the 1850's this development had culminated in the idea that the workers should emulate their employers rather than rely upon their superiority and protection.

In the United States this basically equalitarian idea was given harsher overtones in the glorification of the struggle for survival. But in retrospect that may well have been an episode which was as short as the "Gilded Age." For while the open-shop campaign asserted the employers' sovereignty within the plant, scientific management was already prescribing what to do with that sovereignty with the more or less tacit suggestion that science was a substitute for managerial discretion. During the 1920's industrial psychology advanced this theme by elaborating techniques of testing and personnel management which were applied to the workers, while the old praise of virtue and success continued unabated with regard to employers and managers. Yet, this invidious distinction may have been short-lived also if one takes the "human relations" movement since the 1930's to mean that managers as well as workers act in response to group-pressures and emotional involvement. Such equalitarian undertones of the managerial "images of man" cannot hide the existing differences of status and reward. But these "images" suggest that the equalitarian traditions of the West have been brought in line with the organizational changes of economic enterprises which put a premium on the "bureaucratic arts." Even at the level of managerial ideologies they contrast sharply with a tradition which maximizes the differences among men not merely by differential rewards, but also by a rigid, if frequently shifting, political orthodoxy.

At the end of his essay on the *Protestant Ethic* Max Weber observed that the dissolution of Puritan asceticism into the utilitarianism of capitalist entrepreneurs still needed to be investigated. Works like those of Leslie Stephen and Elie Halevy are major contributions in this respect. But it may be suggested that this line of inquiry tends to isolate the ideas of the rising middle classes from the social context in which they are developed. An emphasis on that context tends to direct attention to those "ruling ideas of the ruling class" which are concerned with the related images of "the entrepreneur" and "the worker" and hence with the place of both in an emerging industrial society. The study here under review has attempted to show that in England the entrepreneurial ideologies of the early 19th century came to make a positive moral appeal to the worker in lieu of the earlier identification of poverty with a fall from Divine grace. Though only one of many factors, this appeal was of significance for the civic reintegration of the rising working class and hence for the dissipation of the revolutionary potential of early industrialization. The contrast with Russia tends to emphasize the importance of such appeals on the part of the ruling class. Indeed such contrasts are needed for a proper characterization of shared understandings among groups of very unequal status.

The successful industrialization of a country presupposes an ethic of work performance. In his essay Weber had investigated the religious ideas in which the work-ethic of the rising middle classes of Western Europe had originated. Today, the industrialization of countries like Russia and Japan suggests that this requisite work-ethic may originate in different ways, above all by nationalist appeals implemented through political coercion.[11] And this difference in the origin of the requisite work-ethic is also related to an important difference in timing. To be successful today industrialization cannot depend upon a prolonged education of the masses before introducing modern large-scale enterprises, as the countries of Western Europe could. But to do so simultaneously means that no such interval is possible between the persuasion of the elite and the persuasion of the masses as occurred in England between the agitation of the Puritan divines in the late 16th and early 17th centuries and the education of the masses from the 1760's to the 1830's. A comparison of managerial ideologies in England and Russia suggests, rather, that successful industrialization today may depend upon the simultaneous development of large-scale industry and of a work-

ethic among the masses. In this respect Russia may be likened to
Germany and Japan. The development of all three countries poses
the question whether today a work-ethic among the masses can be
created without the political accentuation and manipulation of
status differences in the name of nationalist goals.

SOCIAL STRATIFICATION AND
THE POLITICAL COMMUNITY

In the developing areas of the world new class-relations emerge, as one after another country adopts democratic institutions and initiates industrial growth. In the "developing areas" of Europe a comparable process took place since the French Revolution and during much of the nineteenth century. This essay seeks to enhance our understanding of the modern problem by a re-examination of the European experience with special reference to the relation of social stratification and the political community in the nation-state.[1]

This re-examination has a theoretical purpose. The social and political changes of European societies provided the context in which the concepts of modern sociology were formulated. As we turn today to the developing areas of the non-Western world, we employ concepts that have a Western derivation. In so doing one can proceed in one of two ways: by formulating a new set of categories applying to all societies or by rethinking the categories familiar to us in view of the transformation and diversity of the Western experience itself. This study adopts the second alternative in the belief that the insights gained in the past should not be discarded lightly and that a reassessment of the Western experience may aid our understanding of the developing areas of the non-Western world.

The problem before us is the transformation of Western Europe from the estate-societies of the Middle Ages to the absolutist re-

An earlier version of this essay was published in *European Journal of Sociology*, I (1960), pp. 181–210.

gimes of the eighteenth century and thence to the class-societies of plebiscitary democracy in the nation-states of the twentieth century. In the course of this transformation new class-relations emerged, the functions and powers of centralized national governments increased and all adult citizens acquired formal legal and (at a later time) political equality. Attempts to understand this transformation gave rise to social theories that were necessarily a part of the society they sought to comprehend. Though their scientific value is independent of this fact, our understanding is aided when we learn how men come to think as they do about the society in which they live. Such self-scrutiny can protect us against the unwitting adoption of changing intellectual fashions; it can alert us to the limitations inherent in any theoretical framework. Since the present essay deals with social stratification in relation to the political community, a critical assessment of some of the assumptions implicit in studies of this relationship constitutes a part of our inquiry.

A glance at the history of social thought since the Renaissance suggests that this relation has been viewed in terms of three perspectives: that society is an object of government, that politics and government are a product of society, and thirdly that society and government are partly interdependent and partly autonomous spheres of social life.[2]

Inevitably, this division of social theories since the Renaissance is arbitrary. Each of the three orientations can be traced back much further; and there are many linkages among these orientations which blur the distinctions between them. But it is also true that these perspectives have recurred in the history of social theory and that they provide us with useful benchmarks for the reconsideration of "society and the state" which is the particular purpose of this essay.

❧ THEORETICAL PERSPECTIVES

The idea that society is an object of state-craft goes back in the Western tradition to the medieval tracts containing "advice to princes". From an education of character designed for the sons of rulers this idea was developed into an instrument of state counsel by Machiavelli. In the eighteenth century Montesquieu drew upon this tradition in his theory of law in which he combined the old precepts of state-craft by a personal ruler with an analysis of the social and physical conditions which would facilitate or hinder the exercise of authority under different systems of rule.[3] A view of society as an object of state-craft was closely related to the rise of absolutism in Europe, as Friedrich Meinecke has shown in his study of ideas concerning "reasons of state" and the rights and duties of rulers.[4] In this intellectual perspective a high degree of passivity on the part of society had been presupposed. The masses of the people were excluded from all political participation and became an object of governmental attention primarily as a source of tax revenue and military recruitment. Accordingly, this intellectual perspective lost its appeal wherever absolutism declined and political participation on the part of the people at large increased, although in inchoate form it has come back into fashion through the growth of the welfare-state.

As attention came to be focussed on the conditions facilitating or hindering the ruler's purpose, "Machiavellism" gradually blended with the second perspective, the idea that politics and government are products of society. In post-Renaissance Europe this idea came to the fore in the attacks of the Enlightenment philosophers on the established privileges of the church and the aristocracy. These privileges were seen as unjust usurpations arising from the vested interests of established institutions, while politics appeared as a by-product of established prerogatives. If this orientation tended to sociologize politics, its application to the past politicized history. With unabashed forthrightness writers like Voltaire surveyed and judged past events in terms of the eighteenth century concept of a universal human nature and its inherent morality. By distributing praise or blame among contestants of the past they made history appear as a story of ever-changing conflicts among vested interests, suggesting that all governments are mere by-products of contemporary partisanship.

During the eighteenth century such judgments were made in the belief that "man" was endowed by God with certain universal moral attributes. During the nineteenth century this belief and the theory of natural law were replaced increasingly by attempts to develop a scientific study of human nature and the political community. As mentioned earlier, Saint-Simon marked this transition: he proposed to make morals and politics into a "positive science" by basing both on the study of physiology which concerned the truly universal properties of man. In this way speculation would be replaced by precise knowledge with the result that political problems would be solved as simply as questions of hygiene. The outstanding feature of this approach was the tendency to reduce the manifest diversity of social and political life to some underlying, basic element, that presumably could be understood with scientific precision. During the nineteenth century ever new elaborations of this reductionist approach were advanced, from proposals of a "sociology" based upon biological facts through various explanations in terms of climate, race and the struggle for survival to Marx's theory of history as ultimately determined by the imperative that men "must be able to live, if they are to 'make history'." [5] Many of these theories of society accepted the scientific optimism of the nineteenth century and assumed that a knowledge of the "underlying" forces of society or nature provides the clue to human power and that in one way or another such knowledge could be translated into action.

The third intellectual perspective, that society and government are partly interdependent and partly autonomous spheres of social life, deserves more extended consideration, since it reflects (and provides insight into) the structural transformation of Western societies which is the focus of this essay. Here again we may begin with the Enlightenment, especially with those philosophers who emphasized the cleavage between bourgeois *society* and the *state*. That cleavage existed as long as each man's private concerns were at variance with his duties as a citizen. It was towards a solution of this problem that Rousseau made his many attempts to reconcile man in the "state of nature" whose virtues and sentiments were as yet unspoiled by civilization, and man as a citizen who must subordinate himself to the community but without doing violence to his dignity as a man.[6] This speculative contrast between man's potential morality and his actual conduct, and this effort to base the political community on the first rather than the second, were replaced in the nineteenth century by explanations which accounted for man's ethical capacities *and* his actual behavior in terms of human nature in society.

An outstanding example of such an explanation is found in the work of Emile Durkheim, which illuminates both the theoretical perspective of liberalism and the transformation of Western society which is examined below. As a sociologist Durkheim wished to study morality empirically, as a phenomenon arising "naturally" from the group-affiliations of the individual. But as a political liberal Durkheim also knew that such group-affiliation would obliterate the personality of the individual, unless the state intervened to guarantee his freedom. It will be seen that in this way Durkheim altered and continued the tradition of the Enlightenment; for him society itself was the "state of nature" for each individual, but as such it was also differentiated from the legal order and representative government of the "civil state".

From the beginning of his work Durkheim was concerned with a scientific analysis of the moral problems raised by the Enlightenment. He praised Rousseau for developing a construct of the *civil state* or society that was superimposed on the "state of nature" *without doing violence to the latter*. But he also criticized Rousseau's conception of the individual person as isolated, which made it difficult to see how any society was possible.[7] Durkheim applied a similar criticism to the utilitarian doctrine, which indeed he regarded as inferior to the Enlightenment tradition in that it made the social nexus entirely dependent upon the exchange relationship on the market while abandoning the earlier concern with the moral pre-conditions of the civil state.[8] The supposition underlying these approaches, that a basic conflict existed between "man in nature" and "man in society", appeared to Durkheim to be factually incorrect. By a study of the exterior social constraints which compel individuals to act alike regardless of personal motivation he proceeded to demonstrate that society was possible because man was naturally social. In a series of studies of suicide, the family, crime, religion and the division of labor he showed that the moral norms governing individual behavior originated in each person's group-affiliation and hence that Rousseau had been wrong in postulating a conflict between man in a "state of nature" and man in society. In other words, Durkheim "solved" Rousseau's problem by making the individual completely subordinate to society.

> Every society is despotic, at least if nothing from without supervenes to restrain its despotism. Still, I would not say that there is anything artificial in this despotism: it is natural because it is necessary, and also because, in certain conditions, societies cannot endure without it. Nor do I mean that there is anything intolerable about it: on the contrary, the individual does not feel it any more than we feel the atmosphere that weighs on our shoulders. From the moment the individual has been raised in this way by the collectivity, he will naturally desire what it desires and accept without difficulty the state of subject to which he finds himself reduced.[9]

Thus, if society is jeopardized, this is due not to a hypothetical conflict between society and the individual, but to a state of *anomie* in which his group-affiliations no longer provide the individual with norms regulating his conduct in a stable fashion. Where such group-norms are weakening, as in modern society, the social order can be rebuilt only on the basis of strengthened group-norms. Accordingly, Durkheim concluded his studies with the proposal of a new corporatism, based on modern occupational groups, so that "the individual is not to be alone in the face of the State and live in a kind of alternation between anarchy and servitude."[10]

As these studies progressed Durkheim continued to espouse the "moral existence of the individual". As a life-long liberal he was not willing to postpone this humanistic component to the indefinite future, as Marx had done. And as a sociologist he had demonstrated both man's fundamentally social nature and the seemingly inevitable tendency of increasing "individual variations," as the division of labor increased and the "common conscience" of the group became more general and permissive.[11] But if individualism is inevitable sociologically, why be concerned with safeguarding it politically? This combination of a sociological determinism with political liberalism arose, because like Tocqueville, Durkheim became concerned with the *secular transformation of group-constraint.* The associational ties of the province, the parish and the municipality one after another lost their significance for the individual. As a result, a "great gap" had been created between the state and the individual in the structure of European societies.[12] Durkheim's proposal to bridge this "gap" by a new corporatism did not provide a political solution to the problem, as he himself recognized. The individual would be saved in this way from anomie and loneliness vis-à-vis the state, but he would also be oppressed by the secondary group to which he belonged.

Durkheim's answer to this question deserves extensive quotation, since it is not generally familiar.

> In order to prevent this happening, and to provide a certain range for individual development, it is not enough for a society to be on a big scale; the individual must be able to move with some degree of freedom over a wide field of action. He must not be curbed and monopolized by the secondary groups, and these groups must not be able to get a mastery over their members and mould them at will. There must therefore exist above these local, domestic—in a word, secondary—authorities, some overall authority which makes the law for them all: it must remind each of them that it is but a part and not the whole and that it should not keep for itself what rightly belongs to the whole. The only means of averting this collective particularism and all it involves for the individual, is to have a special agency with the duty of representing the overall collectivity, its rights and its interests, vis-à-vis these individual collectivities [. . .]
>
> Let us see why and how the main function of the State is to liberate the individual personalities. It is solely because, in holding its constituent societies in check, it prevents them from exerting the repressive influences over the individual that they would otherwise exert. So there is nothing inherently tyrannical about State intervention in the different fields of collective life; on the contrary, it has the object and the effect of alleviating tyrannies that do exist. It will be argued, might not the State in turn become despotic? Undoubtedly, provided there were nothing to

counter that trend [. . .] The inference to be drawn from this comment, however, is simply that if that collective force, the State, is to be the liberator of the individual, it has itself need of some counterbalance; it must be restrained by other collective forces, that is, by those secondary groups [. . .] *And it is out of this conflict of social forces that individual liberties are born.*[13]

For these reasons Durkheim defined political society as "one formed by the coming together of a rather large number of secondary social groups, subject to the same one authority which is not itself subject to any other superior authority duly constituted." [14]

Durkheim's sociological theories do not prepare us for this political solution of his problem.[15] The emancipation of the individual from the "despotism of the group" appears in the bulk of his work as a result of the increasing division of labor and the related attenuation of custom and law. Though as a political liberal Durkheim valued this "range of individual development", as a social philosopher he feared its consequences for social morality where these consisted in the isolation of the individual and the loss of regulative norms of conduct (anomie). Accordingly he sought to safeguard the individual against the dangers of anomie by his re-integration in the "secondary groups" of society (corporations based on the occupational division of labor). Yet at the same time he called on the aid of the state to preserve individual liberties against the "despotism" with which these groups would seek to control the individual. Implicit in this approach is, therefore, a "dualism" whereby man's psychological and moral attributes are explained in terms of his membership in the society, while the society as a whole is characterized by an overall process (the increasing division of labor), which accounts among other things for man's capacity to alter these attributes through state-intervention in the interest of justice.[16]

This incongruity between Durkheim's sociological and political theories was symptomatic of the liberal tradition in the nineteenth century. Even the classic formulation of this tradition contained, as Elie Halévy has shown, two contradictory principles. Arising from the division of labor in a market-economy man's "propensity to truck, barter and exchange one thing for another" tended to reveal a "natural identity of interests" which enhanced unaided the general interest of society. Yet the quantity of subsistence is insufficient to allow all men to live in abundance and this insufficiency is aggravated by the failure of men voluntarily to limit their numerical increase. Hence it follows, by an exception to the first principle, that the State should protect the property of the rich against the poor as well as educate the latter so that they will restrain their instinct of procreation. In this way the State acts to ensure the "artificial identification of interests." [17]

In its classic or its Durkheimian version the liberal tradition is marked by a "dualism." Society and government constitute two interdependent, but partially autonomous spheres of thought and action. From a theoretical standpoint this tradition is unsatisfactory because it constantly shifts from the empirical level, as in the analysis of market-behavior or the individual's group-affiliation, to the ethical and political level, as in the demand that the state should act to prevent the undesired consequences of market-behavior or group-affiliation. Still, historically, this perspective can be explained by the unquestioned fact that the societies of nineteenth and twentieth century Europe witnessed a juxtaposition between society as an aggregate of interrelated groups and the nation-state with its identifiable culture and institutional structure.

STRUCTURAL PERSPECTIVES

Medieval Political Life.   In turning now from theoretical perspectives to problems of social structure it will prove useful to begin, however sketchily, with the pre-conditions of representative government in the West.[18] In the problematic relations between the "estates" and the power of royal government, say since the eleventh and twelfth centuries, we have to do with group-formations in society and the exercise of legitimate authority and hence with the relation between society and government which was discussed above in theoretical terms.[19]

Characteristic of the political communities of this early period was the fundamental assumption that the personal ruler of a territory is a leader who exercises his authority in the name of God and with the consent of the "people." [20] Because he is the consecrated ruler and represents the whole community, the "people" are obliged to obey his commands; but he in turn is also responsible to the community. This idea of a reciprocal obligation between ruler and ruled was part of an accepted tradition; it can be traced back to ancient Roman and Germanic practices, was greatly strengthened by Christian beliefs, but became formal law only very gradually.[21]

These characteristics of medieval kingship were closely related to the political conditions of royal administration. Each ruler possessed a domain of his own which he governed as the head of a very large household. On the basis of the economic resources derived from this domain, and in principle, on the basis of his consecrated claim to legitimate authority, each ruler then faced as his major political task the extension of his authority over a territory beyond his domain. Secular rulers had to rely upon those elements of the population which by virtue of their possessions and local authority were in a position to aid the ruler financially and militarily, both in the extension of his territory and the exercise of his rule over its inhabitants. From a pragmatic political standpoint this was a precarious expedient, since such aid of local notables could enhance their own power as well as that of the ruler.

As a result, secular rulers typically sought to offset the drive towards local autonomy by a whole series of devices which were designed to increase the personal and material dependence of such notables on the ruler and his immediate entourage.[22] This typical antinomy of the pre-modern political community in Western Europe became manifest with every demand by secular rulers for increased revenue and military service. And to the extent that such demands were followed up by administrative measures, local notables typically responded by uniting into estates that could exact further guarantees or increases of their existing privileges by way of compensating for the greater services demanded of them.

A second characteristic of medieval political life was, therefore,

that certain persons and groups were exempted from direct obedience to the commands issued by, or in the name of, the ruler. This
"immunity" guaranteed that within the delimited sphere of their
authority these persons and groups were entitled to exercise the legal powers of government. This institution goes back to the privileged legal position of the royal domains in Imperial Rome, a privilege which was subsequently transferred to the possessions of the
church, the secular local rulers (i. e. the landed nobility under feudalism) and during the eleventh and twelfth centuries to the mu-
nicipalities. This system of negative and positive privileges (which
may be called "immunities" and "autonomous jurisdiction") became the legal foundation of representative government in Western Europe, because it accorded positive, public rights to particular
persons and groups within the political community. This institution of public rights on the part of certain privileged subjects is
more or less unique to Western Europe. Perhaps the most important factor contributing to this development was the fundamental
influence of the church, which through its consecration of the ruler
and through the autonomy of its organization restrained the power
of secular rulers and re-enforced the political autonomy of the secular estates.[23]

In this setting a political life in the modern sense could not exist.
Rather, the political community consisted of an aggregate of more
or less autonomous jurisdictions, firmly or precariously held together by a king to whom all lords and corporate bodies owed allegiance, and under whose strong or nominal rule they fought or bar-
gained with him and with each other over the distribution of fiscal
and administrative preserves. Consequently, politics at the "national" level consisted for the most part of a species of "international" negotiations among more or less autonomous jurisdictions,
within the confines of a country that sometimes possessed only a
precarious cultural and political unity. In such a community the
coalescence of interests among individuals was not based on voluntary acts, but on rights and obligations determined by birth, such
that each man was—at least in principle—bound to abide by the
rules pertaining to his group lest he impair the privileges of his fel-

lows. Classes or status-groups in the modern sense could not exist, because joint action occurred as a result of common rights and obligations imposed on each group by law, custom, or special edict. Thus, every group or social rank encompassed the rights and obligations of the individual person. Under these conditions a man could modify the personal and corporate rule to which he was subject only by an appeal to the established rights of his rank and to the benevolence of his lord, although these rights might be altered collectively in the course of conflicts and adjustments with competing jurisdictions. As Max Weber has stated,

> the individual carried his *professio juris* with him wherever he went. Law was not a *lex terrae*, as the English law of the King's court became soon after the Norman Conquest, but rather the privilege of the person as a member of a particular group. Yet this principle of "personal law" was no more consistently applied at that time than its opposite principle is today. . . . All volitionally formed associations always strove for the application of the principle of personal law on behalf of the law created by them, but the extent to which they were successful in this respect varied greatly from case to case. At any rate, the result was the coexistence of numerous "law communities", the autonomous jurisdictions of which overlapped, the compulsory, political association being only one such autonomous jurisdiction in so far as it existed at all.[24]

In Western Europe this medieval political structure of more or less loosely united jurisdictions was superseded gradually by absolutist regimes marked by a relative concentration of power in the hands of the king and his officials and by a gradual transformation of the king's relation to the privileged estates.[25] The variety and fluidity of conditions under these absolutist regimes were as great as under the feudal political structure. For example, the nationwide powers of the king developed much earlier in England than on the Continent, partly as a legacy of the Norman conquest. However, the insular condition with its relative ease of communication together with legal tradition antedating the conquest both in Normandy and in England also made for an early and effective growth of "countervailing" powers. None of the Continental countries achieved a similar balance with the result that their absolutist political structures revealed either a greater concentration of royal power and correspondingly a greater destruction of the estates as in France or an ascendance of many principalities with some internal balance between king and estates but at the expense of overall political unity, as in Germany. Still, by the eighteenth century, most European societies were characterized by absolutist regimes in which the division of powers between the king and oligarchic estates as represented by various "constituted bodies" was at the center of the political struggle.[26]

The French Revolution with its Napoleonic aftermath destroyed this system of established privileges and initiated the mass democracies of the modern world. We can best comprehend this major transformation of the relation between society and the state if we leave the complicated transitional phenomena to one side and focus attention on the contrast between medieval political life and the modern political community which has emerged in the societies of Western civilization. To do so, it will prove useful to take the work of Tocqueville as our guide.

Tocqueville's Interpretation of "the Great Transformation." Tocqueville's analysis has power because it covered a very long time-period and because the French Revolution unquestionably marked a transition despite all equally unquestioned continuities. Also, in his admittedly speculative fears about a tyranny of the future, he used a "logic of possibilities" that enabled him to cope intellectually with contingencies he could not predict. By extending the scope of his analysis he made sure that he was dealing with genuine distinctions between different patterns of social relations and political institutions at the beginning and the end of the time-span he chose to consider.

In his famous study of the French Revolution Tocqueville showed how the *ancien régime* had destroyed the century-old pattern of medieval political life by concentrating power in the hands of the king and his officials and by depriving the various autonomous jurisdictions of their judicial and administrative functions.[27]

In pointed contrast to Burke's great polemic against the French Revolution Tocqueville demonstrated that in France the centralization of royal power and the concomitant decline of corporate jurisdictions had developed too far to make the restoration of these jurisdictions a feasible alternative. The nobility no longer enjoyed the rights it had possessed at one time, but its acquiescence in royal absolutism had been "bought" by a retention of financial privileges like tax-exemption, a fact which greatly intensified anti-aristocratic sentiment. Through the royal administrative system of the *intendants* the rights of municipal corporations and the independence of the judiciary had been curtailed in the interest of giving the government a free hand in the field of taxation. As a result the urban *bourgeoisie* was divested of local governmental responsibility and the equitable administration of justice was destroyed. Noblemen thus preserved their pride of place in the absence of commensurate responsibilities, urban merchants aped aristocratic ways while seeking preferential treatment for themselves, and both combined social arrogance with an unmitigated exploitation of the peasants. In lieu of the balancing of group-interests in the feudal assemblies of an earlier day each class was now divided from the others and within itself with the result that "nothing had been left that could obstruct the central government, but, by the same token, nothing could shore it up." [28]

Tocqueville's analysis was concerned explicitly with the problem of the political community under the conditions created by the French Revolution. He maintained that in the medieval societies of Western Europe, the inequality of ranks was a universally accepted condition of social life. In that early political structure the individual enjoyed the rights and fulfilled the obligations appropriate to his rank; and although the distribution of such rights and duties was greatly affected by the use of force, it was established contractually and consecrated as such.[29] The Old Regime and the French Revolution destroyed this system by creating among all citizens a condition of abstract equality, but without providing guarantees for the preservation of freedom. Hence, Tocqueville appealed to his contemporaries that a new community, a new reciprocity of rights and obligations, must be established and that this could be done only if men would combine their love of equality and liberty with their love of order and religion. This admonition arose from his concern with the weakness and isolation of the individual in relation to government. Because he saw the trend towards equality as inevitable, Tocqueville was deeply troubled by the possibility that men who are equal would be able to agree on nothing but the demand that the central government assist each of them personally. As a consequence the government would subject ever new aspects of the society to its central regulation. I cite one version of this argument:

> As in periods of equality no man is compelled to lend his assistance to his fellow men, and none has any right to expect much support from them, everyone is at once independent and powerless. These two conditions, which must never be either separately considered or confounded together, inspire the citizen of a democratic country with very contrary propensities. His independence fills him with self-reliance and pride among his equals; his debility makes him feel from time to time the want of some outward assistance, which he cannot expect from any of them, because they are all impotent and unsympathizing. In this predicament he naturally turns his eyes to that imposing power [of the central government] [. . .] Of that power his wants and especially his desires continually remind him, until he ultimately views it as the sole and necessary support of his own weakness.[30]

Here is Tocqueville's famous paradox of equality and freedom. Men display an extraordinary independence when they rise in opposition to aristocratic privileges. "But in proportion as equality was [. . .] established by the aid of freedom, freedom itself was thereby rendered more difficult of attainment."[31] In grappling with this problem Tocqueville used as his base-point of comparison an earlier society in which men had been compelled to lend assistance to their fellows, because law and custom fixed their common and reciprocal rights and obligations. As this society was destroyed the danger arose that individualism and central power would grow apace. To counteract this threat men must cultivate the "art of associating together" in proportion as the equality of conditions advances, lest their failure to combine for private ends encourage the government to intrude—at the separate request of each—into every phase of social life.[32]

We can learn much from these insights. Tocqueville was surely right in his view that the established system of inequality in medieval society had been characterized by an accepted reciprocity of rights and obligations, and that this system had been destroyed as the *ancien régime* had centralized the functions of government. The French Revolution and its continuing repercussions levelled old differences in social rank and the resulting equalitarianism posed critical issues for the maintenance of freedom and political stability. Again, he discerned an important mechanism of centralization when he observed that each man would make his separate request for governmental assistance. In contrast to this tendency as he observed it in France, Tocqueville commended the Americans for their pursuit of private ends by voluntary association, which would help to curtail the centralization of governmental power.

It is necessary, of course, to qualify these insights in view of Tocqueville's tendency to read into modern conditions the patterns of medieval political life. At an earlier time, when landed aristocrats protected their liberties or privileges by resisting the encroachments of royal power, the centralization of that power appeared as an unequivocal curtailment of such liberties. Today, however, that centralization is an important bulwark of all *civil* liberties, though by the same token government can infringe upon these liberties more effectively than before, as Tocqueville emphasized. The collective pursuit of private ends, on the other hand, is not necessarily incompatible with an increase of central government, because today voluntary associations frequently demand more rather than less government action in contrast to the medieval estates whose effort to extend their jurisdictions was often synonymous with resistance to administrative interference from the outside. In contrast to Tocqueville, Durkheim clearly perceived this positive aspect of modern government and, correspondingly, the dangers implicit in group-control over the individual.

It is the State that has rescued the child from patriarchal domination and from family tyranny; it is the State that has freed
the citizen from feudal groups and later from communal groups;
it is the State that has liberated the craftsman and his master
from guild tyranny. . . .

[The State] must even permeate all those secondary groups of
family, trade and professional association, Church, regional areas
and so on . . . which tend . . . to absorb the personality of
their members. It must do this, in order to prevent this absorption
and free these individuals, and so as to remind these partial
societies that they are not alone and that there is a right that
stands above their own rights.[33]

Important as these qualifications are, they should not make us
overlook the reason why Tocqueville's interpretation of the "great
transformation" was illuminating.[34] By comparing an earlier condition of political life with the transformation brought about by
the *ancien régime*, the new condition of equality ushered in by the
French Revolution, and the possibility of a new tyranny in the
future Tocqueville was concerned with "speculative truths" as
he called them. This simplification of different social structures
enabled him to bring out the major contrasts among them, and
these are not invalidated by the short-run and more deductive
analyses that went astray. As I see it, Tocqueville's work becomes
intellectually most useful, if we attempt to develop within his
overall framework a set of categories that may enable us to handle
the problem of the modern political community, which he discerned, in closer relation to the empirical evidence as we know
it today.

To do so it will be useful to summarize the preceding discussion. Medieval political life consisted in struggles for power among
more or less autonomous jurisdictions, whose members shared
immunities and obligations based on an established social hierarchy and on a fealty relation with a secular ruler consecrated
by a universal church. By the middle of the eighteenth century
this pattern had been replaced by a system of oligarchic rule, in
which the king exercised certain nation-wide powers through his
appointed officials while other important judicial and administra-

tive powers were pre-empted on a hereditary basis by privileged status-groups and the "constituted bodies" in which they were represented. In contrast to both patterns modern Western societies are characterized by national political communities, in which the major judicial and executive functions are centralized in the hands of a national government, while all adult citizens participate in political decision-making under conditions of formal equality in the more or less direct election of legislative (and in some cases executive) representatives. Centralization, on the one hand, and formally equal political participation, on the other, have given rise to the duality between government and society discussed above in theoretical terms.

A further theoretical note is in order here. No one doubts the relevance of the distinction between a feudal order and an equalitarian social structure, which Tocqueville analyzed. In any study of social change we require some such long-run distinction so that we can know whence we came and where we may be going, though distinctions of this kind may be tools of very unequal intellectual worth. But while it is the merit of long-run distinctions that they enable us to conceptualize theoretically significant dimensions of social life (within the same civilization over time or between different civilizations), it also follows that these distinctions will become blurred the more closely we examine social change in a particular setting and in the short-run. The following discussion will suggest some concepts that are designed to "narrow the gap" between the long and the short run and hence reduce to some extent the reliance on deductions which characterized Tocqueville's work. But I doubt that the gap can be closed entirely, because in the short-run we are bound to fall back upon Tocqueville's method of logically deduced possibilities of social change, even if we can go further than he did in comparing actual changes with these artificial benchmarks. Two rules of thumb should be kept in mind, however. One is that this partly inductive and partly deductive study of social change in the short-run should not lose sight of the long-run distinctions, for without them we are like sailors without compass or stars. The other is that this retention of the long-run distinctions imparts a dialectical quality to the analysis of short-run changes. Since we do not know where these changes may lead in the long-run we must keep the possibility of alternative developments conceptually open and we can do this by utilizing the dichotomous concepts so characteristic of sociological theory.[35]

The Problem of the Modern Political Community. Centralization means that such major functions as the adjudication of legal disputes, the collection of revenue, the control of currency, military recruitment, the organization of the postal system and others have been removed from the political struggle in the sense that they cannot be parcelled out among competing jurisdictions or appropriated on a hereditary basis by privileged status-groups. Under these circumstances politics are no longer a struggle over the distribution of the national sovereignty; instead they have tended to become a struggle over the distribution of the national product and hence over the policies guiding the administration of centralized governmental functions.

One unquestioned corollary of such centralization is the development of a body of officials, whose recruitment and policy execution was separated gradually from the previously existing involvement of officials with kinship loyalties, hereditary privileges and property interests.[36] A second corollary of centralization has been a high degree of consensus at the national level. In the political communities of Western nation-states no one questions seriously that functions like taxation, conscription, law enforcement, the conduct of foreign affairs, and others, belong to the central government, even though the specific implementation of such functions is in dispute.[37] The "depersonalization" of governmental administration and the national consensus on the essential functions of government have resulted in national political communities characterized by a *continuous* exercise of central authority. This continuity is not affected by the individuals filling governmental positions or the conflicts of interest among organized groups which affect the legislative process. Accordingly, a national

government of the modern type represents a more or less autonomous principle of decision making and administrative implementation.[38] For Durkheim it was the state which alone could
guarantee the "moral existence" of the individual, and in his
judgment the state was capable of having this effect because it
is "an organ distinct from the rest of society."[39] Presumably,
people as members of a political community regard the overall
jurisdiction of this organ as inviolate, because they believe in the
achievement and orderly revision of an overall reciprocity of rights
and duties, whatever the particular political vicissitudes of the
moment.

In the modern political community consensus (or a workable
reciprocity of rights and obligations) is strongest at this national
level, although as such it possesses an impersonal quality that
does not satisfy the persistent craving for fraternity or fellow-
feeling. But this emergence of a national consensus concerning the
functions of the national government has been accompanied also
by a decline of social solidarity at all other levels of group formation. Classes, status groups and formal associations arise from
the coalescence of social and economic interests, other groups are
formed on the basis of ethnic and religious affiliation: in some
measure these collectivities are reflected in voting behavior. Yet
none of them involves a consensus comparable to the acceptance
by all citizens of the idea that the national government possesses
sovereign authority.

This is not a new issue. From the very beginning of the modern
political community, say, since the great debates of the eighteenth
century, social and political theorists have complained of the loss
of social solidarity, for which the vast proliferation of associations did not appear to be a proper palliative. When writers like
Tocqueville and Durkheim stressed the importance of "secondary
groups", they did so in the belief that such groups could counteract
both the isolation of each man from his fellows *and* the centralization of government. Yet much of this analysis remained at a
level where considerations of policy and an element of nostalgia
merged with considerations of fact, especially in the ever-recurring,

invidious contrasts between traditionalism and modernity.[40] Despite the eminent names associated with it, we should discard this legacy of obfuscation. The "great transformation" leading to the modern political community made the decline of social solidarity inevitable, because (if so complex a matter can be stated so simply) no association based on a coalescence of interests or on ethnic and religious affiliation could recapture the intense reciprocity of rights and duties that was peculiar to the "autonomous jurisdictions" of an estate society. The reason is that in these "jurisdictions," or "law communities" (*Rechtsgemeinschaften*) as Max Weber called them, each individual was involved in a "mutual aid" society, which protected his rights only if he fulfilled his duties. This great cohesion within social ranks was above all a counterpart to the very loose integration of a multiplicity of jurisdictions at the "national" political level. In this respect the absolutist regimes achieved a greater integration through centralized royal administration and the people's loyalty to the king, although the privileges of Church and aristocracy also subjected the ordinary man to the autocratic rule of his local master. Where such privileges replaced the "law communities" of an earlier day, the privileged groups achieved considerable social cohesion. But the people were deprived of what legal and customary protection they had enjoyed through their former, passive participation in the reciprocity of rights and obligations.[41] Modern political communities have achieved a greater centralization of government than either the medieval or the absolutist political systems, and this achievement has been preceded, accompanied, or followed by the participation of all adult citizens in political life (on the basis of the formal equality of the franchise). The price of these achievements consists in the diminished solidarity of all "secondary groups."

This "price" is a by-product of the separation between society and government in the modern political community. Whereas solidarity had been based on the individual's participation in a "law community" or on his membership in a privileged status group possessing certain governmental prerogatives, it must arise now from the social and economic stratification of society aided by the equality of all adult citizens before the law and in the electoral process.[42] On this basis exchange relations and joint actions may develop to the exclusion of "governmental interference" or in quest of governmental assistance or with the aim to achieve representation in the decision making bodies of government.[43] Though it certainly has an impact on the national government, individual and collective action on this basis does not account for the governmental performance of administrative tasks, or, in the larger sense, the continuous functioning of the national political community.

In the societies of Western civilization we should accept, therefore, the existence of a genuine hiatus between the forces making for social solidarity independently of government and the forces accounting for the continuous exercise of central authority in the national political community.[44] This existing pattern is the result of a slow and often painful process. As the central functions of the national government became gradually accepted, organized groups within the society demanded representation in this national political community. Accordingly, "political community" refers not only to the central functions of government and the consensus sustaining them, but to the much more problematic question whether and how the groups arising within the society have achieved a national reciprocity of rights and obligations. For at the beginning of European industrialization in the nineteenth century new social groups were in the process of formation and had yet to learn (in the words of Tocqueville) what they were, what they might be or what they ought to be in the emerging national community of their country.

᪥ IMPLICATIONS FOR A COMPARATIVE STUDY
OF SOCIAL STRUCTURES

During the eighteenth and nineteenth centuries the societies of Western civilization industrialized and became democratic. We should utilize the knowledge gained from this experience as we turn today to a study of the "developing areas" of the non-Western world. This task is difficult because our theories of the "great transformation" in the West have been a part of that transformation. The preceding discussion has separated theoretical reflections on this transformation from a consideration of changes in the institutional structure. While retaining the contrast between medieval and modern society it has discarded the nostalgia so often associated with that contrast. Moreover, the distinction between society and the state proves useful, in view of the institutional duality which exists in this respect in the "developing areas" of yesterday and today.[45] In this concluding section I attempt to reformulate this contrast in general terms so as to facilitate a comparative study of social structures.

My thesis is that for our understanding of "society" and "the state" in the nations of Europe since the French Revolution the third perspective (mentioned above, pp. 225 ff.) is most useful, if it is considered as an analytical framework rather than as the political theory of liberalism. In the utilitarian contrast between the "natural identity" and the "artificial identification of interests," in Durkheim's concern with group integration and state-interference, or, to cite an American example, in W. G. Sumner's distinction between "crescive" and "enacted" institutions we have repeated references to two types of human associations. One of these consists in affinities of interest which arise from relations of kinship, the division of labor, exchanges on the market place and the ubiquitous influence of custom. The other consists in relations of super- and sub-ordination which arise from the exercise of instituted authority and compliance with its commands.[46] The distinction refers to a universal attribute of group-life in the sense that, however interrelated, these two types of human association are not reducible to each other.[47] From an analytical viewpoint it is necessary to consider "society" and "the state" as interdependent, but autonomous, spheres of thought and action which coexist in one form or another in all complex societies, although the separation of these "spheres" is perhaps greatest in modern Western societies.[48]

This distinction lends itself to a comparative study of social structure and the political community. In medieval Europe two types of rule were "competing" with each other as Machiavelli pointed out:

> Kingdoms known to history have been governed in two ways: either by a prince and his servants, who, as ministers by his grace and permission, assist in governing the realm; or by a prince and by barons, who hold positions not by favour of the ruler but by antiquity of blood. Such barons have states and subjects of their own who recognize them as their lords, and are naturally attached to them. In those states which are governed by a prince and his servants, the prince possesses more authority, because there is no one in the state regarded as a superior other than himself, and if others are obeyed it is merely as ministers and officials of the prince, and no one regards them with any special affection.[49]

Government as an extension of the royal household and government based on the fealty between landed nobles and their king and leader thus represented two types of social structure as well as two types of instituted authority.

Again, in the societies of Western civilization at the beginning of the present era this duality between society and the state is reflected in two far-reaching developments, which were eventually followed by a third. A market economy emerged based on contract or the ability of individuals to enter into legally binding agreements, while gradually the exercise of governmental authority was separated from kinship ties, property interests and inherited privileges. These developments occurred at a time when the determination of governmental policies and their administrative implementation were confined to a privileged few, but in the course of the nineteenth century this restriction was reduced and eventually eliminated through the extension of the franchise.

If we consider these developments in retrospect we can summarize their effects on society and the state. The growth of the market economy and the adoption of universal franchise have given rise to interest groups and political parties which mobilize collectivities for economic and political action and thereby "facilitate the interchange between [. . .] the spontaneous groupings of society" and the exercise of authority.[50] On the other hand, the "depersonalization" of governmental functions has accompanied a centralization of legislative, judicial and administrative decision-making and implementation which now facilitates the "reverse interchange" between the state and society.[51] The efficacy of these "interchanges" will vary not only with social cleavages and party-structures as Lipset has shown, but also with the "depersonalization" of government and the propensities of rule-abiding behavior among the people at large. On the whole Western societies are characterized in these respects by a cultural tradition which ensures the containment of group-conflicts within a gradually changing constitutional framework and a high degree of probity in office and popular compliance with rules.

But it is well to remember that even in the West the centralization of government and the democratization of political participation have on occasion created a hiatus that has proved more or less intractable. A striking case in point is the Italian experience with its "negative interchange" between society and the state, as exemplified by the "anti-government organization" of the Sicilian *Mafia* which among other things "protects" the society against governmental encroachments.[52] An extreme case like this serves to remind us that all Western societies have had to grapple with a duality that ranges from the juxtaposition of private concerns and public obligation in each citizen to the juxtaposition of solidary groups based on common interest and appointed officials acting in their authorized capacity.

To say that this hiatus is bridged by "interchange" from both sides only refers to the end-product of a prolonged balancing of group interests and formal institutions. In this respect the great issue of the nineteenth century had to do with the question whether and on what terms the disfranchised masses would be accorded the rights of national citizenship. The resolution of this issue could be eased *or* complicated through the continued confinement of politics to an elite of notables and through the natural as well as legal obstacles standing in the way of effective political organization. The balance between oligarchic resistance and popular political activation, the rise of central power and the later development of citizenship on the part of all adults posed the problem of how a new reciprocity of rights and obligations could be established *at the national level.* In several European countries this problem of a national political community came to the fore at a time when the "new" social classes of employers and workers began to make their bid for political participation and to cope as well with the problem of their reciprocal rights and obligations. Ideological controversy was at its height as these and other groups became capable of organized action and as long as they were denied their bid for equal participation in the political process. But as one after another social group has been admitted to such participation, they have in each case used their newly acquired power to pressure the national government into enacting and implementing a guaranteed minimum of social and cultural amenities. In this way a new reciprocity of rights and obligation among conflicting groups could be established by the "welfare state" at the national level and where this has occurred ideological controversy has declined.[53]

Clearly, this statement does not apply to the "developing areas" of the world today. Instead, we are witnessing ever new attempts to mobilize the "voiceless masses" through democratic ideas and institutions and at the same time provide these masses with the amenities of the "welfare state." This means that all the cleavages of the social structure are given political articulation simultaneously, while governments attempt to plan economic development and provide the minimum essentials of a welfare state. If it be argued that such governments possess only an uncertain authority and relatively little experience, it will be answered that they must make the attempt nevertheless because only on this basis will the mobilized masses positively identify themselves with the new nation.[54] As a consequence of these conditions, ideological controversy is waged with unparalleled intensity, while political leaders attempt to establish a functioning governmental machinery and protect it against the continuous assault of politics and corruption.

In their increasing preoccupation with the "developing areas" of Asia and Africa since World War II Western scholars have had to grapple with the applicability of concepts which had been formulated in the context of Western experience. Since a simple application of these concepts is found wanting the further we move away from that experience, it is not surprising that some scholars decide to discard them altogether in an attempt to comprise in one conceptual scheme all political phenomena, Western and non-Western. The spirit of this enterprise is best conveyed in the following quotation:

> . . . the search for new concepts . . . reflects an underlying drift towards a new and coherent way of thinking about and studying politics that is implied in such slogans as the "behavorial approach". This urge towards a new conceptual unity is suggested when we compare the new terms with the old. Thus, instead of the concept of the "state", limited as it is by legal and institutional meanings, we prefer "political system"; instead of "powers", which again is a legal concept in connotation, we are beginning to prefer "functions", instead of "offices" (legal again), we prefer "roles"; instead of "institutions", which again directs us toward formal norms, "structures"; instead of "public opinion" and "citizenship training", formal and rational in meaning, we prefer "political culture" and "political socialization". We are not setting aside public law and philosophy as disciplines, but simply telling them to move over to make room for a growth in political theory that has been long overdue.[55]

In this approach politics is to be considered a universal phenomenon and as a result the distinction is discarded between societies which are "states" and those which are not, and that just at a time when leading groups in the "developing areas" are directly concerned with the organization of states and the development of governmental machinery.[56]

The preceding discussion has suggested that this is not a new problem even in the Western experience. The rise of absolutism promoted the centralization of governmental power. But no one reading the record of mercantilist regimes can avoid the conclusion that the efficacy of that central power was often as doubtful as

is the efficacy of highly centralized governments in the "developing areas" of today. Again, the destruction of many intermediate
centers of authority and the consequent emancipation of the
individual through the institution of a national citizenship inevitably accentuated all existing cleavages within the society by mo-
bilizing the people for the electoral struggle over the distribution
of the national product. Thus, centralization of power and national citizenship gave a new meaning to the duality between
society and the state, as Tocqueville observed long ago, and as we
have occasion to witness in the "new nations" of the non-Western
world today. It may be true, of course, that some of these "developing areas" are confronted by such an accentuation of cleavages
within their social structure and such a lack of effective government, that anarchy reigns, or a political community can be established only by a "tutelary democracy" or a dictatorship as safeguards against anarchy. Meagre resources in the face of staggering
tasks, the relative absence of a legal and governmental tradition,
and the precipitous political mobilization of all the people greatly
increase the hazards even aside from the additional aggravation
of the Cold War. The efforts to cope with these difficulties certainly command our earnest attention and no one can be sure of
their outcome. In view of that uncertainty we should try to
preserve the insights we have gained from the Western experience
into the social foundations of government *and* the political foundations of society. If a balance is achieved between these perspectives we may be able to utilize our knowledge for an understanding of contemporary social change.

TRADITION AND MODERNITY RECONSIDERED

ᵃᵍ ELEVEN ᵍᵃ

Modernization is a term which became fashionable after World War II. It is useful despite its vagueness because it tends to evoke similar associations in contemporary readers. Their first impulse may be to think of "the modern" in terms of present-day technology with its jet-travel, space exploration, and nuclear power. But the common sense of the word "modern" encompasses the whole era since the eighteenth century when inventions like the steam engine and the spinning jenny provided the initial, technical basis for the industrialization of societies. The economic transformation of England coincided with the movement of independence in the American colonies and the creation of the nation-state in the French revolution. Accordingly, the word "modern" also evokes associations with the democratization of societies, especially the destruction of inherited privilege and the declaration of equal rights of citizenship.

These changes of the eighteenth century initiated a transformation of human societies which is comparable in magnitude only to the transformation of nomadic peoples into settled agriculturalists some 10,000 years earlier. Until 1750 the proportion of the world's active population engaged in agriculture was probably above 80 per cent. Two centuries later it was about 60 per cent, and in the

An earlier version of this essay was published in *Comparative Studies in Society and History*, IX (April 1967), pp. 292–346. Published by Cambridge University Press.

industrialized countries of the world it had fallen below 50 per cent, reaching low figures like 10 to 20 per cent in countries that have a relatively long history of industrialization. In Great Britain, the country which pioneered in this respect, the proportion of the labor force engaged in agriculture reached a low of 5 per cent in 1950.[1]

Wherever it has occurred, the modernization of societies orig- inated in social structures marked by inequalities based on kinship ties, hereditary privilege and established (frequently monarchical) authority. By virtue of their common emphasis on a hierarchy of inherited positions, pre-modern or traditional societies have certain elements in common. The destruction of these features of the old order and the consequent rise of equality are one hallmark of modernization; hence the latter process shows certain uniformities. These changes in the social and political order were apparent before the full consequences of the industrial revolution were understood. As a result, most (if not all) thinkers of the nineteenth century

> . . . exhibit the same burning sense of society's sudden, convul- sive turn from a path it had followed for millennia. All manifest the same profound intuition of the disappearance of historic values—and, with them, age-old securities, as well as age-old tyrannies and inequalities—and the coming of new powers, new insecurities, and new tyrannies. . . .[2]

And, as Professor Nisbet adds, "sociology in Europe was developed almost wholly around the themes and antitheses cast up by the two revolutions and their impact upon the old order." [3] We owe many insights to this intellectual tradition. Yet today there are indications that this perspective gave an oversimplified view of traditional societies, of modern societies, and of the transition from the one to the other. Oversimplification resulted from ide ological interpretations of the contrast between tradition and modernity, and from undue generalizations of the European expe- rience. Today, a more differentiated and balanced analysis of modernization should be possible; the following discussion is presented as a contribution to that end.

Its first part deals with an aspect of the history of ideas. The

rise of industrial civilization in Europe engendered a new conception of society, invidious contrasts between tradition and modernity, and a theory of social change culminating in the work of Karl
Marx and most recently in a revival of theories of social evolution.
My effort will be to show how our conceptual vocabulary in studies
of modernization developed. The second part offers a methodological critique of this intellectual tradition and proposes an alternative conceptualization of the contrast between tradition and modernity. In the third part I shall attempt to develop a comparative
approach to the study of modernization and illustrate it by application to the field of social stratification.

⚮ PERSISTENCE AND CHANGE OF IDEAS ABOUT MODERN SOCIETY

A New Perspective. The sense that the late eighteenth century
represents a hiatus in intellectual perspective as well as a new
departure in the history of Western civilization is as common
among scholars as is the related connotation of the term "modern"
among people at large. Before the 17th and 18th centuries, the
world of nature and of man was conceived as an emanation of
Divine providence. Since then our thinking has been restructured
in all fields of learning. As the idea of God became fused with
that of Nature, the concept of the universe created at the beginning of time was gradually replaced by the idea of an infinitely
various and endlessly active process of evolution. The idea was
applied in parallel fashion to our understanding of the growth of
knowledge, to a new conception of God as in Schelling's *Natur-
philosophie,* and to an ethical interpretation of world history as in
Kant's view that "all the excellent natural faculties of mankind
would forever remain undeveloped" if it were not for man's
nature with its quarrelsomeness, its enviously competitive vanity,
and its insatiable desire to possess or to rule.[4] Here was one of
many schemes by which thinkers of the late eighteenth and early
nineteenth centuries linked the fractious qualities of individual
men with the concept of a self-contained regularity or lawfulness
attributed to the social world. While Kant used a teleological

construction in this respect, classical economists like Adam Smith asserted that man's propensity to truck, barter, and exchange one thing for another gave rise to actions obeying an impersonal law of supply and demand. By their actions in society individuals conform to a regularity or higher principle without intending to do so. Phrases like the "end of nature" or the "invisible hand" by which Kant and Smith referred to such a higher principle may be considered a survival of an earlier belief in Divine providence or a harbinger of later concepts of "society" and "economy." In any case, they helped to usher in a new view of the social world as an impersonal structure possessing attributes or principles of its own.

The following discussion presents an historical sketch of ideas about the new, industrial society in the making—with special emphasis upon the effects of that society on different social classes. My purpose is to show that the invidious contrast between tradition and modernity is the master-theme which underlies a great diversity of topics and influences our understanding of modern society to this day.

In his *Essay on the History of Civil Society*, first published in 1767, Adam Ferguson attributed the progress of a people to the subdivision of tasks (Adam Smith's division of labor) which at the same time improves the skills of the artisan, the profits of the manufacturer, and the enjoyment of consumers.

> Every craft may engross the whole of a man's attention, and has a mystery which must be studied . . . Nations of tradesmen come to consist of members, who beyond their one particular trade, are ignorant of all human affairs, and who may contribute to the preservation and enlargement of their commonwealth, without making its interest an object of their regard or attention.[5]

Ferguson's discussion formulates ways of looking at modern society which have become commonplace. The division of labor necessarily restricts the understanding of those who specialize. In so doing it also increases their productivity and the wealth of the country. Hence, private ends, a lack of conscious concern for public welfare, and public benefits go together. This laissez-faire doctrine is joined, as Marx already noted, with a theory of social action, at least in rudimentary form. By only attending to his business, each man is distinguished by his calling and has a place to which he is fitted. In Ferguson's view the differences among men are a direct outcome of the habits they acquire in practicing different arts: "Some employments are liberal, others mechanic. They require different talents, and inspire different sentiments." [6] In his assessment of these corrolaries of specialization, Ferguson combines the older conventional wisdom with insight into the emerging problems of modern society. The old division of society into a leisured, ruling minority and the bulk of a working population is reflected in his view that social rank depends on the work men do. Those who must eke out a mere subsistence are degraded by the "objects they pursue, and by the means they employ to attain it." Those who belong to the superior class are bound to no task and are free to follow the disposition of their mind and heart.

At the same time, Ferguson is well aware that increasing division of labor exacts a price. The ends of society are best promoted by mechanical arts requiring little capacity and thriving best "under a total suppression of sentiment and reason." [7] Another Scotch philosopher, John Millar, points out that art and science improve with the division of labor, but produce in the worker, who is employed in a single manual operation, a "habitual vacancy of thought, unenlivened by many prospects, but such as are derived from future wages of their labor, or from the grateful returns of bodily repose and sleep." [8] The human cost of manual labor under modern conditions of production is thus a theme from the very beginning of industrial society.

It was argued that this human cost is inevitable. The burdens of the laboring classes under the new conditions are simply a new form of the ancient division of society into masters and servants. Attempts to relieve these burdens only decrease the wealth of a country and hence ultimately aggravate the lot of the workers themselves.[9] Yet this advocacy of the traditional rank-order under new conditions did not in the long run match the significance of another, much more critical body of opinion.

Conservative and Radical Critiques of Industry. In many parts of Europe men of letters viewed the discrepancies between rich and poor with alarm and with a feeling that the destitution of the people represented a new phenomenon and an increasing threat to the social order. The ideas of a growing bifurcation of society into two opposed classes, as well as the doctrine of pauperization, which are familiar to modern readers from the writings of Karl Marx, were in fact beliefs spelled out by many European writers during the seventeenth and eighteenth centuries.[10] Their sense of crisis is reflected in ideas about social rank which sought to take account of the changes occurring in industrializing societies. To exemplify these ideas, indicate something of their ubiquity, and show how strongly they have influenced modern social thought, I shall take examples from Germany, France, and the United States. These judgments about social ranks in a period of transition reflect both the experience and moral sense of men of different social ranks and the moral sense with which the writer himself regards the role of different groups in that transition.

The first example contrasts a conservative and a humanist critique of commercialization in late eighteenth-century Germany. In 1778 the publicist Justus Möser complained in an article on "genuine property" that in his day the German language had lost its capacity to designate an owner's inalienable relationship to his property.[11] At one time ownership of land included associated rights in addition to those of proprietorship, such as the right to hunt, to vote in the National Assembly, and others. These rights had been known by distinctive terms which gave a clue to the specific rights an owner enjoyed in perpetuity. He could sell or otherwise dispose of the land itself, but he could not divest himself of these rights any more than a purchaser of the land could acquire them. Möser's critique of the change of language is thus at the same time an indictment of moral decay resulting from an easy transfer of property. The relationship between an owner and his property is in his view a source of personal identification and social stability. These are ensured as long as ownership of land confers on the proprietor rights and privileges which give him status in the community and can be obtained by inheritance only, not by purchase.

The humanist critique of commercialization looks at first glance very similar to that of Möser. Trading as well as the ownership and care of property undermine an individual's integrity, because his every act and thought turns on considerations of money and economic expediency. Man is ruled by that which should be at his service. In his novel, *Wilhelm Meisters Lehrjahre*, originally published in 1796, Goethe expresses this view when he writes:

> What can it avail me to manufacture good iron whilst my own breast is full of dross? Or to what purpose were it to understand the art of reducing landed estates to order, when my own thoughts are not in harmony? [12]

But Goethe's hero goes on to relate this anticommercial view to the conflicting personal values of the *Bürger* and the aristocrat. The latter, he claims, has polished manners in keeping with his lofty social position, but he does not cultivate his heart. The *Bürger* cannot make such pretensions. For him the decisive question is not "who he is," but what "discernment, knowledge, talents, or riches" he possesses.

> He must cultivate some individual talent, in order to be useful, and it is well understood that in his existence there can be no harmony, because in order to render one talent useful, he must abandon the exercise of every other.[13]

Thus, to Goethe's hero, the aristocrat has high social standing but a cold heart, the *Bürger* may gain distinction by his attainments, but only the artist is in a position to pursue the "harmonious cultivation of his nature." [14]

The resemblance between these views does not go beyond their common rejection of commerce. Möser looks backwards towards a society characterized by a rank-order of privilege and subordination based on land and the rights associated with landownership. He attributes to that society not merely stability, but ideal qualities of mind and feeling such that man's relations to his fellows are in harmony and his work an adequate outlet for his capabilities.

Against this mythical image of the past, the commercialization of property appears as a decay of civilization. During the century and a half which followed, Möser's praise of inalienable, prescriptive rights was associated again and again not only with the benevolence of paternalistic rule but also with the warmth of personal relations and the sense of personal belonging, made possible by a closely knit, hierarchic community. Against this benign view of tradition Goethe's hero defines his own position by referring to the empty, cruel heart which goes together with the polished manners of the aristocrat. Bourgeois man stands forth by virtue of his *individual achievements,* which represent greater personal worth than the ease and poise which are an unearned, and hence unmerited, byproduct of inherited privilege. The *Bürger* may lack manners, but at least his individual attainments establish his personal worth. Yet like Ferguson and Millar, Goethe's hero decries the stultifying effects of specialization. The merit of achievement is only relative, for in the ordinary man it is the result of a one-sided development; all his other capacities are sacrificed so that he may be useful. This praise of man's protean capacities—here put as the artist's many-sided cultivation of his personality—has been associated ever since with the radical critique of bourgeois civilization. An emphasis on achievement as an attribute of that civilization entirely misses this inherent ambiguity of the value of individual striving and creativity.

The two opinions from late eighteenth century Germany reflect a provincial setting in which economic change was slow, but in which imaginative men witnessed more rapid changes taking place in England and France. The classic document portraying this response is Goethe's epic poem *Hermann und Dorothea* in which the upheavals of the French revolution are commented on from afar and in eloquent contrast to the well-being and contentment of an average, small-town *Bürger* family.[15] Under these circumstances reflections about the effects of commerce on the ranks of society tended to be abstract, whether they consisted of nostalgic references to the past or humanistic celebrations of personal values.

With the advance of commerce and industry during the first

decades of the nineteenth century, critical reflections on the impact of these changes continued. Invidious contrasts between tradition and modernity, and between one-sided utility and individual creativity, were elaborated and reiterated, but with more direct attention to the nature of work. Across an interval of more than two generations one may compare the contrast between Möser and Goethe's hero in Germany with the contrast between de Bonald and Proudhon in France. According to Bonald, industry has increased the material wealth of the country, but it has also produced civic unrest and moral decay. Members of families employed in industry

> . . . work in isolation and frequently in different industries. They have no more acquaintance with their master than what he commands and what little he pays. Industry does not nourish all ages nor all sexes. True, it employs the child, but frequently at the expense of his education or before he is sufficiently strong for such work. On the other hand, when a man has reached old age and can no longer work, he is abandoned and has no other bread than that which his children may provide or public charity bestow. . . .
>
> The [industrial laborer] works in crowded and sedentary conditions, turns a crank, runs the shuttle, gathers the threads. He spends his life in cellars and garrets. He becomes a machine himself. He exercises his fingers but never his mind. . . . Everything debases the intelligence of the industrial worker. . . .[16]

In this critique of industry emphasis on the incapacities resulting from specialization are related to the industrial worker and his family. To eke out a subsistence, members of the family are dispersed, they work in isolation, and have no human relationship with their employer. In addition, industry as a whole abuses the child and gives no care to the aged.

In all these respects agricultural work is superior. On the land the different classes work alongside each other and at the same tasks; hence there is no social isolation between them. Children and old people are cared for and productively employed at tasks commensurate with their capacities. Agricultural work is not only healthy in contrast with industrial, it also furthers the intelligence of the peasant or farm laborer. Cultivation of the land demands attention to varied tasks, furthers neighborly cooperation, and through contact with natural processes lifts thought "to that which endows the earth with fertility, gives us the seasons, makes the fruit ripen." [17] Where Möser emphasizes the social stability and moral worth achieved by inalienable property rights, Bonald emphasizes that similar values are inherent in the nature of agricultural work. For Bonald as for Möser, the material benefits of commerce and industry are not worth the price in human values they exact. For both, the traditional social order represents sociability, meaningful human relations, proper security, care for young and old, and man's opportunity to develop his capacities to the full. In all these respects industry is said to fail; its sole accomplishment is the increase of wealth.

This critique of industry is not very different at points from Proudhon's radical attack upon the new industrial order (1846). Proudhon also believes that specialization has a destructive effect upon the individual. Like Bonald he deplores the helplessness of industrial workers and feels that the advance of technology turns men into machines.[18] But their common critique of industry and praise of agriculture shows that Proudhon and Bonald see the same facts in entirely different terms. For example, both agree that agricultural work is many-sided, not one-sided and stultifying like industrial work. Yet Proudhon finds this praiseworthy as the foundation of individualism, not like Bonald as the foundation of neighborliness and cooperation. Proudhon sees the agricultural proprietor as the solitary man who tills the soil for his family and does not depend upon the assistance of others; "never have peasants been seen to form a society for the cultivation of their fields; never will they be seen to do so." This ability to maintain his family by his own efforts makes the peasant into the ideal anarchist. By contrast Proudhon emphasizes that certain industries "require the combined employment of a large number of workers" involving subordination and mutual dependence. "The producer is no longer, as in the fields, a sovereign and free father of a family; it is a collectivity." [19] Thus, for Proudhon, industry is the locus of an enforced collectivism, mutual dependence, and subordination, whereas agriculture enhances freedom and individualism. He favors agriculture, because he rejects the "hierarchy of capacities" as a "principle and law" of social organization.[20] By contrast, Bonald accepts inequalities among men as a fact of nature which is merely recognized by society. For him the distinction between industry and agriculture turns on the question of which activity furthers the community, not the individual; and in this respect industry enhances human isolation, while agriculture promotes human solidarity.

Clearly, both writers structure the evidence to suit their purpose. For Proudhon neighborly assistance disappears from the agricultural community, because he searches for a personification of the individualism which is his ideal; for Bonald the harshness of the peasant's struggle with nature, and the human abuse which is endemic in close neighborly relations, disappear in the roseate image of the community modelled on the familial pattern. Much the same is true of the two views of industry. For Proudhon the *relative* freedom of the industrial worker does not exist, and he ignores the fundamental subordination of the farm laborer in agriculture. Bonald, on the other hand, sees the worker's freedom only in its negative side, as human isolation in contrast to a benign solidarity in agriculture. One man idealizes agriculture as the bulwark of traditional society; the other, however, mistakenly, as the principal means of leveling social differences, decreasing mutual dependence, and enhancing individual freedom. Transparent as they are, such ideological constructions have had a profound influence upon the contrast of tradition and modernity down to the present.

To these examples I wish to add a brief reference to similar arguments on this side of the Atlantic. They will show something of the persistence of the intellectual tradition I am characterizing, even under quite divergent conditions. In the United States conservative views like those of Bonald had been openly expressed during the first decades following the Declaration of Independence. During the 1830's the public disclosure of these views became politically inexpedient, even among New England conservatives.[21]

At the same time, the belief in inequality became a matter of deep conviction in the Southern states. In this regional context, conservative views became linked with an attack on Northern industrialism, on the one hand, and a defense of slavery, on the other. In his *Sociology for the South*, George Fitzhugh denounced men of property who are masters without the feelings and sympathies of masters, engaged in the selfish struggle to better their pecuniary condition and hence without time or inclination to cultivate the heart or the head.[22] Fitzhugh reiterates the theme which is already familiar to us: that the division of labor may make men more efficient, but also confines the worker to some monotonous employment and makes him an easy prey of the capitalist, who considers him solely in monetary terms.[23] In this setting the standard argument against the division of labor, which Marx emphasized so much, is used in a defense of slavery! For Fitzhugh contrasts the moral destitution of the free laborer, hated by his employer for the demands he makes and by his fellow workers because he competes for employment, with the moral attainments and domestic tranquillity of the South, which is founded upon the parental affection of the masters and child-like obedience of the slaves.[24]

This view is strangely echoed by Orestes A. Brownson, a New England cleric and radical Christian who had identified himself with the workers in the 1830's, and later became converted to Catholicism. Brownson contrasts the moral degradation imposed on both employers and workers with the benign features of paternalism:

> Between the master and the slave, between the lord and the serf, there often grow up pleasant personal relations and attachments; there is personal intercourse, kindness, affability, protection on the one side, respect and gratitude on the other, which partially compensates for the superiority of the one and the inferiority of the other; but the modern system of wages allows very little of all this: the capitalist and the workman belong to different species, and have little personal intercourse. The agent or man of business pays the workman his wages, and there ends the responsibility of the employer. The laborer has no further claim on him and he may want and starve, or sicken and die, it is his own affair, with

which the employer has nothing to do. Hence the relation between the two classes becomes mercenary, hard and a matter of
arithmetic.[25]

This language is not essentially different from that of the *Communist Manifesto*; it culminates in the contrasting images of
exploiters and exploited, of haughty indifference, on the one hand,
and injured hostility, on the other. Brownson even uses Marx's
symbol of the worker as an appendage to the machine, though
the phrase may have been common among social critics of the
mid-nineteenth century.

The examples I have cited suggest that from the late eighteenth
century on men of letters were made deeply anxious by what they
considered the moral crisis in human relations, brought on by the
coming of industry. Karl Mannheim has pointed out that critics
like Möser and Goethe or Bonald and Proudhon were deeply
divided in their political views but nonetheless based their opposition to industrial society on grounds that are similar to quite a
striking extent.[26] Industry depends upon the division of labor and
as that division progresses men cease to be masters of the machines
they use and instead become their victims. As labor becomes more
monotonous, workers are increasingly deprived of the opportunity
to develop and apply their human faculties. More generally, the
specialized development of one capacity in the interest of productivity and commercial success entails the atrophy of many or most
other capacities. Industrial man appears as the counterimage of
Renaissance man, and that at all levels of the social structure. At
the same time, commercialization loosens the ties which bind men
to each other. Freedom from paternal rule and the hierarchy of
rank is obtained for the individual, but only at the price of fraternity. The ties among men lose their basis in sentiment and
the sense of moral obligation and come to depend on economic
interest alone. As equals men compete with one another rather
than cooperate and as employers and workers they strike bargains
solely in terms of material advantage.

These themes have been standbys of social thought for almost
two centuries.[27] They owe their profound emotional appeal to the

invidious linkage between the transition to an industrial society and the decline of the two ideas of individual creativity and human fraternity. Obviously, conservatives attribute both of these values to a largely symbolic, hierarchic order of the past, but implicitly (and sometimes explicitly also) radical critics of industrial society use the same clichés. By their incorporation in the work of Karl Marx these clichés have become a dominant influence on modern thought because of the unique way in which Marx combined the sense of moral crisis described above with his claim that his approach represented a scientific study of society. Reflections on Marx's theories are legion; here they will be pursued only to the extent that the reader can form an independent judgment of the differences between the presentation which follows and the most influential treatment of social classes in the process of modernization.

The Marxian Perspective. "The history of all hitherto existing societies is the history of class struggles." The *Communist Manifesto* begins with this sentence, yet Marx's work as a whole does not contain a sustained analysis of social classes. The third volume of his lifework, *Das Kapital,* breaks off after four paragraphs of a chapter which was to be devoted to this topic. The paradox has often been commented on, but it is more apparent than real. Probably Marx had said what he had to say about social classes, since it is not difficult to summarize his views.[28]

For Marx classes are but the agents of social change, their ultimate determinant is the organization of production. His reasons for this assumption go back to early philosophical considerations. Today these would be considered existentialist in the sense of inferences derived from basic exigencies of human experience. Men cannot live without work; they also propagate their kind and hence enter into the social relations of the family. Men use tools to satisfy their needs; as needs are satisfied, new needs arise and techniques of production are improved. The proliferation of needs and improved techniques put a premium on cooperation based on some division of labor, for divided labor increases productivity.

How labor is divided depends on the organization of production, specifically on the distribution of property in the means of production. It is, therefore, the position the individual occupies in the organization of production, which indicates to which social class he belongs.

In the unfinished chapter on class, Marx distinguishes between wage-laborers, capitalists, and landlords which form the three great classes of capitalist society, and he emphasizes the "infinite distinctions of interest and position which the social division of labor creates *among* workers as *among* capitalists and landowners." [29] In a complex society, individuals are distinguished from one another in a great many ways, even when they belong to the same class. Thus, individuals who depend entirely upon wage-labor may still differ greatly in terms of income, consumption patterns, educational attainment, or occupation. Efforts to ascertain class membership by grouping people in terms of their similar share in the distribution of material goods, skills, and prestige symbols, only produces statistical artifacts in Marx's view. For him "class" refers to a process of group formation in which people are united despite the "infinite distinctions of interest and position" which divide them.[30] To be sure, a shared position in the organization of production is the necessary condition of a social class. But only the experience gained in making a living, and particularly the experience of economic and political conflict, would prompt workers, capitalists, or landowners to develop a consciousness of class and become united in action. Marx specified a number of conditions that would facilitate the process. Where communication of ideas among individuals in the same class position is easy, repeated economic conflicts will lead to a growth of solidarity and a sense of historic opportunities. Profound dissatisfactions arise from an inability to control the economic structure in which the ruling class curtails the economic advance of the group and subjects it to exploitation. In Marx's view a social class becomes an agent of historical change when these dissatisfactions lead to the formation of political organizations. A fully developed class is a politically organized group, capable of overcoming in action the distinctions of interest and rank that divide it.

This interpretation of social class was based in the first instance on Marx's detailed observations of the English labor movement which he himself systematized in the following words:

> Large-scale industry assembles in one place a crowd of people who are unknown to each other. Competition divides their interests. But the maintenance of their wages, this common interest which they have against their employer, brings them together again in the same idea of resistance—*combination*. Thus combination has always a double aim, that of putting an end to competition among themselves, to enable them to compete as a whole with the capitalist. If the original aim of resistance was that of maintaining wages, to the extent that the capitalists, in their turn, unite with the aim of repressive measures, the combinations, at first isolated, became organized into groups, and in face of the unity of the capitalists, the maintenance of the combination becomes more important than upholding the level of wages. This is so true that English economists have been astonished to observe the workers sacrificing a substantial part of their wages in favour of the associations, which in the eyes of the economists were only established to defend wages. In this struggle—a veritable civil war—all the elements for a future battle are brought together and developed. Once arrived at this point the association takes on a political character.[31]

This conception of class as a group gradually emerging to self-consciousness and political organization was at once analysis and projection. Analysis in so far as Marx systematized his observations of emerging working-class movements in England from the late eighteenth to the middle of the nineteenth century.[32] Projection in so far as Marx generalized from this analysis, both with regard to the formation of classes in the past (for example, that of the bourgeoisie under feudalism) and with regard to the development of a revolutionary working class in the future. The latter views applied not only in England but in all countries undergoing a capitalist development such as England had experienced since the eighteenth century. We should understand what gave Marx confi-

dence in predicting that the struggle he analyzed would eventuate
in a revolutionary overthrow and reconstitution of society.

The first point to be mentioned is Marx's acceptance and
dramatic elaboration of the ideas briefly described above. Like
Ferguson, Millar, Möser, Goethe, Bonald, Proudhon, Fitzhugh,
Brownson, and a host of others, Marx was deeply impressed by
the moral crisis which capitalism had wrought in man's relation
with his fellows and his work. To cite Marx's views on alienation
at this point would be to repeat many of the moral reflections
cited earlier (albeit in more Hegelian language) and what has
been elaborated in a thousand ways by critics of modern society
since his day.[33] But Marx's elaboration of widely shared beliefs
assumed special significance. The reason is, I believe, that for him
the mounting alienation of men was part of an economic process
in which repeated and severe depressions together with the capitalists' restrictive practices would create an ever-increasing discrepancy between the forces and the organization of production,
or, in simpler language, between the economy's capacity to satisfy
human needs and the satisfaction of needs which is actually
achieved. Marx's economic analysis seeks to support this interpretation, and in view of the importance he attached to it he had no
reason to feel that he had neglected the analysis of social class.
His analysis is distinguished from the many other writers who
developed similar themes by the belief that he had proved man's
alienation to be a symptom of the *final* phase of "pre-history."

Secondly, Marx welcomed the technical and economic changes
which were revolutionizing the old order but, he saw the difference
between then and now in a very special way. Earlier epochs were
marked by "manifold gradations of social rank," but the modern
era tends towards a simplified antagonism between bourgeoisie
and proletariat. While this prediction has not stood the test of
time, it is of a piece with his view that all previous history is pre-
history. Never before had the social world been stripped of all its
traditional practices and religious beliefs; only now had it been
revealed as it really is, capable of a rational ordering by men who
have come within reach of satisfying all their desires. Eventually,

the classless, communist society of the future would establish both a true fraternity among men and on that basis an opportunity for each to develop and apply his capacities. Though he refused to speculate about this new order, Marx was emphatic that world history was nearing its decisive turning point. In his view man's productive potential had become so great that the deprivations of inequality and hence the substitute gratifications of religious beliefs had become obsolete. For the same reasons human relations have become transparent so that the social order is now capable of being "consciously regulated by freely associated men in accordance with a settled plan." [34] Marx believed that this equalitarian society of the future would bring about a complete break with the past, leading to a cessation of class struggles and freeing men from being at the mercy of circumstances not of their own choosing. For the first time in history men had the opportunity to establish a rationally planned society. To cope with this world historical turning point, Marx devoted his life work to an analysis of those cumulative conditions, endemic in the capitalist organization of production, which would bring about the final revolutionary struggle.

The third point to be noted is the famous paradox of Marx's determinism. On the one hand, he predicted that the contradictions inherent in capitalism would inevitably produce a class-conscious proletariat and a proletarian revolution. On the other, he assigned to class-consciousness, to political action, and to his own scientific theory a major role in bringing the inevitable about. The paradox is "resolved" once it is remembered that for Marx the eventual revolution as well as the subjective actions and ideas which help bring it about, are consequences of the mounting contradictions between the potential for productivity and the actuality of exploitation. Marx "explains" the eventual political maturity of the proletariat, the constructive role of "bourgeois ideologists" as well as his own scientific theory as creative responses to contradictions which are the product of capitalism.

For Marx "all hitherto existing societies" encompass the "prehistory" of class struggles as contrasted with the classless society of the future. All his attention is focused on analyzing the last phase of that pre-history. Accurate, scientific understanding of this phase is indispensable for guiding political action, but capitalism also jeopardizes all constructive and undistorted use of intelligence. Between these two positions there is a fundamental ambivalence. Marx wants to know, accurately and dispassionately, but since his own theory of the socio-historical foundation of knowledge casts doubt upon the possibility of a science of society, he also wants to make sure that the knowledge gained will play a constructive role in human affairs. Science "shows" that alienation must get worse, and the worse alienation gets, the more it will function as the historical precipitant of the truth which will make men free. Accordingly, his lifelong work on economic theory, cast in a scientific mold, and his moral vision of an ultimate revolt against alienation, support each other. In his view a moral and world-historical crisis is upon us because we face the prospect of immiseration—relative deprivation and the loss of fraternity and creativity—just when an era of plenty has become possible. Marx's confidence in the contribution of his own theory was greatly reinforced by this coincidence—as he saw it—of a moral and an historical crisis. But at the same time we should note that this combination of a moral concern,. a world-historical perspective, and a scientific stance greatly reinforced the invidious contrast between tradition and modernity as the foundation of a scholarly understanding of modernization.

Critique of an Intellectual Tradition. The interpretations of modernization which I have reviewed, established an intellectual tradition which has remained predominant down to the present. By their frequent reformulations of the contrast between tradition and modernity, such writers as Ferdinand Toennies, Emile Durkheim, and, among American sociologists, Charles Cooley, Robert Park, Robert Redfield, and Talcott Parsons have strongly reinforced that tradition. For all their diversity, these and related writers have the idea in common that "traditional society" and "modern society" constitute two systems of interrelated variables. The tendency is (1) to treat societies as "natural systems," (2) to search for the "independent variables" which—if altered initially —will cause changes in the related, but dependent variables in the process of transition from one type to the other, (3) to conceive of the transition as one of declining tradition and rising modernity, and, finally, (4) to assume that social change consists of a process that is internal to the society changing.

Marx was probably the most prominent expositor of this approach. England was the first country to industrialize. In Marx's view she exemplified the "laws of capitalist development" which he had analyzed in *Capital*. Writing in 1867, in his preface to the first edition of that work, Marx declared England to be the classic ground of the capitalist mode of production. He explained his analytic procedure in the following terms:

> The physicist either observes physical phenomena where they occur in their most typical form and most free from disturbing influence, or, wherever possible, he makes experiments under conditions that assure the occurrence of the phenomenon in its normality. In this work I have to examine the capitalist mode of production, and the conditions of production and exchange corresponding to that mode. Up to the present time, their classic ground is England. That is the reason why England is used as the chief illustration in the development of my theoretical ideas. If, however, the German reader shrugs his shoulders at the conditions of the English industrial and agricultural laborers, or in optimist fashion comforts himself with the thought that in Germany things are not nearly so bad, I must plainly tell him, "*De te fabula narratur!*"
>
> Intrinsically, it is not a question of the higher or lower degree of development of the social antagonisms that result from the natural laws of capitalist production. It is a question of these laws themselves, of these tendencies working with iron necessity towards inevitable results. The country that is more developed industrially only shows, to the less developed, the image of its own future.[35]

Marx made these predictions on the assumption that the same organization of production generates everywhere the same or similar transformations of social classes and the political structure. As an empirical proposition, this assumption is misleading because it treats societies as if they were entirely self-contained structures, each evolving in terms of given, internal tendencies. Actually, once industrialization had been initiated in England, the technical innovations and the institutions of the economically advanced country could be used as a model to move ahead more rapidly than England had while mitigating or even avoiding the problems encountered by the pioneering country. I shall consider this possibility in more detail below; Marx himself also noted it but did not think it significant. Instead, he declared that his analysis of the advanced country could help to "shorten the birth-pangs" of similar developments in other countries. By making social change in the long run entirely dependent upon the economic structure, Marx precluded recognition of the importance which international emulation and governmental initiative, nationalism and the diffusion of ideas could have in countries that followed in the wake of English industrialization. It is a measure of the surpassing influence of the intellectual and ideological tradition culminating in Marx that basically similar assumptions still inform many recent and empirical studies of "development." Some of these studies will here be considered in brief review in order to substantiate this statement.

Studies of social change typically operate with a "before-and-after" model of the society under consideration. The earlier and the later social structure are distinguished by two sets of dichotomous attributes, and one has great difficulty in resisting the view that each set constitutes a generalizable system of interrelated variables. On that assumption societies can be classified according to the degree to which they exhibit one set of attributes rather than another, resulting in a rank-ordering of countries in terms of their relative modernization. An example of this procedure appears in Daniel Lerner's well-known study *The Passing of Traditional Society*.

The great merit of Lerner's study consists in its candid use of Western modernization as a model of global applicability. For Marx, England, as the country that is "more developed industrially," exemplified universal "laws of capitalist development";

for Lerner, Western modernization exhibits "certain components and sequences whose relevance is global." [36] He recognizes that the "North Atlantic area" developed first and rather gradually, while other countries came later and sought to develop more rapidly, but like Marx before him he dismisses this as a secondary consideration. As Lerner sees it, the central proposition is that in the process of modernization, then as now, four sectors or dimensions are systematically related to one another, namely urbanization, literacy, media participation, and political participation.[37] The author appears to regard the following statement as central to his purpose:

> The book seeks to explain *why* and show *how* individuals and their institutions modernize together. It denies a unique role to "human nature" or to "social determinism." Having no taste for beating dead horses, we do not even acknowledge these as issues, but go directly to a "behavioral" perspective. To wit: social change operates through persons and places. Either individuals or their environments modernize together or modernization leads elsewhere than intended. *If new institutions* of political, economic, cultural behavior *are to change in compatible ways, then inner coherence must be provided* by the *personality matrix* which governs individual behavior. We conceive modernity as a participant style of life; we identify its distinctive personality mechanism as empathy. Modernizing individuals and institutions, like chicken and egg, reproduce these traits in each other.[38]

This vigorous assertion of a behavioral perspective rejects a psychological as well as a social determinism, but is still beholden to the conventional contrast between tradition and modernity.[39]

Professor Lerner puts the case in a conditional form which is hard to reconcile with his emphasis on behaviorism. He says in effect that either new institutions change in compatible ways (meaning, presumably, ways similar to the Western model), or modernization leads elsewhere than intended (meaning, presumably, in directions differing from the Western model). He believes that the high association between urbanization, literacy, media participation, and political participation in modern societies points to an underlying, systemic coherence (which Lerner calls "the

participant style of life") such that societies can be ranked in
accordance with their degree of tradition, transition, or modernity.
Yet I do not believe there is any assurance that once initiated
economic growth will be self-sustaining or that new institutions
will change in "compatible ways." Professor Lerner himself asserts
that "traditional societies exhibit extremely variant "growth" patterns; some are more urban than literate, others more media
participant than urban." [40] Such "deviations from the regression
line" are due to the fact that "people don't do what, on any
rational course of behavior, they should do" [41]—hardly a consistent,
behaviorist position. And although Professor Lerner recognizes
that in the emerging nations people have not done what according
to his model they should have done, he still considers his model
validated by events.[42]

In recent years Lerner's work has been followed by a whole
series of studies which compile attribute-checklists on which the
countries of the world are ranked by the degree to which they
approximate the characteristics of Western industrial societies.[43]
Such an approach rests on an application of evolutionary theory
to very short time-periods despite earlier warnings that this is
highly questionable even from the standpoint of evolutionism.[44]
If the earlier and the later social structure constitute two generalizable systems of interrelated variables, it may be logical to
infer that the transition from one to the other is characterized
by admixtures of attributes from both, and over time by a decline
of attributes from the first and a rise of attributes from the second.
Yet attribute-checklists of the relative modernization of countries
do not easily avoid the implication that change once initiated
must run its course along the lines indicated by the "Western
model," and that in the transition to modernity all aspects of the
social structure change in some more or less integrated and simultaneous fashion. Only on these assumptions is it reasonable to
ignore the timing and sequence of modernization of countries in
their several and distinct aspects.

Just this timing and sequence can make a crucial difference for
the success or failure of the effort to modernize.[45] In his introduc-

tion to Lerner's book, David Riesman notes that the transitional individual is defined as one who attends to the mass media, but cannot read, to which he appends the disturbing question: "What will a society look like which is dominated by such 'post-literate' types?" [46] This question points to the possibility of a "transition" of long duration, a contradiction in terms which arises from evolutionist assumptions and leads to a questionable nomenclature about "developing" or "transitional" societies which may never become developed enough to be called modern. Related questions are raised as efforts at modernization in these so called developing countries have led, or are leading, to changes of sequence and timing as compared with the Western model. For example, in many European countries the franchise was extended rather slowly, while in many newly independent countries universal suffrage has been adopted all at once.[47] Such a difference is ignored where countries are merely ranked at one point in time in terms of the degree to which the franchise has been extended to the adult members of their populations. The matter is not necessarily improved by the addition of another index, say that of literacy, because such data—even if they were reliable—would not reveal the level of education attained by the population. More generally, checklists of attributes of modernization are not likely to yield reliable inference, if—without regard to sequence and timing—their several items are interpreted as indices of approximation to the Western model.[48]

Nevertheless, comparative studies of modernization necessarily rely on the Western experience when they *construct* developmental sequences. This practice becomes hazardous only when past experience is used to extrapolate to the future of "industrializing" societies. In their book, *Industrialism and Industrial Man*, Clark Kerr and his associates explicitly emphasize that the "logic of industrialism" they have constructed involves abstractions on the assumption that the "transition stage of industrialization" has passed. Indeed, they emphasize that tendencies *deductively* arrived at (albeit by illustrative reference to the experience of "developed" societies) are not likely to be fully realized in the *actual* course of history. Yet, throughout the volume phrases recur which betray a confusion between these two levels of analysis. On the same page tendencies are alternately called logically constructed and inherent (33–34), emphasis on the contrast between abstraction and history is followed by the assertion that "the empire of industrialism will embrace the whole world" (46), industrialization is called an "invincible process," while the uncertainties of the future are relegated to variations of length and difficulty in the transition or to the several types of past industrializations (19–20, 47 ff.). Perhaps the most arresting feature of this deterministic view of the future is that the "industrialism" of the whole world is predicated, not on the organization of production as in Marx, but on the initiating or manipulating actions of five different elites whose capacity to "industrialize" whole societies is simply assumed. Exceptions, delays, and what not are seen as deviations which "cannot prevent the transformation in the long run," [49] while neither the possibility of failure nor that of unprecedented types of industrialization is given serious consideration. Seldom has social change been interpreted in so managerial a fashion, while all contingencies of action are treated as mere historical variations which cannot alter the "logic of industrialism." Though the recognition of alternate routes to industrialization is a distinct improvement over the unilinear evolutionism of the study by Lerner, the authors abandon the gain they have made when they predict one system of industrialism for all societies in much the same way as Marx predicted the end of class struggles and of history for the socialist society of the future.

✎§ AN ALTERNATIVE APPROACH TO TRADITION AND MODERNITY
The studies cited above may suffice as examples of the persistent influence of an intellectual tradition which originated with the emergence of industrial society in Western Europe. Necessarily, studies of social change rely on historical experience. But Western modernization has been accompanied throughout by a particular intellectual construction of that experience, prompted by moral or reforming impulses often presented in the guise of scientific

generalizations. Theories of social evolution have had a particularly important influence in this respect in that they tend to use historical experience to construct contrasting ideal types of tradition and modernity and then use that contrast to make contingent generalizations about the transition from one to the other. In this section, I turn to a critical assessment of evolutionism and to the proposal of an alternative.

Ideal Types Are Not Generalizations. At a minimum, considerations of change involve two terminal conditions so that the word "change" refers to the differences observed before and after a given interval of time. Without knowing in what respects a later social structure differs from an earlier one, we would not know what changes to look for and explain. Accordingly, we are obliged to characterize the earlier (pre-modern) and later (modern) social structure by two lists of mutually disjunctive attributes.

The abstract formulation of such contrasts can be as seriously misleading, however, as the moral evaluations reviewed earlier. The point may be illustrated by using Talcott Parsons' contrast between universalism and particularism as attributes of modernity and tradition, respectively. In Europe traditional society, though particularistic in many respects, involved a major element of universalism through the Christian faith and the institutions of the Catholic church; in China traditional society involved other universalist elements through Confucianism and the examination system; even in India, where Hindu religion and the caste system fostered an extreme particularism, the basic cultural themes of that particularism spread throughout the sub-continent. Evidently, "particularism" characterizes traditional societies only in some respects, while in others it is combined with a "universalism" which may be as different as Catholicism, Confucianism, or the ideas of reincarnation. Hence, the disjunctive characterization of "tradition" and "modernity" by such abstract terms as "particularism" and "universalism" exaggerates and simplifies the evidence, as Max Weber pointed out in his discussion of the ideal type. Such characterization says nothing about the strength or generality with which any one attribute is present. Also, the use of one or several abstract terms to characterize either tradition or modernity tends to mistake labelling for analysis, since apparently societies vary not only in the degree but also in the kind of their universalism or particularism. At this abstract level it is quite probable that no society is without some elements from both ends of the continuum, leading some writers to use phrases such as "the modernity of tradition" or "the tradition of the new." [50]

These problems are compounded when we turn from the contrast between social structures "before and after" to a consideration of change from the one to the other. In this respect we can be guided by Max Weber's own discussion of this problem:

> *Developmental* sequences too can be constructed into ideal types and these constructs can have quite considerable heuristic value. But this quite particularly gives rise to the danger that the ideal type and reality will be confused with one another.[51]

Accordingly, ideal-typical constructs of development must be sharply distinguished from the actual sequence of change, but this distinction is "uncommonly difficult" to maintain. For in *constructing* a developmental sequence we will use illustrative materials in order to make clear what we mean and hence may confuse the sequence of types with a course of events.

> The series of types which results from the selected conceptual criteria appears then as an historical sequence unrolling with the necessity of a law. The logical classification of analytical concepts on the one hand and the empirical arrangements of the events thus conceptualized in space, time, and causal relationship, on the other, appear to be so bound up together that there is an almost irresistible temptation to do violence to reality in order to prove the real validity of the construct.[52]

The hazards referred to by Weber have not gone unnoticed. Following the tradition of Maine, Durkheim, and Toennies, Robert Redfield compared four contemporary communities in Yucatan. He emphasized that his method was not to be recommended to those wishing to raise questions as to whether changes in any of the characters are related to or conditioned by changes in any of the others, and as to how they are interrelated. . . .

But while Redfield clearly stated that he had not answered such questions, he nevertheless supposed that

> there is some natural or interdependent relation among some or all of the characters in that change with regard to certain of them tends to bring about or carry with it change with respect to others of them. . . .[53]

In thus seeing his problem as one of causal "relations among variables" Redfield unwittingly disregards his own warning concerning the disjunction between ideal types and historical sequences. We should try to understand why this confusion is as widespread as Weber already suggested.

In operating with a "before-and-after" model of the society under consideration, one has difficulty in resisting the view that the two sets of attributes characterizing the earlier and the later social structure constitute generalizable systems of empirically interrelated variables. But in adopting this view, we entirely ignore that the specification of a list of attributes is ideal-typical and hence simplifies and exaggerates the evidence. If we are to avoid mistaking ideal types for accurate descriptions, we must take care to treat the clusters of attributes as *hypothetically*, not as actually, correlated. We need these clusters to distinguish between social structures, we illustrate them by historical examples, but these are still abstractions, constructs that should be used as tools of analysis. Redfield, for example, suggested that the relative isolation and the occupational homogeneity of communities coexisted in many instances and was perhaps causally related. No doubt there are many isolated communities with relatively little division of labor, but degree of isolation and occupational differentiation are correlated very imperfectly, and over time communities have varied independently in both dimensions. If one wishes to get away from the artificiality of ideal types one can visualize two overlapping frequency distributions in which either isolation or occupational heterogeneity are treated as the dependent variable. Such distributions would approximate historical reality more closely, whereas the ideal type of an isolated and homogeneous community is best employed as a *suggestion* for the investigation of isolated communities with considerable division of labor, or non-isolated communities that are relatively homogeneous.[54]

That these cautions are often ignored may be illustrated by reference to two related and quite common lines of reasoning. One of these has to do with the notion of "prerequisites." Beginning with the contrast between tradition and modernity (in one of its many versions) the analyst takes all the basic traits of modernity to be prerequisites of modernity, a procedure which implies that regardless of time and place all countries must somehow create all the conditions characteristic of modernity before they can hope to be successful in their drive for modernization. But

> Obviously, some of the factors listed are not prerequisites at all, but rather something that developed in the course of industrial development. Moreover, what can be reasonably regarded as a prerequisite in some historical cases can be much more naturally seen as a product of industrialization in others. The line between what is a precondition of, and what is a response to industrial development seems to be a rather flexible one.[55]

Such a distinction could be made only if the specific processes of industrialization are analyzed. However, causes and consequences tend to become confused, if instead a uniform process is assumed such that countries entering upon industrialization at a later time will repeat in all essentials the previous industrialization of some other country.[56]

Another line of reasoning involves an undue generalization of a limited historical experience (rather than working back from present characteristics to necessary prerequisites). For example, the decline of kinship ties and the concomitant rise of individualism were aspects of Western modernization. Today we are learning how many meanings and exceptions were in fact compatible with this overall tendency, though these are quite properly ignored when we construct an ideal typical sequence. But, rather than using that sequence as an analytical tool to show how and why actual historical developments deviate from it, we use it to make contingent predictions about the future of "developing" societies. To be sure, no one is likely to say simply that these societies will develop; he states instead that they will not develop unless kinship ties decline. There are at least three things wrong with this procedure: (a) it ignores the exaggerations and simplifications which went into the ideal type in the first place, and hence blinds us to the role which kinship ties and collectivism played in the modernization of Western Europe; (b) it also blinds us to the possible ways in which kinship ties and collectivism might be, or might be made, compatible with the modernization of other areas (tacitly we have misused the ideal type as a generalization); (c) it diverts attention from the very real possibility that modernization may never arrive at modernity, so that terms like "development" or "transition" are misnomers when applied to societies whose future condition may not be markedly different from the present.

These critical considerations do not stand alone. Several writers have examined the assumptions of the intellectual tradition which I have characterized and have also found it wanting. Elkan and Fallers have examined specific local developments, like the mobility of wage labor in Uganda, and shown in what respects this experience differs from the mobilization of a work-force in early industrial England.[57] In his discussion of the changing craft traditions in India, Milton Singer has questioned the assumption of a uniform recapitulation of the process of industrialization, and the tendency to employ the concept of "tradition" as a generalization rather than an ideal type.[58] Similar questions have been raised and systematized by Neil Smelser, who distinguishes clearly between ideal-typical constructs of, and generalizations about, social change, and who emphasizes that the latter are difficult to achieve. Even if the "vicious circle of poverty" is broken, subsequent changes of the social structure will vary with the pre-industrial conditions of the country, the particular impetus to develop, the path which modernization takes, the significant differences that persist in developed economies, and finally with the impact and timing of dramatic events.[59] As Wilbert Moore has pointed out in a similar context:

> The manner in which history prevents its own replication creates difficulties in generalizations that will unite historical and contemporary experience and deal with the diversity that optional paths of change introduce. . . . In addition to minimum, required sequences and results, what is needed, and is mostly not at hand, is the construction of limited-alternative or typological sequences where total generalization is improper.[60]

Strictures of this kind are of rather recent date, though Gerschenkron had already expressed them in 1952. They have not replaced the dominant, evolutionary approach to the comparative study of modernization.

The impetus to generalize even where generalization is improper, derives not only from the intellectual tradition I have traced. It derives also from the desire to put policy directives on a "scientific" basis, and from the indispensability of ideal types in studies of social change. The fact that time and again the distinction between tradition and modernity has been oversimplified does *not* mean that we can dispense with that contrast entirely. Studies of social change are not possible without a "before-and-after" model of the social structure in question.

The Contrast Restated. The contrasts between pre-modern and modern social structures may be formulated along the several dimensions that are conventionally distinguished in the analysis of social structures. The problem of the causal interrelation among these dimensions is one of empirical research which cannot be replaced by logical deductions, as long as the evidence argues against the assumption of one uniform process of modernization. Nor is it proper to turn the two attribute-checklists by which we may distinguish tradition from modernity into two systems to which certain properties are imputed. For in this way a set of separate or separable attributes is transformed into the structural propensities of a collective entity. Such reification is closely related to the moralism and scientism that has characterized many reactions to industrialization, as we have seen.

Smelser has suggested the concept of "structural differentiation" as a basic analytical tool for the study of modernization. He sees the transition between tradition and modernity as involving changes in several spheres of life. In technology there is a change from simple techniques to the application of scientific knowledge, and in agriculture from subsistence farming to the commercial production of agricultural goods. In industry human and animal power are replaced by power-driven machinery. And with industrialization the population shifts increasingly from the farm and the village to the city and the economic enterprises located in it. These processes of change consist of, or are accompanied by, structural differentiation in the sense that in each case an earlier structure that combines several economic functions is eventually replaced by a later one characterized by greater specialization, or by a greater division of labor as the older writers called it.[61] Smelser is careful to point out that, while these processes may occur jointly, it is also true that each has occurred independently of the others. He emphasizes that structural differentiation in such other realms as the family, religion, and stratification is not simply a consequence of "industrialization" alone; it has occurred in "pre-industrial" areas, for example as a result of colonialism.[62] In this way, "structural differentiation" provides us with a summary designation of the contrast between "tradition" and "modernity" without prejudging the systemic character of either term. The designation allows us to investigate the causal relation between different processes of structural differentiation.

Such investigations are needed, if we are to employ the indispensable, ideal-typical contrasts between "before" and "after" without imparting a spurious, deductive simplicity to the transition from one to the other.[63] A case in point is the cultural ramifications of changes in economic institutions which are properly conceived as instances of structural differentiation. The German historian Otto Brunner has shown that in the pre-modern societies of

Europe the facts of economic life were typically incorporated in treatises on estate or household management, in which instructions concerning agriculture and the keeping of accounts occurred side by side with advice on the rearing of children, marital relations, the proper treatment of servants, and related matters. Technical and economic considerations were very much a part of the moral approach to human relations. This juxtaposition belongs to a world in which the household or estate typically constituted a unit of production, consumption, and social life, whereas the separation of morals from economics belongs to a society in which the family household is typically separated from the place of work.[64] In this case, the change in economic institutions and in intellectual outlook may be considered related instances of "structural differentiation," but it should be clear that this relationship is complex and requires detailed investigation.

Such investigations can help us avoid the ambiguities which remain at the abstract level, because terms like differentiation are not as neutral and unequivocal as one would wish. Following Durkheim, Smelser notes that modernization involves a "contrapuntal interplay" between differentiation "which is divisive of established society, and integration which unites differentiated structures on a new basis." [65] Here certain cautions are needed to avoid the value-implications of the evolutionary model. A traditional economy is characterized by little differentiation between economic and familial activities *within* more or less self-sufficient households or estates. *Within* the family and the community a high degree of integration exists in the sense, say, that the authority of social rank and religious norms are accepted without question. But we must take care not to commit the romantic fallacy so prominent in the intellectual tradition I have surveyed.

First, high integration and lack of differentiation *within* the family and community go together with much fragmentation *among* them. Second, within families and communities everyday life is one of "proud and cruel publicity," as Huizinga puts it. Since all activities occur within the household or estate, personal interdependence is not only benign but also extremely coercive; it fosters sentimental attachments but also the most intense personal hatreds; it encourages fraternity but also mutual surveillance and suspicion. When structural differentiation is divisive of the established family households, not only their group solidarity and stable norms (integration of established society) are disrupted, but also their lack of privacy, their personalized cruelties and oppressions from which no member of the household could previously escape. This disruption of the household as one form of integration goes hand in hand with integration between households through increased interdependence. It is also accompanied by increased differentiation *within* these structures—increased privacy and freedom from personal coercion. A modern economy is characterized, therefore, by the separation of family household and workplace (structural differentiation) and by increased interdependence of the family with the market or of workers in the factory (integration on a new basis). Only assiduous attention to the liabilities and assets of each structure can avoid the ideological implications of the ideal-typical contrast between tradition and modernity. Otherwise, we merely nurse the discontents of industrial society by contrasting the liabilities of the present with the assets of the past.

To avoid this pitfall, it is useful to summarize the preceding discussion in explicit contrast to the received conventions of sociology. Social structures may be distinguished by the solidarities they achieve. Typically, traditional societies achieve intense solidarity in relatively small groups isolated from one another by poor communication and a backward technology. These groups create for their individual participants an intensity of emotional attachment and rejection which modern men find hard to appreciate and which they would probably find personally intolerable. Typically, modern societies achieve little solidarity in relatively small groups and by virtue of advanced communication and technology these groups tend to be highly interdependent at an impersonal level. In this setting individual participants experience an intensity of emotional attachment and rejection at two levels which hardly exist in the traditional society, namely in the nuclear family at its best and its worst, and at the national level where personal loyalties alternate between being taken for granted in ordinary times and moving up to fever pitch during national crises or other direct confrontations with alien ways of life.

Analogous considerations apply to the invidious personification of modernity and tradition. We saw that the stultifying effects of the division of labor became a major theme of social philosophers from the beginning of industrialization. Generations of writers have reiterated the theme with different contrasting images of man ranging from "the aristocrat" and "the medieval craftsman" to the several versions of "the Renaissance man" of protean capacities who has been the daydream of intellectuals from Goethe's Wilhelm Meister and Baudelaire's *Dandy* to Herbert Marcuse's "Multi-dimensional Man." [66] This romantic utopia of intellectuals in an era of industrialization must be taken seriously indeed, since the ideal images of a culture affect the changing social structure. But the idea of unlimited creativity by "the individual" or "the people" is as much a chimera as is that of a womb-like security and warmth in human relations attributed to a bygone age. These are projections of the discontents of intellectuals with a civilization that induces in them an intense ambivalence between elitism and populism—a point to which I return in the following discussion.

The contrast between tradition and modernity may be recast accordingly. It is probably true that traditional societies are characterized by universally accepted cultural norms. But this goes together with the subservience of men of letters to the church and to private patrons, and with the prevalence of illiteracy in the general population. It is, therefore, not accidental that terms like "ideology," and "intellectuals" originated in Europe during the eighteenth century, when traditional beliefs were challenged, men of letters were emancipated from their previous subservience and literacy increased along with printed materials and a market for literary products. The universal cultural norms of traditional society also go together with a low level of productivity and communication and with a consequent fragmentation of the social structure in economic, legal, and political terms. One implication of this fragmentation is the prevalence of force and fraud and of jurisdictional disputes among a large number of solidary groups which depend for their cohesion not only on common norms but also on the imperatives of self-help and defense.[67] In each of these solidary groups and in the polity as a whole, society tends to be divided sharply between rulers and ruled. Those of gentle birth have a disproportionate share of the wealth, privileged access to positions of formal authority, enjoy sociability, leisure, and culture, whereas the bulk of the population lives in the drudgery of physical labor and in poverty, without access to literacy, culture, or positions of influence, and without recognized means of airing their grievances. In this setting the term "society" is applied only with difficulty, since the people themselves live in fragmented subordination, while their rulers constitute "the society" because they are the persons worthy of note in the country. These attributes may suffice as a contrast-conception for a reformulation of modernity.

It is probably true that modern societies are characterized by relatively few cultural norms that are universally accepted, and this goes together with a relative emancipation of men of letters and a nearly universal literacy in the general population. Structural differentiation in technology and communications has led to high levels of productivity and a high degree of impersonal interdependence. Associated with this interdependence are the attributes of the nation state which were noted earlier. The adjudication of legal disputes, the collection of revenue, the control of currency, military recruitment, the postal system, the construction of public facilities, and others have been removed from the political struggle among competing jurisdictions and have become the functions of a national government. Another and related characteristic of modern society is the process of fundamental democratization by which "those classes which formerly only played a passive part in political life," have been stirred into action.[68] The old division between rulers and ruled is no longer clear-cut, since the ruled have the vote, and the rulers are subject to formal controls at many points. Status distinctions no longer coincide with hereditary privileges. In this setting the term "society" is appropriately applied to all people in a country who constitute that society by virtue of their interdependence and equality as citizens.

The foregoing discussion has attempted to "de-ideologize" the conventional contrast of tradition and modernity. At this general level the contrast holds good for many societies that have undergone a process of modernization. Most "traditional societies" lack means of rapid communication so that the bulk of the population lives in relatively small enclaves isolated from one another. However, if one goes beyond such generalities, one is obliged also to go beyond the simple contrast discussed here. What is true of *all* traditional societies is by the same token not very illuminating about any one of them. For example, a key-feature of the European experience was the tie-in of universal cultural norms with the organization of the Church and hence with the enduring, if rather unstable balancing of centralizing and decentralizing tendencies of government which culminated in the development of representative institutions.[69] In countries like Russia and Japan universal cultural norms came to prevail in a manner that is quite different from this Western-European pattern. The study of social change in these societies would, therefore, require a more specific conceptualization of the contrast between tradition and modernity, in order to be analytically useful. The general contrast here discussed should be only the beginning of analysis, though often it has been mistaken for analysis itself.

Another limitation becomes apparent when one applies these concepts to colonial and post-colonial societies. Can any colonial society be said to have the characteristics of "tradition"? Does it have universally accepted norms? And since the prevailing norms surely do not apply to the subject population, in what sense can one in fact speak of one society? To contrast the past and present social structure one should take account of at least two traditions: the native tradition and the tradition of a dual society created by the colonizing country. Analogous questions apply to the European frontier settlements abroad, as in the United States, Canada, Australia, and New Zealand, but here the native populations were not strong enough to create the problem of a dual society, while the imported culture of the European settlers already represented a major break with the medieval tradition. The point of these comments is to suggest that several models of change are needed and are preferable to any attempt of forcing all types of change into the Procrustes bed of the European experience.

That ideal types of social change are of limited applicability, makes them more, not less useful. Once the weakness of the most general formulation as well as the limitations of the Western-European model are observed, it is then appropriate also to recognize the utility of focussing attention on the area in which the breakthrough to modernity was achieved first. The following analysis attempts to spell out the implications of this breakthrough and to interpret the process of modernization in the light of the foregoing discussion.

✑ MODERNIZATION IN COMPARATIVE PERSPECTIVE

Theoretical Orientation. As European societies approached the "modern era," men of letters came to think about differences of social rank with an awareness of a new society in the making. Although political and ideological rather than scholarly, these ideas about modern society have strongly influenced the concepts with which social scientists have approached the study of modernization. At this point it is useful to state the common denominator of this intellectual tradition in terms of three related tenets.

A. The industrial revolution in England and the contemporary political revolution in France had a profound cultural impact, frequently leading men of letters to formulate pervasive and invidious contrasts between the old and the new social order. As a result "tradition" and "modernity" came to be conceived in mutually exclusive terms, not only as a conceptual aid but also as a generalized, descriptive statement about the two, contrasting types of society. Related to this approach is a conception of each type of society as a social system, characterized by the functional interdependence of its component parts and a balance of forces among them. Hence, "traditional" and "modern" societies appear as two types of societies, each with its own, built-in tendency towards self-maintenance or equilibrium.

B. From the vantage-point of Europe in the late eighteenth and early nineteenth centuries, both revolutions and much of the social change that followed appeared as phenomena that were internal to the societies changing. This mode of explanation goes back to influences emanating from Plato and characteristic of Western philosophy down to the present.[70] In the late eighteenth century this intellectual tradition was reflected in interpretations of the growth of commerce and industry. Specifically, many writers of the period considered the division of labor a major factor in promoting social change. To a man like Ferguson that growth depended ultimately on the subdivision of tasks, which determines the ideas and actions of men, provides the basis for the difference between social classes, and gives rise to political actions.

The view that social change is the product of internal social forces has a certain basis in historical fact, difficult as it is to separate facts from reflections upon them. Most observers of early industrialization thought economic change the primary factor, whether they believed that governmental measures reflect that change, as the radicals did, or that these measures were needed to avert its worst consequences, as the conservatives did. In England, the work of the classical economists enhanced this consensus, because opposition to mercantilist policies argued for less regulation of economic affairs and hence for a secondary role of government. As governmental controls over the economy were reduced, as guild regulations were abandoned, as labor mobility increased along with population, trade, and manufacture, it became very plausible to consider that society and economy possess a "momentum" of their own, while government merely responds to the impact of social forces. At this time, office holding was still a form of property ownership so that the idea of authority as an adjunct of ownership partly described the society. In addition, the industrial revolution first occurred in England; among the continental countries England (along with Holland) lacked an absolutist tradition with its basis in a standing army, and she was also characterized by a more permeable upper class than the countries of the Continent. It was indeed a unique constellation of circumstances which gave new emphasis to the old view that social change is internal to the society changing, that social change originates in the division of labor, and that, consequently, government or the state are products of the social structure. It may be suggested that this intellectual perspective unduly generalizes from a very limited phase of the English experience.

Accordingly, both the intellectual tradition of Europe and the specific historical constellation at the end of the eighteenth century encouraged explanations of social change which emphasize the continuity and interconnectedness of changes *within* society, a tendency which was reinforced when modern nationalism came into its own. As a result a certain lawfulness was attributed to the social structure, while the relative autonomy of government and the impact of external factors upon every society were ignored or minimized. Paradoxically, this perspective also prevailed during a period of absolutist regimes, of European overseas expansion and of world-wide industrialization, when societies were increasingly subject to influences from abroad in contrast to the relative integrity of national societies in Western Europe. This cultural and historical background may help to account for the prominence of explanations which attribute change to a society's internal functional differentiation, such as the increasing division of labor, an observation that can alert us to the limitations of this intellectual perspective without questioning its analytic utility in the proper context.

C. The third tenet asserts that ultimately industrialization will have the same effects wherever it occurs. This follows, or appears to follow, from a combination of assumptions rather loosely linked with the preceding points. Where the causes of social change are conceived as intrinsic to a society, industrialization (and, more vaguely, modernization) is considered to have certain necessary and sufficient prerequisites without which it cannot occur. Conversely, once these prerequisites are given, industrialization be-

comes inevitable. The same reasoning is applied to the consequences of the process. Once industrialization is under way, it has
certain inevitable results. In the long run, modernity will drive out
tradition and fully industrialized societies will become more and
more alike.

The three tenets mentioned here are closely related. Their common basis is the conception of society as a structure arising from
a fixed set of preconditions and characterized by mutually rein-
forcing attributes which make the change of the structure appear
as an inevitable modification of interrelated variables. This conception of society is closely related to the theory of social evolution, though that theory is not of direct concern to the present
discussion. But the three assumptions of social system, internal
differentiation, and developmental inevitability form a coherent
approach to the study of industrialization from which the approach
to be discussed below will now be distinguished.

A. Against the view that tradition and modernity are mutually
exclusive, I wish to maintain that even the two revolutions of the
eighteenth century are best understood as culminations of specific
European continuities, i.e. that "modern" elements were evident
long before the modern era. (By the same token the European
tradition, and English society particularly, had distinctive attributes
not found in other civilizations.) The point may be illustrated
with regard to the bases of social action. Kinship ties, religious
beliefs, linguistic affiliations, territorial communalism, and others
are typical forms of association in a traditional social order. None
of these ties or associations have disappeared even in the most
highly industrialized societies; to this day the relative decline of
"traditional" and the relative ascendance of "modern" solidarities
remain or recur as social and political issues. But some of the old
ties or associations were weakened by the ascendance of Christianity, others by the Renaissance and Reformation, and others still
in the course of the struggles between absolutist rulers and the
estates. It may be recalled that Max Weber's lifework documents
the proposition that Christian doctrine and the revival of Roman
law militated against familial and communal ties as foci of loyalty

which compete effectively with the universal claims of legal procedure and the Christian faith. The ethical universalism of the Puritans and its subsequent secularization were later links in this chain of preconditions. By these prior developments in Western Europe men were freed very gradually for such alternative solidarities as those of the nuclear family, social class and national citizenship. In my view there was indeed a breakthrough to a new historical era, but this was the result of continuities reaching back to classical antiquity, which came to a head in a specific time and place owing to the very particular conditions of English society in the seventeenth and eighteenth centuries. This element of continuity was neglected by men of letters who interpreted the emerging industrial society in terms of a cultural conflict between tradition and modernity. However, in other respects continuity was emphasized.

B. Against the conception of change as intrinsic I wish to maintain that following the breakthrough in England and France every subsequent process of modernization has combined intrinsic changes with responses to extrinsic stimuli,[71] and has involved government intervention as a prominent feature of that process. The modernization of societies is *not* to be understood primarily as a result of internal changes in which governments play at best a secondary role. The great lacunae of the interpretations here opposed is their failure to account for the diffusion of ideas and techniques, the prominent role of government, and the rising tide of nationalism, all of which have accompanied the process of industrialization throughout.

The point is a general one. All complex societies have an internal structure and an external setting. Likewise, all complex societies possess a formal structure of governmental authority which differs from, and is relatively independent of, the group formations arising from the social and economic organization of society. For analytic purposes it is legitimate to separate these dimensions and to neglect one or another of them, if this seems indicated by the problem under consideration. But in the comparative study of modernization, and especially one that focuses attention on problems of social stratification, such neglect seems inadvisable. The influence of modernization on the means of communication is international in scope, so that we should attend to the external setting of societies, even where our primary focus is on changes internal to their social structures. Moreover, the secondary or dependent role of government resulted from very particular historical circumstances, as noted earlier, and should not be considered a general, theoretical proposition. The facts are that intellectuals have played a major role in helping to transform the social structure of backward societies and have done so more often than not in reference to prior economic and political developments abroad. Likewise, government officials have played a major role in the development of economic resources, or have supported and implemented an institutional framework in which such a development became easier. To be sure, these are possibilities, not certainties. But to neglect the rather independent role of intellectuals or governmental officials in the process of modernization is to subscribe to the Marxian view that the international setting, the political structure and the cultural development of a society depend in the long run on its organization of production.

C. Against the concept of industrialization as a largely uniform process of structural change I wish to emphasize the importance of diffusion and of government "intervention" for an understanding of this process. England was the first country to industrialize and in Marx's view she exemplified the "laws of capitalist development." We saw that, in his preface to the first edition of *Capital,* Marx had declared England to be the classic ground of the capitalist mode of production. England was more developed industrially than other countries. As they enter upon the path in industrialization, these other countries will undergo developments comparable to those of England because of the tendencies inherent in the capitalist organization of production. Marx made this prediction on the assumption that the same organization of production generates everywhere the same or similar transformations of social classes and the political structure. As an empirical proposition, this assumption is misleading. Once industrialization had

been initiated in England, the technical innovations and the institutions of the economically advanced country were used as a model
in order to move ahead more rapidly than England had; and also
as a warning so as to mitigate or even avoid the problems encountered by the pioneering country. Marx himself noted this
possibility, but did not consider it seriously. He declared that his
analysis of the advanced country could only help to "shorten the
birthpangs" of similar developments in other countries, for the
capitalist mode of production is governed by the same laws or
inevitable tendencies wherever it occurs.

Again, the point is a general one. Industrialization itself has
intensified the communication of techniques and ideas across national frontiers. Taken out of their original context, these techniques and ideas are adapted so as to satisfy desires and achieve
ends in the receiving country. Certainly, such adaptation is affected
at every point by the resources and economic structure of the
country, but Marx tended to make necessities out of contingencies.
He did not give full weight to the historical traditions which affect
the social structure of every country and with it the capacity of a
people to develop its opportunities. Nor did he consider that this
structure is modified materially by the international transmission
of techniques and ideas and by attempts to control the process and
repercussions of industrialization politically. Against the view that
industrialization has the same effects wherever it occurs, I wish to
maintain the importance of timing and sequence as crucial variables. Once industrialization has occurred anywhere, this fact
alone alters the international environment of all other societies.
There is a sense in which it is true to say that because of timing
and sequence industrialization cannot occur in the same way twice.

Accordingly, studies of modernization should be guided by two
considerations which have been neglected in the past. Although it
is true that certain consequences follow from an increasing division
of labor, these are embedded in the *particular* transition from a
pre-industrial to an industrial structure which distinguishes one
society from another. The social structure of a country's "transitional phase" should, therefore, be a primary focus of analysis

rather than be dismissed as a survival of the past. In addition, modernization, once it has occurred anywhere, alters the conditions of all subsequent efforts at modernization so that "the late arrivals cannot repeat the earlier sequences of industrial development." [72] Both considerations, the significance of the transition and the demonstration effects of "earlier sequences" preclude an evolutionary interpretation of the process of modernization.

The reorientation I propose considers the industrialization and democratization of Western Europe a singular historic breakthrough, culminating a century-long and specifically European development. But modernization brings about special discontinuities by virtue of its expansive tendencies so that the relation between the intrinsic structure and external setting of societies assumes special significance. Thus, the internal, historically developed structure of a country and the emulation induced by economic and political developments abroad affect each country's process of modernization.

Towards a Definition of Modernization.   My objective is to define the term so that it refers to change during a specific historical period. I want to show that throughout the designated period the process of change has certain overall characteristics. At the same time I emphasize the distinction between "modernization" and "modernity." Many attributes of modernization like widespread literacy or modern medicine have appeared, or have been adopted, in isolation from the other attributes of a modern society. Hence, modernization in some sphere of life *may* occur without resulting in "modernity." Uncertainty concerning their future existed in the past history of all presently industrialized countries, just as it exists at present in the so-called developing countries. Recognition of this uncertainty provides a better basis for the comparative study of modernization than the alternative assumption that industrialization has the same prerequisites and results wherever it occurs.

In thus preferring uncertainty to a generalizing, systemic analysis we deal in effect with two approaches to the study of social change. The *retrospective* approach employs a "before-and-after" model of society, i.e. some variant of the contrast between tradition and modernity. Such models are indispensable aids in an analysis of social change, which can start from a knowledge of past changes, though with the cautions suggested earlier. The *prospective* approach cannot employ such a model directly, because it seeks to deal with future contingencies. This second approach may still employ the available "before-and-after" models, but its emphasis will be on the diversity of modern societies in the search for clues to the process of transformation. This is the approach I adopt for the remainder of this discussion.

By "modernization" I refer to a type of social change which *originated* in the industrial revolution of England, 1760–1830, and in the political revolution in France, 1789–1794. One can set the inception of the changes here considered differently, and this is in fact advisable for certain purposes. The expansion of Europe, for example, antedated the late eighteenth century; some aspects of modernization like the diffusion of modern weapons can be traced back to the fifteenth century.[73] Also, particular antecedents of modernization can be traced back very far, as in the instance of printing or of representative institutions or ideas of equality, and many others. Nevertheless, there are reasons of scale which make it advisable to separate the transformations of European societies and their world-wide repercussions since the eighteenth century from earlier economic and political changes. Reference was made at the beginning to the massive transformation of agriculture: the changes leading to a declining proportion of the labor force engaged in agricultural production were initiated in the eighteenth century. Similarly, the fundamental elitism of societies prior to the eighteenth century has been replaced, albeit gradually, by a "functional democratization" (Mannheim), and this change may again be traced to beginnings in the eighteenth century. Also, the distinction between rulers and ruled had coincided roughly with the distinction between the literate and the illiterate. That distinction was beginning to break down in the course of the eighteenth century with the slow spread of both literacy and printed matter.[74] These three transformations of the economic, political, and social order may suffice as an indication that it is useful to treat the eighteenth century as a breakthrough to a new historical era, at any rate in studies of modernization.

The economic and political "breakthrough" which occurred in England and France at the end of the eighteenth century, put every other country of the world into a position of "backwardness." Indeed, the same may be said of the two pioneering countries. The economic transformation of England provided a "model" for France, while the political revolution of France instantly became a major focus of political debate in England. Ever since the world has been divided into advanced and follower societies. With reference to the eighteenth and early nineteenth centuries it is appropriate to have this formulation refer to England and France as the "advanced" countries and all others as follower societies, though even then the statement would have omitted earlier pioneering countries such as Holland or Spain. But since that time the process has ramified much further. Follower societies of the past such as Russia or China have become advanced societies, which are taken as models by the satellite dependencies of Eastern Europe or by some African and Asian countries that have won their independence since World War II. Each of the countries that have come to play the role of "pioneer" with regard to some follower society has a history of externally induced changes, though with the success of modernization the emphasis on this extrinsic dimension may become less salient than it was at an earlier time. Accordingly, a basic element in the definition of modernization is that it refers to a type of social change since the eighteenth century, which consists in the economic or political advance of some pioneering society and subsequent changes in follower societies.[75]

This distinction implies a shift in intellectual perspective. The traditional posture of sociological theory conceives of change as slow, gradual, continuous and intrinsic to the societies changing. This view is more or less appropriate as long as we confine ourselves to the enduring characteristics of a social structure which may aid or hinder the modernization of society. As suggested earlier, it is quite appropriate to the interpretation of change in European civilization, and this was the intent of Max Weber's question concerning the combination of circumstances to which the rationalism of Western civilization can be attributed. However, once the two eighteenth century revolutions had occurred, subsequent social changes were characterized by a precipitous increase in the speed and intensity of communication. Ideas and techniques have passed from "advanced" to "follower" societies, and to a lesser extent from "follower" to "advanced" societies. Within a relatively short historical period there are few societies which have remained immune from these external impacts upon their social structures.[76]

Diffusion of ideas and techniques may be a byproduct of expansion by "advanced" societies, but it occurs even in the absence of expansion because of the economic and political breakthrough in eighteenth century Europe. As Gerschenkron has pointed out, leading strata of "follower" societies respond to this breakthrough by introducing the most modern, capital-intensive technology, in order to close the "gap" as rapidly as possible.[77] This tendency is part of a larger context:

> . . . one way of defining the degree of backwardness is precisely in terms of absence, in a more backward country [or "follower" society as I have termed it here], of factors which in a more advanced country serve as prerequisites of development. Accordingly, one of the ways of approaching the problem is by asking what substitutions and what patterns of substitutions for the lacking factors occurred in the process of industrialization in condition of backwardness.[78]

Such substitutions are believed to represent shortcuts to "modernity." They are part of the effort to avoid the difficulties encountered in the modernization of the "advanced" country. This idea of the "advantages of backwardness" did not originate with Leo Trotsky (as has sometimes been supposed) but was expressed already in the late seventeenth century.[79] All aspects of modernity are up for adoption simultaneously, and it depends upon available resources, the balance of forces in the "follower" society, and the relative ease of transfer which aspects will be given priority. The fact that such items as medication, printed matter, educational innovations, political practices like the franchise are more easily transferred than advanced technology requiring heavy capital investment is another aspect of the divergence of processes of modernization.

Many writers have observed that in this setting of "follower societies" governments play, or attempt to play, a decisive role. The special utility of this perspective for comparative studies of modernization is evident from a recent, comprehensive analysis of English, French, and German industrialization since the eighteenth century. In that context, David Landes states that for the governments of Europe "industrialization was, from the start, a political imperative." [80] Governments may be more or less successful in meeting the imperatives confronting them, and their attempts to do so will be affected throughout by the structural attributes of their societies. Generally speaking, governments attempt to play a larger role in the modernization of relatively backward than of relatively advanced societies. Since this generalization applies to "follower societies" since the eighteenth century, and since most societies of the world are (or have been) in that category, the proposition is perhaps only another aspect of modernization, i.e. of the distinction between the two types of societies. The difference can be of strategic importance for modernization, since "follower societies" are by definition lacking in some of the elements of modernity found in "advanced societies." Where governments manage to provide "functional equivalents" or "substitutes" for these missing elements, they may succeed in reducing the backwardness of their societies, but this presupposes a relatively effective government which is an attribute of modernity or advance. [81]

Here again a major shift in intellectual perspective is implied. The view that government is an integral part of the social structure, but may have the capacity of altering it significantly, is not in the mainstream of social theory. The opposite view is more common that formal government and its actions are epiphenomena, the product of forces arising from the social and economic structure of society. This view is related to the "emanationist" and "evolutionary" intellectual tradition, and was reinforced as noted earlier, by a particular historical constellation in early nineteenth century Europe. Writers of otherwise incompatible political views agreed that government is an epiphenomenon, and this uncommon agreement still influences modern social thought. Yet in studies of modernization it is more useful to consider social structure and government, or society and the state, as interdependent, but also relatively autonomous, spheres of thought and action.[82]

The gap created between advanced and follower societies and the efforts to close it by a more or less *ad hoc* adoption of items of modernity produce obstacles standing in the way of successful modernization.[83] In his discussion of the "new states" that have come into being since World War II, E. A. Shils has characterized these obstacles as a series of internal, structural cleavages:

> It is the gap between the few, very rich and the mass of the poor, between the educated and the uneducated, between the townsman and the villager, between the cosmopolitan or national and the local, between the modern and the traditional, between the rulers and the ruled.[84]

Though such tensions exist in "advanced" states as well, they are far more pronounced not only in the "new states" of today but also in the follower societies of the past which can be ranked, albeit roughly, by their degree of backwardness.[85] The analogy between "backward" or "underdeveloped" social structures then and now should not be pressed too much, since the Continental countries possessed many cultural and economic attributes that were relatively favorable to modernization. But it is also true that during the nineteenth century there was a gradient of backwardness within Europe such that the countries to the East paralleled the "gaps" found in the "new states" of today more closely than the countries of Western Europe.[86]

The analogies or parallels noted here are especially close at the cultural level. For the "gap" created by advanced societies puts a premium on ideas and techniques which follower societies may use in order to "come up from behind." Educated minorities are, thereby, placed in a position of strategic importance, while the always existing gulf between the educated and the uneducated widens still further. In a world marked by gradations of backwardness the comparative study of modernization must attend to the "reference society" that becomes the focus of attention in the follower society, especially for the educated minority that seeks to utilize advanced ideas and techniques in order to "catch up." [87] Here one can see at a glance that a focus on the distinction between advanced and follower societies, and on the communications-effects of modernization, necessarily gives prominence to the role of intellectuals and of education, whereas ideas about social change focusing on the internal division of labor necessarily made much of standard social classes like workers and capitalists. It is as typical of backward countries to invest heavily in education in order to "bridge the gap," as it is for an intelligentsia to develop and engage in an intensified search for a way out of the backwardness of their country.[88] A typical part of this search consists in the ambivalent job of preserving or strengthening the indigenous character of the native culture while attempting to close the gap created by the advanced development of the "reference society or societies." [89]

Four aspects of the process of modernization have been distinguished in the preceding discussion:

a. Reasons of scale suggest that since the eighteenth century the external setting of societies, and especially the "gap" created by the early industrialization of England and the early democratization of France, have imparted to the "degree of backwardness" the special significance of a "challenge" to modernization.

b. In their endeavor to bridge this "gap" leading strata of follower societies typically search for substitutes to the factors which were conditions of development in the advanced countries. Within the limitations imposed by nature and history all aspects of modernity (as developed abroad) are up for adoption simultaneously, and the problem is which of the adoptable items represents a shortcut to modernity. Since the achievement of "modernity" is not assured, it is part of this process that the adoption of items of

modernization may militate against "modernity," or may be irrelevant to it.

c. This common setting of follower societies in turn imparts
special importance to government. Typically, governments attempt
to play a major role in modernization at the same time that they
seek to overcome the sources of their own instability which arise
from the special tensions created by backwardness.[90]

d. The division of the world into advanced and follower
societies, together with the relative ease of communication, put
a premium on education as a means to modernization which is
more readily available than the capital required for modern technology. Education and modern communications also encourage
the development of an intelligentsia and a cultural product which
—as Wilhelm Riehl noted as early as 1850—is in excess of what
the country can use or pay for.[91] This recurrent phenomenon is
reflected in a mushrooming of efforts to overcome the backwardness of the country by attempts to reconcile the strength evi-
denced by the advanced society with the values inherent in native
traditions.

Comparative Aspects of Social Stratification. This concluding
section outlines a program of comparative study dealing with
stratification in relation to modernization. In the past that study
has contrasted tradition and modernity in "either-or" terms and
emphasized changes internal to the society studied and largely determined by the division of labor. The present analysis emphasizes
the continuity of social change insofar as the contrast between a
social structure then and now is an artifact of conceptualization.
But modernization may have a disrupting effect on changing patterns of stratification, due to the hiatus between advanced and
follower societies. Governmental intervention is another possible
source of discontinuity, since authority structures are relatively
autonomous. In other words: although social change is a continuous process, it is often affected by factors conventionally considered extrinsic to the social structure. In a process of modern-

ization relations among groups are exposed to such "extrinsic" influences, although other aspects of the social structure (e.g. the family) may be less affected in this manner. Typically, the modernization of societies is accompanied by a nation-wide redefinition of rights and duties. Individuals and groups respond not only to the actions and beliefs of others, but also to the images of such group-relations derived from prior developments in their reference-society. The following discussion attempts to show that these general points bear directly on the study of social stratification.

The simplified contrast between tradition and modernity shows us that medieval society was ruled by a landowning aristocracy and capitalist society by a bourgeoisie owning the means of production. If one conceives of the transition from tradition to modernity as the decline of one set of attributes and the rise of another, one gets the simple picture of a declining aristocracy and a rising bourgeoisie. Possibly Marx has contributed more than anyone else to this conception. His interpretation of the bourgeoisie as the collective, historical agent which "created" the revolutionizing effect of modern industry, has produced a tendency to read a "rising bourgeoisie" back into the last thousand years of European history.[92] The broad effect of this tendency has been to make the merchants of pre-eighteenth-century Europe into direct precursors of nineteenth-century industrial entrepreneurs and to fasten upon them a corresponding degree of striving and social protest, when in fact they fit quite well into the social structure of feudal Europe. The effect is also to antedate the decline of the aristocracy by some centuries in order to provide room for the rising bourgeoisie.[93] But the changes of social stratification in the course of industrialization do not present the simple picture of a declining aristocracy and a rising bourgeoisie. In most European countries the social and political pre-eminence of pre-industrial ruling groups continued even when their economic fortunes declined, and the subordinate social and political role of the "middle classes" continued even when their economic fortunes rose. In Europe this pattern applies rather generally to the period of transition to an industrial society. Here is how Joseph Schumpeter puts the case with reference to England, while pointing out that in modified form the same applies elsewhere:

> The aristocratic element continued to rule the roost *right to the end of the period of intact and vital capitalism*. No doubt that element—though nowhere so effectively as in England—currently absorbed the brains from other strata that drifted into politics; it made itself the representative of bourgeois interests and fought the battles of the bourgeoisie; it had to surrender its last legal privileges; but with these qualifications, and for ends no longer its own, it continued to man the political engine, to manage the state, to govern. The economically operative part of the bourgeois strata did not offer much opposition to this. On the whole, that kind of division of labor suited them and they liked it.[94]

In the modernization of Europe, aristocracies retained political dominance long after the economic foundations of their high status had been impaired and after alternative and more productive economic pursuits had brought bourgeois strata to social and economic prominence. The "capacity to rule" obviously varied among the several aristocracies, as did the degree to which other strata of the population tended to accept their own subordinate position. In Europe, these legacies were eroded eventually, but only after the transition to an industrial society was affected by the general pattern to which Schumpeter refers. This pattern of a continued political dominance by traditional ruling groups even under conditions of rapid modernization reflects an earlier condition of the social structure, when families of high social and economic status had privileged access to official positions while all those below the line of gentility were excluded. Pre-modern European societies were characterized by a vast number of status-differences and clashes of interest of all kinds, but by only "one body of persons capable of concerted action over the whole area of society."[95] That is, a tiny, possessing minority of the well-born was capable of concerted action and hence constituted a class, while the whole mass of unorganized and, under these conditions, unorganizable persons were set apart by their common lack of access to positions of privilege. Accordingly, European societies conformed at one time to a pattern in which class and authority were more or less synonymous terms, but this identity diminished in the course of modernization and was replaced eventually by the principle of separation between office and family status.[96]

This equalization of access to public employment is an aspect of modernization which makes sense of the assumptions we bring to this field of study. In modern sociology government employment is not considered a basis, or an index, of social stratification. Rather, government employment (even in high positions) is seen as a dependent variable, for example when we examine the distribution of public officials by social origin. Yet this perspective presupposes the separation of government office from the claims a family can make by virtue of its social status and economic position. These assumptions were less applicable in an earlier phase of European societies, and today they are less applicable in the follower societies that are economically backward. There, governments play, or attempt to play, a major role in the process of modernization, as we have seen. Under these conditions government employment provides one of the major bases of social mobility, economic security, and relative well-being. In fact, in economically backward countries the government is one of the major economic enterprises. Hence, government officials partake of the prestige of ruling, even if their positions are humble. And in view of the power at the disposal of government, access to government office and influence upon the exercise of authority are major points of contention—in the personalized sense characteristic of societies in which interaction is kinship-oriented.[97] While this importance of government employment is associated with economic backwardness and the weakness of middle strata in the occupational hierarchy, it can also divert resources from uses which might overcome these conditions. In the absence of viable economic alternatives government employment itself becomes a major basis of social stratification,[98] although these new polities frequently institutionalize plebiscitarian, equalitarian principles in the political sphere. This identification of class with authority differs fundamentally from the elitism of medieval European societies, in which only a privileged minority had access to positions of authority.

The preceding sketch suggests several perspectives for the comparative study of ruling classes in the process of modernization. Within the European context it focuses attention on the continued importance of traditional ruling groups throughout the period of modernization. In this respect, further study would have to differentiate between the relatively accommodating development in England and the much more conflict-ridden development of other, follower societies. At the same time, I have suggested that the modernization of Western societies generally shows a gradual separation between governmental office and family status. The continuity between tradition and modernity remains a characteristic of social change throughout, for even the increasing differentiation between office and family in Western Civilization reveals a variety of historically conditioned patterns. There is no reason to assume that future developments elsewhere will be more uniform. The comparative study of ruling groups in the process of modernization can thus combine the three themes, mentioned above: the continuity of change, the effect of extrinsic influences on the changing role of ruling strata, and the relative separation between government and social structure. The same themes may be combined in the study of other social groups.

The patterns of action and reaction which characterize a society's changing structure come most readily into focus as one moves from the top to the bottom ranks of the social hierarchy. Here one may use the simplified contrast between tradition and modernity as a point of departure, because the rise of political participation by the lower strata is a characteristic feature of modernization. In medieval Europe lower strata fragmented in household enterprises of a patriarchal type existed side by side with a ruling class characterized by wealth, high status and high office. Karl Marx has analyzed this condition effectively with regard to the French peasantry:

> The small peasants form a vast mass, the members of which live in similar conditions, but without entering into manifold relations with one another. Their mode of production isolates them from one another, instead of bringing them into mutual inter-

course. The isolation is increased by France's bad means of communication and by the poverty of the peasants. . . . Each individual peasant family is almost self-sufficient; it itself directly produces the major part of its consumption and thus acquires its means of life more through exchange with nature than in intercourse with society. The small holding, the peasant and his family; alongside them another small holding, another peasant and another family. . . . Insofar as there is merely a local interconnection among these small peasants, and the identity of their interests begets no unity, no national union and no political organization, they do not form a class. They are consequently incapable of enforcing their class interest in their own name, whether through a parliament or through a convention. They cannot represent themselves, they must be represented. Their representative must at the same time appear as their master, as an authority over them, as an unlimited governmental power, that protects them against the other classes and sends them the rain and the sunshine from above. The political influence of the small peasants, therefore, finds its final expression in the executive power subordinating society to itself.[99]

Probably, Marx would have agreed that this analysis of peasants in nineteenth century France applied *mutatis mutandis* to the small craftsmen of the towns, to the manorial estates as well as to the independent peasant freeholds in medieval Europe. The family-based enterprise fragmented the lower strata into as many units of patriarchal household rule over family, servants, and apprentices. On the other hand, the heads of households would join with others in guilds, exercise authority in official capacities, join in the deliberation of representative assemblies, and thus constitute a "class" or "classes" in the sense of groups capable of concerted action.

In this setting "fundamental democratization" refers to the whole process of class-formation by which the fragmentation of the lower strata is gradually overcome, not only to the extension of the franchise. Geographic mobility increases, literacy rises along with the diffusion of newspapers, patriarchial rule and household enterprises decline as conditions of work lead to an aggregation of large masses of people in economic enterprises providing opportunities for easy communication.[100] As Marx noted, these conditions gave rise to trade unions, political organizations, and a heightened class-consciousness due to repeated conflicts with employers. He was too preoccupied with "industry" to note that other groups than workers and other means of communication than direct contact at the place of work might come into play.[101] He was also too committed to an evolutionary perspective with its emphasis on the eventual decline of the aristocracy to note the importance of the beliefs which upheld the legitimacy of the traditional "ruling class" even in an industrializing society. Large masses of people at the bottom of the social hierarchy retained their loyalty to the established order, even in the face of the physical and psychological depriva tions so suddenly imposed upon them.[102]

This loyalty is evident in the numerous references to the real and imaginary rights enjoyed under the old order. Populist protest based on such references meant, among other things, the demand for equality of citizenship. That equality was proclaimed by the legal order and by the appeals to national solidarity in an era of well-publicized empire-building, but in practice it was denied by the restriction of the franchise, the dominant ideology of class-relations, and the partisan implementation of the law. The rising awareness of the working class in this process of "fundamental democratization" reflects an experience of *political alienation,* a sense of not having a recognized position in the civic community of an emerging industrial society. During the nineteenth century nationalism was so powerful in part because it could appeal directly to this longing of the common people for civic respectability, a longing which was intensified by acute awareness of development in other countries. When this quest was frustrated and as ideas of the rights of labor spread during the nineteenth century, people turned to the socialist alternative of building a new civic community to which they too could belong.[103] This general interpretation of working-class agitation in Europe may be contrasted with the problems encountered today under conditions of greater economic backwardness and greater advance abroad.[104]

In employing the English development as the prototype of later developments in other countries, Marx mistook the exception for the rule, a consideration which applies to his analysis of an emerging working class. As English workers attained a level of group-consciousness in the late eighteenth and early nineteenth centuries, they became aware of England's per-eminent position as a world-power. In follower societies the lower strata rise to an awareness of the relative backwardness of their society. Also, early working-class agitation in England occurred in an anti-mercantilist context which militated against protective legislation during a transitional period of greatly intensified deprivations. In follower societies the greater reliance on government makes social legislation a natural concomitant of early industrialization.[105] In England the work-force in the early factories was separated effectively from the land, and population increase in the countryside as well as the city roughly corresponded to the increasing demand for labor. In many follower societies the work-force retains its familial and economic ties to the land and population increase in city and country is well in advance of the demand for labor.[106]

These contrasts vary with the degree of industrialization achieved locally and the degree of governmental control over internal migration, to mention just two relevant considerations. The permanent separation of workers from their ties to the land obviously facilitates the growth of class consciousness and of political organization in Marx's sense of the word. On the other hand, a continuation of these ties may result either in a weak commitment to industry (and hence weak group solidarity), and/or in the emergence of segmental peasant-worker alliances in urban and national politics. Where this latter alternative exists, one can begin to appreciate how important it is to consider such phenomena in their own right, rather than treat them as transitions that are expected to disappear with increasing modernization. We do not know after all what forms modernization might take where separation between town and countryside fails to occur, at least for a considerable period of time.[107]

Having considered ruling and lower strata, I wish finally to turn to a brief analysis of education and intellectuals, again using the guidelines of the preceding discussion. In the case of England, education had been a privilege associated with high status until, in the course of religious controversies, several sectarian groups instituted private school systems so as to preserve the integrity of their beliefs. The idea of making education available beyond these narrow circles immediately raised the question of danger to the social order because workers and peasants would learn to read and write. This apprehension is quite understandable when one considers that the basic dividing line between those who officially ranked as "gentlemen" and the vast majority of the people was identical with the division between the literate and the illiterate. Still, the social mobilization of the population due to commerce and industry undermined the old hierarchy of ranks. The effort of ensuring that people would retain their old regard for rank led to the gradual spread of education with a strong emphasis on religion. This spread of education was not unlike the parallel problem of military conscription: both were aspects of a "fundamental democratization" which gave unprecedented political importance to people who could read and—in times of emergency—had guns.[108]

These issues are transformed in follower societies which seek to achieve the benefits of an industrial society, but by a speedier and less costly transition than occurred in England. In these societies popular and higher education seem to provide the easiest shortcut to industrialization. By this means the skill level of the population is raised while the highly educated increase their capacity of learning advanced techniques from abroad. For these reasons governments in follower societies usually push education, even though in so doing they also jeopardize their own political stability. They may attempt to avert such dangers through restrictions of the franchise, censorship, control of associations, etc.; one can differentiate between follower societies of the nineteenth and the twentieth centuries in terms of degrees and types of control over a mobilized population.

Such contrasts in the role of education are paralleled by contrasts in the role of intellectuals. Many educated persons engage in intellectual pursuits from time to time, but the term "intellectuals" is usually (if vaguely) restricted to those persons who engage in such pursuits on a full-time basis and as free professionals rather than "hired hands." [109] Intellectual pursuits occur in all complex societies, but "intellectuals" as a distinct social group emerged as a concomitant of modernization. In Western Europe men of letters underwent a process of emancipation from their previous subservience to the Church and to private patrons, because industrialization created a mass public and a market for intellectual products. The whole process was one of great complexity, but it can be simplified for present purposes. Intellectuals tended to respond to their emancipation by a new cultural elitism, and to the new mass-public by responses which vacillated between a populist identification with the people and a strong apprehension concerning the threat of mass-culture to humanistic values.[110] These responses were quite incongruent with the dominant materialism of advanced industrial societies, so that intellectuals experienced a social and moral isolation. During the nineteenth century the great economic and political successes of advanced European societies reinforced, rather than assuaged, the isolation of those intellectuals who took no direct part in that success and questioned the cultural and personal worth of those who did. To the extent that this estrangement resulted from the emancipation and consequent elitism of intellectuals, as well as from their ambivalent reaction to a mass public, it must be considered a concomitant of modernization.[111]

The response of intellectuals briefly sketched here was largely internal to the most advanced societies of Europe. But the breakthrough achieved by the industrial and political revolutions of England and France made other countries into follower societies. The economic advance of England and the events of the French revolution were witnessed from afar by men who rejected the backwardness and autocracy of their own country. Under these conditions cultural life tends to become polarized between those who would see their country progress by imitating the "more advanced countries," and those who denounce that advance as alien and evil and emphasize instead the well-springs of strength existing among their own people and in their native culture. Both reactions were typified by the Westernizers and Slavophils of Tsarist Russia, but the general pattern has occurred again and again. It has been a mainspring of nationalism and of movements for national independence. In this setting intellectuals do not remain estranged witnesses of a development carried forward by others; they tend to turn into leaders of the drive towards modernization.[112]

This discussion has endeavored to provide a framework for the comparative study of modernization and inequality. Such studies have been influenced for too long by a stereotype derived from the Marxian tradition. According to this stereotype, history is divided into epochs, characterized by a predominant mode of production and, based upon it, a class structure consisting of a ruling and an oppressed class. Each epoch is further characterized by a typical sequence of changes in the relations between the two major classes. In the early phase the dominant mode of production is established by a class in its period of revolutionary ascendance. For a time this class is progressive. Its economic interests are identical with technical progress and human welfare, and hence, on the side of liberating ideas and institutions. Eventually however, such an ascending class becomes a ruling class. From a champion of progress in its period of ascendance the class has turned into a champion of reaction in its period of dominance. Increasingly, the ruling class resists changes which would endanger its entrenched position. But meanwhile, within the structure of the old society, a new class has been formed from the ranks of the oppressed, who have no such vested interests and who in due time will overthrow that old structure in order to make way for the material progress which has become technically possible. Within the European context this grandiose simplification appeared to account for the feudal powers of resistance, the progressive, rising bourgeoisie and its gradual transformation into a reactionary ruling class, and finally the class of the oppressed proletariat which has a world to win and nothing to lose but its chains.

It is quite true, of course, that Marx modified this scheme to allow for leads and lags in interpreting the actual historical developments of his time. These modifications may have appeared all the more persuasive because of the passionate moral and intellectual conviction with which Marx adhered to the basic assumptions of the scheme itself. This conviction, I have suggested, was part of the European intellectuals' response to the crisis in human relations brought about by the rise of an industrial society, a response which suggested an "either-or" confrontation between tradition and modernity with its many ramifications.

A critical awareness of this intellectual heritage can assist the reorientation needed in the comparative study of stratification. It prompts us to recognize that the contrast between tradition and modernity is itself part of the evidence we should consider. This intellectual response to the rise of industry has been an aid or hindrance (as the case may be) in each country's modernization, typically marked by the emancipation of men of letters and by the manner in which they assessed their country's backwardness relative to the advances of their reference-societies. Once the unwanted legacies of this intellectual response are discounted, as I have attempted to do in this essay, a rather different approach to the study of modernization emerges.

The division of history into epochs, like the distinction between tradition and modernity, is a construct of definite, but limited utility. These constructs will vary with the purpose of inquiry. While we have found it useful to consider late eighteenth-century Europe as an historical turning point, it is recognized that the process of modernization which reached a crescendo since then, is coextensive with the era of European expansion since the late 15th century, or the "Vasco da Gama era" as Carlo Cipolla has called it. If we want to explain this historical breakthrough in Europe, our emphasis will be on the continuity of intra-societal changes. If we wish to include in our account the worldwide repercussions of this breakthrough and hence the differential process of modernization, our emphasis will be on the confluence of intrinsic and extrinsic changes of social structures. Both emphases are relevant for the comparative study of stratification.

Within this broad context the rise of new social structures as of technical innovations appears as a multifaceted process, not exclusively identifiable with any one social group. Typically, the pioneers of innovation seek the protection of ruling groups rather than defy them, provided of course that such groups exist and can provide protection. The outcome of this process varies with the pressure for innovation and the degree to which given ruling groups themselves participate in innovation or feel jeopardized by it. At any rate, the emphasis upon the continuity of ruling groups in the era of modernization is a first corollary following from the rejection of the "either-or" image of tradition and modernity.

A second corollary involves what Karl Mannheim has called the "fundamental democratization" of modern society. The contrast between the monopoly of rule by a tiny minority of notables and the principle of universal suffrage in modern nation-states is striking and unquestioned. But the growth of citizenship which occurs in the transition from one to the other, involves highly diverse developments in which the relative rights and obligations of social classes are redefined, as the political process interacts (more or less autonomously) with the changing organization of production. In the era of modernization this interaction can be understood best if proper attention is given to the international setting as well as the internal differentiation of social structures.

In the end it may appear—from a mid-twentieth-century viewpoint—that the growth of citizenship and the nation-state is a more significant dimension of modernization than the distributive inequalities underlying the formation of social classes. In that perspective Marx's theory of social classes under capitalism appears as a sweeping projection of certain temporary patterns of early nineteenth-century England. Not the least argument favoring this conclusion is the growth of the welfare state in the industrialized societies of the world, which in one way or another provides a pattern of accommodation among competing social groups as well as a model to be emulated by the political and intellectual leaders of follower societies.[113] My object has been to provide a framework which can encompass these contemporary developments as well as the modernization processes of the past.

SOCIAL AND POLITICAL CHANGES IN THE TWENTIETH CENTURY

✎§ TWELVE ﻬ

Two-thirds of the twentieth century are now past. In the period since 1900 the speed and diversity of change seem unprecedented. The late 1960s have witnessed a rising sense of uncertainty especially in Western societies. To the contemporary observer the future appears more impenetrable than ever. But the present century is accessible to him, as other centuries are not. The question is whether social change during this century is basically different from that of earlier historical periods. I believe the answer is yes.

Since 1900 world population and world urbanization show an accelerated growth for which there is no parallel. Now Asia and Latin America rather than Europe and North America are the areas of most rapid growth. In most industrialized countries the twentieth century has also witnessed the decisive shift of the labor force out of agriculture; only in England did this shift occur much earlier. Other occupational shifts have been equally distinctive: the declining importance of unskilled labor, the rise of managerial, technical, and white-collar occupations, and the employment of women. These characteristic changes of the twentieth century will be surveyed in the first part of this essay.

The second part deals with an outline of political changes. In this century the social and political institutions of Western socie-

This essay was written for a volume edited by Alan Bullock, *The Twentieth Century*, to be published by Thames and Hudson, London, and McGraw-Hill, New York. It is here published in abbreviated form with the permission of the editor and the publishers.

ties have been transformed through the simultaneous growth of mass politics and the welfare state, the rise of bolshevism and fascism, and the great contention between democratic and totalitarian tendencies. On a still larger scale the world of empire in the years before 1914 has been superseded by the world of rich and poor nations since World War II.

The social changes surveyed in Parts I and II suggest that the theories of the nineteenth century have become inapplicable to the experience of the twentieth. These Western European theories conceived societies as self-contained and integrated, a condition approximated by some countries before the turn of the century. Today these assumptions are invalid. Our world has become one in the sense of interdependence. With modern communications and the division of the world into superpowers and satellites, events anywhere can have instant repercussions everywhere. Also, the civic integration of the working class, which so preoccupied the nineteenth century, is no longer the major issue even in the industrially developed societies. It may be contrasted with major civic problems of the 1960s in order to underscore the basic difference of the twentieth century.

INDICATORS

World population stood at 1 billion in about 1825, at 2 billion in 1930 and at 3 billion in 1960. It took millennia to reach the 1825 figure, 105 years to reach the 1930 figure, but only 30 years to reach the 1960 figure. Before 1930, world population grew at a rate between 4 and 7 per cent each decade. Since 1930 it has increased at a rate between 14 and 20 per cent. The general cause of accelerating population growth is clear. Modern medicine and sanitation have wiped out epidemics. Increased agricultural productivity is capable of sustaining a much larger population. Accordingly, death rates have declined rapidly, while birth rates have stayed high. Only when birth rates begin to fall will the rate of growth decline, and then only gradually.

Population growth mirrors a key problem of social change in

the twentieth century. To see this we must compare the history of industrialized countries with the present experience of countries that are economically underdeveloped. Take England and Wales, the pioneers of industrialization. In a period of 175 years (from about 1780 to about 1955) the English birth rate declined from 37 to 16 per 1000, and the death rate from 25 to 4 per 1000. Average life expectancy increased from 40 years in 1850 to 53 in 1900 and 70 in 1955. Other industrialized countries show comparable patterns. Death rates declined first as a result of improved sanitation, hygiene, and the development of modern medicine. As more infants survived, the most compelling reason for large families—to ensure their continuity—lost ground. Gradually, motives for the curtailment of reproduction gained. As industrialization provided people with new opportunities, early marriage and the cost of raising children appeared as obstacles to personal advancement and security.

Now take India by way of contrast. Prior to 1920 her crude birth and death rates were 47 and 40 per 1000 respectively. (Note that these figures are considerably higher than those for England in 1780.) In the decades since 1920 the Indian birth rate has declined somewhat, probably to 44 per 1000. In the same period her death rate has declined to about 20 per 1000. Whereas India's population grew by 11 per cent in the 1920s, it increased by 21 per cent in the 1950s. A 20 per cent increase in a single decade is higher than any rates of increase recorded for Western European countries in the last century and a half. Nor is this Indian figure the most extreme. In the 1950s the population of Ceylon increased by 34 per cent, and countries like Taiwan, Malaya, and Costa Rica had similar rates of growth.

In the countries of Asia and Latin America nothing has led as yet to a major decline of reproduction. But in a few decades the death rates have declined to one-half or less of their former level, a point reached by a country like Sweden only after 130 years. The result is clear. The average growth of the world's population has become very uneven, with Asia and Latin America contributing a large share of the increase. As Kingsley Davis has stated:

The demography of the non-industrial countries today differs in essential respects from the early history of the present industrial nations. . . . Today, non-industrial populations are growing faster and at an earlier stage than was the case in the demographic cycle that accompanied industrialization in the 19th century.[1]

The reasons for this difference are in dispute. Some argue that the falling death rate in nonindustrialized countries is due to a slowly rising standard of living increasing the people's resistance to disease. In this view public health measures and modern medicine merely assist an economic development that is under way. It is hoped this development will eventuate in a declining birth rate and a diminished rate of growth, as it did in Europe. Others regard this as wishful thinking. Medicines and public health measures have had a quick effect. But it takes decades to achieve a rapid rate of economic growth and limit family size in response to new opportunities. In the industrialized countries the rate of reproduction has come to fluctuate with business conditions, but in non-industrialized countries the correlation between population growth and annual gain of per capita income is negligible.[2] In some measure the issue can be resolved only in the future. But it is clear now that formerly unquestioned values such as health and a long life can be problematic, even tragic, in their results when they contribute unwittingly to population growth unmatched by economic advance.

World urbanization is a recent phenomenon. Between 1900 and 1960, the number of people living in cities of 100,000 and over increased from 75 to 525 million, or from 4.7 to 17.5 per cent of world population. The population of all cities of 20,000 or more grew from 14 to 25 per cent. This means that amid general urban growth, the larger cities have grown quickest. In the period 1920–60 the world's population increased by a factor of less than two, but urban population (cities of 20,000 or more) by a factor of three.

Regional differences are pronounced in respect to the number of urban residents and their rates of growth. In 1960 Europe (without the USSR) had the largest *number* of residents in cities of

20,000 and over, followed by East Asia, South Asia, Northern America, the Soviet Union, Latin America, and Africa, in that order. However, this ranking by total number obscures divergent *rates* of growth as well as the divergent proportions of the urban sector in the entire population. Europe's urban population was 41 per cent of its total population in 1960. This urban sector had grown by 18 per cent in the preceding decade. By contrast, East Asia's urban population was only 20 per cent of total population, but the urban rate of growth was 52 per cent.

TABLE 1: URBAN POPULATION (20,000 AND OVER): *its decennial increase (1950–60) and its percentage of total population (1960) in major areas of the world* *

Area	Per cent Decennial Increase (1950–60)	Percentage of Total Population (1960)
Europe (without USSR)	18	41
Northern America	35	57
East Asia	52	20
South Asia	51	14
Soviet Union	56	36
Latin America	67	32
Africa	69	13

* United Nations, Dept. of Economic and Social Affairs, *Urbanization: Development Policies and Planning* (International Social Development Review No. 1; New York: United Nations, 1968), p. 12.

Thus, in the older industrialized regions of the world, the urban sector represents a high proportion of the total population, but the urban rate of growth is relatively low. So many people have already migrated from the land in some countries, that city growth slows down. Some cities grow no more than the general population. In the newer industrialized regions like the Soviet Union, and to a lesser extent North America, the urban sector is already large but its rate of growth is still high. The pattern is reversed in the non-industrial regions of Asia, Latin America, and Africa: the urban sector is small, but its rate of growth very high.

This present-day urbanization of economically underdeveloped countries differs from the past urbanization of industrialized countries. In the past the growth of cities required an enormous influx of people from farms and villages, because urban employment opportunities increased rapidly while death rates were higher in the cities than in the countryside. That influx continued even after sanitation had reduced the high urban death rates. In the United States 27 million people migrated to the cities between 1920 and 1959, with the result that farm population declined from about 32.5 million to 20.5 million. If only the families dependent on agriculture are counted, the farm population is down to 12.9 million, or 6.8 per cent of the United States population. Today, in the economically underdeveloped countries, the towns and cities also grow very rapidly. But while public health measures have lowered their urban death rates, their urban birth rates are almost as high as in the rural areas.

In Latin America and many countries of Asia, urbanization occurs primarily as a result of a rapidly rising population, not because of rural-urban migration. Between 1927 and 1963, Costa Rica's urban population almost tripled, but only 20 per cent of that increase was due to rural influx. In Switzerland between 1850 and 1888 urbanization resembled that of Costa Rica, but there rural-urban migration accounted for 69 per cent of the growth of towns. Thus, nonindustrial societies face the grave dilemma that their rapid urbanization does little to alleviate the simultaneous growth of the rural population. Underemployed farmers are crowding the land, while the growing cities are dotted with shantytowns of squatters, eking out a life of stark deprivation.

Figures on population growth and urbanization reflect the growing discrepancy between rich and poor countries. Where economic advance is slow, public health measures preserve life at the expense of well being: population grows faster than per capita income.

Under these conditions urbanization is not accompanied by a rapid rise of industry and of national income, as it was in nineteenth-century Europe. In South Asia, for example, the growth of cities has occurred together with slow industrialization and, still worse, with a relative stagnation of agriculture.[3] In 1952–56 South Asia's volume of agricultural output of 100 compared with 580 for Europe and 1780 for the United States.[4] Since economic improvement is so often assumed to be a part of industrialization, it is well to remember the crucial importance of a corresponding revolution in agriculture.

The proportion of the labor force employed in agriculture is a convenient measure of the transformation of societies in the nineteenth and twentieth centuries. Shifts out of agriculture indicate not only the growth of the labor force in all other sectors of the economy, but also—if indirectly—the rise in agricultural productivity. In America one farm worker's labor fed seven people in 1900, but thirty-three people in 1965. Great Britain, as the oldest industrialized country, has the longest record of shifts out of agriculture. The proportion of her labor force in agriculture was already

TABLE II. PROPORTION OF LABOR FORCE IN AGRICULTURE, SELECTED COUNTRIES AND YEARS *

U.S.	1870	51	
	1910	32	39% decline in 80 years
	1950	12	
Japan	1872	85	
	1925	52	
	1950	48	52% decline in 88 years
	1960	33	
USSR	1928	71	
	1958	40	31% decline in 30 years

* Data from Simon Kuznets, *Modern Economic Growth* (New Haven: Yale University Press, 1966), pp. 106–7.

as low as 35 percent in 1801, fell to 9 per cent by 1901, and to 5 per cent by 1951. Countries which industrialized later may be compared with these benchmark figures.

The United States had less than 50 per cent of her labor force in agriculture before the turn of the century, whereas for Japan that change occurred after 1925 and for the USSR during the 1930s. In these and other industrialized countries the labor force shifted first into industrial employments, and as these became more labor-saving, into services.[5] These shifts between major branches of the economy were made possible by a second industrial and by a scientific revolution.

In the last decades of the nineteenth century the early age of steam and coal was superseded by the age of steel and electricity, of oil and chemicals. Inventions that are commonplace in our daily lives made their first appearance before or shortly after the turn of the century: the internal combustion engine, telephone and telegraph, bicycles and pneumatic tires, phonographs and typewriters, mass circulation newsprint, synthetic fibres and plastics. Still more important than specific products were basic innovations in the manufacturing process of steel and aluminum. New production processes were developed in the electrical, chemical, and petroleum industries. Artificial fertilizer as a by-product of steel production also greatly increased agricultural productivity. Finally, new methods of food preservation (canning, refrigeration) as well as major advances in shipping and railroad construction largely solved the problem of how to supply great urban centers. It is apparent that the decades at the turn of the century witnessed an economic and technical breakthrough of major proportions. Since that time other breakthroughs were achieved through the development of air transportation, radio, and television.

Yet all of this seems dwarfed by what is happening now. Sixty-five years have elapsed between the Wright brothers' first airplane and man's first landing on the moon. In the past few decades science has grown into a mass collective endeavor. Eighty to ninety per cent of the scientists who have ever lived are alive today. If we take the number of American scientists and engineers to have been

100 in 1900, then this compares with 540 in 1930 and 1640 in 1954. Atomic energy, the electronics industry with its transistors, computers, and automated devices, and now the development of space travel involve not only a profusion of technical innovations, but a concerted national effort. In the United States total annual expenditures for research and development have increased from 5 to 25 billion dollars between 1953 and 1968. In the period between 1940 and 1960 total annual expenditures for institutions of higher education have increased from 758 million to 6,230 million dollars. There is good reason to believe that today we are in the midst of a scientific and technological revolution which is qualitatively different from what went before.

These headlong advances are reflected in the changing occupational structure. In the United States between 1900 and 1960, the share of wage and salary earners in the labor force increased from 75 to 93 per cent. This also means a decline in the proportion of the self-employed from 25 to 7 per cent. Increasingly, the individual is obliged to become a functionary in large organizations, although in some respects this was already true sixty years ago.

In the past sixty years, mounting technical complexities have required an increasingly skilled labor force. A dwindling proportion of farmers and unskilled workers (8 and 9) are a contrast to the more or less steady proportion of skilled workers (6 and 7). Yet the losses of the first category are so great that manual workers as a whole declined by more than 30 per cent. Meanwhile white-collar workers have increased by the 30 per cent that the manual category has lost. The "technostructure" (J. K. Galbraith) requires personnel at the technical, managerial, and clerical levels, and all three categories have doubled, quadrupled, or even increased tenfold. The share of women in all white-collar occupations has increased greatly, although their subordinate role persists. A disproportionate number of typists and sales personnel are women, while a disproportionate number of managers and officials are men. And among professional and technical workers most women are probably laboratory assistants and other subordinate technical personnel.

Selected Occupational Group	Share of Occupational Groups in Total (per cent)			Share of Females in Occupational Group (per cent)	
	1900	1960	1967	1900	1960
1. Professional, technical, and kindred workers	5.7	12.2	13.3	35.2	38.1
2. Managers and officials	0.8	5.8	10.1	0.4	14.4
3. Clerical and kindred workers	4.0	16.0	16.6	24.2	67.6
4. Sales workers	6.0	8.0	6.1	17.4	36.4
5. *White collar workers* (1–4)	16.5	42.0	46.1	24.5	45.7
6. Craftsmen, foremen, and kindred workers	14.1	15.4	13.2	2.5	2.9
7. Operatives and kindred workers	17.1	21.5	18.7	34.0	28.1
8. Nonskilled laborers except farm and mine	16.6	5.9	4.8	3.8	3.5
9. Farm laborers and foremen	23.6	2.6	2.1	13.6	17.3
10. *Manual workers* (6–9)	71.4	45.4	38.9	14.0	15.7
11. Service workers except household	4.8	9.6	10.2	34.3	52.4
12. Household workers	7.3	3.0	2.4	96.6	96.4
13. *Service workers* (11–12)	12.1	12.6	12.6	71.8	63.0

* Data from Kuznets, *op. cit.*, p. 192. Subtotals italicized. The data for 1967 have been added from U.S. Dept. of Labor, *Manpower Report of the President* (Washington: U.S. Government Printing office, 1968) Table A-9 p. 232.

The occupational shift towards greater skill has required better education and more of it. All strata of the population have been affected by this. Among those aged 17, the percentage of high school students increased from 6.4 to 76.2 between 1900 and 1967. Among those aged 18 to 21, the number of students in higher education has increased from 2 to 6.3 million between 1946 and 1967, and is expected to reach 9.6 million by 1977. In a twenty-year period the proportion of these college students has doubled from 22 to 46 out of every 100 persons aged 18 to 21.

The effect of this educational advance has been pervasive. In the civilian labor force, 25 years old or above, the proportion of those who completed high school, rose from 46 per cent in 1957–59 to 55 per cent in 1965–66 and is expected to reach 66 per cent by 1975. This massive development of education has had a substantial effect on productivity. For the period 1929–57 national output per worker increased by 56 per cent and estimates attribute two-fifths of that rise to the increasing education of the work force. Gross National Product in the United States grew from 103 billion dollars per year in 1929 to 780 billion in 1967. During the same period all expenditures for education increased from 3.2 million to 54.6 million dollars, or from 3 to almost 7 per cent of the GNP. Between 1900 and 1965 income increased 32 times, but the labor force producing that income increased only 2.7 times. Clearly, the shift out of agriculture, away from unskilled labor, and towards white-collar work has been accompanied by rapidly increasing productivity and a greatly increased demand for higher levels of education in the work force. These indicators are important clues to social change in the twentieth century.

◄§ POLITICAL CHANGE

The historical turning points of this century have been cataclysmic. Since 1900 there have been two World Wars, each ending with a communist revolution. In the fifty years since the Bolshevik revolution of 1917, Soviet Russia has built up an industrial society and a new world empire. Since 1949 China has begun a similar effort, although her internal consolidation and external role are still in the future. Together the two communist giants encompass almost one-third of the world's population. The years since Hitler's rise to power in 1933 have brought the decline of European empire, the rise of the United States as an industrial and political world power, and the proliferation of national regimes around the world. Since 1945 fifty-one newly established sovereign nations have been recognized as members of the United Nations, increasing the total from 71 to 122. World affairs have been dominated by the contentions between Russia and the United States for political, military, and technical superiority. In Europe and the Far East, Germany, Korea, and Vietnam have been divided. America, Russia, and now also China compete for spheres of influence in Asia, Africa, and the Middle East. And since the 1940s the hazard of nuclear destruction has cast a pall over every move.

Changes in the internal structure of societies have been no less momentous. The two World Wars destroyed whole segments of the population and caused massive migrations, especially in Central Europe. In addition the structure of the population, such as that of the Federal Republic of Germany, reflects the casualties of these wars and the shortages of births resulting from them, as well as from the great depression of the 1930s. In 1960, 25 per cent of the population in the Federal Republic consisted of migrants from other parts of Europe. Perhaps countries like Russia and China were ravaged to the same extent, but we lack comparable statistical information.

The political structure of Western countries was transformed by these upheavals. National organization for modern war, the bolshevik and fascist regimes of the interwar years, and the economic depression of the 1930s led to the political mobilization of great masses of people. To an extent such mobilization was already anticipated by developments preceding World War I.

Until the 1870s the franchise was restricted to owners of property, and parliament was an assembly of dignitaries from the upper strata of society. In the United Kingdom, for example, even the

Reform Bill of 1867 extended the franchise to only one out of thirty persons. In the absence of the secret ballot, election results were manipulated by the ruling oligarchies. These conditions changed with the introduction of universal manhood suffrage in France and the German empire (1871), Switzerland (1874), other countries following suit in the 1890s or later. (In European overseas settlements like the United States or Australia the extension of the franchise occurred earlier.) Note that in most of these cases women received the franchise in the years following World War I, some fifty years later than men, even though they had become a considerable part of the labor force.

The extension of the franchise was the political expression of a changing concept of the lower classes in Western societies. In the nineteenth century and amid rapidly advancing industrialization, pauperism had been considered the overriding social problem. It was attributed to personal failure in life's struggle for survival. In England, franchise restricted to owners of property meant second class citizenship for the five out of six adult males who could not vote. This second class position was reversed by the extension of the franchise—in England a process lasting from the introduction of the secret ballot in 1872 and the Third Reform Bill of 1884, to universal manhood suffrage in 1918. During the same period, the identification of poverty with degradation was abolished step-by-step through an extension of the welfare principle. The young, the old, the sick, and the unemployed were gradually extracted from the category of pauperism by measures designed to provide an assistance that did not carry the stigma of second class status.

The gradual abolition of second class citizenship for the vast majority of the population brought in its train a decline in the politics of notables so characteristic of the nineteenth century. The mass democracy which took its place required political parties which could organize mass participation in the electoral process. In Europe and the countries which modeled themselves after her, this took the form of permanent membership organizations. These parties imposed a discipline on all functionaries and representatives of the party and catered to the diverse interests of the members through a multitude of affiliated organizations. In the United States, party organizations are permanent only at the level of an oligarchic leadership which undertakes to organize a mass following in every electoral contest.

Party policies can be confirmed or altered in broad outline only during periodic elections. But the details that really affect the individual citizen are hammered out in the long intervening periods, through parliamentary debate and committee work, through legislation and administrative implementation. At these levels politics was largely a matter of personal influence during the nineteenth century, involving family relations or social contacts among a relatively small group of the privileged. Here also, the politics of notables has been superseded, not however by mass democracy, but by a politics of organized interests. Although the transactions of parliament and of administrative agencies are related to electoral politics, they are more immediately influenced by those segments of the public capable of organizing and representing their interests to legislators and officials. As government functions expand, so do the efforts to influence policy.

No simple measure of that expansion is available. The size of public employment and government purchases can only serve as a gross index, since government influence extends far beyond its own direct operations. In the United States, in 1966, public employment had reached 14.4 million out of a total labor force of 72.8 million persons, with government purchases of goods and services reaching a total of 154.3 billion out of a Gross National Product of 743 billion dollars. Since roughly one-fifth of all employed persons and of all purchases involve public authority directly, the transactions of parliament and of government agencies have become too important to be left to politicians and officials.

Moreover, governmental decision making is not the exclusive domain of legislators. Policy decisions and control of implementation become the concern of administrators and experts in the many cases in which legislators depend upon and use advice for political ends, or avoid political choices by recourse to "knowledge." In addition, the work of government has been delegated since World War II to what one writer has called "the quasi non-governmental organization." This means that private organizations of many types are engaged in research and production under public contract in fields in which the government does not want to operate directly. It is little wonder that organized interests have been mobilized to exert pressure on government when public decisions are made. Such mobilizations must be considered a public response to modern government, much as mass political parties were a response to the universal franchise.

The structural changes here reviewed—the political mobilization of the people and the transformation of decision making—can be analyzed at a more abstract level as a basis for the consideration of totalitarian regimes in the next section. To do this it is useful to distinguish direct democracy from representative government, or the plebiscitary from the representative component of democratic government. The term "plebiscite" refers to the direct vote on an important public issue by all qualified electors of a community. Where qualifications are at a minimum, all adult members of the community would participate directly in the decisions of public authority. Plebiscitarian rule assumes that the public interest is identical with the public will, and that this will is unified enough for effective public action and ascertainable through direct vote on all major issues. In this view minorities or special interests interfere with the untrammeled formation of public opinion. Even a system of parliamentary representation appears as an inadequate substitute for public decision making, or direct democracy. Public authority should thus be based on a continual plebiscite, as in periodic public opinion polls which would extend the universal franchise to the periods between elections. In practice, such mobilization has occurred, not through periodic polls, but through one-party regimes which carried the principle of political participation by everyone to its logical conclusion.

In a representative government all important public issues are voted upon only by those who have been elected to perform this function by the qualified voters of a community. Such a government will take account of majority opinion whenever possible, but it does not assume that the public interest is identical with the public will. Rather, the public interest, hypothetical as that is, will be preferred to a public opinion that can change quickly and is frequently uninformed. Parliament is the model of representative government, although with the expansion of government functions administrators of particular agencies also respond to the public they serve and in a sense represent them. Moreover, with the devolution of parliamentary functions the distinction between public and private often becomes so blurred that even agents of organized interests claim to be representatives in a quasi-public sense. Such agents have been elected by a private constituency and represent its interests. They pervert the idea of representation when they claim to speak in the name of the public.

Modern democratic governments are an interplay between these two principles. Universal franchise is the model of plebiscitary rule. The direct democracy of the town hall meeting is applied to national affairs, although in practice it is combined with the idea of representation. Parliament is the model of representative government. Representation has an affinity with oligarchic rule, although in practice it is frequently responsive to public opinion. How can this interpretation be related to the wars and dictatorships mentioned at the beginning of this section?[6]

Modern wars and dictatorships are radical applications of the plebiscitary principle. They are so extreme, however, that government by the people is turned into its opposite. In practice, no regime ever conducts its affairs by means of continual plebiscites. Instead, when public issues are decided by direct vote of all adult citizens, the regime becomes one of mass acclamation on staged public occasions. No individual interest is permitted to obstruct the popular will and in its name all people and resources are mobilized. Thus plebiscitary rule has an authoritarian as well as a populist side. But this authoritarian meaning is given a semblance of popular rule by construing the actions of government as a direct decision of "the people," with no representative bodies intervening.

In the era of mass politics and democratic ideals, government by public consent has a powerful appeal. Thus, wartime governments may issue decrees curtailing or suspending partisan politics, but they are likely to proceed as if a universal consent had been given. And the decrees themselves are limited usually to the duration of the war. On the other hand, dictatorships are regimes of perpetual emergency, real or simulated. To meet such emergency, such regimes begin with the destruction of parliamentary institutions. The dissolution of the Constituent Assembly by the bolsheviks in 1917, or the Reichstag fire of 1933 exploited by Hitler, marked the beginning of a para-military destruction of all independent organizations, no matter how nonpolitical. To a modern dictatorship, every organization that is independent is also political.

These first steps result in a continuous mobilization to achieve the national task. In an effort to describe the resulting regimes comprehensively, Professor Robert Tucker refers to "revolutionary mass movement regimes under single party auspices." Although such regimes differ in many respects, they have also much in common. Their overthrow of an "old regime" fulfills the first task of their ideological mission. This overthrow is a plebiscite in action, the result of a mass movement against the establishment. The spearhead and ruling force of the mass movement is the single party. To achieve the necessary unity and drive, the party organizes for political combat by controlling all other organizations of the society. In this way the party claims to express the will of the people, and to act on the basis of a continual plebiscite.

In practice this means the enlisting of masses of people in the activities of trade unions, youth, professional, and other organizations that are formally nonparty in character but operated under party guidance and supervision via directorates from top to bottom in which disciplined party members predominate. A large proportion of the population is thus drawn into the

whirlpool of guided public life, and many may derive an experience of political participation that was denied them under
the old regime.[7]

The price of this mobilization is high. It has been estimated
that some 20 million people perished under the Stalinist regime
in Soviet Russia. A locational map of German prisons, Gestapo
commando posts, and concentration camps under the Nazis would
show the country covered from one end to the other. And the
baffling Great Proletarian Cultural Revolution in China appears
to have been similarly extensive, although we do not know at
what human cost. The point is that total mobilization can be
achieved only by the destruction of all independent organizations
which could mediate between the central power of the state and
the individual. By representing a particular segment of society
each of these organizations would jeopardize the claim of the
single party to represent the people as a whole.

These characteristics of "revolutionary mass movement regimes"
have proved compatible with quite divergent cultural and historical
traditions. The bolshevik regime was the first full scale example,
coming to power in 1917 following the protracted agonies of
Russia's participation in World War I. A single-party regime
initiated the industrialization of the whole country in an economically backward society. This fact destroyed the nineteenth-century
notion that rapid economic growth could only be the product
of a free market and private initiative. Bolshevism thus appeared
as a threat to economically advanced countries in which this conception was widespread. And the defense against this threat
encouraged the rise of fascist movements in many European
countries.

In Italy and Germany, these movements established regimes
of the far right. This proved that the techniques of mass mobilization and single-party rule could also be used in industrially advanced countries. Where national crises are severe enough to
arouse people's anxiety and jeopardize the functioning of institutions, fascism can rise to power on the claim that the national
interest demands a clean sweep of conventional politics, of the

"Establishment," or of *das System,* as Hitler put it. This extremist possibility did not end with Hitler's and Mussolini's defeat in World War II. In the last third of the twentieth century it is a likely threat, where mounting problems at home and abroad polarize the political community and thereby undermine its institutional framework.

The organizational similarities between bolshevism and fascism (or rather between Stalinism and Hitlerism) should not obscure the difference between them. At the ideological level they are a world apart: a universalist materialism and a belief in progress on one side, a racist romanticism and belief in war and national superiority on the other. But in practice, both regimes are nationalist in the extreme. Both are dedicated to advance their country by a civic simulation of perpetual combat against external and internal enemies, a continuation of war by quasi-peaceful means. These common elements of totalitarian regimes have replaced absolute monarchy as an alternate model of rule which competes with Western democracy.

In the second half of the twentieth century all the countries of the so-called Third World face the double task of developing a sense of national identity and achieving rapid economic growth. For that purpose nationalist authoritarian regimes have tended to borrow whatever served their immediate ends: from the bolshevik version of the Marxian tradition, from the national socialist and anti-democratic orientation of fascism, as well as from the older liberal, Christian, and racist ideology of the colonial past. In Europe the rise of bolshevism and fascism signaled the transformation of nineteenth-century political structures. But in Africa and Asia the ideas of European liberalism inspired nationalist movements of independence from Western domination. The mass movement regimes of Europe and these independence movements in many parts of the world combined nationalism with populist, single-party regimes, mostly at the expense of democratic institutions. An account of social change in the twentieth century must summarize how these developments have changed the character of world politics.

In 1900 European population represented one-fourth of world population, having grown by 51 per cent since 1850. The beginning of this century marked a high point of European dominance. Her share in world trade amounted to 65.9 per cent. World production had been increasing rapidly and Europe contributed the lion's share of it. Between 1870 and 1900 production of coal had tripled; between 1850 and 1900 production of iron ore had increased tenfold; between 1860 and 1900 production of petroleum had increased more than 200 times. In 1900 Western Europe produced 54 per cent of the world's pig iron compared with 34.8 per cent for the United States and 7.1 per cent for Russia. Europe's share in the world's manufacturing production was more than 40 per cent in 1913.

This period of industrial growth was also one of imperial expansion. The opening of the Suez canal in 1869 was followed by English and French colonization in Africa. The 1880s and 1890s witnessed European advances in Asia, including Russia's penetration of Siberia and of the inner Asian frontiers of China. From 1876 to 1914 colonial powers of the world annexed eleven million square miles of territory.

Within Western European societies themselves, pauperism had been the major social problem of the nineteenth century. It was the result of rapid industrialization and urbanization. Increasing wealth seemed the answer to pauperism. At the same time workers grew aware of their second class status and this made citizenship the major political problem. Extension of the franchise established equal citizenship and seemed an effective answer to the workers' protest. Both answers appeared readily available in nations enjoying a rising standard of living at home and increasing power abroad. Economic growth at home was linked with political and military expansion abroad. Propagandists of "social imperialism" no longer exhorted the poor to remain content with their station in life, as the evangelists of the early nineteenth century had done. Instead, they sought to enlist the poor in a common national endeavor of overseas expansion. Rich and poor would benefit alike, at the expense of the "inferior races."

Yet European predominance in the decades since 1880 marked at the same time the passing of the European age. A period of strident self-confidence also witnessed growing uncertainty and despair. As John Lester has noted, the praise of life lived to the fullest was increasingly marred by doubt that life was worth living. In 1905 Edward Carpenter wrote that "we are dying slowly and surely of Unbelief—and there can be no deadlier disease." [8] In the midst of unprecedented material achievements and imperial power writers of sensibility noted the undercurrents of the age with profound skepticism. At the turn of the century Europe was already undergoing the transformations which have led to the world of the second half of the twentieth century. Demographic and economic indicators tell that story in one way. A changed international setting and an altered sensibility do so in other ways.

From 1900 to 1950 European population fell from one-fourth to one-fifth of world population. More important, her rate of growth in the decade 1950 to 1960 was down to almost one-half of the world average, whereas in that decade Asia's population increased almost twice as fast and Latin America's almost three times. By 1960, 56 per cent of the world's population and its greatest potential for growth were found in Asia. Europe, the USSR, and North America together encompassed only 28 per cent. In the field of economic growth the passing of the European age was as clearly marked. In 1800 Europe's share in world trade had been 75 per cent and in 1900 65 per cent. By 1956 it had gone down to 43 per cent, a decline of over 20 per cent in five decades. In 1900 Western Europe produced 54 per cent of the world's production of pig iron, but by 1959 her production was down to 30.4 per cent. Simon Kuznets has compared the productive capacity of several European countries with those of the United States, Russia, and Japan. While England and France, for example, increased total production by more than six times the initial level a century ago, the United States and Japan increased total production thirty-four times. If the current growth rate of the Soviet Union is extrapolated for a century, she would have increased her total product seventy-four times the initial level.

The implications of these developments were anticipated by some. In the 1830s, Tocqueville foresaw that the rise of Russia and America would overshadow Europe. In the 1880s the English historian J. R. Seeley declared that once Russia and the United States were mobilized by steam, electricity, and a network of railways, European states like France and Germany would be dwarfed. For its time Seeley's insight was remarkable for the inclusion of Russian industrialization as a major factor in the changing balance of power.

To less prescient observers, the rising imperial role of Russia and the United States remained hidden. In the case of Russia, bolshevism was largely seen as a threat to the social order of other countries, not as the ideology of a world power. Russia was too preoccupied with her internal development to appear plausible as the future center of an empire. The United States became deliberately isolationist after her participation in World War I, and would not join the League of Nations. But these appearances of isolation were shattered by World War II.

The alliance between England, France, the United States, and Russia, the domination of the postwar world by the two superpowers, the revolution in China in 1949, and finally the rise to political prominence of a large number of newly sovereign countries have all shaped a world in which Europe has lost her former preeminence. Divested of her empires, Europe faces great spiritual difficulties. There is not much left of the confidence which still prevailed in 1900, despite the fact that material achievements of industrial societies are very much greater today than they were at the turn of the century. There is a deep chasm between the European cultural tradition and the legacies of depredation which five centuries of Western expansion have left behind. None of the glories of European culture can undo or allay those legacies. In her decline from world eminence, Europe must come to terms with this fact. It is easier, of course, to evade this dilemma, and instead view the superpowers as the twin dangers to civilization. While Russia and now China are seen in the image of an undifferentiated mass of humanity menacing the individual, the United States is seen as a society in which the soul is sacrificed to the machine. Yet the contemptuous rejection of other cultures is not an effective defense of one's own. Indeed, the massive critique of things Russian and American is a form of European self-righteousness, an arrogance coupled with anxiety as the Swiss writer Karl Schmid has put it.[9]

While the dream of Europe as the cradle and center of civilization is not easily relinquished, the two superpowers face burdens of their own. None of the achievements of the United States can efface her guilt in the enslavement and oppression of Negroes. A century after the Civil War, the problem of integrating this submerged tenth of the nation is as unsolved as ever. Nor has American history prepared her people to handle the responsibilities of world power at a time when the United States has become the unwitting heir of Europe's earlier imperial role. There are signs that American democracy will be tested severely, if unresolved problems at home and abroad further polarize the easily aroused segments of the population on the right and the left. Meanwhile, Russia has celebrated the fiftieth anniversary of the Bolshevik revolution (1967). The momentum of her successful industrialization is a tremendous source of national power and internal legitimacy, despite the horrors of Stalinism. But this achievement is marred by the unresolved problems of economic organization, the continual persecution or harassment of ethnic and national minorities, the fitful but pervasive suppression of thought, and perhaps above all the stultifying mediocrity of a top-heavy bureaucracy. It is marred also by Russia's mounting imperial problems with restless satellites in the West and a hostile communist regime of 700 million Chinese in the East. The United States and Russia thus face the last third of the twentieth century with a powerful technical civilization, a materialist culture that alienates their educated elites, and a host of problems that cannot be solved either by American anti-communism or Soviet anti-americanism.

In addition, the Western world has come to be haunted by the stark discrepancies between rich nations and poor. The gulf between them is not new. But the new political independence of poor countries and the remaining scars of colonialism together have made this gulf a potent issue. The poor countries are also the colored nations, so that their hostility to rich nations is frequently joined with anti-Western sentiments born of colonialism and racial discrimination. Thus the legitimacy of rich nations is questioned, because they are also Western and white and as such a reminder of exploitation and inequality. An apparent exception like Japan is only used to demonstrate that in fact the colored people are superior and their poverty is unjustified. Such feelings are widespread in the second half of the twentieth century. They greatly aggravate the domestic problems of many societies of the West. For racial minorities and youths, the poor nations of the world are a symbol of the injustice perpetrated by "the establishment," past and present, and hence a reason to attack its legitimacy.

✑§ CURRENT PROBLEMS

Nineteenth-century theories of society did not explain this crisis of legitimacy in the midst of affluence, nor did they deal with the civic integration of minorities. Such problems will beset us for the rest of this century. We have no comprehensive theory to analyze them. But even in its absence we can take a measure of our time by finding out why the old theories are inapplicable.

Note that all such theories were a product of Western thought, as was the idea of a scientific study of society. These theories were developed in societies that had pioneered the industrial and democratic revolutions of the modern world. These revolutions occurred at the center of world empires. It is not surprising that such theories depicted societies as self-contained units and focused their attention on the division of labor within these units. This division was considered the major determinant of social classes and social change. Several variants of this model developed.

Liberals emphasized the rise in productivity and market exchange as by-products of the division of labor. Conservatives emphasized the division of society into status groups, each with its rights and duties defined as parts of the whole. Radicals saw that division in terms of conflicts between exploiters and exploited. Each of these perspectives emphasized what the other two neglected, but none of them attended to considerations that have since proved important.

Similarly, the international setting of societies was neglected as well as the existence of groups formed on the basis of sex, age, or ethnic identity, rather than on an economic basis. The importance of boundaries for the economy and the nationwide division of labor made it plausible to consider "society" in isolation from other societies. It also seemed clear that being a citizen politically and being a member of society were two aspects of the same reality. Tacitly, these theories identified the term "society" with the nation state. This identification has proved faulty. To analyze some of the urgent problems facing us today, it will be useful to examine the range of facts which come into view when these assumptions are called into question.

Nineteenth-century theories treated society as if it were an island, isolated from countries beyond its shores and without effect upon them. To be sure, these theories took some notice of the international setting. Liberal theory was concerned with international trade. Conservative theory emphasized the inequality of nations as a natural outgrowth of power politics. Radical theory construed international affairs as a continuation of the national class struggle by other means. Yet these considerations remained only peripheral extensions of the idea that the division of labor within society is the main determinant of stability and change. The manifest historical importance of the diffusion of techniques and ideas was neglected.

After four centuries of European expansion it seems paradoxical to think of societies as if they were self-contained units. Rather, societies around the world have suffered massive dislocations due to conquest or economic dependence. Moreover, the industrial and democratic revolutions in England and France towards the end of the eighteenth century were emulated by other countries. Conquest and economic expansion as well as industrial techniques and democratic ideas have made the world one. Yet it is in this world that the idea of "society as an island" has come into prominence.

True, the earliest European expansion had a rather superficial impact upon the non-European world. But the economic and political revolutions of the eighteenth century became an instant object of attention, since they promised to relieve poverty and secure freedom. Both English industrial advance and French democratic ideas provided models to imitate or even to rival. And since England and France were world empires, imitation also seemed to imply a promise of national power. The attempt to emulate "the West" was already notable in Eastern Europe during the eighteenth and nineteenth centuries, but has become more prominent still in the "underdeveloped" countries of the twentieth century.

The diffusion of techniques and ideas gives special importance to the educated elite, which had little or no place in theories that judged social groups in relation to the division of labor. As mentioned earlier, the idea of adopting the techniques and avoiding the errors of more advanced countries, dates back to the beginning of the modern era. Since then, the world has become divided into societies that have achieved high levels of industrialization, and others which have not, but are trying against great odds to build up their economies. The breakthrough by the "Western" countries has been witnessed from afar by men who stand uneasily between modernity and tradition. Such men do not remain estranged witnesses of a materialist civilization as so many did in Western Europe. Instead, they try to become the intellectual and political leaders in the drive towards modernization. They are aware that the attractions of Western wealth and power pose a threat to the native tradition. The resulting ambivalence corresponds to the cultural and institutional divisions within these countries. For a small number of people have adopted ideas and practices from abroad, while the mass of the population is still beholden to native traditions.

The social and political problems posed by this division are intractable. In the nineteenth century, the autocratic regimes of Eastern Europe or the Far East attempted to cope with them. These were strictly regimes of notables. They sought to regulate society by government edict and a corresponding bureaucracy. In 1861, when Tsar Alexander II decreed the emancipation of the Russian serfs, he remarked to Bismarck in an interview: "God only knows what might be the ultimate outcome of the current transaction between peasants and landowners, if the power of the Tsar was not strong enough to give an unconditional guarantee of leadership." [10] This absolutist approach required the government to regulate not only a gradual increase in legal equality, but also social relations arising from inherited privilege, from economic relations, and from religious, ethnic, and linguistic divisions of the population. We know today that many autocratic regimes failed in their attempt to superintend the transition to the modern world.

The problems of these autocracies and of the now emerging nations can be contrasted with the rise of the European nation states. Generally, the European nations began their development with a unification and centralization of governmental functions and an extensive diminution of group differences. This was a gradual development. The new states of the twentieth century face a more difficult task, because through imitation they have accelerated change, making it even more unmanageable. And from the start they are confronted with economic competition from already developed countries. Most of the newly sovereign countries arose from movements of independence, which appealed to all the people, and accordingly established regimes based on a universal franchise. Thus they began their political existence with the full complement of democratic institutions developed in Western Europe. But to achieve national identity and economic growth a national government appears indispensable. And under the conditions of the new states such a government is difficult to establish and maintain with any degree of stability.

Notions like state or citizenship still mean little to people whose social ties remain bound up with blood, race, language, locality, religion, or tradition.[11] Universal franchise and the modern press encourage the public manifestation of these social ties so that the most modern political devices tend to conflict with a national realization of collective aims. Thus, in the new states the divisive tendencies of traditional society are intensified by just those nationalist and democratic developments which in nineteenth-century Europe led to a greater degree of national unity.

Yet this unity of Western nation states, limited as it always was, is now threatened from within. Social divisions other than those of class had existed all along, but in the 1960s they have become political issues. Nineteenth-century theory had assumed that a society encompasses all the people living in the territory of a nation state. However, the meaning of this assumption was limited in various ways. Liberal theory tended to account only for people directly involved in exchange relations, thereby excluding economic dependents of all kinds. Conservative theory tended to account for all people by virtue of their social status, but then placed dependents of all kinds in an inferior position. Nor could conservatives do much with people like intellectuals or foreigners whose status was unclear, or with categories like legal equality or citizenship that applied to everyone. Radical theory tended to account only for people directly involved in employment relationships and encompassed all others by subsuming them under the categories of exploiters and exploited.

The twentieth century has witnessed the social and political emergence of groups which these nineteenth-century theories left out of account: women, racial minorities, youths, the aged, intellectuals, and others. Each of these groups poses problems peculiar to itself in relation to the larger issue of citizenship. With reference to the industrialized nation states I stall discuss the first three groups as segments of the population which were omitted by, or dissatisfied with, the successful development of national citizenship.

Women were the first of the excluded groups to demand a change of status. Under the influence of the French Revolution they had obtained many civil rights during the nineteenth century: liberty of person, freedom of speech and thought, the right to own property and to conclude valid contracts. But political rights were denied them. During the last decades of the nineteenth century a movement for the emancipation of women came to the fore. The right to vote and to stand for an elective office was granted, but only gradually. In some countries, like Switzerland, women are denied political rights to this day. In the field of social rights the record is mixed. Since women were economic dependents for much of the nineteenth century, they were considered proper objects of welfare measures designed to protect them against the most extreme hazards of exploitation and insecurity. However, as they increased their participation in the labor force, women ceased to be considered automatically as dependents and frequently could obtain public assistance only on the same basis as men, perhaps an equivocal gain.[12]

Here the contrast between the new states and the nation states of "the West" is especially striking. Where the ties of blood and tradition remain strong, the position of women is not only that of economic dependents but of social inferiors. In this setting only men have rights. Yet just here the winning of national independence brings with it the full range of political rights for women, not gradually but all at once. The full range of social rights, while also granted, remains on paper. Thus, in the new states, women often remain in their age-old position of social inferiority. Little can be done to ensure them a minimum degree of welfare, but they now have the right to vote and stand for elective office, unlike some women in Europe who have still to win these rights.

The emancipation of women remains an unresolved problem.

For even where it has gone farthest in terms of civil, political, and social rights, it has not resolved the inherent paradox of equalizing the conditions of those who are different by nature. Liberal theory believed the emancipation of women resolved when it advanced their equality of rights before the law and on the market place. But this did nothing to eliminate the social bias against women. In a large number of occupations women are discriminated against to this day. They often receive less pay than men for the same type of work. Nor can formal equalization alter the special role of women in the family. Where women remain in the labor force by staying single or making arrangements for their children, they must compete with men as equals. That competition can have a lacerating emotional effect. And one may wonder what the emotional effects on women are in countries like the Soviet Union, where official doctrine holds them to be equal and where in the absence of occupational choice they must shoulder the same burdens as men.

The case of racial minorities is similar to that of women in some respects. Gunnar Myrdal noted some years ago that prejudice against Negroes and against women is remarkably similar. Both are reputed to be mercurial, childlike, of lesser intelligence, and both suffer from some of the same disabilities like less pay for equal work, employment in menial occupations, greater risks of dismissal, and others. But these parallels of prejudice and social inferiority do not go to the heart of the problem.

Racial minorities, and especially the Negro population in the United States with its history of slavery, constitute a lower class as women obviously do not. An ethnically or racially segregated lower class is a distinctive phenomenon of industrialized societies in the twentieth century. It differs fundamentally from the proletariat of the nineteenth century in the sense that race has been added to class as the reason for a denial of civil, political, and social rights. It differs also from the many countries in Asia and elsewhere, in which racial minorities represent ethnic enclaves that constitute virtually separate societies and economies. For these enclaves are not classes, but distinct ethnic communities. In the

United States, ethnic communities are on the whole integrated economically and to some extent socially. By contrast, the American Negro, the Puerto Rican, and the Mexican-American suffer not only from the disabilities of racial discrimination generally, but constitute a special lower stratum by virtue of their exclusion from the working class.

The citizenship of racial minorities remains an unresolved problem. Members of minority groups are denied rights which are formally theirs, a condition far worse than that faced by workers in the nineteenth century, who could attack the clear symbols of their second class status, like disenfranchisement or the laws prohibiting trade unions. Negro Americans or West Indians in England face a social discrimination so hydra-headed that institutional changes like special guarantees of due process or of the right to vote, important as these are, do not alter their outcast status effectively.

Conservative theory with its belief in natural inequality ignored this problem, but even liberal and radical theory cannot cope with it. For the market does not provide opportunities for those who suffer from massive social discrimination. And the working class will not extend its solidarity to those who find themselves forced to work at lower rates. In this setting, it becomes the task of welfare institutions to prevent the worst deprivations. The schools must attempt to raise the skill level of these outcast groups. And while these institutions become arenas of racial conflict, the major political and economic institutions ignore the problem as long as possible and for the most part confront it only when they must.

I conclude this survey of current problems with a brief reference to the question of youth. It is not customary to consider this a problem of citizenship. However, citizenship means active participation in public affairs, and when youths come of age they acquire the formal right of participation. In the nineteenth century, entry into citizenship did not present a major problem, because youths could join the forward movement of Western societies, whether this consisted in movements of emancipation, the settlement of continents, or an imperial mission. But as noted earlier in this discussion, there were many countries in the nineteenth century which did not enjoy this forward movement. Economically backward and politically repressive, countries like those of Eastern Europe witnessed progress only from afar. In such countries men of letters were often the spokesmen of a youth chafing under the prospect of careers that would only frustrate their personal and national ambitions. To these youths and to their modern peers in the countries of Asia and Latin America, a social order first had to be created in which citizenship would be worthwhile.

In the twentieth century, entry into citizenship has become a critical concern in ways quite unsuspected during the nineteenth century. As long as the franchise was limited, the target was clear. Demands for lowering the voting age and eliminating property qualifications were in the end satisfied, except in oligarchic regimes incapable of this adaptation. But once these demands were met, it became apparent that the right to vote was meaningful only if the values attached to that right were accepted. And this in turn depended on the credibility of the institutional structure. Once the right to vote at age twenty-one can be taken for granted, the critical question becomes whether those who turn twenty-one are committed to uphold the structure in which they now have a right to participate. In Western Europe social critics have questioned that structure throughout, but with particular insistence since the end of the nineteenth century. And the great writers of the twentieth century have treated the ideas of liberal democracy with indifference or hostility.[13] For youth such indifference or hostility has become a passionate concern during the great crises of our era.

In the large context sketched here, these "generational revolts" have a logic of their own.[14] They have occurred at the crises of Western civilization which jeopardized hitherto prevailing assumptions. World War I destroyed the balance of power among states. The great depression witnessed the destruction of the market mechanism as traditionally conceived. And following the recovery from the ravages of World War II the 1960s have been marked by a sense of crisis arising from the prospect of nuclear destruction, the worldwide confrontation of the superpowers, and the unresolved legacies of five centuries of Western expansion.

What then is the prospect before youth today? No one can answer this question, but the reasons for our uncertainty are familiar. In our time the speed and diversity of change have been so unprecedented that the preoccupations of earlier decades seem already curiously old fashioned. Who still considers it vital to discuss central planning vs. the market principle, when partially planned economies have developed under both socialist and capitalist auspices? Who still looks to world government as the solution to international problems, when in fifty years of effort since the founding of the League of Nations only regional alliances and precariously maintained détentes have shown some slight promise of results. Even the horrors of totalitarian rule have dimmed somewhat, as other kinds of one-party rule have been adopted widely, although the harshness of dictatorship remains. Also, fissures have come to divide the communist bloc and the nuclear threat as well as the consequences of the arms race have put accommodation on the agenda of the superpowers.

In the second half of this century there are two changes, however, which are unprecedented in their implications. One is a transformation of radical protest, the other a transformation of the belief in progress through knowledge. Both signify a great, perhaps a fatal, weakening of the Enlightenment tradition.

In the mid-nineteenth century Marx had turned his back on utopianism by rejecting speculations about the future and basing present actions upon economic and historical analysis. His was a rationalist approach to capitalist society and the road of the labor movement to revolution and a socialist society of the future. Perhaps Lenin was the first to modify this rationalism by organizing the revolution in a backward country and making his party independent of working class support. Mao Tse Tung has carried this modification further, though his voluntarism is still limited by the insistence that the party or the army must win and retain the support of the peasant masses. With men like Castro, Guevara, and Debray and with spokesmen of the New Left this rationalist tradition of radical protest has been eroded. A secular religion based on the charismatic prestige of insurrection has taken the place of both analysis of social conditions and the search for popular support. The Marxian belief in theory and practice has been abandoned.[15]

Equally noteworthy is the declining belief in reason within the citadel of Western science. Since the discovery of atomic energy the prestige of science has been questioned and with it the remaining legacies of the Enlightenment. For all the indispensable knowledge that it alone can develop, science has created powers of destruction so great that agonizing questions are raised concerning the unconditional quest for knowledge. And with these questions comes a renewed concern with the large-scale alterations of the natural environment which are a by-product of headlong and heedless advances in technology. Yet, as noted earlier, science and scholarship presuppose a belief in knowledge "for the benefit and use of life" (Bacon), a belief in the perfectability of man. They do not flourish amidst preoccupation with destructive repercussions, or where the value of knowledge is doubted. The last decades of this century may well witness a crisis of conscience, raising long overdue questions concerning the purpose of knowledge. The prospect inspires anxiety and hope, but hardly confidence.

NOTES

NOTES FOR CHAPTER ONE

[1] The point is elaborated in Chapter 5 of this volume. For a comparison with parallel assumptions in the natural sciences cf. the discussion in Ernst Cassirer, *Substance and Function and Einstein's Theory of Relativity* (New York: Dover Publications, 1953), pp. 364–66, 389–93.

[2] Cf. Sigmund Freud, *New Introductory Lectures to Psychoanalysis* (New York: W. Norton, 1933), pp. 111–12: "Where Id was, there shall Ego be."

[3] A separate study is needed to explore the implications of recruitment. Opinion among practitioners has changed often with regard to the "proper" attitude of the analyst to the patient. Apparently, the training analysis is not sufficient as an index of competence, and indeed many conscientious analysts submit themselves to analysis at regular intervals. Since psychoanalysts had to fight for recognition, they have a vigorous professional association that watches the recruitment process in a manner encouraging to orthodoxy. As with Marxism there is much here which encourages "the self-confirming hypothesis." Cf. also Kurt Mittenzwey, "Zur Soziologie der psychoanalytischen Erkenntnis" in Max Scheler, ed., *Versuche zu einer Soziologie des Wissens* (Munich: Duncker and Humblot, 1924), pp. 365–75

[4] Selig Perlman, *Theory of the Labor Movement* (New York: Macmillan, 1928), pp. 5–9, 41–42, 68.

[5] The use of this invidious term is intentional. By it I want to refer to the common practice of taking a profound idea out of the context of thought in which it had its place without considering the effect which this has on the meaning of the idea itself.

[6] See Theodor Reik, *Listening with the Third Ear* (New York: Farrar, Strauss and Company, 1949), p. 513.

[7] It is perhaps as a reaction against this vulgarization that the neo-Freudian school has emphasized the importance of the self-system during recent years. See the writings of Karen Horney, Erich Fromm, Heinz Hartmann, Erik Erikson, David Rapoport, and others.

[8] I base the preceding characterization on my reading of Emile Durkheim, *Sociology and Philosophy* (Glencoe: The Free Press, 1953), pp. 63–97 and *Education and Sociology* (Glencoe: The Free Press, 1956), pp. 113–34. Other writings of Durkheim are also relevant, but the two volumes cited contain Durkheim's more programmatic pronouncements.

[9] For Freud's statement of faith in science see his *The Future of Illusion* (Garden City: Doubleday & Co., 1957), pp. 98–102.

[10] For an instructive characterization of this "generation of intellectuals" cf. Stuart Hughes, *Consciousness and Society* (New York: A. A. Knopf, 1958).

[11] See Emile Durkheim, *Professional Ethics and Civic Morals* (Glencoe: The Free Press, 1958).

[12] See Anna Freud, *Ego and the Mechanisms of Defense*, rev. ed. (New York: International Universities Press, 1967).

[13] Cf. the further discussion of this point on pp. 35ff.

[14] The distinction between theories of the middle range and general social

theory, introduced by Robert K. Merton, is similar in intent, by noting the difference between hypothesis construction for the explanation of specific causal relations and theory construction for cataloguing the dimensions of societies as social systems. The strategy suggested in the text is designed with references to this second interest, as spelled out in the following essays.

[15] Since aspects of this problem with special reference to Marx, Tocqueville, Durkheim, and Weber are explored in "The Age of Ideology" reprinted in this volume, I confine myself at this point to a brief characterization.

[16] Cf. the argument for the unity of Marx's thought in Robert Tucker, *Philosophy and Myth in Karl Marx* (Cambridge: University Press, 1965), Chp. xi, and passim. Marx's views are analyzed in the larger historical context by Nicholas Lobkowicz, *Theory and Practice* (Notre Dame: Notre Dame University Press, 1967), passim. See also the illuminating article by Lewis Feuer, "Karl Marx and the Promethean Complex," *Encounter* XXXI (December 1968), pp. 15–32.

[17] Scientists reject the view that knowledge is a by-product of history to which Marxists would rejoin that it is inseparable from the conditions of human existence. Of course no one denies that the pursuit of knowledge is affected by society and history. But there is little agreement on how this is to be assessed.

[18] A workable degree of approximation can ensure the productive continuation of scientific inquiry and is thus a pragmatic criterion. For further discussion cf. pp. 63–68.

[19] See the telling exposition of this evolutionist approach to the growth of knowledge by Robert K. Merton, "The Precarious Foundations of Detachment in Sociology," in Edward Tiryakian, ed., *The Phenomenon of Sociology* (New York: D. Appleton-Century, 1970), passim. By way of contrast cf. Karl Popper, *The Poverty of Historicism* (London: Routledge and Kegan Paul, 1961), passim, where the unpredictable growth of knowledge is made the basis of an anti-evolutionist and anti-historicist argument.

[20] The earlier distinction between natural science and *Geisteswissenschaft* or *Kulturwissenschaft* has clearly become obsolete in this respect. German philosophers like Wilhelm Dilthey or Heinrich Rickert who emphasized the difference in the objects studied by these two kinds of disciplines, worked with a nineteenth-century conception of science. In the light of more recent developments the idea of a "unity of knowledge" has been restored by showing that in the natural sciences knowledge also has an indispensable subjective component. Some implications of this development are discussed below in Chapters 3 and 4. For an outstanding exposition of this view see Michael Polanyi, *Personal Knowledge* (London: Routledge and Kegan Paul, 1958), passim. The subjective dimension which for Dilthey distinguished the cultural from the natural sciences, is now claimed as a characteristic of the latter as well.

NOTES FOR CHAPTER TWO

[1] Francis Bacon, "Novum Organum," in E. A. Burtt, ed., *The English Philosophers from Bacon to Mill* (New York: The Modern Library, 1939), pp. 40–41.

[2] See Daniel Bell, *The End of Ideology* (Glencoe: The Free Press, 1960), pp. 369 ff., passim. Cf. Seymour M. Lipset, *Political Man* (Garden City: Doubleday & Co., 1960), pp. 403 ff. The references in these and related writings are to the "end of ideology" in the West; it is acknowledged that there may have occurred a "rise of ideology" in Asia and Africa.

[3] In principle there is also the possibility of a postideological epoch, but this eventuality lies in the future as long as we are witnessing the "end of some ideologies" rather than the "end of ideology." The more accurate phrase has less punch, however.

[4] Carl Becker, *The Heavenly City of the Eighteenth Century Philosophers* (New Haven: Yale University Press, 1932), p. 47.

[5] For a brilliant portrayal of this earlier world view with special reference to social and economic thought, see Otto Brunner, *Adeliges Landleben und Europäischer Geist* (Salzburg: Otto Müller Verlag, 1949), Chap. 2. In the field of literary history, parallel materials are found in Erich Auerbach, *Mimesis, The Representation of Reality in Western Literature* (Garden City: Doubleday & Co., 1957), passim. For a contrast between these premodern perspectives and the "Age of Ideology" I am indebted to Brunner, "Das Zeitalter der Ideologien," *Neue Wege der Sozialgeschichte* (Göttingen: Vandenhoeck & Ruprecht, 1956), pp. 194–219.

[6] *American College Dictionary* (New York, 1947), p. 599.

[7] Bacon, *op. cit.*, pp. 28, 62. The subtitle of the essay is "Aphorisms Concerning the Interpretation of Nature and the Kingdom of Man."

[8] For an acute analysis of the modernity of Bacon's approach in relation to classical conceptions of knowledge and action, see Hans Jonas, "The Practical Uses of Theory," *Social Research*, XXVI (Summer 1959), pp. 127–50.

[9] The quoted phrases are found in Bacon, *op. cit.*, p. 64.

[10] Bacon, *op. cit.*, p. 65.

[11] The fundamental commitment of scientists to a hedonistic and secular world view is examined in detail in the study by Lewis Feuer, *The Scientific Intellectual* (New York: Basic Books, 1963).

[12] The most comprehensive treatment of this development is contained in Ernst Cassirer, *The Philosophy of the Enlightenment* (Boston: The Beacon Press, 1955). Directly pertinent to the present discussion are Charles Van Duzer, *Contribution of the Ideologues to French Revolutionary Thought* (Baltimore: The Johns Hopkins Press, 1935); and Hans Barth, *Wahrheit und Ideologie* (Zürich: Manesse Verlag, 1945), pp. 54–70.

[13] See J. W. Stein, *The Mind and the Sword* (New York: Twayne Publishers, Inc. 1961), p. 88, and passim. The term "ideology" was coined by Tracy in order to distinguish his "scientific" approach from conventional philosophy or metaphysics. See *ibid.*, p. 186, n. 33.

[14] *Ibid.*, pp. 94, 107. Similarly, Cabanis—in his *Rapportis du physique et du mortal* (1802)—sought to analyze morality by research in physiology, a method that would make progress in education and the social sciences as rapid as it had been in the natural sciences. See p. 82.

[15] See Barth, *op. cit.*, pp. 15–35; and Stein, *op. cit.*, pp. 141–71 for accounts of this episode.

[16] A given proposition might be true but impractical and politically beneficial (from some point of view); it might be true, practical, but politically

dangerous (from some point of view); and so forth. Since truth, practicality, and political effect have been involved in the pejorative meaning of ideology ever since Napoleon, confusions abound, especially since utility or political effects have often been employed as tests of truth in order to strengthen or weaken the appeal of theories under the guise of the prestige of science. These confusions, however, are an important part of nineteenth-century intellectual history.

[17] Edmund Burke, *Reflections on the Revolution in France* (Chicago: Henry Regnery Co., 1955), pp. 126–27.

[18] In the passage preceding the one quoted, Burke polemicizes against Rousseau, Voltaire, and Helvétius: "We know that we have made no discoveries, and we think that no discoveries are to be made, in morality; nor many in the great principles of government, nor in the ideas of liberty, which were understood long before we were born, altogether as well as they will be after the grave has heaped its mould upon our presumption. . . . In England we have not yet been completely embowelled of our natural entrails; we still feel within us, and we cherish and cultivate, those inbred sentiments which are the faithful guardians, the active monitors of our duty, the true supporters of all liberal and manly morals. . . . We preserve the whole of our feelings still native and entire, unsophisticated by pedantry and infidelity. . . . We fear God; we look up with awe to kings. . . . Why? Because such ideas are brought before our minds, it is natural to be so affected; because all other feelings are false and spurious, and tend to corrupt our minds. . . ." *Ibid.*, pp. 125–26.

[19] Cf. Leo Strauss, *Natural Right and History* (Chicago: University of Chicago Press, 1953), pp. 307–11, for an extended statement of these contrasts derived from Burke's writings.

[20] Cf. the detailed discussion of this point in *ibid.*, pp. 294–323.

[21] For this formulation of Weber's in his essay "Science as a Vocation," see H. H. Gerth and C. Wright Mills, eds., *From Max Weber: Essays in Sociology* (New York: Oxford University Press, 1946), pp. 150–51. It is a convenient summary of the assumptions underlying much social thought in the nineteenth century; its significance for Weber's approach is considered later.

[22] Such reticence is not universal. Cf. George Lundberg, *Can Science Save Us?* (New York: Longman, Green & Co., 1961), passim.

[23] Cf., for example, the telling arguments against premature consideration of these questions of purpose in Robert K. Merton, "Social Conflict over Styles of Sociological Work," *Transactions of the Fourth World Congress of Sociology*, III (Louvain, 1961), pp. 21–44.

[24] The paradox was first formulated by the Greek philosopher Zeno in the statement: "A Cretan says all Cretans are liars." Since the person making the statement is himself a member of the group of whom a lack of veracity is asserted, an infinite chain of mutually contradictory assertions follows. For our purposes the analogous statement would be: "Social scientists say that every man's knowledge of society is the product of that society," although this application lacks the simplicity of the classic model.

[25] Quoted in Barth, *op. cit.*, p. 67.

[26] Frank E. Manuel, *The New World of Henri Saint-Simon* (Cambridge: Harvard University Press, 1956), p. 134.

²⁷ Quoted in *ibid.*, p. 135.

²⁸ Sigmund Freud, *The Future of an Illusion* (Garden City: Doubleday & Co., n. d.), p. 98. The numbered statements in the text are based on pp. 95–102.

²⁹ *Ibid.*, p. 99.

³⁰ *Ibid.*, p. 102.

³¹ Although the contrast between Saint-Simon and Freud suggests a diminution of hope concerning the benefits to be derived from knowledge, proof of this trend in the climate of opinion is a more complex affair and is not attempted here. Even in the eighteenth century there were great skeptics of the promise of science as applied to human affairs—men like Edmund Burke and Montesquieu—and this skepticism had numerous spokesmen throughout the nineteenth century along with the more dominant expressions of belief in progress. Hans Barth's *Wahrheit und Ideologie* contains a detailed philosophical analysis of changing conceptions of man and truth that supports the interpretation offered here.

³² Karl Marx, *Capital* (New York: The Modern Library, 1936), p. 89. The present discussion of Marx's view of knowledge may be compared with his analysis of social class and change, discussed on pp. 263–68.

³³ *Ibid.*, p. 91.

³⁴ *Ibid.*, pp. 90–91.

³⁵ *Ibid.*, pp. 91–92.

³⁶ See, for example, Karl Marx, *A Contribution to the Critique of Political Economy* (Chicago: Charles Kerr, 1904), p. 12.

³⁷ See, for example, Marx, *Capital*, pp. 12–13, preface to the first edition.

³⁸ Karl Marx and Friedrich Engels, *Manifesto of the Communist Party* (New York: International Publishers, 1939), p. 19. My italics.

³⁹ See note 35 above for the source of this wording.

⁴⁰ From Tocqueville's letter to Henry Reeve, dated March 22, 1837, in Tocqueville, *Memoir, Letters and Remains*, II (Boston: Ticknor & Fields, 1862), pp. 39–40. Tocqueville's work is analyzed further on pp. 135–38 with reference to comparative studies and on pp. 234–40 with reference to social change.

⁴¹ There is a similar argument in Marx, but it is very general and unclear, while Tocqueville is specific and lucid.

⁴² Tocqueville, *op. cit.*, I, p. 376. From a letter to M. Stoffels, February 21, 1835.

⁴³ Quoted phrases are taken from the letter to Stoffels, *ibid.*

⁴⁴ From a letter to M. de Kergorlay, November 13, 1833, *ibid.*, I, p. 299.

⁴⁵ From a letter to M. Stoffels, January 3, 1843, *ibid.*, I, p. 392.

⁴⁶ *Ibid.*

⁴⁷ *Ibid.*, I, pp. 299–300. From the letter to Kergorlay, already cited.

⁴⁸ *Ibid.*, I, p. 393. From the letter to Stoffels, January 3, 1843.

⁴⁹ *Ibid.*, I, pp. 374–75. From a letter to M. Stoffels, January 12, 1833.

⁵⁰ See *Ibid.*, II, pp. 84–5, for a vigorous statement to this effect in a letter to M. de Corcelle, October 11, 1846.

⁵¹ See Karl Marx and Friedrich Engels, *Die Heilige Familie* (Berlin: Dietz

Verlag, 1953), p. 138. Italics in the original; my translation. Marx constantly re-examined the labor movements in various countries for evidence of a rising class-consciousness in his sense of the word, but his judgments in this respect were notably unstable in terms of his own theoretical assumptions.

[52] Tocqueville, *op. cit.*, II, p. 230. From a letter to M. de Corcelle, September 17, 1853.

[53] *Ibid.*, II, pp. 13–14. From a letter to M. de Corcelle, April 12, 1835.

[54] Tocqueville, *Democracy in America* (New York: Vintage Books, 1954), II, p. 352.

[55] Tocqueville, *Memoir*, I, pp. 13–14. From the letter to De Corcelle, April 12, 1835.

[56] Tocqueville, *The European Revolution and Correspondence with Gobineau* (Garden City: Doubleday & Co., 1959), pp. 231–2. From letter to Gobineau, December 20, 1853.

[57] Tocqueville, *Memoir*, I, p. 382. From the letter to M. Stoffels, July 24, 1836.

[58] *Ibid.*, I, p. 400. From the letter to M. Stoffels, July 21, 1848.

[59] *Ibid.*, II, pp. 305–6. From the letter dated January 7, 1856.

[60] *Ibid.*, II, p. 335. From the letter to Madame Swetchine, October 20, 1856.

[61] Emile Durkheim, *The Rules of Sociological Method* (Chicago: University of Chicago Press, 1938), p. xi, from the author's preface to the first edition.

[62] Emile Durkheim, *Montesquieu and Rousseau* (Ann Arbor: University of Michigan Press, 1960), pp. 3 ff.

[63] *Ibid.*, pp. 6–7.

[64] *Ibid.*, p. 10.

[65] *Ibid.*, pp. 10–11.

[66] *Ibid.*, p. 12.

[67] My restatement here is brief in keeping with the purpose of the present discussion. Cf. the further discussion of Durkheim's work in a political context in Chp. 10, pp. 226–30.

[68] Cf. Durkheim's simultaneous insistence upon the collective origin and the individual manifestation of ideas and sentiments in *Rules, op. cit.*, pp. liv, n. 5, and lvi, n. 7. It may be added that Durkheim's strongly antipsychological argument, which is part of his case for sociology as an autonomous discipline, should be read in the context of nineteenth-century psychology with its emphasis on instincts and psychophysical parallelism.

[69] These points are discussed in Durkheim, *The Division of Labor in Society* (New York: The Free Press, 1960), pp. 283 ff, and passim. Note also a later essay, published in 1898, discussed in Edward Tiryakian, *Sociologism and Existentialism* (Englewood Cliffs: Prentice-Hall, 1962), p. 57.

[70] I am indebted to Tiryakian, *op. cit.*, for his analysis of this late phase of Durkheim's thought.

[71] See his discussion of law and occupational groups in *The Division of Labor, op. cit.*, pp. 174 ff., and preface to the second edition. His efforts to

clarify the concepts of normality or "social health" are contained in *Rules*, Chap. III.

[72] Emile Durkheim, *Suicide* (London: Routledge & Kegan Paul, 1952), p. 169.

[73] *Ibid.*

[74] Tiryakian, *op. cit.*, p. 35.

[75] The phrase is taken from Tocqueville's letter to Mrs. Grote, in *Memoirs*, II, p. 321.

[76] Durkheim, *Montesquieu and Rousseau, op. cit.*, pp. 8–9.

[77] *Ibid.*, p .55. My italics.

[78] To consider these criteria a quality inherent in the phenomena is tantamount to the nonideological world-view discussed earlier or its organological legacy in a man like Durkheim. That is, facts and values are like emanations of the divine will just as body temperature and the limits of variation compatible with health are attributes of the biological organism. See below pp. 112–14, 130–33 for further discussion of this approach.

[79] "Denn gerade wegen der Unmöglichkeit, in der historischen Wirklichkeit scharfe Grenzen zu ziehen, können wir nur bei Untersuchung ihrer konsequentesten Formen hoffen, auf ihre spezifischen Wirkungen zu stossen." Max Weber, *Gesammelte Aufsätze zur Religionssoziologie* (Tübingen: J. C. B. Mohr (Paul Siebeck), 1947), I, p. 87.

[80] I add this phrase because the term Weber employs is *Sinn* not *Bedeutung*, sense rather than meaning, although the latter word has been used in the translations.

[81] Cf. Leo Strauss, *op. cit.*, for a comprehensive compilation of the evaluative terms that can be found in Weber's empirical works like his essays on the sociology of religion. Strauss criticizes Weber for his constant use of value judgments in his research, but he fails to note the basic difference between assessments based on ideal types and value judgments in the sense of personal evaluations.

[82] Cf. Reinhard Bendix, "Max Weber's Interpretation of Conduct and History," *American Journal of Sociology*, LI (May 1946), pp. 518–26.

[83] See Weber's discussion in "Science as a Vocation," in Gerth and Mills, *op. cit.*, passim.

[84] This end has occurred, however, where a new orthodoxy has put a stop to the uncertainties endemic in the pursuit of knowledge—hardly the meaning that those who coined the phrase had in mind. One should note in this connection the pejorative use of "ideology" in Soviet terminology as a label by which Western thought is set off from the truth of Marxism-Leninism.

[85] An example of such questioning, which goes beyond the fashionable cultural pessimism, is contained in the impressive work of Friedrich Wagner, *Die Wissenschaft und die gefährdete Welt* (München: C. H. Beck, 1969), passim.

Notes for Chapter Three

[1] Mannheim's concept goes back to a formulation of Alfred Weber's. See Karl Mannheim, *Ideology and Utopia* (New York: Harcourt, Brace & Co.,

1949), pp. 136 ff. and Karl Popper, *The Open Society and Its Enemies* (Princeton: Princeton University Press, 1950), pp. 398 ff.

² Thomas S. Kuhn, *The Structure of Scientific Revolutions* (Chicago: University of Chicago Press, 1964), pp. 10–11.

³ Robert K. Merton, "The Ambivalence of Scientists," *Bulletin of the Johns Hopkins Hospital*, vol. 112 (February 1963), pp. 77–97. See also the same author's Presidential Address, "Priorities in Scientific Discovery," *American Sociological Review*, XXII (December 1957), pp. 635–59.

⁴ See Max Weber, *Gesammelte Aufsätze zur Wissenschaftslehre*, 3rd ed. (Tübingen: J. C. B. Mohr (Paul Siebeck), 1968), p. 184.

⁵ Talcott Parsons, "Evaluation and Objectivity in Social Science: An Interpretation of Max Weber's Contribution," *International Social Science Journal*, XVII (1965), p. 50.

⁶ Much of the difficulty in obtaining a concise view of Marx's theory stems from the fact that it was meant to be a tool for political action in this sense, although Marx claimed scientific validity for his work at the same time. These two sides are not integrated in Marx's own work, but they become quite separated whenever that work has become influential academically. Sociologists who accept and develop aspects of Marx's theory, cannot also simulate the exile politics of mid-nineteenth-century Europe which provided the setting for Marx's activist conception of theory.

⁷ Max Weber, "The Meaning of 'Ethical Neutrality' in Sociology and Economics," in *The Methodology of the Social Sciences*, trans. and ed. by E. A. Shils and H. A. Finch (Glencoe: The Free Press, 1949), pp. 5–10, and passim.

⁸ Cf. Reinhard Bendix, "Social Science and Social Action in Historical Perspective," *Ethics*, LVI (1946), pp. 208–18.

⁹ *Chicago Today*, III (1966), p. 53. In the paragraph just preceding this quotation Professor Rubin ventures to "state that you will encounter more warm human feeling in an African village than you will in a high powered research laboratory." Apparently, this outworn cliché still has appeal despite its checkered history of some two thousand years. Cf. Henry Baudet, *Paradise on Earth* (New Haven: Yale University Press, 1965), passim, for a knowledgable summary of this tradition; and Robert L. Heilbroner, *The Future as History* (New York: Grove Press, 1961), Chap. 1 and passim, for a perceptive statement on the decline of optimism.

¹⁰ Roger Revelle, "The Failures of Western Science," *New York Times, News of the Week* (December 31, 1967).

¹¹ Cf. the discussion of the Baconian perspective by Hans Jonas, "The Practical Uses of Theory," *Social Research*, XXVI (1959), pp. 127–50. Cf. chapter 2, n. 8.

¹² Some years ago I suggested that social scientists welcome such utility and rigor as they attain, but for the rest should claim the recognition that is their due by an appeal to the value of scholarship and enlightenment. Cf. Reinhard Bendix, *Social Science and the Distrust of Reason*, University of California Publications in Sociology and Social Institutions, vol. I (Berkeley: University of California Press, 1951), p. 42.

¹³ J. Bronowski, *The Common Sense of Science* (New York: Random House, n. d.), pp. 102–3.

[14] Ernst Cassirer, *Substance and Function and Einstein's Theory of Relativity* (New York: Dover Publications Inc., 1953), pp. 357–58. The work was originally published in 1923.

[15] *Ibid.*, pp. 364, 388.

[16] He may note that Heisenberg rejects various critiques of the Copenhagen interpretation of Quantum theory on the ground that they are based on the old ontological assumptions. See Werner Heisenberg, *Physics and Philosophy* (New York: Harper & Row, 1962), Chap. 8, and passim.

[17] Cassirer, *op. cit.*, p. 421. Again the layman can but ask whether the statistical laws established by Quantum theory leave the principle of covariancy intact as an effective resolution of the philosophical problem of relativity.

[18] Wylie Sypher, *Rococo to Cubism in Art and Literature* (New York: Random House, 1960), pp. 264–65. See also the instructive comment in Martin Esslin, *The Theatre of the Absurd*, rev. ed. (Harmondsworth: Penguin Books, Ltd., 1968), pp. 414–15.

[19] This intellectual tradition is traced from the eighteenth century to the present in Judith Shklar, *After Utopia* (Princeton: Princeton University Press, 1969), pp. 37–61, 80–96, and passim.

[20] Max Weber especially emphasized that the highest degree of *impersonality* is the specific *personal* ideal of scientists and represents an austere, moral commitment. See particularly his essay "Science as a Vocation" which has been reprinted many times.

[21] See Erwin Schroedinger, *Mind and Matter* (London: Cambridge University Press, 1958), p. 49, who states that "we never observe an object without its being modified or tinged by our activity in observing it." A link between Schroedinger's ideas and certain tendencies in modern painting has been suggested by Wylie Sypher, *Loss of the Self in Modern Literature and Art* (New York: Random House, 1962), pp. 122–23. The parallels between art and science are explored by James Ackerman, E. M. Hafner, George Kubler, and Thomas Kuhn in *Comparative Studies in Society and History*, XI (October 1969), pp. 371–412.

[22] Cf. Daniel Bell's very apt characterization of the nihilist implications of these trends in his book *The Reforming of General Education* (New York: Columbia University Press, 1966), pp. 307–12. The related comments in the text are addressed to the special problem of detachment and objectivity.

[23] Cf. the extended discussion of this transformation by Clark Kerr, *The Uses of the University* (New York: Harper & Row, 1966), passim.

[24] Statement by Chancellor Heyns to the Berkeley Division of the Academic Senate, May 23, 1969, reprinted in *University Bulletin*, vol. 17 (June 2, 1969), p. 191.

[25] Intolerance is familiar enough from the rightist attacks on academic freedom. That it now informs segments of the New Left has recently been stated with gratifying clarity by Herbert Marcuse, in Robert Wolff, Barrington Moore, and Herbert Marcuse, *A Critique of Pure Tolerance* (Boston: The Beacon Press, 1966), passim. Lately, Professor Marcuse has been depending on the principle of tolerance, established within the university, to defend his academic position against attacks by the American Legion. One

wonders how long he will be able to attack what he calls "repressive tolerance" and still continue to benefit from the protection it affords him. The moral ambiguity of his position is intensified still more by the fact that his cultural critique of industrial society coincides in important respects with the conservative and even fascist critiques of that society. For an analysis of this intellectual congruence between rightist and leftist extremism cf. Ernst Topitsch, *Die Freiheit der Wissenschaft und der politische Auftrag der Universität* (Neuwied: Hermann Luchterhand Verlag, 1968), passim. See also my related analysis in "Tradition and Modernity Reconsidered," reprinted below, esp. pp. 255–63.

[26] This argument is of a piece with the demand that disciplinary proceedings at universities should observe all the safeguards of civil law. Oddly enough, this argument is reminiscent of an idea advanced some years ago by Clark Kerr, former president of the University of California. Focusing attention upon the many ways in which corporations and trade unions infringe upon employees or members, Kerr advocated a Bill of Rights which would protect the individual against such infringements. It should be noted, however, that Kerr's proposal emphasized the limited purpose of corporations or trade unions positively, whereas student spokesmen frequently reject the limited purposes of universities. Cf. Clark Kerr, "What Became of the Independent Spirit?" *Fortune* (July 1953), pp. 110–11, 134–36.

[27] The relative neglect of undergraduate education in American universities is not only a by-product of specialization, as has often been noted, it also has resulted from the decline of educational ideals which could orient teachers and students alike. The inchoate dissatisfactions of beginning students are matched by the many, but inchoate experiments in undergraduate education. It does not seem appropriate to interpret the failure of many such experiments as an unresponsiveness to student demand.

[28] See Erwin K. Scheuch, "Soziologische Aspekte der Unruhe unter den Studenten," *Das Parlament, Beilage aus Politik und Zeitgeschichte* (September 4, 1968), pp. 7–17. Scheuch attributes the intensification of these concerns to certain structural transformations in the position of middle-class occupations and in the career problems and prospects of university students.

[29] There is no need to document the latter, but by now it is necessary to recall the former. See, for example, Richard Hofstadter, *Social Darwinism in American Thought*, rev. ed. (Boston: Beacon Press, 1955), passim. For a survey of "scientific arguments favoring Imperialism" cf. J. A. Hobson, *Imperialism* (London: Allen & Unwin, 1938), Part II. Hobson was a foremost critic of imperialism; his book was originally published in 1902.

[30] Karl Schmid, *Hochmut und Angst* (Zürich: Artemis Verlag, 1958), pp. 28–29. Schmid focuses on a critical analysis of the European intellectual's "arrogant and anxious" reaction to the two world powers of Russia and the USA. But many of his points apply generally to the Western intellectual reaction to the postwar world.

[31] This is a major theme in the report by Caleb Foote, Henry Meyer, et al., *The Culture of the University: Governance and Education*, Report of the Study Commission on University Governance, University of California, Berkeley (January 15, 1968). According to its minority critics this report comes "perilously close to asserting that if the university cannot involve its students in courses, let it at least involve them in administration." See *The*

Challenge to the University, Dissenting Report, Study Commission on University Governance, University of California, Berkeley (April 4, 1968), p. 2. The parallel between these ideas on university government and Lenin's ideas in *State and Revolution* should not be overlooked.

[32] Max Weber, "Science as a Vocation," in H. H. Gerth and C. W. Mills, eds., *From Max Weber, Essays in Sociology* (New York: Oxford University Press, 1947), pp. 138, 140, and passim.

[33] Don K. Price, *The Scientific Estate* (Cambridge: Harvard University Press, 1967), p. 105.

[34] Cf. *ibid.*, p. 204, and passim.

NOTES FOR CHAPTER FOUR

[1] This quotation is taken from, and the preceding statement is indebted to, an editorial on "Academic Freedom" which appeared in *The Times Literary Supplement* of October 10, 1968. With regard to the parallel noted in the text it is instructive to reread the work of Carl Schmitt, *Die geistesgeschichtliche Lage des heutigen Parlamentarismus* (Berlin: Duncker & Humblot, 1961), pp. 41 ff., which was originally published in 1926.

[2] Raymond Aron, *The Opium of the Intellectuals* (London: Secker & Warburg, 1957), p. 323.

[3] Peter L. Berger and Thomas Luckmann, *The Social Construction of Reality* (New York: Doubleday & Co., 1966), pp. 113–15. Berger and Luckmann distinguish between monopolistic and pluralistic cultural situations. The utility of that distinction is evident in the Soviet experience, in which a monopolistic construction of reality appears as "science" to insiders, who look on all competing world views as "ideological," while outsiders consider the "monopolistic construction" as ideological. There are, of course, numerous variants of such conflicting perspectives. Historically, monopolistic cultural situations have occurred very frequently.

[4] Cf. the work by Hans Barth, *Wahrheit und Ideologie* (Zürich: Manesse Verlag 1945) and the related discussion on pp. 18–29 above.

[5] A peculiar combination of these two intellectual traditions is the tendency of some sociologists to describe the ideas operative in social life in the minutest detail, but to consider these ideas entirely in manipulative terms. The writings of Erving Goffman are representative of this genre, which combines the idealist approach (social situations conceived entirely in terms of the participants' ideas of them) with an interpretation that reduces social conduct to a strategic game of maximizing status assets.

[6] Cf. Reinhard Bendix, *Social Science and the Distrust of Reason,* University of California Publications in Sociology and Social Institutions (Berkeley: University of California Press, 1951), p. 42, and passim.

[7] Kenneth Burke, *Permanence and Change* (New York: New Republic, 1936), p. 70. See p. 134 for a fuller reference to this passage.

[8] Dilthey's first major contribution is contained in his *Einleitung in die Geisteswissenschaften,* published in 1883. The shift from philosophy to a theory about philosophizing as a clue to human nature and history is most

clearly expressed in a late essay entitled "Die Typen der Weltanschauung," published in 1911. These and other relevant materials are found in his *Gesammelte Schriften* (Stuttgart: B. G. Teubner, 1957–60), vols. I and VIII. Carlo Antoni, *From History to Sociology* (Detroit: Wayne State University Press, 1950), pp. 1–38; and R. G. Collingwood, *The Idea of History* (Oxford: Clarendon Press, 1946), pp. 171–76, provide two perceptive introductions to Dilthey's work in English.

[9] Wylie Sypher, *From Rococo to Cubism* (New York: Random House, 1960), pp. 265, 267–68. My italics.

[10] Max Weber, *Gesammelte Aufsätze zur Wissenschaftslehre*, 3rd ed. (Tübingen: J. C. B. Mohr 1968), pp. 212–13. My translation and italics.

[11] *Ibid.*, p. 214.

[12] *Ibid.* The metaphoric language makes the translation more than usually proximate. But the passage conveys Weber's meaning well and provides an intriguing counterpoint to Hegel's famous metaphor: "When philosophy paints its grey in grey, then has a shape of life grown old. By philosophy's grey in grey it cannot be rejuvenated but only understood. The owl of Minerva spreads its wings only with the falling of the dusk." See T. M. Knox, trans. and ed., *Hegel's Philosophy of Right* (Oxford: Clarendon Press, 1958), p. 13.

[13] Cf. Karl Mannheim, *Ideology and Utopia* (New York: Harcourt, Brace & World, 1936), pp. 118–46 for his typology of political ideologies and pp. 282–83 and passim for his discussion of *relationism*. Mannheim's exposition of relativism and relationism was contained in an article in the *Handwörterbuch der Soziologie* (1931), which was included in the American edition of his earlier *Ideologie und Utopie* (1929).

[14] See Arnold Gehlen, *Die Seele im technischen Zeitalter* (Rowohlts deutsche Enzyklopädie; Reinbeck b. Hamburg: Rowohlt Taschenbuch Verlag, 1957), pp. 27–33. Cf. the similar comments by Hans Freyer, "Gesellschaft und Kultur," in Golo Mann, ed., *Die Welt von Heute* (vol. X of Propyläen Weltgeschichte; Berlin: Propyläen Verlag, 1961), pp. 532 ff. and 550 ff.

[15] Wylie Sypher's statement and the quotations from Gide are taken from Sypher, *From Rococo to Cubism, op. cit.*, pp. 300–301, 305. The representativeness of such views is perhaps suggested by the fact that they were already expressed in the early nineteenth century by the German poet Novalis. See Hugo Friedrich, *Die Struktur der modernen Lyrik* (Rowohlts deutsche Enzyklopädie; Hamburg: Rowohlt Taschenbuch Verlag, 1956), pp. 28–29.

[16] Friedrich, *op. cit.*, p. 35.

[17] *Ibid.*, p. 39.

[18] It is startling to discover that this common theme was already articulated by Rousseau. See *ibid.*, p. 24.

[19] Sypher, *From Rococo to Cubism, op. cit.*, p. 306.

[20] For this formulation I am indebted to the lectures of the late Louis Wirth.

[21] For clarification of the points discussed here I am indebted to Gerhard Frey, *Die Mathematisierung unserer Welt* (Stuttgart: W. Kohlhammer Verlag, 1967), pp. 121 ff. For an illuminating analysis of sociological theory construction cf. Arthur Stinchcombe, *Constructing Social Theories* (New York: Harcourt, Brace & World, 1968).

[22] Here we should be on our guard against a direct application of formula-

tions from one field to another. In his discussion of mathematics Frey points out that the formalized object-language of that discipline is always embedded in a richer meta-language and that meta-theoretical predicates like true or false, tautological or contradictory, can only be formulated in the latter. See Frey, *Mathematisierung, op. cit.*, pp. 129–30. Similarly, one may speak of the meta-theoretical criteria in terms of which the validity of sociological propositions is ascertained. But meta-theoretical statements about the conditioning of sociological knowledge, for example the "class bias" of a perspective chosen for study, has to be clearly distinguished from the criteria of validity.

[23] Even the "Marxists" among us no longer believe in a universal historical process. In this respect Mannheim's approach was only a half-step away from Marx in that Mannheim contented himself with a political reductionism of ideas that borrowed Marx's class terminology but somehow omitted his theory of history. Still further away from Marx is Jürgen Habermas's recent survey of presuppositions in a wide variety of theoretical approaches. See his *Zur Logik der Sozialwissenschaften* (Beiheft 5 of Philosophische Rundschau; Tübingen: J. C. B. Mohr (Paul Siebeck), 1967). Though highly illuminating in its critique of other positions, the book fails to give an account of its own vantage point.

[24] Cf. the earlier analysis of Marx and Weber in the essay "The Age of Ideology, Persistent and Changing," reprinted above, where these points are analyzed in more detail.

[25] When this is ignored, "explanation" easily becomes redundant or trite. In the case of modern lyrics, for example, an analyst might account for all its diversity by reference to the alienation of the artist from bourgeois society. He might be right, but how much of the phenomenon would he explain?

[26] See W. H. Auden, "The Knight of the Doleful Countenance," *The New Yorker* (May 25, 1968), pp. 157–58.

[27] For a political and constitutional elaboration of this idea cf. the searching analysis by Don K. Price, *The Scientific Estate* (Cambridge: Harvard University Press, 1967), esp. Chaps. 5 and 7.

[28] The relation between modern social theory and certain organismic analogies is reviewed in some detail in Cynthia E. Russet, *The Concept of Equilibrium in American Social Thought* (New Haven: Yale University Press, 1966), passim. A more analytic approach to the same material is contained in Walter Buckley, *Sociology and Modern Systems Theory* (Englewood Cliffs: Prentice-Hall, 1967), passim. Note also the historical perspective analyzed by Robert A. Nisbet, *Social Change and History* quoted above.

[29] As an example cf. Dahrendorf's critique of Lewis Coser's analysis for its overemphasis on the integrative effects of conflict in contrast to its disruptive effects. See Ralf Dahrendorf, *Gesellschaft und Freiheit* (München: Piper Verlag, 1962), pp. 122–24.

[30] Not always. China possessed such a conception and the encounter with the West led to its disintegration. A brilliant analysis of this disintegration is contained in Joseph Levenson, *Confucian China and its Modern Fate* (Berkeley: University of California Press, 1958), I, passim.

[31] When the Dutch economist J. D. Boeke advanced his theory of a "dual economy" in an interpretation of the colonial experience in South East Asia, he was criticized because contrasts between traditional and modern economic and political patterns exist in Western European countries as well. See Ben-

jamin Higgins, "The 'Dualistic Theory' of Underdeveloped Areas," *Economic Development and Cultural Change,* IV (1955–56), pp. 106–8.

[32] This point is elaborated in the essay "Tradition and Modernity Reconsidered," which is reprinted as Chapter 11.

NOTES FOR CHAPTER FIVE

[1] "To confine ourselves to the large social formations resembles the older science of anatomy with its limitation to the major, definitely circumscribed organs such as heart, liver, lungs, and stomach, and with its neglect of the innumerable, popularly unnamed or unknown tissues. Yet without these, the more obvious organs could never constitute a living organism. On the basis of the major social formations, the traditional subject of social science, it would be similarly impossible to piece together the real life of society as we encounter it in our experience." K. Wolff, ed., *The Sociology of Georg Simmel* (Glencoe: The Free Press, 1950), p. 9. See also pp. 10–13, and 187–88.

[2] By the phrase "sense of the 'real' " we refer not to formally stipulated assumptions, but to the intuitive feeling for what is significant in society and basic for a scientific theory of society. The multiplicity of social theories is in part attributable to this psychological involvement of social theorists. Yet, the assessment of theories should be independent of this consideration, for the criteria by which a theorist defines "the social fact" must be abstract themselves as well as explicit, so that they may be judged by others. This theoretical level must be maintained, else theorists would merely argue about why they make statements, rather than about what they say. Nonetheless, this psychological precondition helps explain, and also takes into account, the peculiar perspectivism of theorizing about society.

[3] This tendency creates controversies due to the attempt to impose a theoretical perspective, developed on the basis of certain substantive interests, on *all* substantive interests. It is partly for this reason too, perhaps, that so much criticism of sociological theories has an undertone of emotionalism.

[4] See Talcott Parsons, *The Social System* (Glencoe: The Free Press, 1951), vii, p. 38 "The title, *The Social System,* goes back, more than to any other source, to the insistence of the late Professor L. J. Henderson on the extreme importance of the concept of system in scientific theory. . . . 'The fundamental starting point is the concept of social systems of action. The *inter*action of individual actors, that is, takes place under such conditions that it is possible to treat such a process of interaction as a system in the scientific sense and subject it to the same order of theoretical analysis which has been successfully applied to other types of systems in other sciences.' "

[5] Cf. the related discussion of the "principle of polarity" in Morris Cohen, *Reason and Nature* (Glencoe: The Free Press, 1953), passim.

[6] Alexis de Tocqueville, *Democracy in America* (New York: Random House, 1945), II, p. 352.

[7] Georg Simmel, *Conflict and the Web of Group Affiliations* (Glencoe: The Free Press, 1955), 140–41.

[8] Robert E. Park, *Race and Culture* (Glencoe: The Free Press, 1950), p. 42.

See also Robert E. Park, *Human Communities* (Glencoe: The Free Press, 1952), pp. 258–9 and passim.

[9] Max Weber, *Economy and Society*, ed. and trans. by Guenther Roth and Claus Wittich (New York: The Bedminster Press, 1968), I, p. 4.

[10] Max Weber, "Kritische Bemerkungen zu den vorstehenden 'Kritischen Beiträgen'," *Archiv für Sozialwissenschaft* XXV (1907), p. 248. A fuller quotation of this passage is given on pp. 144–45.

[11] Max Weber, *Economy and Society, op. cit.*, III, esp. pp. 1260 ff., 1322 ff.

[12] The term "role" was originally derived from this reference to the "roll" in the hands of the actor. Its modern usage together with the term "status" go back to Ralph Linton, *The Study of Man* (New York: D. Appleton-Century Co., 1936). Cf. David Bidney, *Theoretical Anthropology* (New York: Columbia University Press, 1953), for an illuminating exception to the foregoing characterization.

[13] Ralph Linton, *The Cultural Background of Personality* (New York: D. Appleton-Century Co., 1945), pp. 19, 22, and passim. Italics added.

[14] Within this conceptual framework it is quite feasible to handle the fact that a relatively isolated community is found which is individualistic, lacking in solidarity, and secularized, for such a finding does not disprove the utility of the variables which are subsumed under the concept "folk society." Cf. the questionable criticism of Redfield in Oscar Lewis, *Life in a Mexican Village* (Urbana: University of Illinois Press, 1951), pp. 427–40. Much the same criticism has been leveled at Weber's concept of "bureaucracy," because administrators were found to engage in actions which are out of keeping with the formally stipulated conditions of their work. Cf. Alvin Gouldner, "On Weber's Analysis of Bureaucratic Rules," in R. K. Merton, et al., eds., *Reader in Bureaucracy* (Glencoe: The Free Press, 1952), pp. 48–51; and Peter Blau, *Bureaucracy in Modern Society* (New York: Random House, 1956), pp. 35–36. The trouble with these critiques is that they do not distinguish between concept formation and the formulation and testing of hypotheses. In cases where such critiques are justified, it would be necessary to replace the discarded with a new concept, which is more serviceable. As it is, a concept is criticized and then used anyway.

[15] As Redfield has shown in his *Folkculture of Yucatan*, these comprehensive terms are in fact composites of many paired concepts. To subsume a number of these (like isolation, homogeneity, predominance of the sacred) under one ideal type like "folk society" may suggest a closer degree of association than is useful. But not to do that also raises problems, for a concept like "competition" has many usable opposites like "communication," "cooperation," "solidarity," and others, which are in fact interrelated. Cf. also the analysis of pattern variables in Talcott Parsons, *op. cit., The Social System*, pp. 46–51, 58–67, 101–12 which represents a systematic decomposition of *Gemeinschaft* and *Gesellschaft*.

[16] An example may make this clearer. Recently Robert Bierstedt noted that Weber's concepts of traditional and rational authority differ from his concept of charisma in the sense that the latter refers to leadership, not to authority. Implicitly Weber appears to have acknowledged this point since he referred to charismatic leaders under conditions of traditional and of rational authority. But then the question may be asked what concept we should use for leadership which is noncharismatic, an eventuality for which Weber employed the phrase

"routinization of charisma" though he did not explicitly formulate this idea as a contrast conception. Cf. Robert Bierstedt, "The Problem of Authority," in Morroe Berger, Theodore Abel, and Charles Page, eds., *Freedom and Control in Modern Society* (New York: Van Nostrand Co., 1954), pp. 67–81. It may be added that the absence of an opposite term is often due to the linguistic difficulty of finding an equally appropriate word for both concepts. "Routinization of charisma" is not as neat nor as positive as "charisma."

[17] Leonard Broom and Philip Selznick, *Sociology* (Evanston: Row, Peterson & Co., 1955), pp. 124–26.

[18] This formulation is identical with Redfield's statement: "In every primitive band or tribe there is civilization, in every city there is the folk-society." See Robert Redfield, "The Natural History of a Folk Society," *Social Forces,* XXXI (March 1953), p. 225.

[19] In addition, such universal propositions can also reveal the limitations of sociological analysis. That is, their claim to universality can be refuted, when instances are found in which, for example, no impersonal qualities enter into a primary relationship.

[20] Functionalists would say here that societies must find some balance between intimacy and impersonality in human relationships, if man's basic needs are to be satisfied sufficiently for societies to survive. This formulation attributes the results of man's problem-solving activities to "the society" which is said to have properties of its own that are in some sense independent of these activities. And one of these properties is thought to consist of some given, but unknown degree of satisfaction which is indispensable for the survival of society. Thus, functional propositions will refer given attributes to "society," while propositions using paired concepts would refer such attributes to social actions with their anticipated and unanticipated consequences.

[21] Cf. the related comments on the "dialectic of opposites" in Robert Redfield, *The Little Community* (Chicago: University of Chicago Press, 1955), Chap. IX.

[22] Karl Deutsch has suggested such a measure in his calculation of "input-output" ratios of foreign mail, showing among other things that in 1928–38 Germany and the United Kingdom had a similar excess of foreign mail sent out over foreign mail received (.65 for Germany and .70 for the U.K.). But the U.K. was the center of an empire with no restrictions on international communications, while for half this period Germany was a dictatorship whose censorship isolated the country culturally and politically, even if the volume of foreign mail remained unaffected. Cf. Karl Deutsch, "Shifts in the Balance of Communication Flows," *Public Opinion Quarterly,* XX (1956), pp. 147–48. Some logical techniques for handling the problems of typology which are involved here, are discussed in Paul F. Lazarsfeld and Allen H. Barton, "Qualitative Measurement in the Social Sciences: Classification, Typologies, and Indices," in Daniel Lerner, ed., *The Policy Sciences* (Stanford: Stanford University Press, 1951), pp. 155–92.

[23] A telling illustration of the problem involved is the agonized appraisal of primitive societies in the context of Western expansion and destruction by Claude Levy-Strauss, in *Tristes Tropiques* (New York: Atheneum, Publishers, 1967), pp. 44–45, 118–30.

[24] Weber, *Economy and Society, op. cit.,* I, pp. 302, 305–6. I have re-ordered the wording of this passage slightly. The editors rightly emphasize the

difference between this later formulation and the earlier one, which appears in vol. II, pp. 926 ff. However, aside from the greater conciseness and clarity of the later formulation, both passages show Weber's technique of contrasting ideal-typical formulations with the fluidity and interpenetration of contrasting conditions like class and status in social relations.

[25] *Ibid.*, II, p. 928.

[26] *Ibid.*, II, p. 938.

[27] In this connection Parsons and Shils have stated that goal-directed actions must be analyzed by establishing "primacies among types of interests" so that "the . . . ambiguities intrinsic to the world of social objects" can be resolved. The authors accomplish this resolution of ambiguities by stipulating that the actions of the individual must be examined and classified when he makes his choice, on the knife edge of the present as it were. The discussion of pattern variables appears to be based on the assumption that all choices are dichotomous *in fact* if analyzed minutely enough, whereas for Weber the internal consistency of any action was a *logical* construction. See Talcott Parsons, E. A. Shils, et al., *Towards a General Theory of Action* (Cambridge: Harvard University Press, 1951), p. 91. Our view is that choices are provisional and interests ambivalent. Accordingly, Weber's "as if" construction appears to us less rationalistic than the assumption made by Parsons and Shils.

[28] Swanson has pointed out that Parsons and Shils have failed to derive the classic concepts of collectivities from the "action frame of reference" which they have developed. See Guy E. Swanson, "The Approach to a General Theory of Action by Parsons and Shils," *American Sociological Review*, XVIII (1953), pp. 132–33.

[29] Weber, *Economy and Society, op. cit.*, I, pp. 217–20.

[30] *Ibid.*, I, pp. 229–30. In this passage Weber did not explicitly contrast the last two conditions of employment. It may be added, however, that under traditional authority the chief's arbitrary decisions frequently identify an office with the household official or favorite who occupies it, and the holders of benefices frequently attempt and succeed in appropriating the position. The term "full-time occupation" is not applicable to an administrative staff under traditional authority either. Cf. also Max Weber, *Religion of China* (Glencoe: The Free Press, 1951), pp. 33–104, for an analysis of patrimonial government which shows close approximations to this concept of traditional authority.

[31] Since the first publication of this essay I have elaborated this contrast between employment under legal and traditional authority in my book *Nation Building and Citizenship* (New York: John Wiley and Sons, 1964), pp. 107–15.

[32] This perspective is a corollary of Georg Simmel's emphasis on the reciprocity of all social relations. But attention is focused here on collective actions and institutions rather than upon interactions among individuals.

[33] References to sub-culture emphasize an important aspect of culture, but this terminology also has peculiar disadvantages. Cf. Robert Bierstedt, "The Limitations of Anthropological Methods in Sociology," *American Journal of Sociology*, LIV (July, 1948), pp. 22–30.

[34] Emile Durkheim, *The Rules of Sociological Method* (Chicago: University of Chicago Press, 1938), Chap. 3.

[35] See above Chapter 4, pp. 113–14.

[36] The detailed exposition of Weber's views and their implication is left to the next chapter. The present précis is largely identical with Berger's and my exposition of 1959, published in Gross, ed., *Symposium on Sociological Theory, op. cit.*

[37] Though the term *Kultur* appears occasionally in Weber's text, there is no sustained discussion of it. Probably he wanted to avoid the ethical connotations the term has in German as well as its amorphous quality. Terms like ethics, convention, and style of life can be made group-scientific, as *Kultur* cannot. These terminological choices can now be checked easily with the aid of the index in the English edition of *Economy and Society.*

[38] Weber, *Economy and Society, op. cit.*, II, p. 936.

[39] Weber, *The Protestant Ethic, op. cit.*, p. 182.

[40] Thus, Confucianism is the work of the world-ordering bureaucrats, Hinduism of the world-ordering magicians, Buddhism of wandering mendicant monks, Islam of world-conquering warriors, Judaism of itinerant traders, Christianity of itinerant craftsmen. See Weber, *op. cit., Economy and Society*, II, p. 512, and the detailed discussion of this theme on pp. 468–517.

[41] See Edmund R. Leach, *Political Systems of Highland Burma* (Cambridge: Cambridge University Press, 1954), esp. pp. 1–17 for an anthropological field study which illustrates the usefulness of this perspective. Leach's theoretical position is quite similar to the one discussed in this paper.

[42] Kenneth Burke, *Permanence and Change* (New York: New Republic, 1936), p. 70.

[43] Every social theorist recognizes the deficiencies of this procedure. The practice persists, nevertheless, presumably because sociologists are not satisfied with the unscientific character of political judgments. Yet, in the absence of agreed-on criteria of "social health" it remains a political judgment whether or not a given number of strikes impairs the desired cooperation or cohesion in society. As Merton has stated, "Embedded in every functional analysis is some conception, tacit or expressed, of functional requirements of the system under observation. . . . This remains one of the cloudiest, and empirically most debatable concepts of functional theory." See Robert K. Merton, *Social Theory and Social Structure* (Glencoe: The Free Press, 1949), p. 52.

[44] This experimentation with what is possible can be identified in the boundary-extending activities of individuals, whether these consist of criminal activity and all other forms of deviance or of scientific research and all other forms of creative work. But this identification does not preclude the search for "hidden" results (say, the boundary-extending implications of boundary-maintaining actions, or vice versa), which our paired concepts suggest. Cf. Talcott Parsons, *The Social System, op. cit.*, for a different view of "boundary maintenance" in a social system.

[45] Letter to John Stuart Mill of December 18, 1840 in *Memoirs, Letters and Remains of Alexis de Tocqueville* (Boston: Ticknor and Fields, 1862), II, p. 68. Some of these letters were referred to in Chapter 2 above, where they were related to Tocqueville's concept of knowledge. In the present context they are related to his approach to comparative analysis.

[46] *Ibid.*, II, pp. 230–31, 237, 272.

[47] Letter to Stoffels, dated February 21, 1835, in *ibid.*, I, p. 376.

[48] Letter to Louis de Kergorlay, October 19, 1843, in *ibid.*, I, p. 342.

[49] Alexis de Tocqueville, *Democracy in America* (New York: Random House, 1954), II, p. 336.

[50] Letter to Mrs. Grote, July 24, 1850, in *Memoirs, op. cit.*, II, pp. 104–5.

[51] Letter to M. de Corcelle, April 12, 1835, in *ibid.*, II, pp. 13–14: "You suppose my view of the prospects of democracy to be more gloomy than it is. . . . I have endeavored, it is true, to describe the natural tendency of opinions and institutions in a democratic society. I have pointed out the dangers to which it exposes men. But I have never said that these tendencies, if discovered in time, might not be resisted, and these dangers, if foreseen, averted. It struck me that the republicans saw neither the good nor the evil of the condition into which they wished to bring society. . . ."

NOTES FOR CHAPTER SIX

[1] Cf. Neil Smelser, "The Optimum Scope of Sociology," in Robert Bierstedt, ed., *A Design for Sociology*, Monograph No. 9 (Philadelphia: American Academy of Political and Social Science, 1969), pp. 8–9.

[2] The perspective here emphasized was formulated by Georg Simmel, *Conflict and the Web of Group Affiliations* (Glencoe: The Free Press, 1955). For modern developments of this position see Ralph Turner, "Role-Taking: Process versus Conformity," in Arnold Rose, ed., *Human Behavior and Social Processes* (Boston: Houghton Mifflin Company, 1962), Chap. 2; and William J. Goode, "A Theory of Role Strain," *American Sociological Review*, XXV (1960), pp. 483–96.

[3] Max Weber, *Economy and Society*, trans. and ed. by Guenther Roth and Claus Wittich (New York: The Bedminster Press, 1968), I, pp. 321–22.

[4] Weber, *op. cit.*, II, pp. 399–400.

[5] *Ibid.*, p. 402.

[6] *Ibid.*, p. 400.

[7] *Ibid.*, p. 401.

[8] Max Weber, "Kritische Bemerkungen zu den vorstehenden 'Kritischen Beiträgen,'" *Archiv für Sozialwissenschaft*, XXV (1907), p. 248. I have simplified the sentence structure in this translation to ensure intelligibility.

[9] A brilliant analysis of the first phase of that process is now available in Clifford Geertz, *Islam Observed* (New Haven: Yale University Press, 1968), passim.

[10] Cf. on this point Reinhard Bendix, "The Protestant Ethic Revisited," *Comparative Studies in Society and History*, IX (1967), pp. 266–73.

[11] Points one and two are covered in the essay itself. Point three was examined in Weber's supplementary essay on the Protestant Sects. The assumptions as well as Weber's defense are contained in a number of answers to critics which are now published in Max Weber, *Die Protestantische Ethik, Kritiken und Antikritiken*, ed. by Johannes Winckelmann (München: Siebenstern Taschenbuch Verlag, 1968), passim.

[12] William Haller, *The Rise of Puritanism* (New York: Harper and Row, 1957), p. 154.

[13] For details see the striking interpretation of Herbert Schoeffler, *Auswirkungen der Reformation* (Frankfurt: Vittorio Klostermann, 1960), pp. 189–324. I have used this analysis in a comparative study of Japan. See Reinhard Bendix, "A Case Study in Cultural and Educational Mobility: Japan and the Protestant Ethic," in Neil J. Smelser and Seymour M. Lipset, eds., *Social Structure and Mobility in Economic Development* (Chicago: Aldine Publishing Co., 1966), pp. 262–79.

[14] Accordingly Weber calls references to "national character" a confession of ignorance, as well as historically inaccurate. "Cavaliers" and "Roundheads" in seventeenth-century England were not only two parties, but radically different human types, whereas English and Hanseatic merchant adventurers were quite similar in outlook and behavior despite their different cultural and national backgrounds. See *The Protestant Ethic, op. cit.*, pp. 91–92.

[15] Hugo v. Hoffmannsthal, *Selected Prose*, Bollingen Series XXXIII (New York: Pantheon Books, 1952), p. 370.

[16] A more exhaustive and systematic discussion at least of the first two models is contained in Walter Buckley, *Sociology and the Modern Systems Theory* (Englewood Cliffs: Prentice-Hall, 1967).

[17] See Talcott Parsons, Edward Shils, et. al., *Towards a General Theory of Action* (Cambridge: Harvard University Press, 1951), p. 107; and Talcott Parsons, *The Social System* (New York: The Free Press, 1951), pp. 204–5. In sociology this perspective goes back to Durkheim and Spencer, though on other grounds Durkheim was a severe critic of Spencer.

[18] The historical significance of this position is discussed on pp. 191–94.

[19] Perhaps it should be called the coercion-and-revolt model. It is related to the dichotomic conception of social classes which has a long intellectual history. For a perceptive analysis, cf. Stanislaw Ossowski, *Class Structure in the Social Consciousness* (London: Routledge and Kegan Paul, 1963).

[20] See Samuel P. Huntington, *Political Order in Changing Societies* (New Haven: Yale University Press, 1968), esp. Chaps. 1 and 4.

[21] Weber, *Economy and Society, op. cit.*, I, p. 31. Weber refers to a legitimate order as possessing validity (*Geltung*), but this is not easily understood. Viability appears to convey the same meaning.

[22] *Ibid.*, I, pp. 31–32.

[23] Accordingly, the empirical difficulties in studying legitimacy are formidable. The study by Gabriel Almond and Sidney Verba, *The Civic Culture* (Princeton: Princeton University Press, 1963) is an important attempt in this respect.

[24] Weber, *Economy and Society, op. cit.*, I, p. 241.

[25] Weber, *Economy and Society, op. cit.*, I, p. 242.

[26] I am indebted for this phrase to Dankwart Rustow, *A World of Nations* (Washington: The Brookings Institution, 1967), p. 165.

[27] The preceding two paragraphs paraphrase an earlier discussion. See Reinhard Bendix, "Reflections on Charismatic Leadership," in R. Bendix et. al., eds., *State and Society* (Boston: Little, Brown and Co., 1968), p. 620.

[28] Weber, *Economy and Society, op. cit.*, I, pp. 217–18.

[29] Weber, *Economy and Society, op. cit.*, I, p. 215.

[30] Weber, *Economy and Society, op. cit.*, I, p. 226.

[31] Weber, *Economy and Society, op. cit.*, II, pp. 655–57. The distinction of formal and substantive rationality applies to Weber's concepts of instrumentally rational and value-rational action. Cf. *op. cit.*, I, pp. 24 ff. for an analysis of the conceptual ramifications of that division.

[32] Cf. Gerhard Leibholz, *Strukturprobleme der modernen Demokratie* (Karlsruhe: Verlag (F. Müller) 1958), pp. 280–81.

[33] Weber, *Economy and Society, op. cit.*, II, p. 491.

[34] Joseph Schumpeter, *Capitalism, Socialism and Democracy*, 3rd ed. (New York: Harper and Bros., 1950), p. 137. Cf. also the summary of Weber's analysis of feudal and patrimonial ideologies in R. Bendix, *Max Weber, An Intellectual Portrait* (Garden City: Doubleday & Co., 1962), pp. 361–69.

[35] Schumpeter, *op. cit.*, pp. 137–38.

[36] For details see Reinhard Bendix, *Work and Authority in Industry* (New York: Harper and Row, 1962), passim.

[37] These shifts can be followed in the work of Talcott Parsons. His *The Structure of Social Action* (1937) began with the verdict that "Spencer is dead." By contrast his book *Societies, Evolutionary and Comparative Perspectives* (Englewood Cliffs: Prentice-Hall, 1966) is explicitly evolutionist, and not only Spencer but also Max Weber are interpreted in this framework. Cf. Parsons's introduction to Max Weber, *Sociology of Religion* (Boston: The Beacon Press, 1963). For the intellectual background of evolutionism cf. Robert A. Nisbet, *Social Change and History* (New York: Oxford University Press, 1969).

[38] In passing I note that since World War II, twentieth-century Marxism appears to go through its anti-evolutionist phase, as did "bourgeois" social theory in the heyday of pragmatism some fifty years ago. See, for example, the review by Norman Birnbaum, "The Crisis in Marxist Sociology," *Social Research*, XXXV (Summer 1968), pp. 348 80, which documents the decline of the evolutionist element in Marxism, but does not focus on its implications.

[39] Max Weber, *Economy and Society, op. cit.*, III, p. 1121.

[40] See above pp. 64–68.

[41] Jacob Burckhardt, *Force and Freedom* (New York: Pantheon Books, 1943), pp. 255–92, 301–46.

[42] Weber, *Economy and Society, op. cit.*, I, pp. 25–26.

[43] Weber, *Economy and Society, op. cit.*, I, p. 30. I have reordered Weber's phrasing in the interest of brevity.

[44] Max Weber, *The Methodology of the Social Sciences* (Glencoe: The Free Press, 1949), pp. 27 ff.

[45] Cf. Max Weber, *The Protestant Ethic and the Spirit of Capitalism* (New York: Charles Scribner's Sons, 1958), pp. 13–27.

[46] Weber, *Economy and Society, op. cit.*, II, pp. 882–83.

[47] Weber, *Economy and Society, op. cit.*, II, p. 754.

[48] Weber, *Economy and Society, op. cit.*, II, p. 755.

[49] Weber, *Economy and Society, op. cit.*, II, p. 775.

[50] Weber, *Economy and Society, op. cit.*, II, pp. 768–69 ff.

[51] Weber, *Economy and Society, op. cit.*, III, p. 1116.

[52] Robert Nisbet, *op. cit.*, pp. 166–88.

[53] Weber, *Economy and Society, op. cit.*, II, pp. 882–89.

[54] Cf. Karl Löwith, *Meaning in History* (Chicago: University of Chicago Press, 1949), pp. 8–10, and passim. The belief in eternal recurrence is found in India and China as well as in classical antiquity. Its significance as a prelude to theories of evolution is analyzed in Nisbet, *op. cit.*, pp. 29–61.

[55] Cf. here R. G. Collingwood's spirited attack upon the propositional calculus of his philosophical colleagues in *An Autobiography* (London: Oxford University Press, 1939), Chap. 5. He asserts that the same proposition may have several meanings, depending upon the questions to which it may be an answer. Hence, a logic of propositions without inquiry into these prior questions is a futile undertaking. Similarly, Weber's compendium of sociological concepts seeks to separate the formulation of concepts from the questioning process of scholarly inquiry.

NOTES FOR CHAPTER SEVEN

[1] In part it is due to these difficulties of chronological delimitation that sociologists and historians do not get along well intellectually, yet they need each other, for historians use sociological concepts and sociologists ought to derive part of their evidence from history.

[2] I prefer to avoid the term "ideal type" since it requires too many explanations of its meaning to be useful. Cf. the earlier discussion of "paired concepts" on pp. 122ff.

[3] The "pattern variables" as formulated by Talcott Parsons are an aid in this respect, provided their application to specific structures is spelled out. "Universalism," for instance, may be an attribute of urbanism and of bureaucracy, but it is necessary to explicate how this characteristic, which distinguishes urban from folk and bureaucratic from patrimonial administration, becomes manifest in each, and how these manifestations may be linked. Moreover, sociologists interested in social change have often used the logical compatibility among such pattern variables as universalism, achievement, affective neutrality, self-orientation, and others as if this indicated an empirical coherence among these several elements. Thus, they harken back to William G. Sumner's "strain of consistency (of the folkways) with each other, because they all answer their several purposes with less friction and antagonism when they cooperate and support each other." See William G. Sumner, *Folkways* (Boston: Ginn and Co., 1940), pp. 5–6. One would suppose that Sumner was too much of an evolutionist to be aware of the Hegelian legacy in this approach, and given the decreasing interest in the history of ideas among sociologists, a number of them may no longer be aware of the evolutionary theory implicit in their use of "pattern variables."

[4] The following critique of developmental generalizations is considered in greater detail below in Chapter 11.

[5] N. V. Sovani, "The Urban Social Situation in India," *Artha Vijnana*, III (June-September 1961), pp. 85–105, 195–222. The expectation to which Sovani refers should be qualified in the light of some evidence concerning the compatibility between Western urbanism and a "modified extended family," as discussed by Eugene Litwak, "Occupational Mobility and Extended

Family Cohesion," and "Geographic Mobility and Extended Family Cohesion," *American Sociological Review*, 25 (February and June 1960), pp. 9–21, 385–94. See also Sidney M. Greenfield, "Industrialization and the Family in Sociological Theory," *American Journal of Sociology*, 67 (November 1961), pp. 312–22.

⁶ *Urbanization in Asia and the Far East*, Proceedings of the Joint UN/UNESCO Seminar, Bangkok, August 8–18, 1956, Tensions and Technology Series (Calcutta: 1957), p. 87.

⁷ Hence, Parsons's propositions that are true of all societies take a form such as the following: "From the point of view of functioning of the social system, it is not the needs of all the participant actors which must be met, nor all the needs of any one, but only a sufficient proportion for a sufficient fraction of the population." See *The Social System* (Glencoe: The Free Press, 1951), p. 28. Such a statement cannot be falsified or verified, and its remoteness from the evidence is suggested by the fact that the history of all societies records controversies over the meaning of phrases like "sufficient proportion" and "sufficient fraction." Compare the critical comments of T. H. Marshall concerning the use of the term "social system" in "The Welfare State: A Sociological Interpretation," *Archives Européennes de Sociologie*, II (1961), pp. 285–86.

⁸ I note in passing, but with emphasis, that all these are moral issues and that it greatly curtails the "sociological imagination" if this moral dimension is neglected. Some sociologists manage to write even about values or power, as if values existed outside a moral framework or power involved simply a distinction between a few "bad guys" and the masses of the people whose deprivations are a synonym of their virtue. The intellectual challenge of sociological concepts can only gain if the moral issues inherent in them are laid bare.

⁹ Perhaps the simplest statement of this issue is contained in Max Weber, "Agrargeschichte des Altertums," *Gesammelte Aufsätze zur Sozial und Wirtschaftsgeschichte* (Tübingen: J. C. B. Mohr (Paul Siebeck), 1924), p. 280, where an enumeration of different varieties of craftsmen is followed by the assertion that it is necessary, nevertheless, to make do with one concept of the "ancient Greek craftsman" to refer to all of them.

¹⁰ See, for example, Milton Singer, "The Great Tradition in a Metropolitan Center: Madras," *Journal of American Folklore*, 71 (July-September 1958), pp. 347–88.

¹¹ Cf. the discussions of the editors, Louis Dumont and D. Pocock, and of F. G. Bailey in *Contributions to Indian Sociology*, I (April 1957), pp. 26–27, and passim; III (July 1959), pp. 88–101; and IV (April 1960), pp. 82–89.

¹² See the striking characterization of these distinguishing features of the Indian village in B. B. Misra, *The Indian Middle Class* (London: Oxford University Press, 1961), pp. 310–12.

¹³ Max Weber, *Ancient Judaism* (Glencoe: The Free Press, 1952), pp. 270–71, 281, 287–88, 290–92, 295, and my summary statement in *Max Weber, An Intellectual Portrait* (Garden City: Doubleday & Co., 1962), pp. 247–48.

¹⁴ The point has been discussed above in Chapter 5. It is reiterated here in brief form as an aspect of comparative studies.

¹⁵ Cf. the lucid statement of this difference between natural and historical

systems in E. E. Evans-Pritchard, *Social Anthropology* (London: Cohen and West, 1960), pp. 56–62.

[16] For a fuller statement of this distinction in the work of Max Weber and an analysis of its intellectual derivation see Bendix, *Max Weber, op. cit.*, pp. 476–77, and passim.

[17] These illustrations are taken from my work. My hope is that other scholars interested in comparative studies will accept my characterization of this level of analysis.

[18] For an attempt to formulate these three models with the aid of Tocqueville's analysis see "Social Stratification and the Political Community," reprinted herein as Chapter 10.

[19] Cf. the discussion of this contrast in my essay, "The Lower Classes and the 'Democratic Revolution'," *Industrial Relations*, I (October 1961), pp. 91–116.

[20] This approach is developed in my book *Nation-Building and Citizenship* (Garden City: Doubleday & Co., 1969).

[21] Examples are the Latin American countries that have in common the Spanish colonial heritage, European frontier settlements like the United States, Canada, Australia, and New Zealand that have the British legacy in common, and others. Such groupings are not always that simple and there are countries, like Japan, that probably are in a category of their own. Such historical clustering of social structures may then be analyzed with the aid of sociological universals, but I confess to considerable skepticism concerning the use of such universals in the absence of an attempt to spell out in what respects two or more social structures are alike or different. I have made such an attempt in a comparison of German and Japanese modernization in *ibid.*, Chap. VI.

[22] Cf. Chapters 10 and 11 for examples of such analysis.

NOTES FOR CHAPTER EIGHT

[1] Reinhard Bendix, *Work and Authority in Industry* (New York: John Wiley and Sons, 1956).

[2] The laboring poor are asked to prove their virtue by obedience, but they are also told that their dependence results from a natural inferiority. Similarly, the ruling classes are said to be responsible for the deserving poor, and if they do not meet this responsibility, it is only, they say, because the poor who suffer are not deserving.

[3] In Russia the landed aristocracy never succeeded in making itself the unavoidable intermediary between the ruler and the people, in contrast with Western Europe where the ruler's administrative and juridical authority ended in effect at the boundaries of the estate, though this contrast merely states the end-result of protracted struggles over the division of authority. Cf. Max Weber, *Economy and Society*, trans. and ed. by Guenther Roth and Claus Wittich (New York: The Bedminster Press, 1968), III, pp. 1064–68.

[4] Lenin's statement that "the Russian is a bad worker" and his advocacy of the Taylor system and of electrification as the road to socialism are indica-

tive of the fact that the problems of complex industrial reorganizations came to the fore at once. Cf. Chapter 9, p. 215 for the relevant citation.

[5] See Bendix, *Work and Authority, op. cit.*, pp. xvii–xviii, 1–2.

[6] George Herbert Mead, *Movements of Thought in the Nineteenth Century* (Chicago: University of Chicago Press, 1936), p. 21.

[7] *Ibid.*, p. 17.

[8] Georg Friedrich Wilhelm Hegel, *Phänomenologie des Geistes* (Leipzig: Felix Meiner, 1928), pp. 143, 147. My paraphrasing attempts to convey Hegel's meaning without use of his language. The relevant passages are readily accessible in C. J. Friedrich, ed., *The Philosophy of Hegel* (New York: Modern Library, 1953), pp. 399–410.

[9] Alexis de Tocqueville, *Democracy in America* (New York: Random House, 1945), II, p. 195. Some phrases in the preceding paragraph are taken from this chapter of Tocqueville's work.

[10] *Ibid.*

[11] See Bendix, *Work and Authority, op. cit.*, pp. 34–46, 150–62. I deal with this aspect in more detail in Chap. 9 and in *Nation-Building and Citizenship* (Garden City: Doubleday & Co., 1969), pp. 89–126.

[12] For a perceptive analysis of this development see T. H. Marshall, *Class, Citizenship and Social Development* (Garden City: Doubleday & Co., 1964), pp. 65–122. The statement in the text refers specifically to England. Social rights have been instituted in other ways, sometimes in order to withhold the establishment of civil rights as in Imperial Germany.

[13] An expanded statement of this point will be found in Chapter 9.

[14] This section repeats points made in Chapters 5 and 6 in a theoretical context. Its purpose is to show their relevance for empirical studies.

[15] The quoted phrase occurs in Burckhardt's definiton of the objective of culture history, which "goes to the heart of past mankind (because) it declares what mankind *was, wanted, thought, perceived,* and *was able to do*. In this way culture history deals with what is constant and in the end this constant appears greater and more important than the momentary, a quality appears to be greater and more instructive than an action. For actions are only the individual expressions of a certain inner capacity, which is always able to recreate these same actions. Goals and presuppositions are, therefore, as important as events." See Jacob Burckhardt, *Griechische Kulturgeschichte* (Stuttgart: Alfred Kroener, 1952), I, p. 6.

[16] Cf. H. Stuart Hughes, *Consciousness and Society* (New York: A. A. Knopf, 1958) which gives a perceptive analysis of this "generation."

[17] By "ideologies" I do not refer to attitudes of the type that can be elicited in a questionnaire study, but to the "constant process of formulation and reformulation by which spokesmen identified with a social group seek to articulate what they sense to be its shared understandings." See *Work and Authority, op. cit.*, p. xxii. I call these articulations "ideologies" in the specific sense of "ideas considered in the context of group-action." All ideas may be analyzed from this viewpoint; hence I depart from the identification of "ideologies" with false or misleading ideas.

[18] For example, at the turn of the century American employers asserted their absolute authority over the workers but this assertion lacked content

until the bureaucratization of industry brought to the fore experts who worked out methods for the exercise of authority. Again, the Tsar's assertion of authority over all the people inadvertently encouraged the peasants to appeal to the Tsar for redress of grievances. This procedure is adapted from that used by Max Weber in his sociology of religion.

[19] The sentence immediately following this quotation reads: "The tradition of all the dead generations weighs like a nightmare on the brain of the living." See Karl Marx, *The 18th Brumaire of Louis Bonaparte* (New York: International Publishers, n. d.), p. 13. I do not accept this polemical exaggeration, since traditions are enabling as well as disabling, but the emphasis upon the impact of cultural tradition on current ideologies is more in line with the facts than the effort to explain the latter solely in terms of the problems the businessman encounters in his work. Such an interpretation leads to an elimination of ideological changes, and of differences between ideologies, since all ideologies are in this sense responses to the strains endemic in modern society. Cf. Francis X. Sutton et al., *The American Business Creed* (Cambridge: Harvard University Press, 1956), passim, where the change of business ideologies over time is denied and where these ideologies are explained in exactly the same terms as nationalism and anti-capitalism. See also the comments of Leland Jenks, "Business Ideologies," *Explorations of Entrepreneurial History*, 10 (October 1957), pp. 1–7.

[20] *Work and Authority, op. cit.*, p. xx.

[21] Cf. the earlier discussion of this point in Chapter 7, pp. 180–84.

[22] *Work and Authority, op. cit.*, p. 251. To avoid a possible misunderstanding I add that this assertion, which is elaborated in *ibid.*, pp. 244–51, is in my judgment compatible with the endeavor to put managerial decision making on a more scientific basis. The substitution of machine methods for manual operations is obviously an on-going process that has greatly curtailed the areas of possible discretion, although machine methods also create new opportunities for discretionary judgments. But while these methods and organizational manipulations may curtail and reallocate the areas in which discretion is possible or desired, and may in this way achieve greater efficiency, they cannot, I believe, eliminate discretion.

[23] Cf. *Work and Authority, op. cit.*, pp. 248–49, for a fuller statement.

[24] Hence they will do so even for the purpose of achieving the objectives of the party itself. Cf. Joseph Berliner, *Factory and Manager in the USSR* (Cambridge: Harvard University Press, 1957) which documents that the most successful Soviet managers use subversion to implement plan goals as well as for their personal convenience. This fact suggests that "good faith" can be inculcated in many ways, even by the systematic distrust of all subordinates, provided of course that the distrust has a higher rationale, such as the utopian and nationalist ideology of Russian communism.

[25] A case study of totalitarianism in the context of industrial relations is contained in *Work and Authority, op. cit.*, Chap. 5. For a generalized treatment of this approach to totalitarianism cf. Bendix, *Nation-Building and Citizenship, op. cit.*, Chap. V.

NOTES FOR CHAPTER NINE

[1] The relevance of European industrialization in this respect is discussed by Alexander Gerschenkron, "Economic Backwardness in Historical Perspective," in Bert F. Hoselitz, ed., *The Progress of Underdeveloped Areas* (Chicago: University of Chicago Press, 1952), pp. 3–29. See Chapter 11 below for a more detailed discussion.

[2] For a survey of what is known see Wilbert Moore, *Industrialization and Labor* (Ithaca: Cornell University Press, 1951), Part I.

[3] In the book I state my reasons for this assumption. For a brief summary see above, pp. 194–97.

[4] Alexis de Tocqueville, *Democracy in America* (New York: Random House, 1954) II, pp. 194–95, as quoted above on p. 193.

[5] Cf. the discussion by David Mitrany, *Marx Against the Peasants* (Chapel Hill: University of North Carolina Press, 1951), pp. 205–6, and passim, who emphasizes the paradox that communism has been successful in predominantly agrarian countries. For a comparative analysis of agrarian upheavals in England and France in the seventeenth and eighteenth centuries see Barrington Moore, *Social Origins of Democracy and Dictatorship* (New York: Harcourt, Brace & World, 1967), Chaps 1 and 2.

[6] Statement of the Metropolitan Filaret of Moscow in 1839, advising the police on how the peasants could be quieted, cited in John S. Curtiss, *Church and State in Russia* (New York: Columbia University Press, 1940), p. 30.

[7] The polemical literature initiated by Marx always reserved its most caustic invectives for the hypocrisy of employers, who admonished starving workers to work hard, live frugally, and be content with their lot. Yet the contrast with Russia suggests that this moralizing approach differed significantly from a demand for submission as such. The selfish interests which no doubt dominated both approaches cannot explain the difference between them, nor is the repeated "discovery" of these interests very illuminating in itself.

[8] *Lenin, Selected Works* (New York: International Publishers, n.d.) VII, pp. 332–33. It may be added that Lenin inveighed against the Left-Wing Childishness and Petty-Bourgeois Mentality (in *ibid.*, pp. 351–78) of those who feared that labor discipline would restore capitalism, alienate the workers, diminish their initiative, and thereby jeopardize productivity.

[9] Quoted in Franziska Baumgarten, *Arbeitswissenschaft und Psychotechnik in Russland* (München: R. Oldenbourg, 1924), pp. 111–12. The phrase "Communist Americanism" reflects the enthusiasm for technology in the early 1920s, when "America" was the symbol of technological advance. To emulate and surpass the West was a popular goal before it was claimed that Russia was in every way superior to the West. This shift became known at the end of World War II, but it probably began during the first years of Hitler's regime in Germany. See Klaus Mehnert, *Stalin vs. Marx* (London: G. Allen and Union, 1952).

[10] A widespread enthusiasm for technology developed in Russia at the same time that the most advanced techniques of production were introduced, while in England these two phases were separated by two or three generations. In

this respect, Russia is, however, rather typical, since broadly the same contrast may be made between England and Germany or Japan.

[11] Because of his concentration on the differences between Western European and Asiatic civilizations, Weber even slighted the case of Germany. Although he analyzed the contrast between the Lutheran and the Calvinist traditions in the sixteenth and seventeenth centuries, he did not take up the interesting problem of how the emotionalism and submissiveness of Lutheranism was transformed in the nineteenth century into a quasi-military activism which also proved to be an effective work-ethic for industrialization.

NOTES FOR CHAPTER TEN

[1] The two terms used in the title of this paper were chosen in preference to the more conventional terms "society" and "state," although in the text both are used. My reason is that "social stratification" emphasizes (as "society" does not) the division of individuals into social ranks which provide the basis of group formation that is of interest here. "Political community" in turn emphasizes the consensus between governors and governed within the framework of a polity, while the term "state" puts the emphasis upon the administrative aspect of government, at any rate in English usage. Both aspects must be considered together, but I did not wish to emphasize the latter in the title.

[2] For easy identification it would be desirable to label these three approaches, but it is awkward to do so since every label has misleading connotations. "Society as an object of state-craft" may be considered a Machiavellian approach, but this perspective is also characteristic of the social-welfare state which is not "Machiavellian" in the conventional meaning of that term. Government considered as a "product of society" might be called the sociological perspective, but this is also characteristic of Marxism which should not be identified with sociology, and then there are sociologists like Max Weber and Robert MacIver who do not adhere to this view. The theory of a partial dualism between society and government is a characteristic feature of European liberalism, but to call it the "liberal orientation" carries overtones of a specific political theory which need not be associated with this approach. In view of such difficulties I have decided to avoid convenient labels and repeat the three phrases mentioned in the text.

[3] The development suggested here is traced in Friedrich Meinecke, *Die Entstehung des Historizismus* (München: R. Oldenbourg, 1946), Chap. III. The partly scientific orientation of Machiavelli and Montesquieu is discussed in Leonard Olschki, *Machiavelli the Scientist* (Berkeley: The Gillick Press, 1945); and Emile Durkheim, *Montesquieu and Rousseau* (Ann Arbor: University of Michigan Press, 1960).

[4] See Friedrich Meinecke, *Die Idee der Staatsräson* (München: R. Oldenbourg, 1925), passim. The work is available in English translation under the title *Machiavellism*. The relation between this concern with "reasons of state" and the development of factual knowledge about society is discussed in Eli Heckscher, *Mercantilism* (New York: Macmillan 1955), II, pp. 13–30, 269 ff.; and Albion Small, *Origins of Sociology* (Chicago: University of

Chicago Press, 1925). See also Carl J. Friedrich, *Constitutional Reasons of State* (Providence; Brown University Press, 1957).

⁵ Cf. Chapter 2 above for a fuller analysis of this perspective.

⁶ Karl Löwith has shown that this contrast goes back to ancient Greek and Christian ideas and he has traced the development of this theme during the nineteenth century. See his book *Von Hegel zu Nietzsche* (Zürich: Europa Verlag, 1941), pp. 255–65 ff. See also the judicious restatement of Rousseau's position in R. R. Palmer, *The Age of the Democratic Revolution* (Princeton: Princeton University Press, 1959), I, pp. 119–27.

⁷ Emile Durkheim, *Montesquieu and Rousseau, op. cit.*, pp. 65, 137, and passim.

⁸ See Emile Durkheim, *The Division of Labor in Society* (Glencoe: The Free Press, 1947), pp. 200–206, and passim.

⁹ Emile Durkheim, *Professional Ethics and Civic Morals* (Glencoe: The Free Press, 1958), p. 61. Published for the first time in 1950 in a Turkish edition of the French manuscript, these lectures were delivered by Durkheim in 1898, 1899, and 1900 at Bordeaux and in 1904 and 1912 at the Sorbonne. As will be shown below, they contain Durkheim's political theory and their repeated delivery together with the well-known preface to the second edition of *The Division of Labor* (published in 1902) indicate that for Durkheim this aspect of his work was of great importance. It is a symptom of the tendency of our own time that this political aspect has been neglected or ignored by most scholars who have been influenced by Durkheim's sociological theories.

¹⁰ I take this telling phrase from Marcel Mauss's introduction to Emile Durkheim, *Socialism and Saint-Simon* (Yellow Springs: The Antioch Press, 1958), p. 2. Durkheim's elaboration of his views on the corporate society may be found in the second preface to his *The Division of Labor, op. cit.*, pp. 1–31. Cf. especially the following summary statement of his position: "A society composed of an infinite number of unorganized individuals, that a hypertrophied state is forced to oppress and contain, constitutes a veritable sociological monstrosity. . . . Where the State is the only environment in which men can live communal lives, they inevitably lose contact, become detached and thus society disintegrates. A nation can be maintained only if, between the State and the individual, there is intercalated a whole series of secondary groups near enough to the individual to attract them strongly in their sphere of action. . . ." *ibid.*, p. 28. In the preceding account I have only restated the familiar themes of Durkheim's work. The best analytical exposition of these themes is contained in Talcott Parsons, *The Structure of Social Action* (Glencoe: The Free Press, 1949), Chaps. viii–xi, though this statement was written before Durkheim's unpublished lectures on the state became available.

¹¹ Emile Durkheim, *The Division of Labor, op. cit.*, pp. 283 ff.

¹² *Ibid.*, pp. 27–28, 218–19.

¹³ Emile Durkheim, *Professional Ethics and Civic Morals, op. cit.*, pp. 61–63. My italics.

¹⁴ *Ibid.*, p. 45. This formulation is indebted to Montesquieu and Tocqueville.

¹⁵ Cf. the reference to this paradox in E. Benoit-Smullyan, "The Sociologism of Emile Durkheim and his School," in H. E. Barnes, ed., *An Introduction*

to the History of Sociology (Chicago: University of Chicago Press, 1948), pp. 518–20.

¹⁶ See Division of Labor, op. cit., pp. 386–88.

¹⁷ Elie Halévy, The Growth of Philosophical Radicalism (London; Faber and Faber, 1928), pp. 90–91, 118–20, 489–91, and passim.

¹⁸ The following statement relies on the work of Otto Hintze, "Weltgeschichtliche Bedingungen der Repräsentativverfassung," Historische Zeitschrift, CXLIII (1930), pp. 1–47; and by the same author, "Typologie der ständischen Verfassungen," Historische Zeitschrift CXLI (1929), pp. 229–48. Hintze's contributions are corroborated and extended in Dietrich Gerhard's "Regionalismus und Ständisches Wesen als ein Grundthema Europäischer Geschichte," Historische Zeitschrift, LCXXIV (1952), pp. 307–37.

¹⁹ This characteristic feature of medieval political life will be contrasted below with the problematic relation between social stratification and the political community in modern Western societies.

²⁰ The quotation marks refer to the ineradicable ambiguity of this term in medieval society. The "people" were objects of government who took no part in political life. Yet kings and estates frequently justified their actions by speaking in the name of the "people" they claimed to represent. In fact, "consent of the people" referred to the secular and clerical notables whose voice was heard in the councils of government. See the discussion of this issue in Otto Gierke, Political Theories of the Middle Ages (Boston: The Beacon Press, 1958), pp. 37–61. It may be added that this ambiguity is not confined to the Middle Ages, since all government is based in some degree on popular consent and since even in the most democratic form of government the "people" are excluded from political life in greater or lesser degree. These differences of degree, as well as the qualities of consent and participation are all-important, of course, even though it may be impossible to do more than formulate proximate typologies.

²¹ Cf. Max Weber, Economy and Society, ed. by G. Roth and C. Wittich (New York: The Bedminster Press, 1968), II, pp. 839–64 and passim.

²² In his analysis of traditional domination Max Weber distinguished patrimonial from feudal administration, that is, the effort of rulers to extend their authority and retain control either by the use of "household officials" or by their "fealty relationship" with aristocratic notables of independent means. These two devices are by no means mutually exclusive, since "household officials" were usually of noble birth and in territories of any size demanded autonomy, while "feudal" notables despite their independence frequently depended upon the ruler for services of various kinds. Contractual obligations as well as elaborate ideologies buttressed the various methods of rule under these complementary systems. For an exposition of Weber's approach cf. R. Bendix, Max Weber, an Intellectual Portrait (Garden City: Doubleday & Co., 1960), pp. 334–79.

²³ A systematic analysis of this role of the church is contained in Max Weber, Economy and Society, III, Chap. XV. A brief résumé of this chapter is contained in Reinhard Bendix, Max Weber, op. cit., pp. 320–26. For a detailed historical treatment of the consecration of secular rule cf. Ernst Kantorowicz, The King's Two Bodies (Princeton: Princeton University Press, 1957).

²⁴ Weber, Economy and Society, op. cit., II, pp. 696–97. In this connection

it should be remembered that the privileges or liberties of medieval society were associated with duties that would appear very onerous to a modern citizen. Also, these individual or collective "privileges" frequently resulted from compulsion rather than a spontaneous drive for freedom, as is vividly described in Albert B. White, *Self-government at the King's Command* (Minneapolis: University of Minnesota Press, 1933). The title itself illuminates the combination of royal power and compulsory local autonomy, which was typical of England, but not found to the same extent elsewhere in Europe. Still, the privileges of an estate also had the more ordinary meaning of rights (rather than duties), and this was true to some extent even of the lower social orders. Cf. the discussion of this problem by Herbert Grundmann, "Freiheit als religiöses, politisches und persönliches Postulat im Mittelalter," *Historische Zeitschrift*, CLXXXIII (1957), pp. 23-53. A detailed case study of medieval political life is contained in Otto Brunner, *Land und Herrschaft* (Brünn: Rudolf M. Rohrer Verlag, 1943).

[25] Cf. Weber, *Economy and Society, op. cit.*, III, Chaps. XII and XIII for the distinction between feudalism and patrimonialism as the two aspects of "traditional domination" which were present throughout the European Middle Ages. The development towards absolutist regimes is best seen, therefore, as a relative shift of emphasis in Western European institutions, which varied from country to country.

[26] For a comparative account of this political structure in eighteenth-century Europe cf. Palmer, *The Age of the Democratic Revolution, op. cit.*, I, Chap. III, and passim.

[27] Alexis de Tocqueville, *The Old Regime and the Revolution* (Garden City: Doubleday & Co., 1955), pp. 22-77. For a modern appraisal of the survival of corporate and libertarian elements under the absolutist regimes of the eighteenth century cf. Kurt von Raumer, "Absoluter Staat, Korporative Libertät, Persönliche Freiheit," *Historische Zeitschrift*, CLXXXIII (1957), pp. 55-96.

[28] Alexis de Tocqueville, *op. cit.*, p. 137.

[29] *Ibid.*, pp. 15-16.

[30] Tocqueville, *Democracy in America* (New York: Random House, 1945), II, p. 311. In advancing this thesis Tocqueville referred, for example, to the innovative activities of manufacturers that were characteristic of democratic eras. Such men engaged in "novel undertakings without shackling themselves to their fellows," they opposed in principle all governmental interference with such private concerns, and yet "by an exception of that rule" each of them sought public assistance in his private endeavor when it suited his purpose. Tocqueville concluded that the power of government would of necessity grow, wherever large numbers of mutually independent men proceeded in this manner. See *ibid.*, p. 311, n. 1.

[31] *Ibid.*, p. 333.

[32] *Ibid.*, pp. 114-32.

[33] Emile Durkheim, *Professional Ethics and Civic Morals, op. cit.*, pp. 64-65.

[34] A fuller critical appraisal of Tocqueville's facts and interpretations is contained in the essay by George W. Pierson, *Tocqueville in America* (Garden City: Doubleday and Co., 1959), pp. 430-77, though Pierson

slights Tocqueville's theoretical contribution which is emphasized in the text.

[35] Cf. the discussion of this perspective in Chapter 5 above.

[36] As an ideal type, Weber's concept of bureaucracy is based on the assumption that this process of separation of modern from patrimonial administration has been completed. See his *Economy and Society, op. cit.*, III, Chap. XI. For an exposition of the contrast between patrimonial and bureaucratic administration see pp. 127–29 above. There are many indications, however, that patrimonial characteristics recur. See the discussion by Guenther Roth, "Personal Rulership, Patrimonialism, and Empire-Building in the New States," *World Politics*, XX (January 1968), pp. 194–206. In the Western context the separation of bureaucratic from patrimonial administration is traced comparatively by Ernest Barker, *The Development of Public Services in Western Europe, 1660–1930* (New York: Oxford University Press, 1944).

[37] Admittedly, these matters are in flux and in this respect significant differences exist within Western civilization. Still, no one can be in doubt in the instances in which this fundamental assumption has come into question, as in the American Civil War or more recently in the critical conflict between the national government in France and the French settlers in Algeria. The Southern opposition to school integration is *not* a comparable development, I believe, since even in the more extreme cases it is combined with an acceptance of national jurisdiction on which there is no sharp disagreement. But the political reintegration of the South has been and may continue to be painfully slow, because the federal political structure appears to militate against national policies.

[38] Neither medieval political life nor the absolutist regimes of the eighteenth century nor yet many of the "developing areas" of the modern world knew or know a government of this type, because adjudication and administration were and are decentralized, personal, intermittent, and subject to a fee for each governmental service.

[39] E. Durkheim, *Professional Ethics and Civic Morals, op. cit.*, pp. 64–82.

[40] For a survey of this line of thought, disguised as it is in theoretical disquisitions, cf. Robert A. Nisbet, *The Quest for Community* (New York: Oxford University Press, 1953).

[41] Tocqueville tended to obscure this distinction by identifying this reciprocity in the earlier estate societies of medieval Europe with the later symbiosis of absolutist rule and aristocratic privilege, though he was quick to point out how absolutism tended to undermine the aristocratic position. On the increase of aristocratic privilege just prior to the French Revolution cf. Palmer, *op. cit.*, Chaps. II–IV.

[42] Max Weber has stated that in the legal systems of the older type "all law appeared as the privilege of particular individuals or objects or of particular constellations of individuals or objects. Such a point of view had, of course, to be opposed by that in which the state appears as the all embracing coercive institution. . . . The revolutionary period of the 18th century produced a type of legislation which sought to extirpate every form of associational autonomy and legal particularism." The extension of the market economy and bureaucratization "replaced the particularist mode of creating law . . . in two ways: the first is the formal, universally accessible, closely limited, and legally regulated autonomy of association which may

be created by anyone wishing to do so; the other consists in the grant to everyone of the power to create law of his own by means of engaging in private legal transactions of certain kinds." Max Weber, *Economy and Society, op. cit.,* II, pp. 698-99.

[43] Demands for representation are difficult to distinguish from demands for privileged jurisdictions or outright benefits, because representation in decision-making bodies may be used to obtain these privileges or benefits. It is clear at any rate that voluntary associations are not the unequivocal counterweight to centralized power for which Tocqueville was searching in his study of American society. Instead, voluntary associations frequently demand governmental assistance even where they reject it in principle, and in this respect they act in much the same way as individual manufacturers tended to do a century ago, according to Tocqueville's observations. Voluntary associations are a protean phenomenon. They are evidence of consensus within the society, especially where they pursue private ends as an alternative to governmental assistance and regulation. But they may also be evidence of dissent within the national political community, in so far as they enlist the national government in the service of parochial interests, and hence seek to secure from the government privileges that are denied to other groups.

[44] Incidentally, this hiatus is reflected in the very widespread and sanguine juxtaposition of patriotism with the most extreme selfishness of individuals and groups.

[45] The term "state" is needed to designate the continuing political identity of the nation irrespective of the governments embodying this identity from time to time. Where monarchical institutions have survived, they represent this identity separately from the ruling government. Such institutional separation is not possible under democracies. In this discussion the terms "state" and "political community" or "polity" are used interchangeably since all three refer with different emphasis to the apparatus and the consensus which sustain the political identity of the modern nation.

[46] Like all such distinctions there is a good bit of overlap between the two types. Affinities of interest which arise from the social structure forever engender relations of super and sub-ordination, while the exercise of instituted authority forever produces, and is affected by, affinities of interest.

[47] Hence, the ideas that society is an object of state-craft or that all governmental institutions are the product of social forces represent perspectives that are useful only as long as their partiality is recognized.

In a recent article Raymond Aron stated the case against the Comtean as well as Marxian tendency to reduce all politics and government to forces arising from the socioeconomic substructure. "Contre l'un et l'autre, nous avons appris que la politique est une catégorie éternelle de l'existence humaine, un secteur permanent de toute société. Il est illégitime de se donner, par hypothèse, l'élimination de la politique en tant que telle ou de caractériser une société par sa seule infra-structure." See Raymond Aron, "Les sociologues et les institutions représentatives," *Archives européennes de sociologie,* I (1960), p. 155. The present analysis is in agreement with this position and I assume that Professor Aron would agree that the sociological level of analysis likewise possesses a certain autonomy. Perhaps it is symptomatic for modern social science that the most elaborate systematization of social theory to date acknowledges society, culture, and personality, *but not politics,* as relatively autonomous levels of analysis. Cf. Talcott Parsons, E. A.

Shils, et al., *Toward a General Theory of Action* (Cambridge: Harvard University Press, 1951), pp. 28–29. Cf. also the learned critique of this reductionist tendency in Sheldon S. Wolin, *Politics and Vision* (Boston: Little, Brown and Co., 1960), Chaps. IX–X.

[48] As I see it, this is the viewpoint from which Weber developed the analytical framework of his posthumously published *Wirtschaft und Gesellschaft*. The fundamental distinction of that work is not the one between "economy" and "society," but between society and domination and hence between groups arising from the pursuit of "ideal and material interests," on the one hand, and relations of super and sub-ordination arising from beliefs in legitimacy, administrative organization, and the threat of force. For details of this interpretation cf. my book *Max Weber, op. cit.*, passim. A lucid exposition of the fundamental assumptions of this approach is contained in Robert MacIver, *The Web of Government* (New York: Macmillan, 1947), Chap. XIII.

[49] Niccolò Machiavelli, *The Prince and the Discourses* (New York: The Modern Library, 1940), p. 15.

[50] See Seymour M. Lipset, "Party Systems and the Representation of Social Groups," *Archives européennes de sociologie*, I (1960), p. 51. In this article Professor Lipset presents comparative materials on the interrelation of different representative systems with different social structures.

[51] Cf. Philip Selznick, *TVA and the Grass Roots* (Berkeley: University of California Press, 1949), which may be considered a case study of this "reverse interchange."

[52] Cf. the analysis by E. J. Hobsbawm, *Social Bandits and Primitive Rebels* (Glencoe: The Free Press, 1959), Chap. III. See also Roger Vailland's novel *The Law* which illustrates the anarchical propensities through which either formal compliance with, or the symbolic re-enactment of, the law is used to subvert all "rule-abiding behavior."

[53] There is, thus, a close relationship between this *gradual* establishment of "social rights" and the decline of ideology, although it must be kept in mind that this decline in the West may be the consequence of the Cold War and the rise of ideology in the rest of the world as much as it is a result of the welfare state. Different aspects of this complex phenomenon are discussed in T. H. Marshall, *Class, Citizenship and Social Development* (Garden City: Doubleday & Co., 1964), pp. 65–122; Otto Brunner, "Das Zeitalter der Ideologien," *Neue Wege der Sozialgeschichte* (Göttingen: Vandenhoeck and Ruprecht, 1956), Chap. IX; Daniel Bell, *The End of Ideology* (Glencoe: The Free Press, 1960), part III; E. A. Shils, "Ideology and Civility," *Sewanee Review* LXVI (1958), pp. 450–80; and Seymour M. Lipset, *Political Man* (New York: Doubleday & Co., 1960), pp. 403–17. The limitations of this development are noted on pp. 338–48.

[54] For a comparative analysis of the cleavages facing the "new nations" and the related liabilities of government cf. E. A. Shils, "Political Development in the New States," *Comparative Studies in Society and History*, II (1960), pp. 268–82, 379–411.

[55] Gabriel Almond, "A Functional Approach to Comparative Politics," in Gabriel Almond and James S. Coleman, eds., *The Politics of the Developing Areas* (Princeton: Princeton University Press, 1960), p. 4.

[56] The concept "state" is discarded on the curious ground that it is based

on a dichotomy which is incompatible with the existing continuity of the phenomena. Professor Almond suggests that with reference to the "developing areas," only the political "input" functions will be analyzed because the formal governmental structure ("out-put" function) is usually not well developed. This decision would seem to reintroduce the distinction which was discarded. Cf. *ibid.*, pp. 12, 17.

NOTES FOR CHAPTER ELEVEN

[1] See Carlo M. Cipolla, *The Economic History of World Population* (Baltimore: Penguin Books, 1964), pp. 24–28. By focusing attention on the technical and economic effects of the process, Cipolla provides a comprehensive formulation of what is meant by industrialization. Nothing like that clarity can be achieved with regard to "modernization," which is more inclusive and refers, albeit vaguely, to the manifold social and political processes that have accompanied industrialization in most countries of Western civilization. The following discussion contains contributions towards a definition of "modernization."

[2] See Robert A. Nisbet, *Emile Durkheim* (Englewood Cliffs: Prentice-Hall, 1965), p. 20.

[3] *Ibid.*, p. 21 n.

[4] Immanuel Kant, "Idea for a Universal History with Cosmopolitan Intent," in Carl J. Friedrich, ed., *The Philosophy of Kant* (New York: Random House, 1949), p. 121. Note the relation of this view to the intellectual tradition traced in Arthur Lovejoy, *The Great Chain of Being* (New York: Harper and Bros., 1961), passim.

[5] Adam Ferguson, *An Essay on the History of Civil Society*, 5th ed. (London: T. Cadell, 1782), pp. 302–3.

[6] *Ibid.*, pp. 308–9.

[7] *Ibid.*, p. 305.

[8] See John Millar, "Social Consequences of the Division of Labor," reprinted in William C. Lehmann, *John Millar of Glasgow, 1735–1801* (Cambridge University Press, 1960), pp. 380–82. This volume contains a reprint of Millar's *Origin of the Distinction of Ranks*, first published in 1771.

[9] Edmund Burke, "Thoughts and Details on Scarcity (1795)," in *Works* (Boston: Little, Brown and Co., 1869), V, pp. 134–35. Burke himself used the laissez-faire doctrine to support his argument. The law of supply and demand governed the wages paid to labor and interference with that law would merely aggravate the condition of the poor. The traditional argument against the injustice of this system is exemplified by William Godwin, *Enquiry Concerning Political Justice and its Influence on Morals and Happiness* (Toronto: University of Toronto Press, 1946), I, pp. 15–20.

[10] Cf. the survey of these opinions by Robert Michels, *Die Verelendungstheorie* (Leipzig: Alfred Kroener, 1928), passim.

[11] Justus Möser, *Sämtliche Werke* (Berlin: Nicolaische Buchhandlung, 1842), IV, pp. 158–62. I owe this reference to the article by Karl Mannheim, cited below.

[12] Johann W. Goethe, *Wilhelm Meister's Apprenticeship*, trans. by R. Dillon Boylan (London: Bell and Doldy, 1867), p. 268. See also Baron Knigge, *Practical Philosophy of Social Life* (Lansingburgh: Perriman and Bliss, 1805), pp. 307–8.

[13] Goethe, *op. cit.*

[14] See Werner Wittich, "Der soziale Gehalt von Goethes Roman 'Wilhelm Meisters Lehrjahre'," in Melchior Palyi, ed., *Hauptprobleme der Soziologie, Erinnerungsgabe für Max Weber* (Berlin: Duncker and Humblot, 1923), II, pp. 278–306.

[15] For documentation of the social and literary life of the period cf. W. H. Bruford, *Germany in the 18th Century* (Cambridge University Press, 1939), passim. The literary and philosophical response to the French revolution is analyzed in Alfred Stern, *Der Einfluss der französichen Revolution auf das deutsche Geistesleben* (Stuttgart: Cotta, 1928), but I know of no comparable summary treatment of the German response to English industrialization. Cf., however, Hans Freyer, *Die Bewertung der Wirtschaft im philosophischen Denken des 19. Jahrhunderts* (Leipzig: W. Engelmann, 1921), for some relevant materials.

[16] M. de Bonald, *Oevres Complètes* (Paris: J. P. Migne, 1864), II, pp. 238–39.

[17] *Ibid.* Note in passing that this contrast between agricultural and industrial work is made in almost identical terms by John Millar, years earlier. The difference between Millar's liberalism and Bonald's conservatism seems to be reflected only in Millar's emphasis on the knowledge of the peasant and Bonald's greater stress on his religion. Cf. Lehmann, *op. cit.*, pp. 380–82. As Max Weber has pointed out, this emphasis on the piety of the peasant is a distinctly modern phenomenon, related to invidious contrasts between town and country. See Max Weber, *Economy and Society, op. cit.*, II, p. 470.

[18] P. J. Proudhon, *A System of Economic Contradictions or The Philosophy of Misery* (Boston: Benjamin R. Tucker, 1888), I, p. 138.

[19] P. J. Proudhon, *General Idea of the Revolution in the 19th Century* (London: Freedom Press, 1923), p. 215. This work was written in 1851.

[20] Proudhon, *Philosophy of Misery*, p. 132.

[21] Cf. Norman Jacobson, *The Concept of Equality in the Assumptions of the Propaganda of Massachusetts Conservatives, 1790–1840*, Ph.D. Dissertation (University of Wisconsin, 1951).

[22] George Fitzhugh, *Sociology for the South* (Richmond: A. Morris, 1854), pp. 233, 235.

[23] *Ibid.*, p. 161.

[24] *Ibid.*, pp. 106–7, 253–54. A major analysis of this Southern ideology in historical perspective is contained in W. J. Cash, *The Mind of the South* (Garden City: Doubleday & Co., 1954), passim.

[25] Orestes A. Brownson, *Works* (Detroit: T. Nourse, 1884), V, pp. 116–17. This passage was written in 1857, after the author's conversion to Catholicism.

[26] Karl Mannheim, "Conservative Thought," in *Essays in Sociology and Social Psychology* (London: Routledge and Kegan Paul, 1953), pp. 74–164.

[27] Different meanings of "alienation" as the common theme of anti-industrial

sentiment are examined in Lewis Feuer's essay on this concept in Maurice Stein and Arthur Vidich, eds., *Sociology on Trial* (Englewood Cliffs: Prentice-Hall, 1963), pp. 127–47. That men of opposite political persuasion have come to employ this concept is analyzed sociologically by René König, "Zur Soziologie der Zwanziger Jahre," in Leonhard Reinisch, ed., *Die Zeit ohne Eigenschaften* (Stuttgart: W. Kohlhammer, 1961), pp. 82–118.

[28] The following account is based in part on Reinhard Bendix and Seymour M. Lipset, "Karl Marx's Theory of Social Classes," in *Class, Status and Power* (New York: The Free Press, 1966), pp. 6–11.

[29] See Thomas B. Bottomore and Maximilien Rubel, eds., *Karl Marx, Selected Writings in Sociology and Social Philosophy* (London: Watts and Co., 1956), p. 179. My italics.

[30] Cf. T. H. Marshall's definition of class as "a force that unites into groups people who differ from one another, by overriding the differences between them." See his *Class, Citizenship and Social Development* (Garden City: Doubleday & Co., 1964), p. 164.

[31] Bottomore and Rubel, *op. cit.*, pp. 186–87.

[32] A recent massive study by E. K. Thompson, *The Making of the English Working Class* (New York: Pantheon Books, 1964), passim, enables us to appreciate this Marxian perspective in that it describes the movements Marx observed with the benefit of another hundred years of scholarship. However, the author faithfully reproduces Marx's own blindness to the strongly conservative elements that were an enduring part of working-class agitation (by treating these elements as a passing phase) as well as to the mounting gradualism of the labor movement (by terminating his study in the 1830s).

[33] A convenient compilation of relevant quotations from Marx is contained in Bottomore and Rubel, *op. cit.*, Part III, Chap. 4. To my knowledge the most comprehensive analysis of this complex of ideas is that of Karl Löwith, *From Hegel to Nietzsche* (New York: Holt, Rinehart and Winston, 1964).

[34] Karl Marx, *Capital* (New York: The Modern Library, 1936), p. 92. Marx attributed religious beliefs and ideologies which disguise the "actual" relations of men in society to the conflicts of interest engendered by its class structure. It was therefore logical for him to anticipate that the advent of a classless society would coincide with the "end of ideology," since then the "need" for ideology would disappear. Cf. the earlier discussion in Chapter 2, pp. 35–40.

[35] *Ibid.*, pp. 12–13 (from the preface to the first edition).

[36] Daniel Lerner, *The Passing of Traditional Society* (New York: The Free Press, 1964), p. 46. The reasoning in this work (originally published in 1958) is paralleled at many points by that contained in Walt W. Rostow, *The Stages of Economic Growth* (Cambridge University Press, 1961). For a critical evaluation of the latter cf. Walt W. Rostow, ed., *The Economics of Take-Off into Sustained Growth* (*Proceedings of a Conference by the International Economic Association*) (New York: St. Martin's Press, 1963).

[37] Lerner, *op. cit.*, pp. 65–68. Cf. also the 1964 preface to the paperback edition.

[38] *Ibid.*, p. 78. My italics.

[39] Cf. the discussion of the "system" of modernity in *ibid.*, pp. 54–65. See also David Riesman's comment on p. 13 of his introduction.

[40] *Ibid.*, p. 65.

[41] *Ibid.*, p. vii (1964 preface).

[42] *Ibid.*, pp. vii–x. The fact that Lerner chooses to ignore what he so clearly recognizes was explained by David Riesman in his introduction to the original edition by "the general belief that there must be a way—a way out of poverty and the psychic constriction of the 'Traditionals'—which links the author of this volume with his own national tradition.—But this very American belief that there is a way is a dream. And Professor Lerner, as a student of communications, understands that it is dreams that inspire not only new wants but new solutions—as well as violent gestures toward modernity. What seems required from his perspective is an allopathic rationing of dreams, enough to spark the religion of progress, of advance without inciting to riot." To which Riesman adds the observation that "the emotional and political fluency of newly-liberated illiterates can be quite terrifying," and that "a movie image of life in America . . . is a radical 'theory' when it appears on the screens of Cairo, Ankara or Teheran." *Ibid.*, p. 10.

[43] See Seymour M. Lipset, *Political Man* (Garden City: Doubleday & Co., 1950), Chap. II and the references cited there. Cf. also Phillips Cutright, "National Political Development," *American Sociological Review*, XXVIII (1963), pp. 253–64; by the same author, "Political Structure, Economic Development and National Security Programs," *American Journal of Sociology*, LXX (1965), pp. 537–50; but also the critical contribution by Stanley H. Udy, Jr., "Dynamic Inferences from Static Data," *ibid.*, pp. 625–27. Meanwhile massive studies along similar lines are underway. See A. S. Banks and R. B. Textor, *A Cross-Polity Survey* (Cambridge: Massachusetts Institute of Technology Press, 1963); and Bruce M. Russett, Hayward R. Alker, et al., *World Handbook of Political and Social Indicators* (New Haven: Yale University Press, 1964).

[44] See Margaret Mead, *Continuities in Cultural Evolution* (New Haven: Yale University Press, 1964), p. 7. The author cites Boas's acceptance of evolution on a planetary scale, but also his rejection of the application of evolutionary concepts to a few centuries since short-run changes can go in any direction—a position accepted by most modern evolutionists.

[45] Despite cautionary comments, the tendency is to substitute a "horizontal" compilation for the "vertical" dimension of history. Cf. Raymond Grew and Sylvia L. Thrupp, "Horizontal History in Search of Vertical Dimensions," *Comparative Studies in Society and History*, VIII (January 1966), pp. 258–64.

[46] David Riesman in Lerner, *op. cit.*, p. 14.

[47] In the countries of Western Europe that extension was relatively gradual during the nineteenth century; the establishment of universal suffrage dates only from the first World War or the early 1920s. See Stein Rokkan, "Mass Suffrage, Secret Voting, and Political Participation," *Archives Européennes de Sociologie*, II (1961), pp. 132–52. By contrast, a compilation shows that of thirty-nine nations that have become independent and joined the United Nations between 1946 and 1962 only seven do not have universal suffrage. The restrictions usually refer to members of Buddhist religious orders, whose rules do not permit them to vote, and to members of the armed forces.

[48] Sometimes, as in statistics on economic growth and democratic trends, data of current trends from one country are superimposed onto the past trend data of another, more advanced country, but the similarity of current with past trends does not resolve the question of sequence and timing. Note the critical analysis of this approach by Simon Kuznets, "Underdeveloped Countries and the Pre-industrial Phase in the Advanced Countries," in Otto Feinstein, ed., *Two Worlds of Change* (Garden City: Doubleday & Co., 1964), pp. 1–21.

[49] Clark Kerr, John T. Dunlop, Frederick Harbison, and Charles A. Myers, *Industrialism and Industrial Man* (Cambridge: Harvard University Press, 1960), p. 49, and passim.

[50] The first phrase occurs several times in Lucian W. Pye and Sidney Verba, eds., *Political Culture and Political Development* (Princeton: Princeton University Press, 1965), passim. The second is the title of a book by Harold Rosenberg.

[51] Max Weber, *The Methodology of the Social Sciences* (Glencoe: The Free Press, 1949), p. 101.

[52] *Ibid.*, pp. 102–3.

[53] Robert Redfield, *The Folkculture of Yucatan* (Chicago: University of Chicago Press, 1941), pp. 343–44.

[54] Cf. the related discussion above in Chapter 5.

[55] Alexander Gerschenkron, *Economic Backwardness in Historical Perspective* (New York: Frederick A. Praeger, 1965), p. 33. My indebtedness to Gerschenkron will be evident throughout; in several respects my analysis represents a sociological extension of points first suggested by him in the context of economic history.

[56] *Ibid.*, p. 40. Cf. also Gerschenkron's critical discussion of Rostow along similar lines in Rostow, ed., *The Economics of Take-Off, op. cit.*, pp. 166–67. See also for a related discussion Albert O. Hirschman, "Obstacles to Development," *Economic Development and Cultural Change*, XIII (1965), pp. 385–93.

[57] Walter Elkan and Lloyd A. Fallers, "The Mobility of Labor," in Wilbert E. Moore and Arnold S. Feldman, eds., *Labor Commitment and Social Change in Developing Areas* (New York: Social Science Research Council, 1960), pp. 238–57.

[58] Milton Singer, "Changing Craft Traditions in India," in Moore and Feldman, eds., *op. cit.*, pp. 268–76.

[59] Neil J. Smelser, *The Sociology of Economic Life* (Englewood Cliffs: Prentice-Hall, 1963), pp. 105–6.

[60] Wilbert Moore, *The Impact of Industry* (Englewood Cliffs: Prentice-Hall, 1965), p. 19. Cf. also the same writer's earlier monograph on *Social Change* (Englewood Cliffs: Prentice-Hall, 1963), Chap. V. Similar critiques of evolutionism are contained in the writings of S. N. Eisenstadt, esp. in two recent essays "Social Change, Differentiation and Evolution," *American Sociological Review*, XXIX (1964), pp. 375–86; and "Social Transformation in Modernization," *ibid.*, XXX (1965), pp. 659–73.

[61] See Smelser, *op. cit.*, pp. 101–2, 106.

[62] *Ibid.*, p. 112.

[63] Cf., for example, the analysis of changes in industrial organization by H. Freudenberger and F. Redlich, "The Industrial Development of Europe: Reality, Symbols, Images," *Kyklos*, XVII (1964), pp. 372–401.

[64] The characterization of pre-modern treatises on economics is contained in Otto Brunner, *Neue Wege der Sozialgeschichte* (Göttingen: Vandenhoeck and Ruprecht, 1956), pp. 33–61. Cf. also the analysis by Peter Laslett, *The World We Have Lost* (London: Methuen and Co., 1965), passim.

[65] Smelser, *op. cit.*, p. 110.

[66] See Cesar Grana, *Bohemian Versus Bourgeois* (New York: Basic Books, 1964), passim, for a sympathetic analysis of this imagery. Herbert Marcuse's *One-Dimensional Man* (Boston: The Beacon Press, 1964) appeared too late to be included in Grana's concluding analysis.

[67] It may well be the present-day absence of a need for self-help and defense which makes the closely knit solidarity of such groups appear oppressive to a modern observer, especially if he discounts the romanticism of past interpretations. By the same token, it may be the absence of that need for self-help and defense which weakens the solidarity of groups in modern societies and allows for the development of individualism. The older pattern often arose from the imposition of taxes in return for privileges, which necessitated the organization of communities for self-help and defense; Max Weber discussed this device under the concept of "liturgy." Cf. Max Weber, *The Theory of Social and Economic Organization* (New York: Oxford University Press, 1947), pp. 312–13. A society like the Russian in which this older pattern was preserved up to the present may well engender customs and attitudes markedly different from those that are familiar to us today. For an insightful discussion of these customs and attitudes see Wright W. Miller, *Russians as People* (New York: E. P. Dutton, 1961), Chap. 5.

[68] See Karl Mannheim, *Man and Society in an Age of Reconstruction* (New York: Harcourt, Brace & World, 1941), p. 44.

[69] See above pp. 230–34.

[70] For the link between the theological conception of emanation with theories of social evolution and functionalism cf. Arthur Lovejoy, *The Great Chain of Being, op. cit.*; Karl Loewith, *Meaning in History* (Chicago: University of Chicago Press, 1949); and the comprehensive historical treatment in Robert A. Nisbet, *Social Change and History* (New York: Oxford University Press, 1969), passim. The intellectual tradition discussed in these works has been criticized very effectively by Ernest Gellner, *Thought and Change* (Chicago: University of Chicago Press, 1964), passim. Gellner's analysis corroborates the present discussion at several points.

[71] So, of course, did the initial development of England, depending as it did on intense competition with Holland. The point that social structures cannot be understood by exclusive attention to their internal developments is a general one. See Otto Hintze, "Staatsverfassung und Heeresverfassung," in *Staat und Verfassung* (Göttingen: Vandenhoeck & Ruprecht, 1962), pp. 52–83. The essay was published originally in 1906.

[72] See Milton Singer, *op. cit.*, p. 262.

[73] Carlo Cipolla, *Guns and Sails in the Early Phase of European Expansion, 1400–1700* (London: Collins, 1965), passim.

[74] The changes in literacy and the availability of printed matter are sur-

veyed for England in Raymond Williams, *The Long Revolution* (London: Chatto and Windus, 1961), pp. 156–72.

[75] The terms of that distinction do not stay put. Before the "modern" period England was a "follower" society while Holland and Sweden were "advanced," especially in the production of cannons. Cf. Cipolla, *Guns and Sails, op. cit.,* pp. 36–37, 52–54, 87 n. In the twentieth century the Russian revolution, the fascist regimes, and the Chinese revolution have added their own modifications of this distinction. Singer, *op. cit.,* pp. 261–62 refers to the same distinction by speaking of "early" and "late" arrivals, but I wish to emphasize the sense of pioneering or backwardness that has animated people in "advanced" and "follower" societies. These terms refer to the evaluations of the participants rather than to my own assessment of "progress" or "backwardness."

[76] There are those who consider societies closed systems. They would counter this diffusionist argument with the contention that societies are not passive recipients of external stimuli, but select among them in accordance with the dictates of their internal structure. This interpretation is an extension of the equilibrium model and as such a secular version of the original, theological belief in "pre-established harmony." That older view was as compatible with the existence of evil in a divinely created world as the functionalist interpretation is compatible with the existence of conflict and change. Neither view is compatible with the possibility of a self perpetuating disequilibrium, or cumulative causation as Myrdal has called it.

[77] Gerschenkron, *op. cit.,* pp. 26, 44, and passim.

[78] *Ibid.,* p. 46.

[79] Cf. the analysis of this complex of ideas in the work of Gottfried Wilhelm von Leibniz (1646–1716), especially the interesting contacts between Leibniz and Peter the Great with regard to the modernization of Russia, in Dieter Groh, *Russland und das Selbstverständniß Europas* (Neuwied: Hermann Luchterhand Verlag, 1961), pp. 32–43.

[80] David Landes, "Technological Change and Development in Western Europe, 1750–1914," in H. J. Habbakuk and M. Postan, eds., *The Cambridge Economic History of Europe; The Industrial Revolution and After* (Cambridge University Press, 1965), Vol. VI, Part I, p. 366.

[81] Note the frequency with which "political unity" appears as an index of modernity in the several lists of attributes presented in Marius Jansen, ed., *Changing Japanese Attitudes Towards Modernization* (Princeton: Princeton University Press, 1965), pp. 18–19, 20–24, and passim.

[82] For a discussion of this point cf. Bendix, *Nation-Building and Citizenship, op. cit.,* pp. 15–29.

[83] On the "ad hoc diffusion" of items of modernity cf. the illuminating discussion by Theodore H. von Laue, "Imperial Russia at the Turn of the Century," *Comparative Studies in Society and History,* III (1961), pp. 353–67; and Mary C. Wright, "Revolution from Without?" *Comparative Studies in Society and History,* IV (1962), pp. 247–52.

[84] Edward A. Shils, "Political Development in the New States," *Comparative Studies in Society and History,* II (1960), p. 281.

[85] Gerschenkron, *op. cit.,* pp. 41–44.

[86] Cf. Landes, *op. cit.,* pp. 354, 358.

[87] The concept "reference society" has been chosen in analogy to Robert Merton's "reference groups." Cf. Robert Merton, *Social Theory and Social Structure* (Glencoe: The Free Press, 1957), pp. 225 ff.

[88] Cf. the succinct overview of the "intelligentsia" by Hugh Seton-Watson, *Neither War Nor Peace* (New York: Frederick Praeger, 1960), pp. 164–87. See also Bendix, *Nation-Building, op. cit.*, pp. 231 ff.

[89] The most sensitive analysis of this bifurcation I have found in the literature is the study by Joseph Levenson, *Modern China and its Confucian Past* (Garden City: Doubleday & Co., 1964), passim. Cf. also Cipolla, *Guns and Sails, op. cit.*, pp. 116–26.

[90] Cf. the analysis of these tensions by Edward A. Shils, "Political Development in the New States," cited above.

[91] Cf. the chapter on "Die Proletarier der Geistesarbeit" in Wilhelm Riehl, *Die Bürgerliche Gesellschaft* (Stuttgart: J. G. Cottasche Buchhandlung, 1930), esp. pp. 312–13.

[92] For a vigorous critique of this tendency cf. J. H. Hexter, *Reappraisals in History* (New York: Harper & Row, 1963), passim. Note also the cautionary comments regarding the problem of historical continuity in Gerschenkron, *op. cit.*, pp. 37–39.

[93] For a more balanced assessment of the European bourgeoisie, cf. Otto Brunner, *Neue Wege der Sozialgeschichte*, pp. 80–115.

[94] Joseph Schumpeter, *Capitalism, Socialism, and Democracy* (New York: Harper and Bros., 1947), pp. 136–37. See also pp. 12–13 for a more generalized statement. Substantially the same observations were made by Frederick Engels in 1892, but the political primacy of the aristocracy and the secondary role of the bourgeoisie appeared to him only as a "survival" which would disappear eventually. See Frederic Engels, *Socialism, Utopian and Scientific* (Chicago: Charles H. Kerr, 1905), pp. xxxii–xxxiv. For an empirical study cf. W. L. Guttsman, *The British Political Elite* (New York: Basic Books, 1963).

[95] Cf. Peter Laslett, *The World We Have Lost, op. cit.*, p. 22 and passim.

[96] Cf. Ernest Barker, *The Development of Public Services in Western Europe, 1660–1930* (London: Oxford University Press, 1944), pp. 1–6 and passim.

[97] Cf. Clifford Geertz, "The Integrative Revolution," in Geertz, ed., *Old Societies and New States* (Glencoe: The Free Press, 1963), pp. 105 ff. Cf. my article "Bureaucracy" in the *International Encyclopedia of the Social Sciences,* 1968 edition.

[98] Cf., for example, the statement that "In Egypt the middle class has been weak in numbers and influence, and civil servants have comprised a large proportion of it." Morroe Berger, *Bureaucracy and Society in Modern Egypt* (Princeton: Princeton University Press, 1957), p. 46.

[99] Karl Marx, *The 18th Brumaire of Louis Bonaparte* (New York: International Publishers, n. d.), p. 109.

[100] See John Stuart Mill, *Principles of Political Economy* (Boston: Charles C. Little and James Brown, 1848), pp. 322–23.

[101] Cf. the analysis of growing class consciousness among workers in Karl Marx, *The Poverty of Philosophy* (New York: International Publishers, n. d.), pp. 145–46; but note also the evidence adduced by David Mitrany, *Marx against the Peasants* (London: Weidenfeld and Nicolson, 1951), passim.

[102] To discount such beliefs because they disappeared eventually is no more plausible than to make the aristocracy's role decline in advance of its eventual demise. Cf. the discussion of the "traditionalism of labor" in my book *Work and Authority in Industry* (New York: John Wiley and Sons, 1956), pp. 34 ff.

[103] For a fuller statement of this interpretation cf. Bendix, *Nation-Building, op. cit.*, pp. 61–74.

[104] As always, the contrast is not absolute. During the nineteenth century, as one went eastwards in Europe, one encountered certain parallels to the "underdeveloped syndrome" of today, namely an increased importance of government and rather weakly developed middle strata. Cf. the illuminating statement by David Landes: "The farther east one goes in Europe, the more the bourgeoisie takes on the appearance of a foreign excrescence on manorial society, a group apart scorned by the nobility and feared or hated by (or unknown to) a peasantry still personally bound to the local *seigneur*." See Landes, *op. cit.*, p. 358.

[105] The debate concerning the deprivations of early English industrialization continues. But whatever its final resolution in terms of the changing standard of living, there is probably less disagreement on the psychological repercussions. The separation of the worker's home from his place of work, the novelty of a discipline which previously had been associated with the pauper's workhouse, the brutalization of work conditions for women and children merely by the shift away from home, and related matters constitute the impressive circumstantial evidence. Note also that the statement in the text makes sense of Germany's pioneering in the field of social legislation as an attribute of an early follower society.

[106] Cf. Landes, *op. cit.*, pp. 344–47 for a summary analysis of the labor supply problem in the English industrial revolution in terms of the current state of research. These findings can be contrasted readily with comparative materials on various follower societies contained in Wilbert Moore and Arnold Feldman, eds., *Labor Commitment and Social Change in Developing Areas, op. cit.*, passim.

[107] Note that Marx and others with him considered that separation as a prerequisite of capitalist development. Cf. the discussion of the distinctive position of workers in African countries by Lloyd A. Fallers, "Equality, Modernity and Democracy in the New States," in Geertz, ed., *Old Societies and New States, op. cit.*, pp. 187–90. See also Richard D. Lambert, "The Impact of Urban Society upon Village Life" in Roy Turner, ed., *India's Urban Future* (Berkeley: University of California Press, 1962), pp. 117–40.

[108] In these respects there are of course striking differences between France and England which can be considered symptomatic of the radical and the conservative approach to education and conscription. For a comparative treatment of these issues cf. Ernest Barker, *The Development of Public Services in Western Europe, op. cit.*, Chaps. 2, 5.

[109] The circularity of this statement is unavoidable. In a general sense pursuits engaging the intellect refer to the creation and maintenance (transmission) of cultural values, but each of these terms (cultural values, creation, maintenance, transmission) is the subject of constant debate, and that debate itself is an important intellectual pursuit. Since this debate involves the pejorative as well as appreciative use of these terms, and by that token the endeavor of speakers to "belong" to the positive side of the cultural process (in however marginal a fashion), no one set of defining terms will be wholly satisfactory.

In view of this difficulty the most reasonable alternative is to set up a typology of intellectual pursuits and leave the group of persons called "intellectuals" undefined. For one such attempt cf. Theodor Geiger, *Aufgaben und Stellung der Intelligenz in der Gesellschaft* (Stuttgart: Ferdinand Enke Verlag, 1949), pp. 1–24, 81–101.

[110] Cf. the case study of this process in England by Leo Lowenthal and Marjorie Fiske, "The Debate over Art and Popular Culture," in Mirra Komarovsky, ed., *Common Frontiers of the Social Sciences* (Glencoe: The Free Press, 1957), pp. 33–112.

[111] I avoid the term "alienation" because misuse has made it worthless. For a scholarly treatment of this intellectual response to "bourgeois society" in nineteenth-century Europe cf. Karl Loewith, *From Hegel to Nietzsche*, passim. Cf. also the analysis of the social distance between "intellectuals" and "practical men" in Joseph Schumpeter, *op. cit.*, pp. 145–55 as well as the unusual acceptance of that distance by at least one great artist, William Faulkner, who speaks of writers "steadily occupied by trying to do the impossible" while keeping "out of the way of the practical and busy people who carry the burden of America." See Faulkner's speech on the occasion of receiving the National Book Award in *The New York Times Book Review* (February 6, 1955), p. 2.

[112] See Edward A. Shils, "Intellectuals, Public Opinion and Economic Development," *World Politics*, Vol. 10 (1958), pp. 232–55.

[113] Cf. Gaston Rimlinger, *Welfare Policy and Industrialization in Europe, America and Russia* (New York: John Wiley and Sons, forthcoming).

NOTES FOR CHAPTER TWELVE

[1] Kingsley Davis, "Population," in *Technology and Economic Development* (Harmondsworth: Penguin Books, 1965), pp. 46–47.

[2] *Ibid.*, pp. 50–51.

[3] Gunnar Myrdal, *Asian Drama* (New York: Random House, 1968), I, pp. 467–68.

[4] *Ibid.*, p. 416.

[5] Industry comprises mining, manufacturing, construction, power and light utilities, transportation, and communication. Services include trade, finance, real estate, personal business, domestic and professional service, and government employment.

[6] This distinction was formulated originally by Ernst Fraenkel, *Deutschland und die westlichen Demokratien* (Stuttgart: W. Kohlhammer, 1964), pp. 71 ff.

[7] Robert C. Tucker, *The Soviet Political Mind* (New York: Frederick Praeger, 1963), p. 11.

[8] Quoted in John Lester, *Journey through Despair, 1880–1914* (Princeton: Princeton University Press, 1968), pp. 50–51.

[9] Cf. the earlier reference to this European reaction in the postwar world and to Karl Schmid's *Hochmut und Angst* on p. 88 above. F. R. Leavis's

eloquent plea for English studies in *Times Literary Supplement* (May 29, 1969), p. 572, contains a striking illustration of these themes.

[10] Quoted in Karl Staehlin, *Geschichte Rublands* (Königsberg: Ost-Europa Verlag, 1939), IV, 1, p. 81.

[11] Clifford Geertz, "The Integrative Revolution," in Geertz, ed., *Old Societies and New States* (Glencoe: The Free Press, 1963), p. 108.

[12] The distinction between civil, political, and social rights was formulated originally by T. H. Marshall, "Citizenship and Social Class," in *Class, Citizenship and Social Development* (Garden City: Doubleday & Co., 1964), pp. 71–72, and passim.

[13] Cf. Lionel Trilling, *Beyond Culture* (Harmondsworth: Penguin Books, 1967), p. 150.

[14] Cf. Lewis Feuer, *The Conflict of Generations* (New York: Basic Books, 1969), passim.

[15] On these points I am indebted to the analysis by Richard Lowenthal, "Unreason and Revolution," *Encounter*, XXXIII (November 1969), pp. 22–34.